Deep Sea Hunters: RAF Coastal Command and the War against the U-Boats and the German Navy

Deep Sea Hunters: RAF Coastal Command and the War against the U-Boats and the German Navy

Martin W. Bowman

Pen & Sword
AVIATION

First Published in Great Britain in 2014 by
Pen & Sword Aviation
an imprint of
Pen & Sword Books Ltd
47 Church Street, Barnsley, South Yorkshire S70 2AS

A CIP catalogue record for this book is
available from the British Library.

Typeset in 10/12pt Palatino
by GMS Enterprises

Printed and bound in England by
CPI Group (UK) Ltd, Croydon, CR0 4YY

Pen & Sword Books Ltd incorporates the Imprints of Pen & Sword
Aviation, Pen & Sword Family History, Pen & Sword Maritime, Pen & Sword
Military, Pen & Sword Discovery, Wharncliffe Local History, Wharncliffe
True Crime, Wharncliffe Transport, Pen & Sword Select, Pen & Sword
Military Classics, Leo Cooper, The Praetorian Press, Remember When,
Seaforth Publishing and Frontline Publishing.

For a complete list of Pen & Sword titles please contact
PEN & SWORD BOOKS LIMITED

47 Church Street, Barnsley, South Yorkshire, S70 2AS, England
E-mail: enquiries@pen-and-sword.co.uk
Website: www.pen-and-sword.co.uk

Contents

6

Acknowledgements

I am indebted to all the contributors for their words and photographs. Thanks also go to my fellow author, friend and colleague, Graham Simons, for getting the book to press ready standard and for his detailed work on the photographs; to Pen & Sword and in particular, Laura Hirst; and to Jon Wilkinson, for his unique jacket design once again.

Introduction

Coastal Command is an air force in miniature. Its Sunderlands and Catalinas range the ocean to protect our ships; so likewise do its Beauforts and Blenheims, its Whitleys and Wellingtons, its Hudsons and Liberators, but they are also a bombing force capable of instant use against a wide choice of targets; its Beaufighters and Blenheim fighters join combat with the Luftwaffe at ranges beyond those within the compass of Fighter Command. It is an amphibious force in the sense that, though its element is the air, it makes us of both land and sea to provide it with bases from which to set out against the enemy. Its aircraft fly over the restless waters of the Atlantic, the Channel and the North Sea, over the pack-ice about the shores of Greenland, over the desert scrub and palms of West Africa, over the stern mountains of Norway and Iceland, ever the wide fields of France, over the iron and concrete buildings of Reykjavik, the wooden houses of Trondheim, the brick-built mansions of Rotterdam, the lighted windows of Nantes.
Their Spirit is Serene; Coastal Command; The Air Ministry Account of the Part Played by Coastal Command in the Battle of the Seas 1939-1942.

At the outbreak of war Coastal Command Order of Battle (ORBAT) was eleven GR (General Reconnaissance) squadrons, ten of which were equipped with Avro Ansons; and of the six flying boat units only two had Sunderlands - 204 Squadron at Mount Batten, near Plymouth in Devonshire and 210 Squadron at Pembroke Dock - always known as 'PD'. On 3 September 1939 Coastal Command was equipped with six main types comprising 487 aircraft, the most numerous being the Avro Anson with 301 aircraft. The Anson or 'Faithful Annie' to give it its Service nickname was a military development of the Avro 652 six-passenger commercial aircraft, two of which were ordered by Imperial Airways in April 1934. In May 1934 the Avro Company was invited by the Air Ministry to consider the design of a twin-engined landplane for coastal reconnaissance duties. The design which later became known as the Anson was accepted by the Air Ministry in September 1934 and the prototype first flew on 24 March 1935. In July 1935 Avro's received an initial contract for 174 Ansons and on 6 March 1936,

Ansons entered service on 48 Squadron at Manston, Kent. On Tuesday 5 September 1939 when two Ansons on 206 Squadron were deployed to fight German U-boats, mistakenly attacked two surfaced British submarines with two 99lb depth charges. The HMS *Snapper* received a direct hit on its conning tower but that did no more than break four electric bulbs inside the boat. On 3 December an Anson on 206 Squadron released its bombs onto the conning tower of another surfaced submarine - U-boat this time - and Pilot Officer R. H. Harper received the DFC for his determined attack. Though classified as obsolescent for front-line service by 1940, Ansons continued to fill the gap for many Coastal units until late 1941.

Not surprisingly, the German Unterseeboote was a highly respected adversary. A U-boat for example, could be armed with an 88mm gun and two 20mm guns forward, or four 20mm cannon, or a 37mm gun. Either way, when they cornered one, crews knew they were in for a fight, especially when Karl Dönitz, the U-boat Commander-in-Chief, ordered that U-boats, when attacked, were to remain on the surface and 'slug' it out with their low level attackers.

After the Anson, at the outbreak of war the next most numerous aircraft were 53 Lockheed Hudsons and thirty obsolete Vickers Vildebeest biplane torpedo-bombers which had been in service since 1933. The Hudson was the first American-built aircraft to see operational service with the RAF in the Second World War. The original Lockheed 14, from which the Hudson derived, made its first flight on 29 July 1937. The first Hudson for the RAF first flew on 10 December 1938. The turret was fitted on the Hudsons after arrival in England and was of Boulton Paul type, carrying twin guns. The Hudson first entered service on 224 Squadron at Gosport in the summer of 1939, replacing Avro Ansons. [1]

A flight sergeant in charge of a maintenance party on 224 Squadron who was a pilot until an accident put him on ground duties, said that being the first squadron in the RAF to be equipped with American aircraft, anyone who wanted to know the difference between the English and American language should have come to his workshops then. 'Many of the engineering terms are quite different. Most people know that petrol is gasoline and engines are motors, but did you know that the American equivalent of chassis is 'structure', oil or petrol feed-pipes are collectively called 'plumbing', a hand fuel pump is a 'wobble pump' and a tailplane is a 'horizontal stabiliser'? There are many more curious terms we had to learn when we first got Hudsons. We could have done with a dictionary. We had the very willing assistance of Lockheed and Wright-Cyclone engine experts to smooth the difficulties, but even they unwittingly misled us on occasions. For instance, they would talk about seeing a ship out at sea and while we would look on the water they were watching an aircraft in the sky.

'In a way, we are rather like surgeons who take a pride in performing restorative treatment. We replace broken sections and graft on new metal skin. If you could see the damaged condition in which an aircraft sometimes returns, you would think it could never be repaired. But we can do wonders with a few days in the workshops - or even a few hours - and it comes out again as good as new. When an aeroplane returns with battle-scars we make a thorough examination to check up the full extent of the damage. It's amazing how some bullet-holes hide themselves away. On one occasion we thought we had finished the repairs, but a final check-over revealed a bullet-hole through a bolt holding a wing in place. The bullet had neatly removed the core of the bolt without damaging anything else, so it was difficult to see that anything was wrong. Then, sometimes, a scrap of shrapnel will play havoc with the complicated wiring system of the instrument panel. When something goes wrong with that box of tricks, you need the patience of Job to put it right again.

'The aircraft repair section of any station is a pretty busy place. All day and all night as well, you hear the buzz of electric drills, the rattle of compressed air riveters, the hum of paint-sprayers and the roar of engines. It's not a peaceful life, but it's a very interesting one. There's plenty of work for us all, from the youngest reservist to the station engineer officer. Talking of youngsters, I have a very useful lad who is a modern counterpart of the chimney-sweep boys of the past. He's only four feet six inches and of course is called Tich and is the only person on the station small enough to crawl right to the tail end of the fuselage of a Hudson. He was away one day and another rigger took his place. This man got to the end but became wedged and we couldn't move him. It took two hours' work to get him out. He had gone in feet first and got stuck on his back between a couple of cross-bracing struts and the roof. We had to turn him over on to his stomach and pull on his shoulders to get him out. After that, Tich reigned supreme in his own sphere.

'One of our most interesting jobs was repairing a Hudson which became known as the 'corkscrew plane'. It was badly damaged near Norway and limped home with rudder controls away. The crew almost baled out, but decided to try and put it down and made a sort of side-slip landing in the dark. They were all safe, but the aircraft was a mess! We got to work that night. The tail control wires were all wrapped round each other like a ball of wool after the cat's got it. We had to rebuild the entire port tailplane, but that aircraft was flying again within five days and is still doing its patrols today. We did a quick-change act on another Hudson which came back 300 miles over the sea with one engine seized up. The pilot radioed that one engine had packed up and the moment he landed we had a new engine and all accessories ready. The aircraft arrived back in the evening and we had it flying again the next day. It's a great help to us that the engine unit of a Hudson is amazingly compact. Each of the two 1,100 hp engines is held to the wing by only a very few main bolts. We can take out one engine and bolt another in position in a quarter of an hour and it only takes another couple of hours to connect all the pipe-lines, controls and exhaust system ready for starting up. Every man on the maintenance side knows the responsibility of his work. The crews of out aircraft give us their complete confidence. Their successes against the enemy are ample reward for our work. They place their lives in our hands and we do our best to be worthy of the trust.'

Hudsons maintained constant patrols over the French beaches during the evacuation of the British troops at Dunkirk in May 1940 and also made low-level bombing attacks on German troops in the vicinity of the beaches. On several occasions, although only reconnaissance aircraft, Hudsons engaged in air combats with German aircraft. A Hudson on 206 Squadron went to the aid of Fleet Air Arm Skuas under attack by Bf 109E fighters and with concentrated fire from its turret drove the enemy off. The Flight Lieutenant leader of the flight of three Hudsons recalled: 'We were suddenly attacked by a flight of Messerschmitt fighters, which came screaming down out of the sun. We dived towards the sea in order to prevent them from getting beneath us and to allow our rear gunners to get to work. The Messerschmitts had the advantage of being faster than we were, so we remained in tight formation and dodged and twisted to break up their attacks. They were flying up behind us, shooting as they came and then breaking away on either side to turn and renew the attack. Our Lockheeds were going hell for leather. I was wrenching the stick right over from side to side and keeping the engines at maximum boost the whole time. The air-speed indicator was showing about fifteen or twenty mph more than the maximum claimed by the American manufacturers. Even then I had something in hand because as leader I had to make sure that the other two were keeping up with all I was doing. The nose cannons of the Messerschmitts were firing at us all the time. Puffs of smoke came from them with unpleasant regularity, like someone hurriedly blowing a lot of smoke-rings. In all we had fifteen attacks from each of them. Then they ran out of ammunition and went home. Our Lockheed Hudsons were still flying as well as ever, although the attacks had lasted for more than half an hour. By that time we had led them about 150 miles from land and there was just a chance that the Messerschmitts would not have enough petrol to get back.

'When we landed, we found that only one of our Lockheeds was at all badly hurt. It had received two cannon shots in the wings, one in the cabin and one in the tail. Quite a lot of metal skin was blown off the wings, but the flying performance was very little impaired. One shell had come from behind, ripped through the wing to the main spar - and exploded there. The upper and lower surfaces of the wing looked like a sort of colossal nutmeg grater. By a stroke of good luck neither the flap nor aileron controls were affected. We tested the engines of all three aircraft. There wasn't a thing wrong with any of them.'

On another occasion three Hudsons on 220 Squadron attacked forty Junkers Ju 87 Stuka dive bombers and destroyed five of them, damaging two more. The event was described in a contemporary account by David Masters.

'On the evening of 31 May 1940 in a mess somewhere on the east coast of England, Flying Officer Ronald Nicholas Selley read with troubled eyes a note advising him that his brother was missing. He turned to his friend Flying Officer Hilton Aubrey Haarhoff. 'If we do meet anything we'll give them what for,' he said quietly. Both the young men were South Africans who flew together in a Hudson aircraft which was manned by a crew of four, a wireless operator, a navigator, an air gunner who was Flying Officer Haarhoff and the pilot Flying Officer Selley. The Hudson is a useful long distance reconnaissance aircraft which can carry a good load of bombs for offensive purposes and is armed with twin guns in the pilot's cockpit and a nice sting in the tail where Flying Officer Haarhoff sat in the turret with his two guns. But in those Dunkirk days all aircraft became fighters, as the German dive bombers over the beaches learned to their cost.

On 1 June a battle flight of three Hudsons took off to relieve the dawn patrol over Dunkirk. It met the other battle flight about midday over Dover, inward bound for their base. Selley flew on the port side of the outward bound formation at about 1,000 feet. In the Channel, sea-power was working its miracle. Haarhoff gazed on the greatest and most miscellaneous collection of shipping he had ever seen in his life. There were tugs towing barges and tugs towing yachts, with motor boats of all sizes, some, towing lifeboats, with torpedo boats and destroyers coming and going on their errand of mercy and deliverance. Up and down the coast by Dunkirk the formation of Hudsons patrolled for fifteen minutes each way. Once some Spitfires dropped out of the clouds and mistakenly attacked the leader, who had difficulty in evading them. Another time a Hudson chased an enemy aircraft which fled for its life right into the fog of black smoke with which the burning oil blanketed the town and the smoke, seeping into the cockpit of the Hudson, nearly choked the gunner. Not a ripple stirred the sea. It was so calm that Haarhoff could see bottles floating about; once or twice he saw a body amid rafts and overturned boats and drums and barrels; a bombed destroyer was lying on its beam near the beach. There was the remarkable pier of lorries formed by army drivers to help the evacuation and one or two other wrecks nearby, among them an overturned steamer.

'It was a miracle: not a breath of wind during the vital days. When I saw all the little craft passing across I was thrilled,' said Wing Commander T. H. Carr DFC who flew another Hudson during those historic hours.

Selley noted the moving figures and boats and all the wrecks and the flotsam and jetsam on the sea, with its huge patches to tell of oil which would never fall into the German hands. A couple of days earlier he had seen a table floating four miles from shore with three men upon it and closer examination revealed a bicycle. In that emergency one of those men was literally fighting for his life, yet he still refused to relinquish his bicycle and had dragged it after him on to the table before they floated away. The pilot of the Hudson soon brought a steamer to the spot, but the captain was out to save life, not bicycles and the South African pilot watched the men being picked up while the cycle which one had risked. So much to save went floating away on the table top.

About 3 o'clock in the afternoon the Hudson sighted forty Junkers 87s. As these were unseen by the Spitfires patrolling above open cloud at 4,000 feet, the three Hudsons were ordered to break formation and attack. Selley sped off to attack eight Junkers 87s that were about five miles away. 'As we approached,' said Haarhoff afterwards, 'we could see them circling in about a two mile radius. Each one was doing a steep climb with a stall turn at the top and then came over in a very steep dive straight down. It was a very pretty and impressive sight and they were doing it with such regularity and uniformity that they might have been at Hendon flying pageant. I'll never forget it as long as I live. We saw about forty altogether and they seemed to split up into two bunches of twenty. I took a bunch of eight Junkers 87s which had twelve more flying at 200 feet above them. When we came in to attack they all joined in one big circle at about 1,200 feet. We just went straight into them. We thought there were a lot, but we didn't mind. It was our job to look after the fellows below and we had to do it.'

Regardless of the risk, Selley flew alone in that ring of twenty enemies. It might have been a performing circus with the South African as the ring-master. Round and round he went with them. He tried at first to follow one down and get it while it was diving, but the dive was too steep for the Hudson to follow, so he decided to time his attack to coincide with the moment that an enemy aircraft climbed in front of him before it did its stall turn and dive. We attacked as one came up and as he stall turned we just leapt across and shot him down. As we circled with them, Haarhoff picked them off going round and as they came up I got them with my front guns. I shot ·down two with my front guns and damaged two more, one badly, but we did not see him go in. Haarhoff shot one down into the sea and damaged another, but we did not see that go in either.'

The extraordinary thing is that the Hudson was not hit. Unable to stand up to the guns of the avenging South Africans, the Germans fled and gave them the skies to themselves. That was how Selley and Haarhoff eagerly and fearlessly attacked twenty enemy aircraft and each was awarded the DFC. Five minutes after routing the Junkers they saw two lifeboats adrift full of men which they circled while the other Hudsons flew off to find a ship to pick them up. Almost simultaneously three Junkers 88s and three Heinkel 111s with an escort of two Messerschmitt 109s hove in view to bomb the boats. At once the South African made a head-on attack. Those eight German aircraft had not the courage to face that lone Hudson. They turned away over Dunkirk and gave the tugs which came on the scene a chance to take the lifeboats in tow.

Later in the week a Wing Commander of the Coastal Command beheld not the least amazing sight in those amazing times. 'For two or three days after the evacuation ended, Tommies were leaving the coast in rowing boats, on rafts, bits of wreckage, in fact anything that would float and putting out in the Channel where we were sighting them and sending ships to pick them up,' he remarked when it was all over. 'Some Tommies swam out to a ship that was lying on her side and took refuge in her. When I came along, the ship seemed to be deserted. Then I saw a man poke his head through a porthole and look up very cautiously. He observed us carefully and when he saw it was a British aircraft he started to wave frantically. In a few seconds men's heads began to pop up through the portholes to right and left and hands began to wave to us for succour. It was a most astounding sight. At one moment the ship was dead, the next it sprang to life. The men had been in hiding there for three days when we saw them and directed a ship to their rescue.'

The British pilots who witnessed Dunkirk from the air conjure up an unforgettable picture of the continual pall of smoke under which they flew, of beaches lined with men walking into the water with their rifles held over their heads as they climbed into little boats which rowed them to the bigger boats further out. 'It was' as Pilot Officer Lloyd Bennett DFC remarked afterwards 'one continual traffic, almost a bridge of boats. The Channel was very small for our Hudsons and I circled so much one day that I mistook a burning town on the other side for Dover and thought the war had moved over to our side. I was quite surprised to find we were all right.' It is possible to make a mistake like that in daylight, the difficulty of fixing a position at night after taking violent evasive action can be imagined.' [2]

At the outbreak of war Coastal Command was equipped with three types of flying-boats, the most numerous being 27 Short Sunderlands, the last of a long line of flying boat designs in RAF service and without question the finest boat to see service in Coastal Command. The others were 17 Saro London and nine Supermarine Stranraer obsolete biplane flying-boats which had been in service since 1936. These two types were superseded by the Sunderland, which was produced as a military development of the renowned 'C' Class Empire flying-boat resulting from a 1933 Air Ministry Specification. The prototype Sunderland flew at Rochester, Kent on 16 October 1937 and was the first British flying-boat to incorporate power-operated turrets as part of its defensive armament. These were so effective in combat that the Sunderland was nicknamed the 'Flying Porcupine' by the Germans The first Sunderland entered RAF service on 28 May 1938 when L2159 was flown to Seletar, Singapore to join 230 Squadron on 22 June 1938. In Britain Sunderlands first entered squadron service in the summer of 1938, being issued to 210 Squadron at Pembroke Dock. In both 230 and 210 Squadrons the Sunderland superseded Singapore III biplane flying-boats.

Of fifty types of aircraft used by Coastal Command during the years 1939-45, the Sunderland was the only one in front line service from the first to the last day of the European war. The crews who manned these flying boats were perhaps the most individualistic of all in the RAF. Among the naval-oriented terms used by these fliers, one of the best-known was their reference to their huge aircraft as 'boats', a word which immediately identifies anyone who ever served on Sunderlands. It was also said that the mark of a boat veteran was the green-stained cap badges worn by some, testimony too many hours on patrol over the salt waters of the Bay of Biscay and the Atlantic Ocean, which comprised their main hunting grounds in the U-boat war.

In September 1939, 210 Squadron had six Sunderlands on strength and 204 Squadron at Mount Batten began receiving its Sunderlands from July 1939. Four of 210 Squadron's pilots, who flew Sunderlands on operations during the first month of war, were Australians from an RAAF detachment at Pembroke Dock which had arrived in England in July to receive and fly back a complement of Sunderlands to Australia for RAAF use. In the event, the Australians were given additional RAAF and RAF personnel and formed the nucleus of 10 Squadron RAAF, which on 3 January 1940 joined 15 Group Coastal Command and was declared operational with effect from 1 February; flying its first operational sortie five days later.

Until the spring of 1940 the war at sea had gone steadily in Britain's favour.[3] Even the Germans' victorious campaign had cost the Kriegsmarine one-third of its cruisers and almost half its destroyers. However, in April the sea war flared up again. Units of Bomber Command found themselves called upon to bolster 18 Group Coastal Command, which was responsible for Britain's Northern Approaches. Germany's occupation of Norway, the subsequent overrunning of France and the Low Countries and Italy's intervention in the war changed the situation in the war at sea radically. U-boats and E-boats began operating with deadly effect from French Atlantic bases. Soon aircraft such as the four-engined Focke Wulf 200, an adapted commercial transport with a range of 2,000 miles, began to menace Britain's Western Approaches and reach out into mid-Atlantic waters previously immune from German intervention. RAF Coastal Command was at once confronted with a series of fresh problems ranging from anti-invasion patrols to long-range escort duties. In June 1940 Air Chief Marshal Sir Frederick Bowhill KCB CMG DSO [4] could only call upon 500 aircraft for such diverse tasks and only 34 of these, the Sunderlands, could only operate beyond 500 miles from Britain's shores. The period between June and October, when U-boats sank 282 ships with only seven U-boats lost to all causes, became known to the U-boat crews as the 'Happy Time'. At first the U-boats attacked shipping in the South-West Approaches. During June sinkings by U-boats peaked at 63 ships. By August they became bolder, following up on the surface during the day and delaying closing in on convoys until nightfall. To escape detection by the Asdics [5] they remained on the surface and attacked under cover of darkness. Coastal Command did not have an answer to such tactics and from the beginning of June to the end of 1940 over 300 million tons of Allied and neutral shipping was sunk.[6]

The only salvation available to RAF crews was ASV (Air to Surface Vessel) radar. Relatively few aircraft in Coastal Command were fitted with the device and those that were did not always perform as efficiently as crews would like.

By the middle of 1941 the shortage of Very Long Range (VLR) aircraft as opposed to long-range aircraft was still causing problems. As the U-boat campaign intensified stop gap measures were tried such as procuring Blenheims from Bomber Command. Bases were established In the Hebrides, Northern Ireland and Iceland but very valuable locations were denied the British in neutral Eire. By May 1941 the U-boats were largely reduced to operating off West Africa or in the Central Atlantic, the latter being beyond the range of Coastal Command aircraft. In June 1941 Bowhill was posted to form Ferry Command while Air Marshal Sir Philip Joubert took over Coastal Command. Joubert inherited a force of forty squadrons and more than half the aircraft were now fitted with ASV (Air to Surface Vessel) radar. Joubert's overriding task was to increase the effectiveness of his ASV aircraft and create airborne U-boat killers. He pressed for heavier types of anti-submarine bombs, bomb sights for low level attack and depth charge pistols which would detonate at less than fifty feet below the surface. He encouraged tests, first started by Bowhill, with various forms of camouflage, in order to render the attacker invisible for as long as possible. As a result all anti U-boat aircraft were painted white on their sides and undersurfaces.

Footnotes

1   By the outbreak of war 224's Hudsons were operating from Leuchars and had been joined by a second squadron (233) at Bircham Newton. A third Hudson squadron (220) was also in the process of converting from Ansons at Thornaby. Over 200 Hudson Is had been delivered by the middle of 1940 and orders were placed for an additional 150 aircraft. Orders for 20 Hudson IIs and 414 Hudson IIIs followed. Over 800 Hudsons were delivered to the RAF against British contracts before the introduction of Lend-Lease. The first version supplied under Lend-Lease was the Hudson IIIA, 382 of which were delivered and were followed by 309 Hudson Vs and 450 Hudson VIs. To these were added the 30 Hudson IVs diverted from a RAAF contract. Total deliveries of Hudsons to the RAF were just over 2,000. In Coastal Command they were operated on Nos. 48, 59, 206, 220, 224, 233, 269, 279, 280, 320, 407, 500 and 608 Squadrons. *Aircraft of the RAF Since 1918* by Owen Thetford (Putnam 1979).
2   *So Few; The Immortal Record of the RAF* by David Masters.
3   Between April 1940 and March 1943 Bomber and Coastal Commands laid nearly 16,000 mines at a cost of 329 aircraft. These mines sank 369 vessels, totalling 361,821 tons. During the same period Bomber, Coastal and Fighter Commands delivered 3,700 attacks on ships at sea at a cost of 648 aircraft that resulted in the sinking of 107 vessels, totalling 155,076 tons.
4   'Ginger' Bowhill, who had originally entered the Royal Navy as in 1898 as a midshipman, had taken over as AOC-in-C Coastal Command vice Philip Joubert on 18 August 1937.
5   Term applied to Sonar equipment used for locating submerged submarines. ASDIC (an acronym for 'anti-Submarine Detection Committee' the organization that began research into this device in 1917) emitted a distinct 'ping' when locating the target.
6   The second 'Happy Time' for the U-boats came with the entry into the war by America following the Japanese attack on Pearl Harbor on 7 December 1941. The US Navy failed to learn from the bitter experience suffered by the Royal Navy and shipping losses off the American eastern seaboard 'grew to ridiculous proportions'. Between January and June 1942 567 ships were sunk at a cost of 21 U-boats. *U-boat Fact File* by Peter Sharpe (Midland Publishing Ltd 1998).

The torpedo struck Compass Rose as she was moving at almost her full speed: she was therefore mortally torn by the sea as well as by the violence of the enemy. She was hit squarely about twelve feet from her bows: there was one slamming explosion and the noise of ripping and tearing metal and the fatal sound of sea-water flooding in under great pressure: a blast of heat from the stricken fo'c'sle rose to the bridge like a hideous waft of incense. Compass Rose veered wildly from her course and came to a shaking stop, like a dog with a bloody muzzle: her bows were very nearly blown off and her stern was already starting to cant in the air, almost before the way was off the ship.

At the moment of disaster, Ericson was on the bridge and Lockhart and Wells: the same incredulous shock hit them all like a sickening body-blow. They were masked and confused by the pitch-dark night and they could not believe that Compass Rose had been struck. But the ugly angle of the deck must only have one meaning and the noise of things sliding about below their feet confirmed it. There was another noise, too, a noise which momentarily paralysed Ericson's brain and prevented him thinking at all; it came from a voice-pipe connecting the fo'c'sle with the bridge - an agonized animal howling, like a hundred dogs going mad in a pit. It was the men caught by the explosion, which must have jammed their only escape: up the voice-pipe came their shouts, their crazy hammering, their screams for help. But there was no help for them: with all executioner's hand, Ericson snapped the voice-pipe cover shut, cutting off the noise.

The Cruel Sea **by Nicholas Monsarrat.**

Chapter 1

Norwegian Campaign

On 8th April 1940 at 2 o'clock in the afternoon, a Sunderland flying boat sighted a battleship of the 'Scharnhorst' class accompanied by two cruisers of the 'Leipzig' class and two destroyers. They were a hundred and thirty miles from the Alsboen Light off the West coast of Norway. The ships saw the Sunderland almost at the same moment and opened anti-aircraft fire which was both heavy and accurate. The Sunderland was hit almost at once; two of its tanks were holed and the hull gradually filled with petrol. When it landed at its base it had lost 300 gallons.

That same day German destroyers had been seen at various times in the neighbourhood of the Horns Reef, steaming on a Northerly course. The German attack on Norway had begun.

Throughout the next day aircraft of Coastal Command were very busy reconnoitring the new area of battle. Before midday a London flying boat had reported the presence of a German cruiser of the 'Koln' class in Bergen. This intelligence was confirmed later by a Blenheim and a Wellington. A Sunderland reported one 'Hipper' class cruiser in Trondheim Fjord and Wellingtons enemy warships and possibly transports at Kristiansand (South). The cruiser at Bergen was attacked that afternoon by Wellingtons, which dropped thirty armour-piercing 500-lb bombs from between 4,000 and 6,000 feet. They were met by heavy fire, but thought that they had scored one direct hit on her stern. On the next day a Hudson reported that after a further attack by naval Skuas from the aircraft carrier HMS Furious the cruiser had sunk.

On 12th April a Wellington, put at the service of Coastal by Bomber Command, flew from an aerodrome in Northern Scotland over a thousand miles' of sea to the North of Norway. When it entered Narvik Fjord 'huge rocks towered up on either side of us,' reports the wireless operator. 'Snow drifted down so that we could see only a few yards ahead. The gusts were terrific, bouncing and throwing us about... By then we reckoned we were within about ten miles of Narvik, but we could not continue. Visibility was almost nil... We went about and picked our way down the fjord again... like a boat hugging the shore. Suddenly we saw once more the open sea.' They soon saw something else, a Ju 88 crossing their bows. 'We began to circle each other, two heavy bombers waiting to pounce.' Then the inevitable curtain of snow fell and they lost each other: Near Narvik the compass showed errors of between twenty and thirty degrees, but the Wellington set course for base and landed safely after a flight of fourteen and a half hours.

*When the Wimpy entered Narvik Fjord 'huge rocks towered up on either side of us,' reported the wireless operator. 'Snow drifted down so that we could see only a few yards' ahead. The gusts were terrific, bouncing and throwing us about. … By then we reckoned we were within about ten miles of Narvik, but we could not continue. Visibility was almost nil. … We went about and picked our way down the fjord again … like a boat hugging the shore. Suddenly we saw once more the open sea.' They soon saw something else, a Ju 88 crossing their bows. 'We began to circle each other, two heavy bombers waiting to pounce.' Then the inevitable curtain of snow fell and they lost each other: Near Narvik the compass showed errors of between twenty and thirty degrees, but the Wellington set course for base and landed safely after a flight of fourteen and a half hours. On the next day the Royal Navy entered the fjord and sank seven German destroyers.
By 14th April the German Air Force was in occupation of all the aerodromes in Norway and Denmark...'*
Coastal Command: The Fight for Norway Air (Air Ministry 1942.)

The great consolidation of the Empire Air Force began almost concurrently with the fall of France in May 1940. In this, the Atlantic Delivery Service was a major factor. The service was inaugurated on the night of 10 November 1940 when seven Hudson aircraft, crewed by men from Britain, Australia, South Africa, Norway, Canada and the United States made the first flight under the leadership of Captain D. C. T. Bennett, who later became Air Officer Commanding RAF Pathfinder Force. Headquarters for the Atlantic Delivery Service were set up at Montreal and with the help of the Canadian Pacific Railway Company the service was built up. Pilots and radio operators were at first obtained from British Overseas Airways as a nucleus. Later, service navigators trained under the Joint Air Training Plan became available.[7]

In Coastal Command, Hudsons were just coming into squadrons at the outbreak of war and eventually they completely superseded the shorter range Avro Anson. Hudsons gave excellent service for a number of years on anti-submarine and general reconnaissance duties from bases all round the British coastline and they also served in a maritime role with the RAF in West Africa, the Mediterranean area, the West Indies, in Iceland and in the Far East. They were the first American aircraft to be delivered by air to Britain and the first aircraft in Coastal Command to carry airborne lifeboats for air-sea rescue duties. Hudsons were hard at work over the North Sea from the first day of the war, their main task being to keep a watch for German surface raiders attempting to escape into the Atlantic between Scotland and Norway. A Hudson on 224 Squadron can claim to be the first RAF aircraft operating from the United Kingdom to shoot down an enemy aircraft, on 8 October 1939, when the Hudson succeeded in destroying a Dornier Do 18 flying-boat during a patrol over Jutland.

224 Squadron began operations before war was declared. During the Munich crisis all the Coastal Squadrons were sent to their war stations. 224 Squadron was already at Leuchars, from which they were to patrol the North Sea in venerable Ansons, which could not reach the Norwegian coast and be

able to return. All the German fleet had to do was to cling to the coast and slip out to the Atlantic without being seen, As the threat of war increased the Squadron was equipped with Lockheed Hudsons, Two weeks before the war truly began, 224 sent out its first sortie, disguised as an exercise but actually to report the movements of the German naval units off the coast of Norway, while the Home Fleet was moving from Portsmouth to Scapa Flow.

Wing Commander Terry McComb, CO of 224 Squadron recalled, 'Going to Norway was a big thrill in those days. I know it must seem funny now, but we had all wanted to look at the Norwegian coastline because it had been impossible in our old Ansons, The first member of the Squadron to see it was quite a hero for a few hours. During the exercise the weather was bloody awful and the Squadron suffered its first war casualty; Dingle Bell, the Squadron adjutant, who crashed into a Norwegian cliff.' The aircraft were poorly armed and gun turrets had not arrived. Although they had no gun turrets, 224 aircraft waded into the enemy with two fixed front guns. 'It was not long before we had our first kill. Three Hudsons led by the Flight Commander of 'C' Flight did it. The leader was 'Dog-shooter' Womersley, who always wore drain pipe trousers, a shooting jacket and bow tie.'

The Squadron also took part in photographic reconnaissance. It began with nervous little attempts to photograph the enemy country on the other side of the Channel. A detached flight of 224 Squadron was kept at Thornaby at the beginning of the war to photograph and report on the movements of naval units in the Heligoland Bight. McComb said that photographic reconnaissance was 'a very dirty job' in those days, but that as a result of those flights, information was brought back, making it possible for the Wellingtons and Hampdens to attack enemy ships in force. In those early days the aircraft of 224 Squadron flew battle flights to intercept and shoot down enemy aircraft, they bombed aerodromes in Norway, searched for enemy ships and photographed enemy harbours and attacked shipping. That cumbersome word, specialization, has conquered all these uncertain arrangements and 224 now do little but hunt and kill U-boats at night. [8]

On 31 January 1940 fourteen Hudsons became the first aircraft in Coastal Command to be fitted with ASV radar which enabled the location of U-boats at night or in poor visibility. In February 1940 a Hudson on 220 Squadron directed naval forces to the hideout of the German prison ship *Altmark* (an auxiliary of the *Graf Spee*) in Norway. Many British prisoners of war were set free as a result. A Flight Commander on 224 Squadron gave a talk on the BBC about a raid on Norway. 'When I was last in London I was actually taken for a Scotsman, but, as you may guess, my home is in Canada - Vancouver, British Columbia. In some ways, Scotland is quite like home - pine trees, mountains and plenty of snow in the winter.

'We've been pretty busy in the last few weeks with our American-built Hudson aircraft. It's a mixed type of work that falls to the Coastal Command. We spend most of our time over the North Sea doing reconnaissance work, looking for U-boats and escorting convoys. These are comparatively peaceable occupations, although you may run into German aircraft doing the same job from the other side. But sometimes you get an operation which breaks the monotony. We had a bit of excitement the other day when orders came through for us to attack some shipping in a Norwegian harbour. Our leader was our Wing Commander [Terry McComb] and we had a talk in his office before starting, discussing the method of attack and then we got ready for the flight. Soon after we left we ran into mist, fog and rain and had to fly blind for about half an hour. There was a possibility that the bad weather might spoil the fun, but nearer to the Norwegian coast, it cleared.

In the half light the scores of little islands were a greyish-brown colour, with the sea a darker shade. The wide fjord showed up almost black ahead. We flew into it, keeping level with the tops of the surrounding mountains. We kept on until we had a big, snow-covered mountain between us and the harbour. We skipped over the top of this mountain and flew down the other side so close to the snow that we almost seemed to be tobogganing down it. In a few minutes we were below the snow level, skimming the rocks and the tops of the pines. The wing commander was leading, with five of us streaming along behind. That was just about the moment that the guns opened up on us. Batteries on the mountain-side behind started firing down from above and anti-aircraft posts on each flank and in from let us have all they'd got. Streams of tracer shells coming at us made a criss-cross pattern all round and there were bursts of black smoke ahead where the heavy stuff was exploding. It was really a fireworks display and, actually, it looked very nice - if you were in a position to appreciate it.

'Another few seconds and we were down over the harbour. Machine gunners were shooting from the windows of the hotels on the waterfront. One of our rear gunners sprayed the buildings with bullets as we passed - and the windows emptied like magic. The guns on either side were firing so low that they were probably hitting each other as we went between them. They didn't touch us and, as a matter of fact, none of our six aircraft was so much as scratched. The ships we were after were lying at anchor-some against the quays and some moored in the harbour. We dropped our bombs on and around them and shot off towards the sea. As we looked back, we could see the smoke and flames caused by the explosions. We had an even more spectacular party over the same harbour, later, when we paid a return visit and blew up an ammunition dump. I arrived by myself, a little early for the appointment and decided to start the ball rolling. It was very early dawn and I could just pick out the little huts on the end of the quay which we knew contained ammunition. (I'd seen photographs of them before leaving, taken by another aircraft of the squadron.) 'Two of my bombs and possibly more, scored direct hits on the dumps. We were about 2,500 feet up, but even there the force of the explosion lifted the aircraft as if it were riding a wave.

'We went right over the hill and did a right turn and circled back round the harbour to see what damage we had done. Growing from the remains of the ammunition dump was a huge mushroom of black smoke, going up to 2,000 feet. Its base was a fiery red mass and higher up it was pierced through and through by flames and pieces of burning debris flying through the air. Other aircraft which arrived later saw the fire still burning. We all returned from that trip safely.

'Another job was the occasion when we bombed a group of enemy warships. To give honour where it is due, I must raise my hat to the German naval gunners. We were flying at 15,000 feet, but they kept planting their heavy ack-ack so close to us that we could see the flash of the bursts before the smoke appeared (the burst has to be VERY close for you to see more than just the smoke). We could feel the aircraft vibrating from the explosions. It was continually jerking, as though it had been kicked by a giant. All six of our aircraft were hit by bits of high explosive shell, but we all got back to our base-and I might mention as a tribute to the maintenance staff that the six were all flying again the next day.

'On one of our raids in the north of Norway, we used the Midnight Sun to light us to our objective, which was an aerodrome. We dropped numbers of high explosive and incendiary bombs on that occasion and left several fires behind us. Perhaps our most successful attack on an enemy aerodrome was when we dropped ninety bombs in less than a minute. This particular aerodrome had hardly been used and was tucked into the side of a hill. With infinite trouble, the Germans had built new wooden runways which looked as smooth as a skating rink when we arrived, but were burning merrily after our bombing. We counted forty fires when we left, some of them in the woods where the aircraft were probably hidden and others in the huts around the side of the aerodrome.'

After the collapse of France two squadrons of Hudsons moved to Northern Ireland to strengthen the anti-U-boat force and some of these aircraft took part in the hunting of the *Bismarck* in April 1941. 269 Squadron operated over the Western Approaches from Iceland. [9]

On 30 January 1940 a Sunderland on 228 Squadron laid claim to the first U-boat kill for Coastal Command. Flight Lieutenant E. J. Brooks was flying Sunderland N9025/Y when he attacked U-55 in the North Sea after the enemy submarine had been depth-charged to the surface by the sloop HMS *Fowey*. The destroyer HMS *Whitshed* and the French destroyer *Valmy* escorting Convoy OA.80G arrived on the scene and as the warships opened fire the U-boat crew scuttled their boat and were all rescued except the commander, 31-year old Kapitänleutnant Werner Heidel.[10] From June 1940 Sunderlands on 228 Squadron operated against Italian shipping in the Mediterranean and in November one of these boats flying from Malta carried out a reconnaissance of Taranto prior to the celebrated Fleet Air Arm attack on the night of 11 November by Swordfish aircraft on the Italian Fleet. Preliminary reconnaissance of Taranto harbour showed that the Italians had six battleships at anchor, as well as several cruisers and destroyers.[11]

In April 1940 meanwhile, Sunderland crews in Britain were tasked to monitor German naval activity off Norway and reconnoitre the coast to obtain intelligence for possible future operations. On 1 April 204 Squadron were at Sullom Voe, 201 Squadron at Pembroke Dock and 10 Squadron RAAF at Mount Batten. One writer noted that 'the Australians seemed to be at home beside this ancient water from which Drake left to circumnavigate the world, nearly 400 years earlier. They were housed in two hangars where T. E. Lawrence worked as Aircraftman Shaw from 1929 to 1933. The Australians are not history worshippers and sometimes they treat the past as if it were a cigarette end. But the ghosts of Drake and Lawrence are treated amiably here.'[12]

Three days' later 204 Squadron flew its first operation from Sullom Voe when Flight Lieutenant Frankie Phillips in N9046 took off at 1125 for a convoy escort. Phillips located the convoy in the estimated position. At 1550 while the aircraft was twenty miles away from the convoy on the starboard bow, two Ju 88s were sighted low on the water approaching from the direction of the Norwegian coast. The Sunderland and the enemy aircraft were 50-100 feet above the sea. The Ju 88s circled around the Sunderland for two minutes and then carried out a beam attack on the starboard side at a range of 800 yards, the two aircraft flying past successively on a course parallel to the flying-boat. A desultory engagement took place without any apparent damage to either aircraft. Both turrets and the starboard amidship gunner fired short bursts. The subsequent appearance of four more Ju 88 aircraft led to the belief that the enemy was employing this tactic to draw fire. After three minutes' fighting the two aircraft began to climb turning away from our aircraft and after a three-minute pause, four more Ju 88s appeared from the same direction and immediately delivered a line astern attack on the tail of the Sunderland. The rear gunner, Corporal Little, held his fire till the leading Ju 88 was at 100 yards range. He then opened fire and shot down the leading attacker, which banked steeply and dived into the sea. The second Ju 88 was also hit and was afterwards known to have force-landed. During this attack the first two Ju 88s to arrive were attempting to bomb the Sunderland from a height of 1,500 feet. The bombs however were easily avoided by the fire control officer in the observation dome, directing the pilot away from them. The bombs could be seen falling as soon as they were released and the nearest one burst at least 100 yards from the Sunderland. As soon as the attack of the four aircraft had been broken up by our gunfire, the five remaining Ju 88s immediately made off and the Sunderland made for home, having suffered the following damage: bullets in port inner, starboard middle and starboard inner fuel tanks causing loss of 500 gallons during return flight; bullet holes in hull, fin, instrument panel; trimming gear and fuel jettison systems made unserviceable; one bomb rack damaged; the fire control officer and navigator both sustained face cuts from splinters. Two fuel tanks were hit and the control wires and certain instruments were shot through. Phillips was awarded a DFC and Corporal William Little received the award of the DFM.

Also on 4 April a reconnaissance flight over the Elbe estuary discovered German naval vessels and sixty merchant ships in the Schillig Roads moving northward in formations of five ships. The naval vessels were attacked by six Blenheims without visible result. A patrol sent to the same place on the next day had to be recalled on account of weather; but its leader got through and flying just below clouds, which were down to 200 feet, found the Roads almost empty. On Saturday 6 April a photographic reconnaissance showed that several units of the German Fleet, including the 26,000-ton battle cruisers *Scharnhorst* and the *Gneisenau*, were in the harbours of North-Western

Germany. It was, however, on the night of 6/7 April that the signs of an impending great event became unmistakable. British bombers engaged in the dropping of leaflets reported that a wide stream of motor transport, headlights blazing, was flowing along the autobahn from Hamburg to Lübeck, while at Eckernforde, near Kiel, there was great activity among shipping under the glare of brilliant arc lamps. The Germans made no pretence of concealment. When all is on the hazard they rarely do, believing that speed is more important than secrecy.

Although it was not until 9 April 1940 that German ships of war were seen in Norwegian harbours, they had sailed on the 7th. On 7 April bomber crews were brought to a state of readiness when it was realised that German ships sighted heading for Norway and Denmark the day before were part of an invasion force. During the afternoon twelve Blenheims in two formations of six saw an enemy cruiser and four destroyers at sea. They followed them and four minutes later caught sight of most of the German Fleet, which was then 76 miles NNW of the Horn's Reef. The Blenheims wheeled into the sun and attacked either the *Scharnhorst* or the *Gneisenau*. The leader sent out a message giving the position and course of the German Fleet. This information never got through and only became known some hours later when the aircraft returned. 'The German Fleet was a very grand sight,' said the leader of the Blenheims. 'When they shot at me it was like lightning flashing in daylight all about me.'

Detachments of Wellingtons on 9 and 115 Squadrons that had been sent to Lossiemouth and Kinloss in Scotland sought in vain to find the German ships that same afternoon when they were thwarted by bad visibility. Two of 115 Squadron's Wellington ICs piloted by Canadian Pilot Officer Estelles Arthur Wickenkamp MBE and Pilot Officer Roy Alan Gayford, who was also Canadian, were shot down with no survivors by Bf 110s and three other Wellingtons were damaged. Another force was detailed for the same task the next day were weather-bound.

On 8 April a Sunderland on 204 Squadron flown by the CO, Wing Commander Hyde, who was on a reconnaissance of the Trondheim Fjord, was attacked by two enemy aircraft and damaged before the Sunderland was able to escape. Hyde crawled into the wings and stopped up holes in the fuel tanks, thus enabling the aircraft to make it back to base. At 1400 hours another Sunderland flying boat sighted a battleship of the Scharnhorst class accompanied by two cruisers of the Leipzig class and two destroyers. They were 130 miles from the Alsboen Light off the West coast of Norway. The ships saw the Sunderland almost at the same moment and opened anti-aircraft fire which was both heavy and accurate. The Sunderland was hit almost at once; two of its tanks were holed and the hull gradually filled with petrol. When it landed at its base it had lost 300 gallons. That same day German destroyers had been seen at various times in the neighbourhood of the Horns Reef, steaming on a Northerly course. The German attack on Norway had begun.

In the small hours of 9 April the Germans crossed the Danish frontier and simultaneously German troops landed at Narvik, Trondheim, Bergen and

24

Stavanger. The same day Wellingtons made an attack on enemy cruisers in Bergen roadstead which had been employed in the invasion. It was one of the war's earliest air attacks on German ships of war. One of those who took part was Flying Officer D. J. French, an Australian member on 50 Squadron. For his work in the Bergen attack French was awarded the DFC, first award to an Australian airman in the war.[13] For his work in the Bergen attack French was awarded the DFC, first award to an Australian airman in the war. Aircraft of Coastal Command were very busy reconnoitring the new area of battle. Before midday a London flying boat had reported the presence of a German cruiser of the Köln class in Bergen. This intelligence was confirmed later by a Blenheim and a Wellington. Sunderland L5806 flown by Flight Lieutenant E. J. Brooks having detached to 18 Group in the Shetlands flew an afternoon reconnaissance to Trondheim Fjord. Brooks made use of a cloud cover approach from the north, inland and made the reconnaissance whilst flying in a westerly direction. Landfall at Vikten Island was made at 1600 and the flying-boat proceeded inland above broken cloud at 7-9,000 feet. Through cloud gaps vessels were seen at anchor in harbour, identified as Hipper class cruiser, two destroyers and three large MVs. Northeast of the harbour was the *Nürnburg* and in a fjord North of the town, one destroyer. Engines were de-synchronized and the aircraft constantly retired into cloud. Considerable icing was experienced and heavy snow storms were encountered. Brooks set course due West at 1750 and landed at the Shetlands at 1955.

That afternoon twelve Wellingtons and twelve Hampdens went out to attack the enemy naval forces now in Bergen. Twelve aircraft were recalled and two of the remaining dozen dropped thirty armour-piercing 500lb bombs from between 4,000 and 6,000 feet at dusk. The Wellingtons were met by heavy fire, but thought that they had scored one direct hit on the cruiser's stern. On the next day, 10 April, a Hudson reported that after a further attack by sixteen Skuas of the Fleet Air Arm from the aircraft carrier HMS *Furious* the cruiser had sunk.

The conquest of Norway gave the RAF no opportunity to its bombers in direct support of the British or Norwegian army by attacking the German troops as they advanced or fought. The RAF had no bases for bombers nearer than in Britain, a distance of 400 miles and to keep up any continuous bombing of the battlefield, where nothing but continuous bombing was of any use, would have been impossible. The Luftwaffe concentrated on the aerodrome and seaplane anchorage at Stavanger, the aerodrome at Vaernes near Trondheim and also on Fornebu, the airport of Oslo. In order to maintain the rate of landings, the Germans by 15 April were using passenger aircraft taken from their Continental passenger services. Together with the German ships at Bergen, Kristiansand, Trondheim and elsewhere the newly-occupied aerodromes formed the most obvious targets for Bomber Command. Most of the Luftwaffe aerodromes were attacked by night and usually - for in April it is still winter in Norway - in bad weather. In Norway, Stavanger aerodrome was most frequently bombed, then Bergen, Trondheim, Kristiansand and Fornebu aerodromes. In Denmark, Aalborg and Rye aerodromes were continually bombed and so was Westerland aerodrome on Sylt. Coastal Command bombed and machine-gunned Stavanger many times, beginning on 10 April. Here is the report contained in the official summary of a machine-gun attack by a long-range Blenheim. It is typical of many such.

'Reached Norwegian coast at 1600 hours on 10th (April). At 1604 entered the clouds after seeing five Messerschmitts taking off from Stavanger. At 1610 observed 18 seaplanes (Blohm and Voss) in the harbour, also twenty Heinkels and fifteen Messerschmitts on the aerodrome. Two Heinkels and three Blohm and Voss seaplanes were raked with machine-gun fire from a height of a hundred feet. One Heinkel was destroyed by an explosion and the other damaged. A Bowser pump was set on fire whilst filling a large bomber; 2,000 rounds in all were fired. At 1620 the Blenheim aircraft set course for Bergen, but failed to locate it. At 1815 (on the way home) a Ju 88 was attacked in a position 135 miles from (North coast of Scotland); 500 rounds were fired, which put the port engine and rear gunner out of action and it is doubtful whether the enemy aircraft could have reached its base. Heavy anti-aircraft fire was encountered at Stavanger and our aircraft was hit by explosive bullets. Undercarriage partially collapsed on landing, rendering aircraft unserviceable. The pilot was slightly injured in the hand from splintered glass caused by enemy fire.'

Lack of cloud cover on 11 April prevented six Hampdens from attacking warships in Kristiansand South. Two Blenheim fighters sprayed Sola airfield near Stavanger with machine-gun fire. They were followed towards dusk by six Wellingtons on 115 Squadron operating from Kinloss which delivered a low-level attack which started a large fire. Three of the Wimpys bombed the airfield but one of the remaining three, flown by Pilot Officer F. E. Barber was shot down by German fighters and Flight Sergeant G. A. Powell's Wellington was seriously damaged and he had to belly-land back at Kinloss without hydraulics. He was later awarded the DFM for this operation. That night 23 Whitleys and twenty Hampdens set out to attack German shipping at various locations between Kiel Bay and Oslo. Heavy darkness hampered the operation. One vessel believed to be carrying ammunition which was seen to explode with 'great violence' was the result of a successful attack by one of the Whitleys. One Whitley failed to return.

It was on 12 April that the largest bombing operation of the war so far was mounted when 83 Wellingtons, Hampdens and Blenheims swept a wide area in search of to bomb some of the main units of the German Fleet. These included the *Scharnhorst*, the *Gneisenau* and a cruiser of the Nürnberg class which had been discovered heading south across the entrance to the Skagerrak. There was fog about and they were not seen, but two warships in Kristiansand South were bombed. The Wellingtons and Hampdens detailed for the operation presently found themselves heavily engaged by a swarm of Bf 109s and 110s which pursued them 200 miles out to sea. In this running fight the enemy pilots, again employing beam attacks to excellent advantage, shot down six Hampdens and two of the six Wellingtons on 149 Squadron from Mildenhall and Squadron Leader M. Nolan's Wellington in

38 Squadron's formation of six Wimpys from Marham. Twelve Wellingtons on 9 and 115 Squadrons, which were ordered to make a bombing attack on two cruisers, the *Köln* and the *Königsberg* in Bergen harbour, fared little better. None of their bombs did any lasting damage. This was the last major daylight raid for the Hampdens and Wellingtons. The Blenheim formations were not attacked by German fighters. German radio admitted the loss of five Me 109s.

Flight Lieutenant Van der Kiste on 210 Squadron was airborne in a Sunderland from Sullom Voe at 0500, tasked to look for troopships in the Hardangar Fjord. There were heavy snowstorms over the Norwegian coast and while searching for the objective, heavy anti-aircraft fire was encountered over Hagesund. The Sunderland's starboard middle tank was hit and the hull pierced but the search continued and the flying-boat was hit again over Garvin, the port middle tank and tailplane being hit. The ships were not located. When the Sunderland landed at Sullom Voe at 1130 it had 400 gallons of petrol in the bilges.

On 12 April also, a Wellington on 215 Squadron, put at the service of Coastal by Bomber Command, was flown by a crew on 75 Squadron RNZAF from an aerodrome in Northern Scotland over a thousand miles of sea to the North of Norway for a daylight reconnaissance of Narvik. In May an account of the flight was given to the BBC by 'a Flight Lieutenant'. By way of an introduction a Wing Commander in Public Relations said:

'It'll be a long time before anyone can tell the full story of the Allies' recent expedition to Norway. But one thing can be told even now-that whatever else it has done, the Norwegian campaign has proved once again that the RAF can be relied on to do its job thoroughly under the worst possible conditions. It was no picnic this work of the RAF over Norway, you can take it from me. Behind the official reports of reconnaissance flights, patrols and heavy bombing raids, there is a remarkable story of men and machines engaged in a struggle in which the odds were with the enemy from the start and not only with the enemy but with Nature as well. To put it bluntly, the Nazis got there first and having got there by means as ruthless as they were treacherous, they seized all Norway's available air bases. In the circumstances our fighters had only one base - and that an improvised one - from which to operate. That meant that our long distance bombers and long range fighters had to fly all the way from this country across at least 300 miles of sea before they could even get going with their job. But in spite of this our men and machines put up a fine show...' He then introduced 'a young Dominion pilot who was the captain and first pilot of the aircraft and he told listeners that the flight was even longer than those to Posen and Prague; it was certainly by far the longest over the sea carried out by land planes. During fourteen and a half hours' flying the pilot and crew were only over land for a few minutes.' The Flight Lieutenant began: 'I am a New Zealander. I come from Northcote, Auckland. My second pilot, who was a sergeant observer and acted as navigator, comes from Stratford, near New Plymouth, New Zealand; my wireless operator, who was a leading aircraftman, is also from Auckland. The aircraftman who was the air gunner, is also a New Zealander. We came to England last year to collect Wellington bombers to serve in New Zealand. Before we could get back the war started and we stopped on.

'The flight to Narvik was all kept pretty hush-hush before-hand. At our home station they simply told us to proceed to another station where we were to collect a Wellington for special reconnaissance work. We flew there and saw the Wellington that had been chosen for our flight. She wasn't a new or special type of aircraft - just an ordinary machine they had been using for training.[14]

It was an all-night job getting the aircraft ready, fitting the special tanks, loading up with ammunition, trying out the machine-guns, the wireless equipment and those hundred-and-one gadgets needed for navigation, then we flew to Scotland where we were told to be ready for a take-off the next morning at daybreak. In Scotland we made our final check up and filled up with petrol and oil. Our navigational equipment included bomb-sight and drift-sight, sextant, compasses, charts, pencils, rubbers, dividers, parallel rules, protractors and so on. The whole crew was interchangeable. Everyone had to be able to do everyone else's job, even to piloting at a push, for there was no automatic pilot in the aircraft. We also had with us a Lieutenant Commander from the Navy to assist in identifying ships at sea.

'We carried a collapsible rubber dinghy safely tucked away behind the engine. Then what happens is this: If we have to use it, we pull a wire which forces the dinghy out of the aircraft. It is immediately inflated automatically and ready for use, complete with its own supply of distress signals. In case we were forced down we carried mostly 'hard tack' - tinned beef, sardines and chocolate. Before taking off we removed the oxygen bottles from the aircraft because we didn't intend to hit the heights. That meant a saving in weight. We had two cameras on board, one for vertical pictures and the other for oblique pictures. The next morning at dawn we were told what the job was - we were to reconnoitre the Norwegian coast to the Lofoten Islands and the Vest fjord to Narvik.

'We took off in the early morning, flew once round the aerodrome and then out to sea in a bee-line for Narvik. We skirted the Shetland Islands at a steady speed of nearly 200 mph and we were soon out of sight of land. It was a bumpy day. We ran into some extraordinary weather with heavy rain squalls and finally, just as we were coming near the Norwegian coast we headed into a snowstorm. For quite a while our instruments were registering twenty-seven degrees of frost. As we came in sight of the Norwegian coast we got ready - ready for anything. The wireless operator manned the front gun; the second pilot took over at the astro-hatch, acting as a fire-control officer and the rear gunner took 'his place in his turret. Norway at that moment looked all covered in deep snow, but still it was land and any sort of land was welcome.

'Our real work had now begun, although the weather was steadily getting worse. There was a high wind by now and we were flying in and out of snow and sleet about 3,000 feet above the sea. There were such terrific bumps that the gunners bumped their heads as they were thrown upwards out of their seats. Just as we were going towards Vest fjord we met an enemy aircraft but he sheered off as soon as he saw us. We flew up the fjord through driving snow at only 200 feet. The clouds and cliffs seemed to be closing in on us and when we got to the end of the fjord we swung round, made a sharp turn and went on with our reconnaissance southward down the coast as far as Kristiansand and then we turned for home.

'Up to this time we were too busy to bother about our rations and too excited. Now that the job was done we passed round hot coffee and sandwiches. We had six flasks of coffee with us, beef and ham sandwiches, chocolate, biscuits, chewing-gum, a packet of tea, six bottles of water, a billy-can and a 'Tommy' cooker.

'Nothing very much happened on the way back. That is to say nothing worse than bad weather. We sighted British Naval units in the North Sea, circled round them and exchanged signals by lamp. We were able to give them news of a couple of British destroyers and a merchantman we had seen at the entrance to one of the fjords. All the way home we had a strong wind against us and we were glad to see the Shetland Islands again. The flight covered well over 2,000 miles and the second pilot and I before we finished had shared between us fourteen and a half hours at the controls. As soon as we landed we were given hot drinks before we began to make out our reports and had the photographs we had taken developed.'[15]

On the night of 13/14 April fifteen Hampdens carried out the first RAF minelaying operation of the war. Fourteen aircraft laid mines in sea lanes off Denmark between German ports and Norway. One Hampden was lost. Operating from Wick, a Wellington I on 38 Squadron flown by Pilot Officer George Lesley Crosby ditched 22 miles off Whitby while returning from a reconnaissance sortie. There were no survivors.[16] Eight Blenheims that were sent to patrol the Wilhelmshaven area abandoned the operation and another attempt by eight Blenheims the next day to the same area also ended in failure because of lack of cloud cover. By 14 April the Luftwaffe was in occupation of all the aerodromes in Norway and Denmark. On the night of 14/15 April 28 Hampdens again carried out minelaying off Denmark. Two of the Hampdens failed to return. Night after night the Hampdens went out in secret to drop their mines by parachute and build up more minefields. It had all the hazards of long-range work over the sea. One mine-layer at least got a laugh out of it, for the pilot of a Beaufort of the Coastal Command was approaching the German coast when the captain of a German ship, probably quite assured that only a German aircraft could be flying in that neighbourhood, flashed a warning: 'You are running into danger,' which was very kind and thoughtful of the enemy.

On 15 April eleven Blenheims set out to attack Stavanger airfield. Six bombed and two German aircraft on the ground were hit. All the Blenheims returned safely. Two further Blenheims bombed patrol boats off Wilhelmshaven. One Blenheim was shot down by one of the German boat's defensive fire. That night twelve Whitleys were dispatched to Stavanger airfield where eight aircraft bombed and hits were seen on the airfield. All the Whitleys returned safely. Through all the early months of the war and especially during the Norwegian campaign the weather remained a factor of cardinal importance and it must not be forgotten that in April it is still winter in Norway. To illustrate the appalling weather met with, here is an account by the pilot of a Blenheim, the only one of six which made it to Stavanger on 16 April, the other five returning because of icing conditions in cloud.

'Soon after leaving the English coast,' he said, 'we ran into rain which was literally tropical in its fury. After some time we climbed and then the rain turned to snow. At 13,000 feet the engines of two of the Blenheims became iced up and stopped. One of the aircraft dropped more or less out of control until only 600 feet above the sea, when they started again. The other Blenheim was even luckier. It actually struck the waves at the very moment its engines came to life. It lost its rear wheel, but both aircraft got safely back to base.' In such conditions it is not surprising that only one of that formation of Blenheims reached Stavanger. It was flying very low and a brisk argument was in progress between the pilot and the observer as to their whereabouts. 'Call yourself an observer,' said the pilot. 'Where is the ------- place?' At that moment a piece of anti-aircraft shell removed half the cowling of his cockpit. They knew they had arrived.

On 15 April also Sunderland N6133 flown by Wing Commander Nicholetts, CO 228 Squadron, took the Chief of the British Expeditionary Force in Norway, General Carton de Wiart VC, the one-eyed and one-armed soldier who suffered from the same disabilities as Nelson and possessed similar dauntless courage, to a rendezvous with a Tribal-class destroyer in Namsos Fjord. The Sunderland landed in the fjord at 1645 - just in time to see the destroyer under attack from four Ju 88s and two He 111s, a number of which then machine-gunned the flying boat. Second Lieutenant Elliott was wounded and one enemy aircraft dropped a long stick of bombs ahead of the manoeuvring Sunderland but the pilots managed to evade this attack with no significant damage being caused.

Since the German occupation of Norway, aerodromes at Kristiansand, Oslo and Trondheim had been attacked twice, nine and five times respectively up to the middle of June. In the opening month of the campaign Fornebu was attacked whenever possible. At the end of April it was bombed four times in four days. In all, Stavanger was bombed sixteen times by aircraft of Bomber Command between 11 and 24 April besides being repeatedly attacked by aircraft of Coastal Command and by the Fleet Air Arm. Operations against ports in Germany were also flown by Bomber Command aircraft. On the night of 20/21 April 23 Hampdens laid mines in the Elbe estuary and some of them patrolled seaplane bases at Borkum and Sylt. Thirty-six Whitleys were detailed to bomb various airfields and shipping and 22 bombed targets including airfields at Stavanger and Kristiansand and at Aalborg in Denmark. Shipping was not located and all the aircraft dispatched returned safely.

At dusk on 16 April twenty Whitleys led by the Commanding Officer took off from Yorkshire to attack Stavanger, Vaernes (Trondheim) and Kjeller (Oslo) airfields. Amongst the members of the CO's crew, his navigator and second pilot were new to the work - the former making his first war flight. Clouds were low at the outset, but the pilot climbed to 11,000 feet into a moderately clear layer between upper and lower cloud masses. Setting a course for the southern promontory of Norway to establish a landfall and flying by dead reckoning, they made the sea crossing at 10,000 feet. Owing to cloud the coast-line was missed and the first sight the pilot had of land was when, shortly after 23.00, a snow-covered hill appeared in the bright moonlight through a gap in the clouds. Recognizing the rolling nature of the country, the pilot fixed his position and set a course to cut the south-east coast of Norway in order to make a landfall. Once again the coast was missed. Half an hour later, driving through a gap at 3,000 feet, a flat black surface was seen. The pilot could not determine whether it was land or water. He therefore switched on his landing light and flew down its beam until the reflection revealed the sea. Course was altered to port until the coast-line was picked up at 2,000 feet and identified by the foam of breakers. For the next half-hour the pilot, with his face pressed into the open aperture of his cockpit window, picked his way in and out of cloud, along the intricate coast to the entrance of Oslo Fjord. Continuing in this manner he reached Drammen at 1,500 feet. Great activity was observed alongside the docks on the southern banks of Drammen Fjord. At least ten cargo vessels of all sizes were seen alongside and numerous other ships were moored in the entrance to the fjord. The docks were floodlit and riding lights were displayed. Tempting though this target was, the pilot's task was to find and attack Oslo aerodrome. So, retracing his path, he set a course for the Norwegian capital at 3,000 feet.

At the head of the Oslo Fjord a severe snowstorm was encountered. The aerodrome at Fornebu and the surrounding country were completely obscured. Several attempts were made to penetrate the gloom, the aircraft coming down to a height of 500 feet where it at once met with severe icing conditions. The pilot therefore flew back over enemy shipping in Drammen in the hope that the snowstorm would abate. In this he was disappointed and although Oslo was bathed in bright moonlight, the area of the landing grounds was still invisible. It might have been possible to judge the position of the target in relation to the town; but rather than risk the destruction of non-military objectives the pilot set a course for England, his bombs still on board. He landed safely at his base shortly after 0430, after being in the air for nine and a half hours. No wireless 'fixes' were asked for or received throughout the flight. Because of the weather, only four Whitleys bombed at Trondheim and two at Stavanger. There were no losses.

At dawn on the 17th Stavanger aerodrome was shelled by HMS *Suffolk*; a Hudson spotted for her and had to fight a Ju 88 over the target. Later in the day twelve Blenheims flew in two formations at different heights to Stavanger airfield. The high-flying formation dropped their bombs ten seconds before those flying at a lower level went in to the attack. By keeping formation they drove off repeated attacks by enemy fighters, though two, which became stragglers, were cut off and shot down. That night twenty Wellingtons and Whitleys were sent to bomb Stavanger, Trondheim (Vaernes) and Oslo airfields. Eleven Wellingtons bombed at Stavanger but other targets were not located. One Wellington was lost. Thirty-three Hampdens meanwhile, laid mines off north-west Denmark and all returned safely. On the night of 18/19 April nine Whitleys set out to attack shipping in the Oslo and Trondheim areas but because of bad weather only three bombed. One aircraft failed to return. On 19 April nine Blenheims set out to bomb Stavanger airfield but seven were forced to abandon the task because of bad weather. Only one aircraft bombed an airfield and one Blenheim was lost. That night four Whitleys carried out reconnaissance flights over Northern Germany without incident. On the night of 20/21 April 22 out of 36 Whitley crews dispatched to Norway reported bombing targets including Sola airfield and Kristiansund and at Alborg in Denmark. Twenty-three Hampdens laid mines in the Elbe estuary and some of these patrolled the enemy seaplane bases at Borkum and Sylt. There were no losses from these operations.

Airfields in Norway were attacked on four nights running, 21/22 April to 25/26 April and minelaying was carried out on two of these nights by Hampdens. The raid on 25/26 April saw twelve Wellingtons and six Whitleys attack shipping, airfields and oil-storage tanks at Stavanger and Oslo. Eight of the aircraft bombed without loss. Two Whitleys carried out reconnaissance flights to Aalborg airfield in Denmark and one aircraft failed to return. Twenty-eight Hampdens were dispatched on minelaying sorties but bad weather prevented any mines being laid and three Hampdens were lost. One of the missing Hampdens was the 49 Squadron aircraft of Pilot Officer Arthur Herbert Benson which was shot down near Sylt by Oberfeldwebel Hermann Förster of the 11th Staffel, IV/(N)JG 2 flying a Bf 109D with the cockpit hood removed as a precaution against the pilots being blinded by the glare of searchlights and was probably the first Bomber Command aircraft to be shot down at night by a German fighter. Benson, Pilot Officer Alfred Peter Burdett Hordern, Sergeant Robert Ian Leonard MacKenzie and Leading Aircraftman John Derek Openshaw - were all killed. Sergeant McKenzie's body came ashore and is now buried in the Kiel War Cemetery but the bodies of the other crew members were never found.[17] The attack by RAF Bomber Command on Stavanger, Fornebu and Rye airfields on the night of 2/3 May by twelve Whitleys and twelve Wellingtons was probably the most successful. Twenty-two of the bombers got their bombs away without loss.

'The sheer necessity of locating aerodromes in Norway' wrote David Masters 'sent the great Sunderland flying-boat commanded by Squadron Leader Robert E. [later Sir Robert] Craven roaring across the waters of a Scottish station and heading over the North Sea at 12.30 pm on 27 April 1940. On board were a squadron leader and a warrant officer charged with the difficult task of finding emergency landing grounds and it was Squadron Leader Craven's duty to place his passengers on board the British destroyer HMS *Witherington* in Molde Fjord. The weather was execrable. Everything was blotted out by heavy rain and mist. Visibility was about fifty yards and the cloud was down to 100 feet, nearly at sea level. 'It was absolutely shocking - almost the worst I've ever flown in,' reported Squadron Leader Craven, which, from such an experienced captain of Sunderlands, means that it was indeed bad.

'Directly the Sunderland was settled on her course there came a welcome call to the ward-room for lunch, which the rigger had prepared on the primus stoves in the galley. Going through to his meal, the captain handed over the controls to the second pilot; Pilot Officer Lawrence Latham Jones, a young Canadian who was born at Saskatoon on 21 June 1917. The skipper generally called him Jonah, while other flying-boat officers often referred to him as Slim Jones - a tribute to his spare figure - or Daisy. But during his Norwegian adventure he acquired another nickname, owing to the first-aid which he administered to a wounded man.

'What did you do, Slim?' asked his friends when he got back to the mess. 'Did you give him a shot of morphia?'

The Canadian looked surprised. 'Gee!' he exclaimed. 'I forgot all about it. I gave him a couple of aspirins!' So for many weeks afterwards they called him 'Aspirin' Jones.

'After the captain resumed his seat at the controls, Pilot Officer Jones went through to enjoy his meal in the ward-room. For a couple of hours or more the Sunderland thrashed through the murk. Then the clouds began to break and by the time they were 300 miles away from their station they emerged into brilliant sunshine with a clear sky ahead. Squadron Leader Craven, who has taught more than one captain of a Sunderland how to handle these giant aircraft, sat calmly at the controls, glancing automatically at the revolution counter and the oil temperature. The engines ran sweetly. The pointer of the altimeter remained steady as the Sunderland cruised along. Like all prudent pilots who have flown through 300 miles of bad weather to come out under clear skies, he had a word with his navigator to check their position, just to make sure that he was not off his course. The snow caps of Norway loomed ahead. Making his landfall at Ålesund, the captain flew along Sula Fjord, only to find there was no exit. As German aircraft were busy bombing a wireless station he did a sharp turn and ran out again. That run enabled him to fix his position. Setting his course to the north-east, he flew to Mia Island where he began the day's adventures by flying under a high tension cable, just as some German bombers appeared. They did not attempt to attack with their machine guns but flew overhead and tried to bomb him. The captain promptly took the Sunderland down to within five feet of the water, using the rudder skilfully and darting from side to side to evade the dropping bombs. The enemy had the speed of him, but they found him much too elusive to hit. As he flew toward Ottero Island the bombers drew off, probably to return for more bombs. Flying round Ottero, he skirted the north of the island and turned into Molde Fjord where he came upon the destroyer *Witherington* with two or three merchant ships nearby.

Just as he touched down on the water he sighted twelve Junkers 88s over the town of Molde flying in sections of three. Sweeping over the houses they bombed them heavily, starting many fires and then flew toward the destroyers and flying-boat. Three of the Junkers made straight for the Sunderland whose captain at once opened the throttles and dodged about over the water in the most erratic manner as bomb after bomb came hurtling down. They burst in the sea all around him, but he was too clever for the

German bombers. Coming close to the destroyer as the bombers turned away, he signalled for a boat to be sent off for his passengers. The whaler was quickly alongside. 'I had better go over, too,' said Squadron Leader Craven to Pilot Officer Jones. 'It is up to you to do as you choose. If you think it necessary to go home and leave me, you must do so.' So Pilot Officer Jones took command of the Sunderland while his captain jumped into the whaler with his passengers and was rowed over to the destroyer. A bomb dropped near them on the way. Just as they got on board another fell and the boat in which they had been sitting simply vanished in the explosion, while two of the ratings on the deck of the destroyer were wounded. It was a most astonishing escape. Then the Junkers took up the attack again, some concentrating on the destroyer and others on the flying-boat. Pilot Officer Jones in the Sunderland began taxiing and zigzagging in all directions, as his crew reported the movements of the enemy. Squadron Leader Craven, who had been invited up to the bridge of the destroyer to help to defeat the attack, watched the Junkers closely and advised the commander how to avoid them. 'Port!' he called; 'Now starboard!' As the warship slowed and a bomber made to attack he called: 'Full speed ahead!' and the destroyer sped swiftly out of the way.

'For half an hour the twelve Junkers attacked the destroyer and the flying-boat, but through the skilful manoeuvring, both escaped damage. By that time Pilot Officer Jones saw that the engines of the Sunderland were beginning to overheat through taxiing about over the water, so he decided to take off in order to cool them. He was barely in the air when a Messerschmitt 110 appeared to continue the attack. Diving down on the tail of the Sunderland, the German fighter opened fire with all its guns. But the rear-gunner and the mid ships gunner of the Sunderland were quick on the mark. They met the Messerschmitt with such a heavy fire that in a few seconds it turned away smoking toward the land. After this fight with the Messerschmitt, which cooled off the engines, Pilot Officer Jones touched down once more. Meanwhile his captain was taken in the destroyer to Åandalsnes which was already a mass of ruins. The wooden houses were burned to the ground, the inhabitants had vanished by coach somewhere over the mountains and all was desolation. Up on the snow-clad hills overlooking the harbour the marines who were the first to land had set up a battery. But the German bombers mostly kept out of range. Those marines were sorely puzzled because one day they saw English fighters flying between formations of German bombers and making no attempt to attack. The men on the ground could not understand it. They did not know that those English fighters had no ammunition left, that for the short space of twenty-four hours the pilots had put up an astounding fight against enormous odds and impossible conditions.

'So desperate was the British need for landing grounds that a squadron of Gladiators strove to function from the frozen lake of Lesjeskogen, forty miles from Åandalsnes. In all that area there was not a flat space of ground. Among the advance party sent to prepare a runway was the famous racing motorist Whitney Straight, who was naturalized some years before the war and had been flying in a fighter squadron of the Royal Air Force since the outbreak of war. His efforts in preparing the lake and his courage during the ensuing attacks won for him the Military Cross. In a blinding snowstorm, eighteen Gladiators took off from the deck of the aircraft carrier and alighted on the lake. Without delay they were refuelled and hidden round the verge; but their arrival was soon discovered by the Germans, who sent over two aircraft disguised by Norwegian markings, which were promptly intercepted and driven away by the Gladiators.

'At three o'clock next morning the pilots and few available staff fought to get the first Gladiators in the air, a task which the intense cold made practically impossible, yet the impossible was accomplished. In an hour came the first clashes with the Germans when the Gladiators shot down a Heinkel and drove off two others. There was a brief breathing space and then the German bombers started to come over at 7.30 in the morning to smash up the surface of the lake and did not cease their attacks until 8 o'clock at night.

'There was no cover for the pilots, no protection for the aircraft. Except where the snow had been cleared, the drifts were so deep that no one could move. The pilots were forced to crawl through the snow on their hands and knees. Their clothes froze solid as boards as they struggled in the snow to refuel and restart the engines in order to go up to fight the enemy. They shot down the enemy in the air, but it was the blast of the enemy's bombs which destroyed the Gladiators on the ground and wounded the pilots. Not one Gladiator did the enemy shoot down from the air. The spirit of that little band of men on the frozen lake was unconquerable. They fought Nature and the enemy at the same time. As they struggled in the snow to refuel, the enemy dived and machine-gunned them. They had no respite. As one aircraft after another was destroyed and one man after another was wounded, they set up a machine-gun and attacked the bombers from the ground. Eighty German bombers had the task of wiping them out and nothing could exceed the ferocity of the German attack. Forty times the British pilots succeeded in carrying out sorties against the enemy. At the end when they had used up their ammunition and had little petrol, some of the pilots showed their ascendency over the Germans by driving them off with feint attacks. One out-manoeuvred three of the enemy by trying to crash into them. When they saw him coming at them, they could not face him and turned away, so he managed to land safely.

'Four or five days afterwards a marine straight from Åandalsnes told me how discomfited they were by the strange actions of the British aircraft which completely baffled them. I could not explain it, but the reason is now plain. One pilot whose aircraft went up in flames as he landed tried to start another, but a bomb destroyed it before he could do so. Another pilot had sixteen fights with the enemy. 'I then attacked another three Heinkels during the course of my patrol. How much damage I inflicted I cannot say as there was always another Heinkel to attack. I broke away because I was running short of petrol and not certain of my position. I landed on the lake and saw three Junkers approaching, so I took off again and attacked them, eventually 'forced landing' through lack of petrol. In all I had sixteen combats.'

'Six Junkers were shot down by the Gladiators. Eight more fled from the British pilots with smoke pouring from them as they disappeared among the mountains. But at the end of the day the squadron of Gladiators was reduced to five. The surface of the lake was shattered and no longer usable, for there were 132 bomb craters on it. Despite the losses, the leader was unbeaten. During the night he found a sloping piece of ground on which it was possible. by the exercise of superb skill to take off and land, but the slightest vacillation or lack of judgment meant disaster. While the Germans were sleeping, he removed the surviving aircraft to this spot and fought the hordes of Junkers for a few more hours until the Gladiators dwindled to one solitary aircraft. Those magnificent men, who had nothing to fly, remain undefeated. Had they possessed properly defended bases and their usual ground staff they would have dealt with those Junkers as the Spitfires and Hurricanes dealt with the Luftwaffe in the Battle of Britain.

'It was with the survivors of this invincible band that Squadron Leader Craven took his evening meal amid the ruins of Veblungsnes and they shared with him all they had to offer - corned beef and Canadian whisky! Afterwards he embarked in a launch and made his way back to the Sunderland to see how Pilot Officer Jones had fared and to make things snug in her for the night. Early next day he heard from Whitney Straight that the Messerschmitt attacked by the Sunderland had definitely crashed. Unfortunately Whitney Straight himself was wounded while locating it and was unable to fly for some time. It may be recalled that Wing Commander Whitney Straight was shot down over the Channel on 1 August 1941 and was driven to make a forced landing in France, after coolly ordering his squadron to return to base.

'Leaving her moorings, the Sunderland taxied away and in a few hours was back again in Scotland. Although bombed in turn by more than a dozen Junkers and attacked by the cannon shell and machine-gun bullets of the Messerschmitt, no one on board was touched, while the flying-boat itself had only two bullet holes in it. The brilliant way the pilots handled the Sunderland during those sustained bombing attacks brought both of them the award of the DFC.

'Within two days Squadron Leader Craven was back with his Sunderland at Åandalsnes. Very thoughtfully he carried some food supplies for his Royal Air Force friends who had shared with him their remaining rations. It was essential for him to see General Carton de Wiart. He found the British Headquarters were just a simple little wooden hut, while General Carton de Wiart was so overwhelmed with work at the moment that all he could do was to push over a bottle of whisky and a cup to the Sunderland captain and say: 'Help yourself!' When the Sunderland left Norway she carried with her eleven stretcher cases straight back to the hospital in Scotland. Not one of the wounded uttered a complaint all the way across.

'The French collapse took Squadron Leader Craven to Gibraltar, where he was stationed for some time. He helped in those reconnaissances, which enabled Admiral Sir Andrew Cunningham to deal effectively with the French naval forces at Oran; and one day while flying over the Mediterranean he unexpectedly came upon the Italian fleet steaming in the direction of North Africa. Owing to the bad visibility it was difficult at first to identify the ships, so he circled round them and made sure that they were Italian. All the men on the Sunderland went to action stations and manned the machine-guns as three Italian aircraft approached in formation, but the Italians concluded it was better not to interfere with such a big adversary and discreetly flew off without making an attack.

'Then the captain of the Sunderland brought her down on the sea and started to shadow the ships. For three hours, up till eleven o'clock that night, he kept them under observation; suddenly they changed course and steamed full speed back towards Italy. As the Sunderland did not return, the Air Ministry grew anxious about her and warned all ships to keep a sharp look-out. But she was quite all right and rode safely on the surface of, the sea at her drogues, or sea anchors, all night. Next morning there was a short swell, but by jettisoning his bombs, Squadron Leader Craven was able to take off without mishap. Three hours later he was in Gibraltar harbour.'

On the night of 30 April/1 May 24 Whitleys, sixteen Wellingtons and ten Hampdens were sent to bomb Stavanger, Fornebu and Aalborg airfields. Of these fifty that were dispatched, 35 aircraft bombed and two Wellingtons and a Whitley were lost. A further four aircraft crashed in England on the return. On 2 May, when twelve Blenheims bombed Stavanger and Rye airfields without loss, the Blenheims were completely withdrawn from Norwegian operations because a German offensive in France and the Low Countries was feared imminent. That night, twelve Whitleys and a dozen Wellingtons returned to the nightly attacks on airfields in Norway. Twenty-two of the bombers attacked Stavanger, Rye and Fornebu. Another force of 26 Hampdens carried out minelaying in Oslo Fjord and Kiel Bay and four Wellingtons patrolled enemy seaplane bases. There were no losses from any of these operations.

The last major operation on targets in Norway was on the night of 9/10 May when 23 out of 31 Hampdens dispatched laid mines off Kiel, Lübeck, Warnemünde and in the Elbe. Nine Whitleys that set out to bomb Stavanger airfield were recalled because of bad weather but one crew did not pick up the signal to return and bombed the target. Six Wellingtons patrolled seaplane bases. One of these, a Wellington on 38 Squadron at RAF Marham, was brought to readiness for a security patrol to Borkum in the German Friesian Islands. LAC G. Dick the front gunner, recalls.

'The object was to maintain a standing patrol of three hours over the seaplane base to prevent their flare path lighting up and thus inhibit their mine-laying sea-planes from taking off. We carried a load of 250lb bombs in case a discernible target presented itself. We took off at 2130 hours. Holland was still at peace and their lights, though restricted, were clearly visible, the Terschelling lightship in particular, obliging by giving a fixed navigational fix. After three hours monotonous circling and seeing next to nothing, I heard Flying Officer Burnell, our Canadian pilot, call for course home. The words always sounded like music to a gunner in an isolated turret with no positive tasks to take up his mind, other than endless turret manipulation and endless peering into blackness. I heard the navigator remark that the lightship had gone out and the pilot's reply, 'Well give us a bloody course anyway'. One only had to go west to hit Britain somewhere, or return on the reciprocal of the outward course - drift notwithstanding. After an hour's flying with the magic IFF box switched on for the past thirty minutes, I gave the welcome call, 'Coast ahead!' Much discussion occurred as to where our landfall really was. I told them I thought north of the Humber, which was 150 miles north of our proper landfall at the Orfordness corridor. I was told to 'Belt up'. As a gunner, what did I know about it? (I had flown pre-war with 214 Squadron for two years up and down the East Coast night and day and was reasonably familiar with it.) Probably pride would not let them admit that they were 150 miles off course, in an hour's flying. Eventually, a 'chance light' showed up and we landed on a strange aerodrome, which turned out to be Leconfield. Overnight billets were arranged at 0400 hours for the visiting crew. However, others were on an early start. They switched on the radio at 0600 hours and gave us the 'gen' that at around midnight Germany had invaded Holland, Belgium and France - hence the extinguished lightship. The odd thing was, we had returned with our bombs, as it wasn't the done thing to drop them indiscriminately. We returned to base later on the tenth to be greeted with 'We thought you'd gone for a Burton'. Good news was slow in circulating in those days.'

There were no losses from any of these operations. On 31 days/nights from 9 April to 9/10 May 1940 Bomber Command had flown a total of 93 night and day sorties, from which 36 aircraft (3.9 per cent) were lost.[18] In June and July Whitleys, Hampdens and Wellingtons of Bomber Command continued to raid German ports and sow mines in enemy waters. The Whitley would, eventually, equip four squadrons in Coastal Command. Sergeant Peter R. Donaldson, a Whitley V navigator on 10 Squadron at Dishforth in Yorkshire recalled that 'they were all right to fly. Inadvertently, they had one advantage that saved us: German fighters couldn't believe we were going so slowly and could not work out how to get at us and I used to sit at navigation table and see their tracer bullets going yards ahead the nose of the plane. I don't remember being nervous - maybe I should have been - but I always had a feeling I was going to survive.

'I did my first bombing raid on 20 April 1940. The target was Stavanger. Sometimes, as well as navigating, I was doing the bombing myself, going into the front turret, looking through a bombsight and dropping the bombs. The Whitley carried 500lb bombs, but Stavanger airbase was built on solid rock and the thought occurred to us that whatever we dropped down there wasn't going to have much effect. All in all, I did eighteen night ops and two daylight raids and 8 July was going to be my twenty-first op. We took off at 2100 hours. The target was Kiel, but I made a navigational error and we flew in an easterly direction for longer than we should. I eventually realised my mistake, so we came back on the opposite course, but we were running short of fuel. Flight Lieutenant D. A. French-Mullins, our captain was a fantastic bloke. He said, 'I don't think we're going to make it, so I'm giving the order now that everyone prepare to ditch.' French-Mullins was a fantastic pilot and he made a perfect landing. As soon as we ditched I opened the main exit door and threw out the dinghy. We all got out of the aircraft and were floundering around in the water trying to right the dinghy, except French-Mullins, who used the escape hatch near his piloting position. He got on to the wing of the aircraft and stood there for a little while. 'Donaldson,' he said, 'would you mind moving the dinghy a little closer to where I am?' So I managed to push the dinghy towards him and he just stepped into the dinghy off the wing. Oh, he was cool as a cucumber, was French-Mullins. Eventually, all five of us got into the dinghy and we were all very cold and wet through and feeling a bit miserable - all, that is, except French-Mullins, he was the only one who was dry. 'Anyone want a cigarette?' he asked and handed them round and we all had a cigarette and watched the Whitley gradually sink beneath the waves.'[19] All five crew were rescued by German fishermen and after they had been landed and interrogated, they were ultimately marched off into captivity.

In addition to bombing attacks, reconnaissance flights by all classes of bomber aircraft were made throughout the active period of the Norwegian campaign. The whereabouts of German shipping off the coasts of Germany, in the Belt, in Oslo Fjord and in the numerous fjords on the west coast of Norway were plotted and much valuable information made available for the Royal Navy. Through this period of just one month, Bomber Command was hard-worked, four squadron sorties in six days being nothing unusual. The losses were thirty bombers. More might, perhaps, have been accomplished, but the task was from the outset of the most formidable kind. There was no more than a small force of bombers available and it had to operate at extreme range in thick weather, without fighter support and with information always inadequate and sometimes altogether lacking. Bomber Command did its utmost. All flights were carried out in the spirit of the crew of the Wellington who flew at 300 feet through fierce snow-storms from the north to the south of Norway and back to Scotland in fourteen and a half hours. The spirit of pilots and crews was, indeed, as high at the end of those thirty days as it had been at the beginning. Though they did not know it at the time, for most of them the campaign was a dress rehearsal for what they were about to be called upon to do over Holland, Belgium and France.

Ships were attacked both by day and by night, but mostly by day; aerodromes were attacked by night and by day, but mostly by night. At 400-miles range and with the number of bombers then in service, bombing even of crucial and carefully chosen targets could never be really continuous, but Bomber Command did everything possible to make it so. Bombers were over Stavanger, in a blinding snowstorm, one afternoon and over Stavanger again that night. Convoys creeping across by night were not immune and even in pitch-darkness the bomber's aim was good. On one of the darkest nights a bomber was flying off the coast of Denmark; the crew saw nothing at all and thought no shipping was out. Then someone saw a very faint light below and the bomber dropped a flare. Ten grey ships were steaming north together at about ten knots. From 1,000 feet the bombs were dropped, four in a stick and it was the last bomb that hit. The bomber was thrown thirty feet upwards by an explosion; an ammunition ship was lost to the Germans. But nine ships got through and so it was with the aerodromes and the fighters, bombers and, transport aeroplanes using them. The rate of casualties may have sometimes been higher, sometimes lower, but the invasion went on; our bombers had to come from too far; our fighters, for lack of a base, could not come at all, except that one squadron of Hurricanes fought at Narvik, using an improvised base, hastily cleared of snow and ice, at Bardufoss. The Fleet Air Arm could work from closer at hand, but aircraft of the Fleet Air Arm are not, of course, built for army co-operation, though the Gladiator Squadron from the aircraft carrier HMS *Glorious*, the squadron also used the base at Bardufoss - worked with astonishing persistence and heroism at Narvik in defence of our troops against the German bombers.

Flight Lieutenant Patrick Geraint Jameson, born at Wellington, New Zealand in 1912 and who joined the Royal Air Force in 1936 as a Pilot Officer, was a Hurricane I pilot on 46 Squadron who had flown daily from the *Glorious* to patrol over Narvik since the battle began was to learn how cruel and cold the sea can be, for he was one of the few survivors from the *Glorious* which the Germans sank in those northern waters to add the culminating touch to the Norwegian tragedy. Becoming an assistant clerk after leaving school, Jameson learned to fly privately at Rongotai in 1933. In January 1936 he travelled to England on the SS *Aorangi* at his own expense, joining the RAF on a short service commission. After training he was posted to 46 Squadron in January 1937, becoming a flight commander in March 1939. The squadron was dispatched to Northern Norway on *Glorious*, arriving on 26 May 1940.

During the land battle of Narvik, when the Allies were closing in on the isolated German forces in order to capture the town, from which millions of tons of Swedish iron ore a year have been conveyed to Germany by sea, the information reached the Allied staff that the Germans were landing troops from Dornier Do 26 four-engined flying-boats south of the port. The Germans holding the town were resisting strongly. They had made the most of the natural defences and to overcome their resistance in the shortest time it was essential to prevent reinforcements and supplies from reaching them. Accordingly, on 28 May Jameson was instructed with two other members of his squadron to see if they could locate the flying-boats. Taking off in their Hurricane fighters, they climbed to look round before flying to the coast. In the most systematic way they began their search. The fjords were so winding, the declivities of many so steep, that it was not easy to sight a small object such as a camouflaged flying-boat from any great height. The top of an overhanging cliff could easily conceal from a fast-moving aircraft an enemy aircraft moored at the base. Jameson pushed the control column gently forward to skim the sea in order to scan both sides of the fjords. Easing it back as the fjords narrowed, he climbed to examine them to the innermost end. Fjord after fjord was searched by the three pilots, but no sign of a flying-boat met their eyes.

Eventually a glance at the clock and the fuel indicator told Jameson that in about fifty minutes he would have to return to his base; there was not too much time left for finding the flying-boats - if they existed. 'So I thought I'd go down Romsbachs Fjord where the German headquarters were and have a look there,' he stated afterwards. They flew up the fjord, looking down on the wrecks of the German vessels in Narvik Bay which were the visible sign of the triumph of the Royal Navy on the evening of 13 April. Flying past the port into the further arm of the fjord, exactly as the British destroyers swept on to find and destroy other enemy warships that layout of sight round the corner, Jameson came upon two of the Dornier flying-boats concealed in a little cove. Not only had the Germans chosen their hiding place with care, but they had moored the aircraft in a position which made them difficult to attack. They were tucked close in under the edge of a cliff, with a gun mounted nearby to protect them and augment their own armament. On the opposite side of the fjord the cliff was 800 feet high and any aircraft making a direct attack could do so only by diving over the edge of the cliff and running the risk of colliding with the opposite cliff, for the fjord here was narrow. The risks were accepted by the pilots without a second thought. Circling round, Jameson examined the position to determine the exact spot from which to attack. Calling up his fellow pilots to tell them to concentrate on the first flying-boat and follow him in to the attack, he dived over the top of the cliff and the roar of his guns reverberated through the fjord. A gun on the flying-boat fired back, but the fire soon ceased. He had barely dived over the cliff and fired a short burst when the opposite cliff confronted him and forced him to do a rapid right-hand turn to avoid it, as he climbed to take up position for continuing the attack. The pom-pom ashore strove to drive off the Hurricanes, but one of the other pilots gave it a burst which quickly silenced it.

Soon tongues of flame enveloped the flying-boat as the petrol tank was pierced. Looking down, Jameson saw three men tumble into a dinghy and go ashore, just as he opened his attack on the second flying-boat. This, too, was eventually set on fire and the pilots returned to base to report their success. 'It was my first action,' Jameson has since revealed, 'and I've never been so thrilled in my life. I've done a good deal of deer stalking and wild pig hunting in New Zealand, but they seem tame after that.'

About 3 o'clock next morning, just as he and the other pilots were about to start on their normal patrol, they were told that enemy aircraft were over Narvik. Taking off, they arrived over the town at a height of 4,000 feet. In a few moments one of the pilots called up Jameson. 'I've sighted enemy aircraft,' he said. 'Lead me on to them,' replied the leader, who pulled back the stick to climb quickly after the other pilot. 'He went ahead and shortly afterwards I sighted them and called him back to rejoin formation, but he did not hear. There were three enemy aircraft flying in line astern at 10,000 feet with half a mile between each. The leader was a Heinkel 111 and the others were Junkers 88. He drifted out to attack the leader and I went up to attack the rear Junkers,' said Jameson in describing the action. 'I closed to 150 yards and at my very first burst there was a terrific flash and my windscreen was obscured with oil and glycol. I broke away and circled above for a few seconds and saw that his starboard propeller was stopping and his

41

engine smoking. I went in again to give him another long burst and as I was about to open fire he dropped his bombs and turned away south. I saw his starboard petrol tank between the engine and fuselage burst into flames and followed him down. Just before he crashed on top of a cliff, one of the crew bailed out and alighted in the fjord - I don't know what happened to him.'[20]

On the evening of 7 June Jameson led 46 Squadron in making the first successful Hurricane deck landings on *Glorious* in order that the unit might be evacuated to Britain. In October 1956 RAF *Flying Review* featured an article called *Deck Landing - by Hurricane!* which described Jameson's fantastic feat.

'High, grey cloud covered the sky and a good strong wind was blowing as Flight Lieutenant 'Pat' Jameson began his approach to the smallest airfield he had ever encountered. A little below and a few hundred yards ahead of his aircraft he could see the carrier *Glorious* churning her way through heavy seas in a valiant attempt to give him as much wind over the deck as possible for the landing which awaited him. A Hawker Hurricane had never before landed on an aircraft carrier and was not fitted with an arrester hook. What is more, Jameson had never in his flying career landed on a carrier. If it failed, as naval experts had predicted it would, he and his aircraft would plunge into the icy waters of the Atlantic Ocean off the coast of Norway well inside the Arctic Circle, or crash into the stern of the carrier... Back at Bardufoss airfield in northern Norway, the man responsible for planning the exploit, Squadron Leader Kenneth Brian Boyd 'Bing' Cross, CO of 46 Squadron, waited in vain for news of its success. When, at the end of the brief, abortive Norwegian Campaign the order for evacuation was given in early June, two alternatives were offered Cross. He was told that after his last sorties had been flown, he could burn his aircraft at Bardufoss to prevent them falling into enemy hands, or he could fly them further north to Lakselv. There was a possibility that they could be loaded on to a Norwegian tramp steamer. Squadron Leader Cross, well aware that every available aircraft was needed at home after Dunkirk, looked for another way out. He found it when he heard that the *Glorious* which had carried his squadron to Norway was still deployed not far from the Norwegian coast. He immediately asked Group Captain M. Moore, commander of the RAF Component of the North Western Expeditionary Force, for permission to fly his Hurricanes on to *Glorious* so that both pilots and aircraft could be saved to fight again. 'I hoped you'd say that,' Moore replied when asked, 'but I didn't want to suggest it because the Fleet Air Arm has already decided that such a feat is impossible!'

From that moment, things happened quickly. While still waging an air war against the Germans, Cross found time to fly out to *Glorious* in a Walrus, where he and Captain Guy D'Oyly-Hughes, a former submariner who had been executive officer of *Courageous* for ten months, made detailed plans for the deck landing. The *Glorious* was in company with the *Ark Royal* and it was arranged that, if the *Glorious*'s deck should prove too short, the Hurricanes would come down on *Ark Royal* which had a slightly longer deck. The drawback to the *Ark Royal* was that her lifts could not accommodate the Hurricanes which would have to have their wings sawn off before the deck could be cleared for the next aircraft to land. The *Glorious* was the better choice. By early morning on 7 June plans were complete and the evacuation was timed for that day. The battle against the Germans, however, continued. Soon after dawn, Squadron Leader Cross and one other pilot engaged four He 111Ks over Bardufoss. The Squadron Leader nursed his aircraft back with a shattered windscreen and a punctured oil tank.

Only ten Hurricanes were serviceable after the bitter campaign and the most experienced pilots of the Squadron were selected for the operation. Jameson, one of those chosen, carried out special flying tests in his Hurricane for one hour during the morning. The tail had been loaded with a sandbag in an attempt, which proved successful, to keep the tail down during violent braking. At six o'clock in the evening, Jameson took off for the *Glorious* with two other Hurricanes piloted by Flying Officer Knight and Sergeant Taylor. They were led out by a Swordfish aircraft or the Fleet Air Arm. Jameson was the first to go down. The deck loomed large to meet him as he came in on a steep approach. 'Watch out for the down-draught,' the Navy pilots had said, 'it'll suck you into the stern before you know where you are.' If he kept his approach steep, Jameson knew that he should escape the worst of the turbulence. The boiling waters in the wake of the great ship flashed under his wing and he concentrated every nerve on keeping his aircraft steady. The stern now rushed up to meet him and a gentle surge of power from the engine foiled the down-draught which snatched at his aircraft. He was now over the deck. The down-draught had been overcome, but one question remained to be answered - without an arrester hook, could his aircraft stop before it reached the end of the deck, which must have seemed all too short to the pilot in his fast moving aircraft? The Navy were not using barrier nets as they do today. Jameson was confident, however. His aircraft was weighted with a 14lb sandbag in the tail and he knew that he could brake violently if necessary without tipping the aircraft on to its nose. But violent braking was unnecessary. The experts were proved wrong as the aircraft rolled to a halt with a third of the flying deck still in front of it. Jameson had landed successfully. Within a few minutes the two other pilots had made landings just as successful.

It had been arranged that Jameson should signal back the results as soon as he had landed, but the Navy were keeping strict radio silence and so Cross remained ignorant of the success of the landings until some time later. Because Bardufoss was so far north it was still daylight when, at midnight a lone Swordfish landed on the airfield. The pilot jumped down and handed a message to Cross. Then, for the first time he knew of Jameson's success. Three-quarters of an hour after midnight Cross and the six other chosen pilots flew their Hurricanes behind the Swordfish out to *Glorious*. It was not an easy flight. The biplane plodded along at a steady 90 mph and to fly at this speed the Hurricanes had to put their props into fine pitch and keep twenty degrees of flap down. The pilots sent up a cheer when at last the flashing beacon of the carrier was seen. A Marine who was on the carrier has left this description of the next few minutes. 'The *Glorious* began to get up tremendous speed into wind to help the Hurriboxes land. Round they'd come at about 200 feet so we could see they were OK and then they'd circuit again and line up for the landing, coming in with a mighty gust and lather of spray. One by one the pilots dragged themselves out and vaulted down to the deck for the official de-briefing.'

The vicious down-draught trapped two pilots, but still they managed to make the deck. The only damage caused to any of the ten aircraft which landed was to two tail wheels which were broken. The operation had been entirely successful. Cross and his men went to bed in the early hours of 8 June after nearly twenty-four hours of continuous action, satisfied that they had saved their aircraft which would later add valuable weight to 'The Few' who were fighting in England. Perhaps the most delighted men on the *Glorious* that night however, were the Fleet Air Arm pilots. 'Now we shall be getting Hurricanes,' they said. The Fleet Air Arm did get the Hurricane before the war was over.'

The *Glorious* was short of fuel and steaming at twenty-eight knots, proceeding independently[21] of the main convoy with only two destroyers, *Acasta* and *Ardent,* as escort, when, at about 3:46 pm, in a choppy sea, with good visibility and no cloud, the funnel smoke from *Glorious* and her two escorting destroyers was sighted by the German battle-cruisers *Scharnhorst* and *Gneisenau* on the way through the Norwegian Sea. The German ships were not spotted until shortly after 4:00 and Ardent was dispatched to investigate. *Glorious* did not alter course or increase speed. Five Swordfish were ordered to the flight deck but Action Stations was not ordered until 4:20. Unfortunately, the Swordfish were loaded with anti-submarine bombs, with a view to taking off at a moment's notice to attack any submarines that were sighted and time was necessary to unload the bombs and reload with torpedoes which would have made an effective attack on the cruisers possible. No combat air patrol was being flown, no aircraft were ready on the deck for quick take off and there was no lookout in *Glorious's* crow's nest. She was easy prey for the powerful enemy ships.

The German battle-cruisers fired a ranging salvo, which missed. *Scharnhorst* switched her fire to *Glorious* at 4:32 and scored her first hit six minutes later on her third salvo, at an approximate range of 26,000 yards, when one 11.1 inch hit the forward flight deck and burst in the upper hangar, starting a large fire. This hit destroyed two Swordfish being prepared for flight and the hole in the flight deck prevented any other aircraft from taking off. Splinters penetrated a boiler casing and caused a temporary drop in steam pressure.

Scharnhorst opened fire on *Ardent* at 4:27 at a range about 16,000 yards, causing the destroyer to withdraw, firing torpedoes and making a smoke screen. *Ardent* scored one hit with her 4.7-inch guns on *Scharnhorst* but was hit several times by the German ships' secondary armament and sank about 5:25. While this tragedy was happening, *Acasta* steamed at speed to lay a smoke screen round the *Glorious* to hide her from the enemy cruisers and obscure their target. Even as the smoke screen was being laid, orders were given on the *Glorious* to take up stations and prepare to abandon ship. The aircraft carrier was still moving at full speed. The laying of the smoke screen brought a lull in the firing and the captain, no doubt thinking there might still be a chance of escaping, ordered the men back to action stations. At 4:58 a second shell hit the homing beacon above the bridge of the *Glorious* and killed or wounded the captain and most of the personnel stationed there. The smokescreen became effective enough to impair the visibility until 5:20 when *Scharnhorst* hit the centre engine room on *Glorious* and this caused her to lose speed and commence a slow circle to port. The carrier also developed a list to starboard. The German ships closed to within 16,000 yards and continued to fire at her until about 5:40.

Acasta broke through her own smoke and fired two volleys of torpedoes at *Scharnhorst*. One of these hit the battleship at 5:34 abreast her rear turret and badly damaged her. *Acasta* also managed one hit from her 4.7-inch guns on *Scharnhorst,* but was riddled by German gunfire and sank around 6:20. Without hesitation, the commander of the destroyer sacrificed his ship in his attempt to save the *Glorious*. Estimates were that about 900 men abandoned *Glorious*.

'The thing which struck me most was the way the ordinary seamen carried out orders - absolutely no sign of panic or anything,' a survivor remarked. Then the salvoes of six-inch and eight-inch shells started again, hitting all the time. They shattered the bridge, wrecked the forward part of the ship, started up fires everywhere. The German cruisers had the *Glorious* at their mercy and it was impossible for her to escape. Once more orders were given to prepare to abandon ship. This time she was burning so fiercely that those on board knew she could not last. Without the slightest fuss and without waste of time they began to prepare to save themselves. Carley floats and rafts and planks were got up on the quarter-deck and thrown over to support survivors until they were picked up. The only boat that got away was a little dinghy which was pushed over the stern from the quarter-deck. Men quickly jumped over and clambered into it.

When the *Glorious* began sinking 'Pat' Jameson remembered that his life-jacket was in his cabin down below along with his log book, which contained the notes of all his flying operations and flying times. A pilot's log book is his most precious possession, as it is to the captain of a ship. At that moment of jeopardy he was apparently determined to save his log book, if he lost everything else. He was seen to go down to his cabin, while 'Bing' Cross and two other members of his squadron were on the quarter-deck. Moving rapidly, he attempted to reach his cabin, only to find that he was shut off from it by a water-tight door. Running up to the quarter-deck again, he found that his companions had all disappeared over the side. He took off his flying boots and was just about to jump over when he saw a raft, which was being towed by the *Glorious*, strike a rating, who was swimming in the water, a terrific blow on the head and lay open his brow. He moved along to avoid a similar danger and then jumped over. For a quarter of a mile he swam to a Carley float on which he saw his Commanding Officer. 'Hallo, sir, can I come on your raft?' asked the New Zealand pilot.

There was still one destroyer floating and they were not worrying at all. They thought they would be picked up either by the destroyer or the Germans. A couple of ratings soon reached down and helped him on the raft.

By that time there were about twenty-seven on it. But there were no oars. A rating pointed to one floating about ten yards away and the young New Zealand pilot was seen to dive in and recover it. That oar helped quite a lot, for they were able later to rig it with a sail made out of a pull-over and a shirt. Then the man who was injured by the raft swam along hanging to a plank. He must have been as tough as nails, for it was a great feat of his to get to the Carley float.

Lots of men were floating in their life-jackets; many were hanging to planks of wood; the sea was dotted with them. The German cruisers came to within a mile and a half of them, still firing at the remaining destroyer which fired back as hard as it could. It continued firing right up to the time it sank. The men on the float saw it disappear; they were watching it very intently, hoping when the Germans went that it would pick them up. So the second destroyer went down with colours flying, firing to the end. The Royal Navy on that black day lived up to its finest traditions. By now the *Glorious* was stopped. She was absolutely obscured by smoke. From the Carley float they could see no portion of the ship at all, only those great clouds of smoke on the surface of the sea, so they did not actually see her sink. Amid that shroud of smoke from her burning debris, she vanished beneath the waters, unseen by any human eye.

In those northern latitudes it was light all night. The Carley float was crowded and the waves continually washed right over the men. So cold was the sea that within four hours men started to die from exposure. The strongest among them did what they could to help and comfort the others. They held the heads of the dying men out of the water and when they died the bodies were committed to the sea. Some of the survivors had on so few clothes that it was necessary to remove some of the clothes from the dead to clothe the living in order to keep the spark of life in their frozen bodies.

When the men first got on the Carley float some of them started to sing cheery and popular songs. As the hours went by, they sang a hymn or two. Then as the cold gripped them they fell into silence. They were drenched to the skin and lacked water and food. By next morning ten men were left on the float, among them three members of the RAF; Jameson, his Commanding Officer and an aircraftsman. Eighteen succumbed during that first night. On another float which provided about sixty men with a refuge directly the Glorious went down, only five men came through that terrible ordeal. One or two officers of the Fleet Air Arm who flew the Swordfish on the *Glorious* were also among the thirty-six men who were picked up, while five more men were saved and imprisoned by the enemy.

In the afternoon of the next day it became calm and one survivor remarked that it would have been quite pleasant if they had possessed something to eat and drink and a few more clothes. One man went to sleep and fell overboard, but they were too weak to pull him back. Two others died from exposure. They spoke very little and there were no complaints at all. They just endured and hoped. On the second day the 'Bing' Cross made a suggestion which did much to aid their ultimate survival. 'If we cut the bottom out of the float and put it across the top, we may be able to get a little sleep,' he said. Without delay they set about this task and they found that it was a big improvement. It not only enabled them to snatch a little sleep, but to a certain extent it kept their legs out of the water. That day there was talk of reaching the Shetlands, although the officers knew it was impossible, for they were at least 600 miles away and drifting in the wrong direction. But it was something to talk about and it gave the others something to think about. 'Do you think we'll make the Shetlands tonight?' a rating asked.

'Not tonight, but we'll probably make them tomorrow,' was the encouraging reply. Several times the same question evoked the same answer. It gave hope and helped the weakening men to endure a little longer.

'One of the things which got us down was the fact that we saw a British cruiser squadron of three or four ships searching for us. They put up an aircraft and we saw it taking off and landing, but it did not come in our direction,' one of the survivors stated. 'We saw several of our own aircraft as well as those of the enemy, but they never spotted us.' Who can plumb their agony of mind as they saw those searching ships turn and vanish from sight?

The rating with the injured head clung grimly to life. He grew weaker under the exposure, but he was still alive next day, although he began to wander in his mind. No one could help him. Some were weaker than others, but all were suffering from the exposure and strain. Then a corporal of marines dropped asleep, lost his balance and fell over into the sea. Weak as they were, they managed to grab him before he floated away and after a big struggle dragged him out of the sea to safety. A couple of hours afterwards one of the ratings sighted a trawler. 'There's a ship!' he said.

'We'd been seeing ships before,' said one of the survivors. 'We looked round and saw the ship about two miles away. It was coming towards us. We could see the masts in line. When it got to within one mile of us it turned off - it was an awful moment - but the trawler [the Norwegian tramp steamer the *Borgund* on passage to the Faeroe Islands, arrived late on 10 June and picked up survivors] only stopped to pick up people off another Carley float and then it came on towards us. By this time one of the officers was waving his yellow Mae West and we all shouted as much as we could. They soon came alongside and one of the Norwegians got down the ladder on to the float and made a loop of rope in which he hoisted the worst cases up on board. Those who were not so weak were helped up the ladder. No one could have been kinder to us than those Norwegians - their kindness was beyond praise! They gave up their bunks for the worst cases - there were thirty-six survivors in all. They gave us cigarettes, shared out their only half bottle of whisky among us and made tea and coffee for us. Then they pointed out the best and warmest places in which to sleep, while they slept on deck or anywhere else they could find.'

After picking up the survivors of the *Glorious*, the fishermen set their course for the Faroes, while the cook in the galley made some Scotch broth for them which was the finest food they had ever tasted in their lives. It was rather sad that the injured seaman who had clung so desperately to life should die after being taken on board. The trawler was not equipped with wireless, so her skipper could not inform the British authorities that he had picked up the survivors of the *Glorious*, thus for nearly a week it was feared that there were no survivors at all. So the trawler plugged along in fairly heavy seas at about eight knots, while the Norwegian fishermen lavished all the care and attention in their power upon the men they had rescued, nursing them and feeding them and making them as comfortable as they could in the circumstances. All on board had a bad moment when they heard the sound of an aeroplane. Presently a Heinkel 115 appeared and circled low over them. But it dropped no bombs and they breathed freely again as it turned away. Five hours later they saw it returning and this time they felt sure that it had come to bomb them. But again it merely circled over them and flew away, much to their relief. After a tough passage lasting three days, the *Borgund* arrived at Thorshavn in the Faroe Islands, where British army officers met the 37 survivors of whom two died. *Svalbard II,* also making for the Faeroes, picked up five survivors but was sighted by a German aircraft and forced to return to Norway, where the four still alive became prisoners of war for the next five years. It is also believed that one more survivor from *Glorious* was rescued by a German seaplane. [22]

British and French troops had to withdraw at Åandalsnes and Namsos and Narvik was besieged and finally captured on 8 June. On 10 June, two days after the evacuation of Narvik a Blenheim, one of three on reconnaissance over Trondheim Fjord, sighted the *Scharnhorst* and two cruisers, one of which they thought might not be a cruiser but a pocket-battleship of the Deutschland class. The warships were back from their successful encounter with the *Glorious* two days before. It was decided to assault them where they lay at anchor near a supply ship and twelve Hudsons carried out a pattern bombing attack from 15,000 feet. They dropped 36 250lb armour-piercing bombs, losing one of their number to anti-aircraft fire and another to an enemy fighter. The *Scharnhorst* was probably missed, but both the cruisers and the supply ship received direct hits. This was on 11 June.

On the night of 13/14 June naval aircraft took a hand. The *Ark Royal,* escorted by the *Nelson* and other units of the Home Fleet, arrived at a position 170 miles off Trondheim. At midnight fifteen Skuas took off for the attack. Long-range Coastal Command Blenheims provided fighter cover over the objective, while Beauforts of the same Command created a diversion by attacking the nearby aerodrome at Vaernes in order to prevent, if they could, German fighters from taking off to engage the Skuas. At that time of the year and in that latitude, daylight is perpetual. It was not possible, therefore, to effect surprise. The enemy were prepared and waiting. The Skuas pressed their attack with the greatest determination. Eight of them - more than half - were shot down, but two hits were scored on the *Scharnhorst.*

Two days later a reconnaissance showed that she was still at Trondheim. On 16 and 17 June two attempts by Coastal Command were made to attack her, but clouds, lower than the hill-tops, obscured the harbour. It was not until 21 June that the *Scharnhorst* was again sighted. This time she was at sea - eight miles West of the Utyoer lighthouse - steaming South at 25 knots, with an escort of destroyers. Flight Lieutenant Phillips on 204 Squadron piloting Sunderland N9028 took off from Sullom Voe at 1237 initially escorted by three Blenheims from Sumburgh. A Do 18 flying boat was sighted and was attacked by the Blenheims to no effect; gunner was killed in a Blenheim and all three returned to base, abandoning the Sunderland. While circling to await the Blenheims, five Fairey Swordfish were sighted by the Sunderland. Continuing alone, Phillips altered course and at 1435 sighted an unidentified submarine, submerging fast. At 1445 the Sunderland sighted the *Scharnhorst* accompanied by seven destroyers and their position was reported to base. The flying boat was at once attacked by heavy fire which endured for an hour. During this time its crew watched a torpedo attack on the battle cruiser by the five naval Swordfish which began at 1510. One of the Swordfish was seen to crash into the sea. At 1610 the Sunderland was being shadowed by an He 60, which dropped a bomb falling about 50 yards away. Between 1520 and 1620 Phillips was under heavy and continuous AA fire. At 1625 first three and then one more Me 109 appeared and carried out attacks on both quarters. The Sunderland captain was the same officer who had piloted the Sunderland which had fought six Ju 88s when protecting a convoy on 3 April. The combat with the Me 109s lasted about half an hour. All the Messerschmitts were hit and at 1640 one of these was shot down into the sea in flames. Meanwhile, in the Sunderland, the rear turret had been put out of action very early in the engagement and tanks were punctured. Phillips broke off the engagement and made off for its base shortly before the arrival soon after 1430 of nine Coastal Command Beauforts from a squadron which had been grounded because of trouble with their engines. On hearing that the *Scharnhorst* was at sea every pilot volunteered to take up his aircraft. They were allowed to make the attack.

When they saw these Beauforts, it is probable that the Germans thought that, like the Swordfish, they were carrying torpedoes and that another torpedo attack was imminent. The destroyer escort was seen to deploy so as to intercept, if they could, the torpedoes launched against the capital ship. The Beauforts, however, were loaded with armour-piercing bombs and, flying in a crescent formation, made a dive-bombing attack. At least three bombs hit the *Scharnhorst,* one on its stern, another nearly amidships and the third forward on the port side. The Beauforts were forthwith attacked by Me 109s in number from 45 to 50. Three were shot down; the rest got back to their base. There were no cases of engine failure. Hudsons, one of which was lost, renewed the attack, but encountered fierce opposition from an enemy now fully ready to meet them, for the warships were by then only 25 miles from Stavanger. In this action five aircraft were lost altogether, but the *Scharnhorst* had received sufficient damage to cause her to retire to a floating dock at Kiel. She remained out of action for the rest of the year and did not put to sea again until early in 1941.

Footnotes

7   'Atfero,' as the organization was known at first, was taken over by the RAF in 1941. In January 1942 two Australians and a Canadian created a transatlantic record. The Hudson was one of several aircraft, fresh from US factories, which were awaiting delivery. The two RAAF men and the Canadian were among a number of young men who had just completed training in Canada and were also awaiting transport. The RAAF men were English-born Pilot Officer G. V. Syer, pilot, who was a clergyman in civil life and Pilot Officer R. A. Stevenson, of Sydney, navigator and the Canadian was Pilot Officer A. Harris. Record breaking was not the objective of the ferry flight. The only object then, as it was throughout the war, was to 'deliver the goods,' but soon after take-off Syer found he had a tail wind of 40/50 mph and stayed with it. The Hudson took off from Gander, Newfoundland at 0141 GMT, rising to 20,000 feet to surmount the heavy banks of cloud that filled the pre-dawn sky to that level. Later it rose still higher and stayed in the 20,000 to 30,000 feet band for most of the journey, using oxygen for six and a half hours because of the rarefied atmosphere. It became intensely cold. The temperature fell as low as minus 35° centigrade; the crew's sandwiches froze into inedible rigidity and even the 'hot' coffee in the Thermos flask became icy. Landfall, in Scotland, was made at 0800 GMT within a few miles of the estimated point of arrival. When the crew arrived at Prestwick at 0921 GMT they had clocked 7 hours 40 minutes - 30 minutes better than the previous record set up by a Liberator. Sometime after the flight eye trouble sent Sye back to his former vocation as a padre in the RAFVR. *RAAF Over Europe* (Eyre & Spottiswoode 1946).

8   *Task For Coastal Command* by Hector Bolitho (1946).

9   On 28 May 1943 a Hudson on 608 Squadron operating from Blida in North Africa was the first RAF aircraft to sink a U-boat by means of rocket-projectiles fired from beneath the wings

10   *U-Boat Fact File* by Peter Sharpe (Midland Publishing Ltd 1998).

11   The Swordfish drawn from 815 and 819 Squadrons embarked in *Illustrious* and 813 and 824 Squadrons from *Eagle*, temporarily embarked in *Illustrious*, each specially fitted with long-range tanks in the rear cockpit displacing the third crew member, took off from *Illustrious*, 180 miles from the target. The first strike force, of 12 aircraft, was airborne at 2030 and was followed by a second force of nine aircraft after an hour's interval. Eleven of the Swordfish carried torpedoes, six carried bombs and four were equipped with flares to illuminate the target. The first flare-droppers arrived over the target about 23.00 and the strike force dived to the attack through the middle of a balloon barrage. Despite intense AA fire, they all hit the target and only one aircraft was lost. The second wave, which arrived at midnight, was equally successful and again only one Swordfish was lost. Next day, when the smoke cleared, air reconnaissance showed that three battleships *Cavour*, *Duilio* and *Italia* had all been severely damaged and two of them were under water. Also, the cruiser *Trento* and the destroyers *Libeccio* and *Pessango* had been hit, two auxiliary vessels sunk and seaplane hangars and oil-storage tanks destroyed.

12   *Task For Coastal Command* by Hector Bolitho (1946).

13   French added a Bar for his part in the attack on the *Scharnhorst* and *Gneisenau* and the 10,000-ton heavy cruiser *Prinz Eugen*. These warships made their famous run from Brest up the Channel on 12 February 1942 in an attempt to join the other German surface vessels at Trondheim. *RAAF Over Europe.*

14   Wellington I L4387 LG-L.

15   A second reconnaissance made on 22 April also by a Wellington covered 1,180 miles in eight and a half hours and photographed Trondheim. It saw, among much else of interest, twenty-two German aircraft on 'a frozen lake' at Jonsvatnet, used by the Germans as a makeshift airfield and its signal about this discovery was picked up by an aircraft carrier whose aircraft 'bombed the lake with excellent effect.'

16   Wellingtons on 38 Squadron also operated against Sola airfield and flew the first of three operations to Stavanger on the 16th.

17   Oberfeldwebel Förster gained a further six night victories before reverting to 2./JG 27, scoring another ten daylight victories. He was KIA in North Africa on 14 December 1941 on his 287th operational flight.

18   *The Bomber Command War Diaries* by Martin Middlebrook and Chris Everitt (Midland Publishing Ltd 1985, 1990, 1995). By the end of April the RN had lost four destroyers, three

submarines and a sloop; five other warships suffered damage from bombs; the *Rodney* among them. By air and sea attack the Germans lost four cruisers, eleven destroyers, five U-boats, thirty transport and supply ships and probably ten more. Two of their battleships were severely damaged.

19   Quoted in *The Goldfish Club* by Danny Danziger (Little Brown 2012).

20   Jameson was awarded a half share in the destruction of the two flying-boats and he was awarded the destruction of the Ju 88, the first of his nine victories during the war.

21   Captain Guy D'Oyly-Hughes was granted permission to proceed independently to Scapa Flow in the early hours of 8 June to hold a court-martial of his Commander (Air), J. B. Heath, who had refused an order to carry out an attack on shore targets on the grounds that the targets were at best ill-defined and his aircraft were unsuited to the task and who had been left behind in Scapa to await trial.

22   Therefore the total of survivors was 40, including one each from *Acasta* and *Ardent*. The total killed or missing was 1,207 from *Glorious*, 160 from *Acasta* and 152 from *Ardent*, a total of 1,519.

Recovering from the ordeal, Jameson was awarded the DFC on 19 July and then he was posted to command 266 Squadron at Wittering on 17 September. In early June he became Wing Commander Flying at Wittering and received a Bar to his DFC on 7 October, followed by a Mention in Despatches on 1 January 1942. On 10 March 1943 received a DSO. By late July 1944 he was commanding 122 Wing in 83 Group of 2nd Tactical Air Force in Normandy, initially controlling Mustang squadrons and then Tempests. He remained in the RAF until 6 August 1960, retiring as an Air Commodore. *Aces High* by Christopher Shores and Clive Williams (Grub Street 1994). In a long and distinguished career, 'Bing' Cross reached the rank of Air Vice Marshal K. B. B. Cross CB CBE DSO DFC.

Chapter 2

Wimpys Over The Waves

You may remember a rather exciting film called 'The Dawn Patrol'. If you do, it is just a point of interest for me to begin by saying that I belong to the Royal Air Force Squadron that was represented in it. The squadron dates back to the last war. It is still going strong, taking its share now in the vast work that is being done day and night by the Coastal Command. Lately, our squadron has been doing its bit in making the ports on the other side of the Channel uncomfortable for their temporary tenants. Cherbourg, Brest and Lorient have been most frequently on our daily lists. Lorient was probably a new one on many people. It was a new one on most of us when we were first told to bomb it.

Our attacks on Lorient are now regular news. Lorient - on the Brittany coast about ninety miles south of Brest - has become a U-boat base and maintenance depot. It isn't giving away any secrets to say that our targets there are power stations, naval yards, slipways, torpedo workshops and so on. Some of us have been so often to Lorient lately that we must know the way into and around it better than its temporary German inhabitants. Now we know every yard of the country and its landmarks. We always see Lorient clearly when we attack it - at dusk or dawn, or in light provided by the moon or by our flares. And the enemy always gives us a hot reception. All sorts of stuff come up at us - light and heavy shells, flaming red things which we call 'onions' and what-not.

The other night the armourers of our Squadron were given their first operational flight. Their job is on the ground - to fit and load our bombs. The idea in taking them with us was that they could study what happens when their bombs burst.

'How did you get on?' one of them was asked afterwards. 'Coo - great stuff,' was the reply, 'all the colours of the rainbow. Lovely it was from the gallery seat.' I don't think I would choose the word 'lovely' myself, but let it pass.

I wonder if I can give you a sort of mental picture of how we set about things on one of these raids. An hour before the take-off we assemble in the Operations Room to be told all about the job in hand. Then off everyone goes to attend to his own particular end of things. The observer gets the weather report; a gunner who is also the wireless operator makes certain that the guns are OK. Then he checks up the recognition signals and the wireless frequencies and sees that the pigeons are in their wicker basket - we always take homing pigeons with us. And the pilot gets into his head all he can about the trip and the targets.

Before we leave the ground I test the microphone which enables me to talk to the gunner in the rear turret and to the rest of the crew.

Hello, gunner - are you all right behind?'

And then to the observer: 'Hello, observer, course to steer, please.'
Some of us carry mascots. I always have the joker of a pack of playing cards and a
couple of German bullets - relics of being shot up on one trip.
And now come with me over Lorient. As we approach it the observer suddenly
shouts: 'I see the target - yes, I've got it' 'OK' I say. 'Master switch and fusing
switch on!' These are the switches which control the fusing and the release of the
bombs. Round just once more to make quite certain. The docks and the outlines of
the naval buildings show up a little more clearly. Then I throttle the engines back.
Running on now,' I tell the observer.
OK' he says, 'left-left - that's it - steady - a shade right - hold it - NOW!'
He presses the electric button which releases the bombs.
The aircraft gives a slight shudder as they go through the doors.
Bombs gone! cries the observer.
Down they go; hundredweight after hundredweight of high explosive. My
observer is watching for the results. Have we scored hits or just got near misses? I
see many bright flashes. Then big flames flick skywards like the fiery tongues of
monster serpents. Showers and towers of ruddy sparks burst from the ground.
My observer nearly jumps from his seat, waving his hands in excitement. 'We've
hit it-we've hit it!' he yells. 'We've damned well hit it!' Then home we go - our
umpteenth visit to Lorient on the Brittany coast has ended.
Attack On Lorient Submarine Base by A Flight Lieutenant, BBC broadcast,
November 1940.

No form of attack in the entire Air Force called for as much precision as the dropping of depth charges. The science of using them - and radar - in a heavy aircraft had to be mastered by the aircrews. Air to Surface Vessel (ASV) radar, developed in parallel with Airborne Interception radar, was first demonstrated in trials in 1938. The first operational ASV sets were fitted to Hudson and Sunderland aircraft of Coastal Command but were only capable of looking directly forward and consequently were of limited value. The fist ASV to be fitted to Wellingtons was the sideways-looking ASV MK.II. In trials, aircraft flying at 2,000 feet ASL detected a 10,000 ton ship at 40 miles range, a destroyer at 20 miles and a submarine at eight miles. ASV Mk.II required four antennae on each side of the rear fuselage and a further four antennae on the spine of the rear fuselage[23] Combined with Yagi antennae beneath the wings and lower nose of the aircraft, ASV MK.II provided the radar operator with information on both range and bearing of surface vessels. Ideally, a U-boat had to be fully surfaced and no more than three miles distant for ASV to be effective.

A ship on the surface was still there to be attacked a second time if the Mosquito missed it and a land target was always waiting for a second visit if a bomber missed it the first time. But a diving U-boat was vulnerable for only a few seconds. If fully surfaced when sighted, it could submerge in thirty seconds and still be vulnerable. Thirty seconds later it would be out of harm's way. The difficulties were doubled at night. The contact was picked up by the radar in the dark. A thin line of amber light revolved continuously on a dark glass screen and when this light is interrupted by a blip by the presence of an object outside the aircraft the first promise of a U-boat has come. A whale or a shoal of fish may cause this blip on the screen, or one of the numerous fishing boats that have been such a nuisance during our patrols. When the blip had been received the next task was divided into two periods, there was the brief interval of darkness while the aircraft was flying in and the thirty seconds of the actual attack, after the Leigh Light[24] had been turned on or after the U-boat had been seen in the moon path. During that interval the radar operator must give the pilot accurate information as often as possible and the pilot must plan his approach accordingly. If the approach on the unseen target erred by three degrees, the attack would be abortive. The drift of the aircraft, the possible zigzagging of the U-boat and the fact that it may be submerging must be taken into consideration. This was the problem in judgment for the pilot while he was flying in. From the movement of the blip on the radar screen the pilot must assess the course and speed of the U-boat, by mental arithmetic and instinct. There was neither time nor light for formula to be consulted. And the pilot had to know exactly how much his radar operator was liable to err in a crisis. If the U-boat did not submerge, there was flak to contend with directly the Leigh Light had been turned on. In the minutes of approach the drill of the ten members of the crew had to be as exquisitely concerted as ten separate instruments sounding one chord in an orchestra. It was here that years of training suddenly manifested themselves in one co-ordinated action.

The pilot was flying his heavy aircraft through the dark on the course calculated from the radar operator's directions. The radar operator meanwhile was watching the blip on the screen and operating his complicated radar set. The second pilot is looking after the engines, putting up the revs and boost as required and at the same time he is setting up the automatic camera. The importance of photographs cannot be exaggerated. They were not souvenirs for an album of victories. They must show the depth charges entering the water, two or three seconds before they explode. It is by the position of entry, not the extent of the explosion, that the attack can be assessed.

During these same minutes the navigator had to set up his bombing panel, check the selection of bombs and see that the bomb doors have been opened. Then he would switch on the Leigh Light. Before this the wireless operator must flash signals back to base so that they knew there was a possible target and so that, if the aircraft was destroyed, it would not be a 'silent loss.' The engineer lay in the open bomb bay to watch the effect of the depth charges when they entered the water, the two beam gunners must prepare to do their share of pounding the U-boat when the Leigh Light was turned on and the rear gunner must prepare to give them a further burst when the aircraft had passed over. The front gunner must also be prepared to give the U-boat hell the moment the light was turned on.

A good captain expected his crew to do all this within a matter of seconds so that at the right distance the engines were giving the right speed. Then the orchestra paused to watch for the conductor's baton. It fell, the light was turned on and the target was revealed for this assemblage of preparation. Then the depth charges were dropped in a long stick, by the navigator. The aircraft flew through the flak and over the U-boat and from his point of vantage the rear gunner was able to substantiate the report of the engineer in the bomb bay. It had to be a perfect straddle. The word straddle is important. A direct hit usually caused the depth charge, which was not fused for contact, to break up. A close miss was therefore the perfect way of exploding the depth charge, to do the maximum of harm. Then came the circuit before the aircraft could fly in and seek for evidence. Little wonder that the crew searched the water hoping to see yellow dinghies and white faces peering up into the merciless beam of the Leigh light.

On 21 November 1940 221 Squadron re-formed at Bircham Newton, Norfolk, equipped with Wellington Is. Early in 1941 ASV sets were installed and in March 1941 the squadron began replacing its Mark Is and ICs with Mark VIII 'Stickleback' Wellingtons. By May 1941 the U-boats were largely reduced to operating off West Africa or in the central Atlantic, the latter being beyond the range of Coastal Command aircraft. In June 1941 when Air Chief Marshal Sir Philip Joubert de la Ferté KCB CMG DSO took over Coastal Command, he inherited a force of forty squadrons and more than half the aircraft were now fitted with ASV radar. Joubert's overriding task was to increase the effectiveness of his ASV aircraft and create airborne U-boat killers. He pressed for heavier types of anti-submarine bombs, bomb sights for low level attack and depth charge pistols which would detonate at less than fifty feet below the surface. He encouraged tests, first started by Bowhill, with various forms of camouflage, in order to render the attacker invisible for as long as possible. As a result all anti-U-boat aircraft were painted white on their sides and under-surfaces.

By September 1941 increased shipping losses again prompted the Admiralty to explore the possibility of employing bombers in the war at sea and Air Marshal Harris turned over large numbers of Wellingtons, Whitleys and Blenheims. In September 221 Squadron moved to Iceland, returning in December for transfer overseas. Three crews flew their Wellington VIIIs to Malta while the remainder of the squadron flew to Egypt in January 1942 to begin anti-shipping patrols from bases in the Canal Zone. Meanwhile, the shipping losses in October and November 1941 showed a reduction over those of September. During early 1942 Coastal Command was helped by the transfer of further aircraft from Bomber Command. In April a squadron of Whitleys, eight Liberators and a Wellington squadron (311 Czech) were transferred to Coastal Command. On 7 May Bomber Command relinquished control of 304 (Polish) Squadron, which flew to its new base at Tiree in the Inner Hebrides. Both squadrons were needed urgently and they took up their new role almost immediately. The Poles had a very eventful career in Coastal Command, moving on 13 June 1942 to Dale in South Wales where they joined 19 Group Coastal Command. They flew 2,451 sorties up until 30 May 1945 and attacked 34 U-boats out of 43 sighted. The Czechs also gave sterling service in Coastal Command. 311 operated the Wellington until June 1943 when it converted to the Liberator. 304 commenced operations on 18 May and 311 Squadron took off from its new base at Aldergrove in Northern Ireland on 22 May 1942 for its first operation.

The Bay of Biscay, 500 miles wide, which was the U-boat's route to the wider hunting-fields of the Atlantic Ocean, would become a happy hunting ground for the Wellingtons, Sunderlands, Liberators, Halifaxes,[25] Whitleys and Hudsons of Coastal Command. All flew the Bay patrols and Coastal Command Beaufighters intervened against German long-range fighters which attempted to intercept the U-boat hunting aircraft. Leonard R. Gribble, a thriller writer of such works as *The Scarlet Widow,* wrote *Bombers Fly East* for the Air Ministry in 1942 using his pen-name, 'Bruce Sanders'. He painted a prosaic propaganda picture of British air operations and *Deep-Sea Hunters,* his thrilling chapter on Coastal Command, was no exception:

'Hunting U-boats is a big-game sport for men with patience. One Wellington captain spent 1,300 hours on operational flying before he sighted and attacked his first under-sea victim. There had been plenty of other work and adventure crowded into that long flying period, so the captain, a former student of the Scottish School of Physical Education in Glasgow, was not bored. But he may be forgiven if at times he seriously doubted whether he ever would see a submarine. Another Wellington skipper, a Canadian, Sergeant A. S. Hakala from Sioux Lookout, Alberta got a submarine on the first patrol he made with his crew. It was not beginner's luck this case, for the U-boat's look-out spotted the plane and the aircraft could not arrive before the submarine crashed but the bombs went down to burst just ahead of the feather of foam betraying the sunken periscope. Hakala recalled: 'It was some explosion. The U-boat surfaced groggily until the conning tower and part of the hull were awash. The Wellington readily took this second opportunity, guns blazing away. To my surprise and joy flames and smoke poured from the conning-tower. The bombs must have started it, but I hope the bullets helped.' The U-boat was still on fire when a thick mist came down and the Coastal Command aircraft had to make for home...'

Another contemporary writer, Hector Bolitho, a New Zealander of Cornish origin[26] penned these words: 'I suppose men who serve in submarine craft are specially gifted with courage and that they do not suffer from claustrophobia. Mere day to day existence in such circumstances has enough horror. But this must be intensified when the U-boats crawl through the water, in continuous fear of attack, hearing the far away thuds of other U-boats being bombed - thuds which can be heard fifty miles away under the sea - and the knowledge that must have come to all of them by now, that it is practically impossible for them to surface anywhere within the patrolled area without being sighted by one of our aircraft.'

'Probably the greatest hardship for submariners' wrote Wing Commander J. Romanes 'was the lack of space in which to live and breathe. The craft is 200 feet long, with a maximum internal diameter of 15 feet, the pressure hull being nearly round. Throughout almost the entire length of the boat half of this space is taken up by two big batteries, six main ballast tanks, two quick-diving tanks and many trimming, fresh water and fuel tanks. A third of what is left is occupied by engines and main motors; a quarter of the rest by torpedo tubes and their allied gear. This leaves a very small space to be divided into control room, officers' quarters, crew's quarters, galley, petty officers' quarters and lavatory room. Space overhead is further restricted by pipes to all the ballast tanks with their high and low pressure air lines and associated valves, both hydraulic and hand-operated, battery cables and a mass of other gear. The control room has to house wireless, asdic, echo-sounder, steering and hydroplane operating gear; as well as a watch of ten men. The living quarters are therefore minute, the wardroom, where four officers must live and sleep, being 8 feet by 6 feet, while twenty men live in the fo'c'sle 20 feet long by 7 feet wide forward and 10 feet wide aft. The hammocks alone seem to fill all the available space and the only way to get between them is to crawl.

'The lively behaviour of the boat in a seaway makes movement even more difficult; she literally whips about and it is not uncommon for the officer in the shipside bunk in the ward room to be slung clean out and deposited in the alley way outside. Moreover, the deck is so greasy with diesel oil that even in a slight sea it is a bit of an art to keep on your feet. Normally the submarine dives all day, which at this time of the year means nearly 16 hours, from six in the morning to ten at night. During this time the crew of forty is using up the very limited supply of oxygen in the air which is trapped in the boat. It is not long before the effects of oxygen starvation are felt. It becomes even more of an effort to move about and reading a book is difficult, as you find yourself reading the same lines over and over again. The effects are very similar to flying at a great height without oxygen. To avoid fouling the air more than is absolutely necessary, neither smoking nor cooking is allowed. The lavatories must be used as seldom as possible as they are operated by pressure air and when blown they release a bubble of air which may be seen on the surface. Smells are impossible to prevent and crew, engines; diesel oil and batteries all make their contribution, so that when the hatch is opened on surfacing, fresh air tastes foul and you get a heavy coat of fur on your mouth which makes your first cigarette taste disgusting. Moreover, when the boat is submerged, a powder is put down to absorb some of the carbon dioxide in the boat but it succeeds mostly in making the crew cough violently. Moisture condenses inside the hull of the boat and after a few days there is a perpetual drip everywhere which is most annoying and which makes all the blankets of the bunks wet.'

On 6 June 1942 a Spanish radio report asserted that an Italian submarine [the *Luigi Torelli* of the 1,200-ton Marconi class commanded by Capitano di Corvetta (Lieutenant Commander) Augusto Migliorini] had been beached near Santander. The foreign radio reports that continued to mention the beaching added that two Sunderland flying-boats of Coastal Command, which had attacked the U-boat, had been forced down. The foreign radio reports were misleading. The Sunderlands were back at base. The episode involving the Italian submarine had all started on the night of 3/4 June. Air Marshal Sir Philip Joubert, knowing that only a successful operational demonstration of the capabilities of Leigh Light Wellingtons would carry the day had thrown caution to the wind and despatched four of the five Wellingtons on 172 Squadron into the Bay of Biscay. The *Luigi Torelli* was damaged by Squadron Leader Jeff H. Greswell and the crew on a Wellington on 172 Squadron (one of five Wimpys fitted with the Leigh Light) picked up an ASV contact. His target was outbound from Bordeaux to the West Indies. Greswell homed on the *Luigi*

Torelli by radar and then switched on the Leigh Light but owing to a faulty setting in his altimeter, his approach was too high and he saw no sign of the submarine. However, Migliorini, mistaking the Wellington for a German aircraft, fired recognition flares, precisely pinpointing his boat. On a second approach with the Leigh Light, Greswell got the *Luigi Torelli* squarely in the brilliant beam and straddled the Italian boat with four shallow-set 300lb Torpex depth charges from an altitude of fifty feet. The shattering effect that depth charges had on a submarine crew is described in frightening detail by Secondo Capo Mechanista Carlo Pracchi of the Regia Marina Velella:

'The sounds are coming from starboard, midships. Thuds in the water, three at a time and a few seconds later you hear three rumbles followed by the inevitable shaking. Sound source from 10 o'clock and then from 7 o'clock and louder thuds. It sounds as if every gauge in the control room is shattering. All the valves are shut down. The glass of the depth gauge breaks. From the telephone comes the voice of someone shouting 'Engines... signal leaks or other faults.' We get the boards up to look at the water-level in the bilge tanks. I can see water running down the sides... I look up. In the meantime the bombs go off. I look up again to see where that water is coming from. I can see from the cracks that fortunately it is the varnish peeling off! Higher up I can see drips on the heads of the rivets in the frames. I touch one with my finger and water runs down my arm. Then we get another depth charge and the drips start to run down themselves. That earlier charge exploded underneath and brought us up; one went off overhead and pushed us down. Machine room crew informs: damage. Forward, with a lunatic grin on his face M.N. shows me a rope with knots he has been keeping a tally of the bombs with it. The main relays shut down. The lights have just gone. We'll have to use the emergency lighting. I feel my leg cramp up, then the tingling starts, then shaking. Maybe I'm tired after these hours of tension. I try to snatch a bit of rest sitting down the centre of the aft bulkhead door of the [salvage] box called by the name of the inventor: Garitta Girolami-Arata-Olivati... The effect on my legs doesn't stop; I use my arms to try to suppress it, holding my knees. It makes no difference ... I try to stop just one knee from trembling, but it carries on and only makes my arms shake. In desperation I say: 'Bloody hell I'm just panicking: can't get myself out of it ... I really panic.'[27]

Unsurprisingly, the blasts to *Luigi Torelli* forced Migliorini to abort and he headed to Aviles, Spain.

In the meantime Greswell and his crew spotted a second submarine nearby. It was submerging when spotted with ASV and searchlight. Greswell strafed the submarine with machine-gun fire, having used all its depth charges on the first attack. What saved the second submarine and the *Luigi Torelli* was the failure of the pursuer to get a signal of the attack to the other three Wellingtons on patrol in the area and home them to the place of the attacks. No doubt the coded signal which indicated 'Sighted sub. Am attacking' had been sent to Chivenor but it may not have reached them immediately because of the low level at which the Wellington was flying when the signal was sent or because of atmospheric disruptions. The three other Wellingtons sighted no U-boats but the ease with which they illuminated fishing vessels proved the merits of

58

the Leigh Light.[28]

During the remainder of June the five Leigh Light Wellingtons sighted no fewer than seven U-boats in the Bay of Biscay. Whitleys using conventional methods failed to find any enemy vessels during the same period. The Leigh Light Wellingtons proved so successful that on 24 June Dönitz ordered all U-boats to proceed submerged at all times except when it was necessary to recharge batteries. The morale of U-boat crews slumped with the knowledge that darkness no longer afforded them protection. The work of the Leigh Light Squadrons was the keystone of the success in the air offensive against U-boats in the Atlantic. They enabled night attacks to be made on submarines when they surfaced to re-charge their batteries under cover of darkness. On the night of 5/6 July the Leigh Light Wellingtons chalked up their first true kill when west of La Rochelle in the Bay of Biscay, an American pilot on 172 Squadron, Pilot Officer Wiley B. Howell flying 'H-Harry' sunk the U-502, which was bound for the Caribbean on its third war cruise. Kapitänleutnant (lieutenant commander) Jürgen von Rosenstiel and all 52 hands perished. It was described by 'Bruce Sanders' thus: 'H for Harry', a Wellington, spotted a U-boat surfaced eight miles distant and began stalking it. Closer and closer the Wellington crept out of the sun, handled very clearly by a pilot who was determined to get the submarine if it was at all possible. He proved that it was. He had covered the entire eight miles and was roaring down over the U-boat before its crew awoke to their danger. Three men were still struggling at the conning-tower hatch when the redskin of the skies charged overhead with machine-guns chattering. They tumbled this way and that like broken dolls and the bombs broke across the under-pirate's slim back.'

What 'Sanders' could not mention was the Leigh Light. About a mile from the target, the crew switched the light on to reveal the Type IXC U-boat rolling gently on the surface. Four shallow set 250lb depth charges straddled the boat. When the water settled, the aircrew saw that the water around the submarine had become uncommonly dark. Six days later, Howell and his crew attacked U-159, again using their Leigh Light. The U-boat skipper, Kapitänleutnant Helmut Witte, ordered his gun crew to shoot out the aircraft's Leigh Light. The gunners, blinded by the intense glare, could not obey. U-159 escaped but suffered damage.[29]

From the twentieth day of June 1940 when Mirek Vild (Flight Lieutenant Miroslav Vild) set out with Alois Siska from Bordeaux bound for England in the good ship Ary Sheffer until 1 November 1944 when Mirek completed his last operational flight as a radio and radar operator, few men can have survived so many potential deaths. On his very first operation with 311 (Czech) Squadron from East Wretham, in Norfolk, the Bomber Command Wellington in which he was flying crashed soon after take-off, eventually accounting for five killed and three more seriously wounded. Vild's escape (he was literally blown to the ground from the aircraft) was providential. 25 May 1941 was his lucky day. After six months in hospital at Ely and another three on light duties, recuperating with the Squadron, he was back on the treadmill. Four months later, on 10 August 1942, after 311 had been transferred to Coastal Command and to the airfield at Talbenny in south-west Wales, he was the radio operator on Flying Officer J. Nyult's crew on Wellington HF922 'H-Harry' who claimed their first U-boat destroyed in the Battle of the Atlantic north of Cape Ortegal.[30]

Soon afterwards Vild was obliged to change crews. He joined the crew of Flying Officer J. Vella DFC. On their very next trip, Vild's former comrades were shot down on a patrol in the Bay of Biscay. None of Nyult's crew survived. Vild then had a strange dream about one of his lost friends. He dreamt that, over a glass of red wine, he asked his departed comrade how he found things and what he thought about life. The message that came back was clear: forget your cares and worries and have a drink, for all will be well. Next, Vild was inquiring of his friend what had happened when he was shot down. Was the end very painful? He was anxious to know the answer. But, suddenly, Vild felt a strange sensation in his head; it seemed to become heavy and painful. What was this? he wondered. He wanted to rest and sleep - but he couldn't because someone was now shaking him, telling him he must wake up and get ready for the briefing... Now wide awake, the radio and radar operator found it was raining outside. He didn't at all feel like flying on what would be his 33rd operation. What is more, he noticed that the comrade sitting next to him in the crew-room was looking downcast and glum, whereas normally he was a jolly, spirited and talkative fellow. Vild asked him what was wrong. It turned out that he, too, had just been dreaming and was now apprehensive; dreams, he said, can so often come true. The two remained silent, content to nurse their own thoughts... As the crew were climbing aboard their Wellington, the front air gunner dropped his Thermos flask. It shattered in a dozen fragments on the tarmac. Vild looked down at the broken glass. His face came to life. 'Ah!' he exclaimed, 'broken glass! Broken glass is lucky. We shall be lucky today!'

That day they were patrolling in the Bay of Biscay, searching for U-boats leaving the south-west ports of France for the Atlantic, or returning after days at sea. Suddenly, down below, the crew spotted eight enemy aircraft, one of which was white. They were Ju 88s. Immediately bombs were jettisoned to make the aircraft safer and more manoeuvrable in a fight. The pilot climbed to 3,000 feet and headed west, out into the Atlantic, at full bore. Mirek radioed the bad news of the sighting back to base.

Meanwhile the 88s began climbing for their prey with the white aircraft positioning for the initial, frontal attack. But the Wellington pilot held his course steady, meeting the approaching German head-on. As they began to close, the Czech air gunner started blazing away from the front turret. Down went the 88, plunging seawards... How the 311 crew evaded the unequal attacks, none could truly say, but at the end of the engagement, which seemed like an eternity, the score sheet read: 311 Squadron - three German aircraft destroyed: the enemy - O. Back at base, the crew stepped down thankfully from the aircraft. Once on the ground Vild sought out the front-gunner. 'Are you superstitious?' he asked. 'No' came the positive, monosyllabic response. Vild brushed the negative aside. 'Have no doubt,' he said, 'the broken glass from your Thermos brought us the luck...[31]

During the war ferry flights were frequently fraught with danger not only from the elements but from hunting enemy aircraft. A mixed crew briefed to take a Wellington to the Middle East was attacked by a Junkers 88 off Cape

Finisterre soon after their dawn take-off on 20 July 1942. The Ju 88 dived and at 500 yards opened fire, shattering the Wellington's rear turret and injuring the gunner with broken pieces of perspex. The fire holed the nacelle tanks, shot through the main spar and severed various controls. The rear gunner of the Wellington, his face streaming with blood and with a bullet in his leg, held his fire until the enemy was 150 yards away, then fired. The Ju 88 stopped firing immediately; smoke began pouring from the port engine. Flight Sergeant J. M. Rogers RAAF, who was in the astrodome, saw it go past the Wellington about thirty yards distant and swoop down into the sea. Half-way down it lifted a little as though the pilot were mortally wounded and someone else were trying to pull the aircraft out, but if so it was a vain attempt.

The Wellington landed at Gibraltar. As it touched down the port tyre collapsed and petrol began to stream from bullet holes in the top of the tanks. Soon afterwards the same crew returned to England, where they were chosen to pioneer the West African route for Coastal Command Wellingtons. The first journey began on 3 October 1942 and the trip to Gibraltar was made without incident. On 14 October they left Gibraltar at dawn, flying past Casablanca, to which, a few months later, Australians, among other ferry pilots, were to bring important delegates. As the day progressed, visibility deteriorated and by the time the Wellington was off Dakar it was flying in thick haze, fighting against high winds and made sluggish by its heavy cargo. Seeking Bathurst, which the wireless operator was unable to pick up because of severe interference, the aircraft flew up and down the coast in the haze until night overtook them with almost empty petrol tanks. They sent out an SOS and decided on a crash-landing on a beach. The pilot touched down and ran into a sand dune. There was a crash and the aircraft burst into flames. The back of the aircraft was broken and the fuselage opposite where Rogers, the Australian was sitting, split from top to bottom, enabling him to dive out of the fiery interior into the sand, although he was badly burned in doing so.

The second pilot escaped through the escape hatch in the rear of the fuselage. The wireless operator got out through the astrodome and the pilot through his escape hatch. The pilot's hands were terribly burned in releasing himself from his harness. The rear gunner alone escaped burning, although he was stunned and bruised. He managed to salvage his parachute, tore the silk into strips and bandaged the burns of the others. It was a hot, tropical night, but all were cold from shock and they huddled close to the burning aircraft.

About an hour later, in the darkness beyond the circle of fiery light, the crew saw several vague figures moving. Rogers and his English comrades staggered to their feet, calling out in the few words of Arabic and French they knew and the figures materialized as scared natives who obviously had seen few, if any, white men before. 'By signs they were made to understand the airmen's need of water and half an hour later they came back with a big calabash full of warm, earthy water and the crew drank deeply. Then the natives helped them along the beach to their fishing hut, warned the airmen by signs to beware of leopards and snakes and went off to their village some distance away. The rear gunner kept the fire going through the night. None of them slept; their burns were too painful.

At first light came the roar of an aircraft and a Hudson aircraft appeared, circled and in response to Very lights and a message written by the Australian and the rear gunner in the sand - 'Five, badly burned' - signalled by Aldis lamp that they were to stay by their aircraft and left. Thirty minutes later a Sunderland arrived. It had picked up the Hudson's signal to base. The Sunderland landed about three-quarters of a mile out. Then another Hudson arrived and dropped a dinghy and some food and the Sunderland sent another dinghy in through the surf to take off the crew. The natives returned, collected the airmen's kit and helped get it into the dinghy on a subsequent trip. Rogers thinks the crew left that tribe the richest in Africa, One of the natives, possibly, is still wearing the remains of the blue silk pyjamas he gave him. The crew was flown to a military hospital at Bathurst. There the second pilot died the following morning from fever and burns. The wireless air gunner died four days later. The rear gunner recovered rapidly and went on to the Middle East. Rogers and the pilot were in hospital for two or three months before they returned to Britain on 2 March 1942.

On 4 August 1942 meanwhile, in the Mediterranean, forty miles west of Jaffa, U-372, which had left Salarnis on its eighth war cruise on 27 July, was attacked by Wellington HF913/M on 221 Squadron and Wellington 'N' on 203 Squadron and depth charged and sunk by RN destroyers *Sikh* and *Zulu* and frigates *Croome* and *Tetcott* after a thirteen-hour hunt. The commander, 33-year old Hans-Joachim Neumann and his crew perished.

In September, a detachment on 172 Squadron, operating from Skitten, Caithness was expanded and became 179 Squadron. The primary task of the Leigh Light-equipped Wellingtons was to saturate the Bay of Biscay at night, forcing as many U-boats as possible, to dive and run submerged and then to surface in daylight hours to charge batteries. This tactic increased the effectiveness of the daylight air patrols of the Whitleys, Sunderlands, Catalinas and other aircraft fitted with less sophisticated radar, whose crews relied heavily on daytime visual spottings.

On 16 September Wellington 'E-Ela' on 304 Squadron was airborne at 0930 and within five minutes was setting out on its 140-mile leg to the Biscay area; briefed for a 'routine' U-boat search. The navigator, Flight Lieutenant Minakowski, takes up the story.

'As we approached position 'A' at 1612, six aircraft appeared; one starboard, three to port and two far astern. The sky was cloudless and the weather fine, with visibility between 25-30 miles from our altitude of 1,500 feet. Flying Officer Stanislas Targowski, our pilot, descended to 500 feet when the aircraft were sighted and, when we identified them as Ju 88s, jettisoned our depth charges and went further down to 50 feet.'

The enemy fighters closed in rapidly. At 1615 three Ju 88s bore in from the port front quarter, one after another and Targowski threw the Wellington into violent evasive manoeuvres, almost dipping the wings into the sea. Each time a Junkers came in, he turned to face it head-on, thereby presenting the smallest possible target. Both front and rear gunners opened fire as the first Ju 88 came on and hit one of them and saw it fall into the sea. The wireless operator, after transmitting a signal to base about the attack and the aircraft's location, manned the beam gun. Minakowski's report continues:

'Two Junkers - those originally farthest away - now closed in from starboard, passed us and then attacked. They nearly succeeded. As one attacked on the starboard beam, our Wellington turned head-on towards him and was struck by cannon shells and a machine-gun burst. One of the petrol tanks was damaged and the cabin was filled with smoke from the explosions. All our guns were banging away furiously. Another Hun was hit and pieces fell off him as he turned towards France with smoke streaming out of his starboard engine. Shortly after this a crash resounded in the Wellington and dense smoke filled the fuselage. There were no fumes, however and nobody was wounded. Some clouds appeared on the horizon just then and we made for them.

'Two fighters now attacked us time after time from astern. Both were hit by our gunners who greeted them with accurate fire as they got within close range. Thereafter the enemy's attacks were half-hearted. The clouds were by now much closer, about 1,500 feet up, so Targowski made for them at full speed. He reached them safely and we finally broke away from the enemy. We fixed our position and informed base we would land at Portreath in Cornwall, owing to fuel shortage. The petrol in the starboard tank had all leaked out and the auxiliary oil-delivery tank was damaged. We landed at 1750, having been airborne for 8hr 20min. None of us was hurt.'[32]

On 22 October 'B-Bertie', a Leigh Light-equipped Wellington on 179 Squadron piloted by Flight Sergeant A. D. S. Martin DFM sank the U-412, commanded by 26-year old Kapitänleutnant Walter Jahrmärker, as she entered the Atlantic northeast of the Faeroes, six days out from Kiel on her first war cruise. All 47 hands were lost. Early in November the Squadron was stood down from anti-shipping operations and by the end of the month had moved to Gibraltar. Meanwhile, 544 Squadron had formed at Benson on 19 October 1942 with two flights. 'A' Flight operated Ansons and Wellingtons from Benson while 'B' Flight operated Spitfires in the PR role from Gibraltar. 'A' Flight Wellingtons began flying experimental night photographic operations over France in January 1943.[33]

By January 1943 Coastal Command aircraft had almost ceased to locate U-boats by night. The only solution was to replace the ASV Mark II, which only had a 1½ metre wave-length, with the long overdue ASV Mark III of ten centimetre wavelength. This apparatus which had a PPI display was already in operation having originated from an adaptation of centimetric AI. An American version, developed with the help of British scientists, had been successfully tested in May 1942 although British models would not be available until spring 1943. The new model Leigh Light-equipped Wellington GR.XIV, which was fitted with ASV.III was powered by more powerful Hercules engines and propellers that could be feathered, which enabled the aircraft to fly on one engine in emergencies. Two Coastal Command squadrons - 172 and 407 'Demon' Squadron RCAF - consisting of about fifteen aircraft each, received these new Wellingtons.

In 1943 Coastal Command underwent many changes to its Wellington squadrons. On 9 February 1943 U-268 commanded by 26-year old

Oberleutnant zur see Ernst Heydemann was inbound to Brest returning from its fourth war cruise low on fuel and was found west of St. Nazaire by 'B-Bertie' a Leigh Light-equipped Wellington on 172 Squadron piloted by Flying Officer G. D. Lundon. He dropped four depth charges close to the U-boat and later, German aircraft and patrol boats could find no sign of U-268. The boat and all 45 hands had perished.[34]Ten days' later, on 19 February U-562, which had left La Spezia on its tenth war cruise on 7 February, was bombed north-east of Benghazi by Wellington LB177/S on 38 Squadron piloted by Flying Officer I. B. Butler DFC who was escorting Convoy XT.3. U-562 was also depth charged by the destroyers HMS *Isis* and HMS *Hursley*. All 49 hands including the commander, Horst Hamm, perished.

In March 1943 one of the biggest convoy battles of the war took place when nearly fifty U-boats in six wolfpacks attacked four large eastbound convoys numbering 150 merchantmen and their escorts. U-333, which had been equipped with extra anti-aircraft guns, encountered a Wellington on 172 Squadron in the Bay of Biscay. When the Wellington attacked, the U-boat crew fought back instead of diving and shot the Wellington down in flames, killing the crew.[35]

Confirmation of claims for kills and identification of the actual U-boat 'victims' often posed difficulties. West of Nantes on 10 April 1943 an attack by a Leigh-Light Wellington, 'C-Charlie', flown by Pilot Officer G. H. Whiteley on 172 Squadron using ASV-IV radar, formerly credited with the destruction of U-376 commanded by 28-year old Kapitänleutnant Friedrich-Karl Marks, was actually directed against U-465, inflicting severe damage.[36] U-376 was outbound for a special operation code-named 'Elster' (Magpie) to take aboard German naval officers who escaped from a Canadian PoW camp at North Point on the northern tip of Prince Edward Island on the Canadian east coast. When it failed repeatedly to report its position after sailing, it was posted as missing in the Bay of Biscay effective 13 April 1943.[37] On 26 April U-437 commanded by 29-year old Kapitänleutnant Hermann Lamby left St. Nazaire on its sixth war cruise bound for the mid-Atlantic but he was forced to return after being hit by a stick of Mark XI Torpex depth charges dropped by 'G-George' a Leigh-Light Wellington on 172 squadron piloted by Flying Officer Peter H. Strembridge. Almost immediately 'two separate patches of very large bubbles were seen' reported Strembridge but two flights of Ju 88s and another U-boat helped nurse the badly damaged submarine to safety at St. Nazaire on 30 April. U-437 was heavily damaged and did not re-sail until 23 September when it set out for the North Atlantic.

North-west of Cape Ortegal in the Bay of Biscay in the early hours of 3 July Leigh-Light Wellington 'R-Robert' on 172 Squadron piloted by Flight Sergeant Alex Coumbis, a Rhodesian, picked up U-126 or U-154, which was close by, on radar. Coumbis lined up and attacked a U-boat that proved to be U-126 commanded by 26-year old Oberleutnant zur see Siegfried Kietz, which was returning from West Africa on its sixth war cruise. Nothing more was ever heard from U-126 which was lost with all 55 hands. West of Figueria six days' later the veteran U-435 commanded by 32-year old Korvettenkapitän (Lieutenant Commander) Siegfried Strelow, which was returning from the

Azores area having left Brest on its ninth war cruise on 20 May, was bombed by four depth-charges dropped by Wellington 'R-Robert' flown by Flying Officer E. J. Fisher on 179 Squadron. The U-boat was lost with all 48 hands.[38]

The U-459 commanded by 49-year old Korvettenkapitän Georg von Wilamowitz-Möllendorf sailed from Bordeaux on 22 July bound for refuelling operations in company with two other U-boats, one of which soon developed a bad leak and aborted. On 24 July, late in the day, Flying Officer W. H. T. Jennings piloting Wellington 'Q-Queenie' on 172 Squadron found U-459 and attacked out of low clouds. U-459 remained on the surface and Wilamowitz-Möllendorf's new quad 20mm and twin 20mm guns opened fire. Jennings bravely flew into this very heavy flak barrage and crashed into the starboard side of U-459, demolishing the quad 20mm and other guns and killing or wounding half a dozen of U-459's crew. Utter chaos ensued. The Germans cut away the wreckage of the Wellington fuselage and pushed it into the sea. Upon doing so, they found three unexploded depth charges, two on the bridge and one on the afterdeck. Apparently unaware that the depth charges were fitted with shallow-set pistols, Wilamowitz-Möllendorf rang up full speed and ordered his men to roll them overboard. One or more of the charges exploded as designed beneath the stern of U-459, inflicting horrendous damage. A second Wellington, on 547 Squadron, piloted by Flying Officer J. Whyte arrived on the scene. Upon seeing U-459, which was slowly circling out of control stern down, he attacked, dropping eight depth charges at wave-top level in a close straddle. These explosions dashed any hopes the U-459 crew may have had of limping home. In a second attack run, Whyte dropped several more depth charges and raked the topside with machine-gun fire, killing and wounding more Germans and destroying some of the dinghies. Following this attack, Wilamowitz-Möllendorf ordered his men to abandon ship and scuttle. As the dinghies pulled away, he saluted his men and then went below and opened the vents. Observed by Whyte and his aircrew, the U-459 sank swiftly by the stern. This second Wellington and other aircraft directed the Polish-manned destroyer Orkan to the scene. Seven to eight hours after the first Wellington attacked, the Poles picked up forty-one Germans and one British airman, A. A. Turner, who had been blown out of the crashed Wellington and had climbed into his own dinghy. The Admiralty credited the kill to the first Wellington and in view of his 'high degree of courage' recommended Jennings for a posthumous Victoria Cross.[39]

During the great battle with U-boats in the Bay of Biscay on 30 July 1943 - subsequently officially described as 'the greatest single victory of the war against U-boats' - a formation of three U-boats was annihilated by aircraft of Coastal Command and the USAAF and by sloops of the Royal Navy, in a six hour's engagement. The U-614, commanded by 27-year old Kapitänleutnant Wolfgang Sträter sailed from St. Nazaire on 25 July 1943 on its third war cruise. On the fifth day out while still in Biscay, Wellington 'G-George' on 172 Squadron piloted by Wing Commander Rowland G. Musson found and attacked U-614, dropping six depth charges. Sträter remained on the surface to fight it out with his new quad 20mm and other flak guns, but the depth charges blew the boat to pieces.

Anson on 220 Squadron passing over the stern of HMS *Revenge* which is behind two other RN battleships. The Anson was replaced on 220 Squadron by the Lockheed Hudson in September 1939. (Charles E. Brown)
Inset: Anson cockpit.

The *Bismarck* spotted in Dobric Fjord just before she weighed anchor for her first and last commerce-raiding voyage in the Atlantic.

The frozen lake at Jonsvatnet used by the Germans in Norway as a makeshift airfield. A Wellington spotted 22 enemy aircraft on it. As a result the lake was bombed - 'with excellent results'.

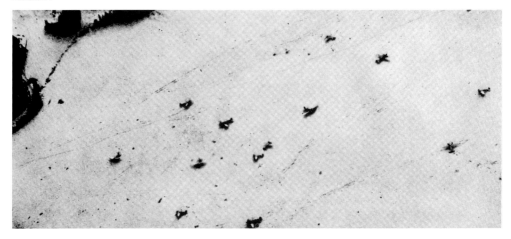

Ålesund a few hours before the successful raid on 29/30 October 1941. Four merchant vessels were sunk and three heavily damaged.

The 26,000-ton battle cruisers *Scharnhorst* (pictured) and the *Gneisenau* or 'Salmon and Gluckstein' (a famous London store) as they were known throughout the Royal Air Force, caused havoc during the Norwegian Campaign and after. During one war cruise the two battle cruisers destroyed 115,622 tons of shipping and the enemy plan was for the *Bismarck* to co-operate with them in the North Atlantic.

In April 1940 at the Australian flying boat base at Mount Batten in Devonshire Wing Commander L. V. Lachal, first CO and (in the flying suits of the day) Squadron Leader W. N. 'Hoot' Gibson DFC; Squadron Leader C. W. Pearce DFC, who followed Wing Commander Lachal as CO; Flight Lieutenant I. S. Podger DFC and Squadron Leader W. H. 'Bull' Garing DFC. When the war in Europe ended Wing Commander Lachal had been appointed air commodore, AOC North-Western Area, Australia and had been awarded the OBE; Squadron Leader Pearce had been promoted to air commodore and gazetted CBE; Squadron Leader Garing had become a Group Captain and made a CBE; Squadron Leader Gibson and Flight Lieutenant Podger were Group Captains.

Liberator GR.III XB-L on 224 Squadron at St. Eval, Cornwall in August 1944. Note the Leigh Light under the starboard wing. The squadron moved to Milltown in September, returning to St. Eval in July 1945.

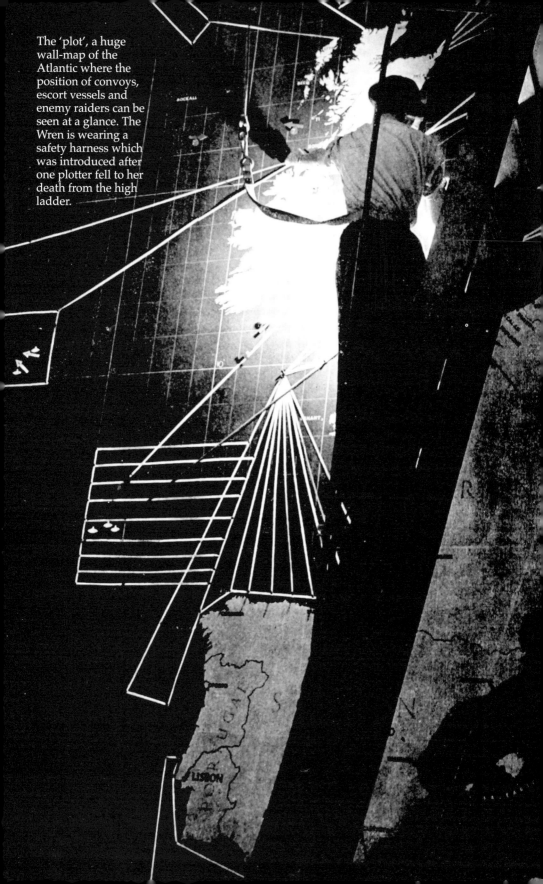

The 'plot', a huge wall-map of the Atlantic where the position of convoys, escort vessels and enemy raiders can be seen at a glance. The Wren is wearing a safety harness which was introduced after one plotter fell to her death from the high ladder.

Whitley GR VII, YG-R of 502 Squadron, based at St Eval in 1942, on anti-submarine patrol. Though something of a hasty improvisation, the GR Whitley units were responsible for sinking or seriously damaging at least 15 U-boats.

A Coastal Command crew stepping lively to their waiting aircraft for a sea patrol in the Atlantic.

Loading a torpedo into the bomb bay of a Beaufort.

A Beaufort is started up by the trolley ack.

Supermarine Walrus ZE-O W2757.

A Walrus at readiness weighed down by oil drums for protection in high winds.

Wing Commander Maechel Anthony 'Mike' Ensor DSO* DFC* AFC flew a total of 67 operations on 500 and 224 Squadrons. He was born on 5 January 1922 at Rangiora, Canterbury in New Zealand. Pilot Officer Ensor's citation for the DFC was on 20 February 1942. A bar to his DFC was awarded on 27 October. On 16 February 1943 he was awarded the DSO. On 6 February 1945 Acting Squadron Leader Ensor, now on 224 Squadron was awarded a bar to his DSO. During his second tour of duty he attacked many enemy U-boats on three occasions. One of the submarines was probably seriously damaged, and from one of the many engagements, Squadron Leader Ensor's aircraft was severely damaged by the heavy and accurate anti-aircraft fire encountered. Left: Ensor with his dog 'Liberator'.

Below Right: Flying Officer William Boris Tilley DFC RAAF of Melbourne, Victoria, a Sunderland pilot on 10 Squadron RAAF. Among his many exploits, on 26 August 1944 he alighted on the water to rescue three survivors from a Wellington on 172 Squadron RAF, clinging to a one-man dinghy after being shot down in the Bay of Biscay while attacking a German submarine. Although it was forbidden for flying boats to alight on the open sea in rescue attempts, Tilley, decided the survivors could wait no longer for surface craft to arrive and touched down to pick them up for a safe return to Mount Batten, Devon. A fourth member of the Wellington crew, Flying Officer R. B. Gray RCAF, refused to risk the lives of the other survivors by overloading the dinghy, although he was seriously injured. He succumbed during their 15-hour ordeal at sea and was awarded a posthumous George Cross.

Below Left: Wing Commander Wilfred E. Oulton DSO DFC on 58 Squadron who sunk U-266 north of the Azores on the night of 14/15 May in Halifax HR746/M while escorting Convoy SC.129.

Handley Page Hampden in flight. Hampdens (and Blenheims and Wellingtons) flew countless sorties against German naval shipping targets early in the war.

Hampdens on 489 Squadron RNZAF which served with Coastal Command as a torpedo and general attack unit. Nearest Hampden is AE361 'C-Charlie'. (IWM)

Ground crewmen on 455 Squadron RAAF bomb up a Hampden in the snow in the winter of 1942.

Catalina I W8406 on 209 Squadron on patrol. Some of the first Catalinas entered service on 209 and 240 Squadrons of Coastal Command at Castle Archdale in Northern Ireland. On 26 May 1941 a Catalina on 209 Squadron spotted the German battleship *Bismarck* after naval forces had lost contact and it was subsequently shadowed by a Catalina on 240 Squadron. (IWM)

Ground crew load up a Catalina with ammunition for the next patrol.

Lockheed Hudson I T9965 on 269 Squadron on patrol flying over the stark and inscrutable face of Iceland - 'black hills bearing no trace of trees or vegetation'. Hudsons first entered service on 224 Squadron at Gosport in the summer of 1939. When war broke out in Europe that September, two squadrons, 224 at Leuchars and 233 at Bircham Newton, Norfolk were operational in Coastal Command. A third squadron, 220, was in the throes of converting from the Anson to the Hudson at Thornaby. A Hudson on 224 Squadron was the first RAF aircraft to destroy a German aircraft in WWII, on 8 October 1939.

At dawn on 28 August the Kingston Agathe and HMS *Durwell* and HMS *Niagara* arrived and the U-boat crew were taken off so that the submarine could be towed to Iceland, escorted all the way by aircraft. After capture U-570 was re-commissioned on 19 September 1941 as HM Submarine *Graph* and used operationally before reverting to training duties. It was wrecked on Islay on 20 March 1944 when on passage to the Clyde from Chatham for extensive refitting.

A Hudson taxies out in Iceland for a night patrol.

Armstrong Whitworth Whitley GR.VII Z9138 WL-R on 612 Squadron getting airborne from Reykjavik, Iceland in 1942. The ASV (Air to Surface Vessel) radar antennae along the top of the fuselage have been deleted by a wartime censor.

The Wellington aircrew saw survivors in the water, 'some wearing life jackets and yellow skull caps.' All waved or defiantly shook fists, but no German survived.[40] On the evening of 24 August Musson took off on a Leigh Light patrol at 2335. He crashed two miles inland from Clovelly thirteen minutes' later. The Wellington caught fire and the DCs exploded. Musson and three of his original successful crew were killed with two others.[41]

By 7 August 1943 Dönitz was facing a grim butcher's bill; for three months past an average of thirty U-boats had been sunk a month and the Allied shipping losses had been reduced' to a relatively negligible quantity'. Fifty-six U-boats were lost in the Bay and in the North Atlantic between 1 June and 1 September 1943 but the nerves of their crews, brave though the great majority were, were near breaking point. 'You've no idea how unnerving is the effect of repeated alarms', observed a prisoner from U-202 sunk on 1 June 1943. 'The loudspeaker begins to sound like the voice of doom'. But perhaps the most significant remark of all was that made by an officer from U-506, sunk on 12 July 1943 in the North Atlantic. 'It's no longer any fun' he said, 'to sail in a U-boat. We don't really mind even a cruiser and we can face destroyers without turning a hair. But if an aircraft is there, we've had it. It directs surface craft to the spot even if it does not attack itself '. These remarks came from the lips of shaken prisoners, but, even after due allowance has been made for their condition of mind it was obvious that by August, 1943, the situation from the German point of view was very serious.

On 17 August 1943 U-403 commanded by 28-year old Kapitänleutnant Karl-Franz Heine who was searching for Convoy Sierra Leone 135, was bombed by Hudson V9220/D flown by Flying Officer P. R. Horbat on 206 Squadron and Wellington HF697 on 697 Free French Squadron off Dakar in Senegal and was lost with all 49 hands. On 24 August, three days after an attack by a Wildcat-Avenger team from the carrier Croatan, escorting convoy UGS 14, 'J-Johnny' a Leigh-Light equipped Wellington on 179 Squadron piloted by a Canadian, Flying Officer Donald F. McRae, found U-134 commanded by Kapitänleutnant Hans-Günther Brosin west of Vigo and attacked in the face of heavy flak. Brosin was returning from American waters and had shot down a blimp in the Florida Straits. McRae dropped six depth charges and claimed U-134 destroyed 45 miles south of Cape Finisterre but he was unable to provide positive evidence of a kill.[42] This was often difficult, to say the least. Sometimes crews did not return to file their claim. On 27 August, Flying Officer R B Gray on 172 Squadron attacked U-534 which was on its third war cruise and was shot down by return fire. The pilot was awarded a posthumous George Cross.

On 6 September Flying Officer Donald McRae attacked U-760 off Cape Finisterre and this time there was no doubt. The U-boat, commanded by Kapitänleutnant Otto-Ulrich Blum, had left La Pallice on its second war cruise on 24 July and on 12 August had been damaged in an attack by an American B-24 and had to return to port. McRae's attack put both diesel engines out of action and U-760 limped into El Ferrol in Spain two days' later only to be interned with its crew.[43] On the night of 18/19 November, 430 miles south-west of Cape Finisterre, McRae was flying Wellington 'F-Freddie' and escorting Convoys SL.139/MK S.30 when U-211 was detected on radar and bombed by

Leigh-Light. The Type VIIC U-boat, which was commanded by 27-year old Kapitänleutnant Karl Hause, had left Brest on 14 October, on its fifth war cruise and was operating as a 'flak trap'. Type VII 'Flak boats' or 'flak traps' were introduced to lure and destroy anti-submarine aircraft. Their first success came on 24 May when west of Gibraltar, the veteran U-441, the first of eight such boats, which was armed with two quad 20mms on bandstands fore and aft of the conning tower and a rapid fire 37mm flak gun on a second, lower bandstand aft, plus nests of machine guns on the bridge and a team of highly trained gunners, shot down Sunderland EJ139 on 228 Squadron flown by Flying Officer H. J. Debden, who also damaged the U-boat's bow area by depth charges. None of the flying-boat crew survived. U-211 went down with all 54 hands.

On 7 September 1943 Pilot Officer E. M. O'Donnell DFC on 407 'Demon' Squadron RCAF carried out an attack in 'W-William' on a U-boat believed to be U-669, commanded by Oberleutnant zur see Kurt Köhl, which was outbound for a special operation code-named 'Kiebitz' to take aboard former U-434 Kapitänleutnant Wolfgang Heyda, who escaped from a Canadian PoW camp at Baie de Chaleurs, New Brunswick on the Canadian east coast. The attack, in which O'Donnell dropped five depth charges, was actually directed against U-584 and they inflicted no damage.[44]

On the night of 10 September a Leigh Light-equipped Wellington on 179 Squadron, piloted by a Canadian, Squadron Leader D. B. Hodgkinson found U-617 commanded by Kapitänleutnant Albrecht Brandi about one hundred miles east of Gibraltar near the coast of Spanish Morocco. Attacking into 'heavy' flak, Hodgkinson dropped six depth charges that disabled U-617.[45] Three hours later, in the early hours of 11 September, another Wellington on 179 Squadron, piloted by Pilot Officer W. H. Bronini, arrived and, in the face of 'intense' flak, dropped six more depth charges. These attacks so badly damaged U-617 that Brandi, could not dive. To avoid certain capture, he drove the boat into shallow water offshore and abandoned ship. After he and the 48 crew reached the beach, Spanish troops took them into custody. Hodgkinson was awarded the DFC.[46]

Among Australians serving in the Leigh Light Squadrons was Pilot Officer M. H. 'Max' Paynter on 612 Squadron. At three o'clock on a black morning in October 1943, when the water was covered in a thick sea mist he piloted a Wellington in one of the many Leigh Light operations in the Bay of Biscay. The Wellington had been sent out to search for a dinghy previously reported in the Bay and it was flying low when an unidentified object was picked up on the detector apparatus. Paynter switched on the Leigh Light and in a few seconds it swivelled round on to a fully surfaced U-boat. As soon as the light went on, red and white and green tracer bullets streamed up from the submarine's guns and the glass of the Leigh Light was shattered and the tail of the aircraft hit. Paynter's navigator, Pilot Officer J. W. McKay RAAF had moved along to man the front gun and at 300 yards could see the gun crew clearly. He opened fire and saw his tracer ricocheting off the deck. Then the Wellington swept in from the beam and dropped a stick of depth charges across the conning tower. McKay kept firing until they passed over and the fire from the submarine slackened and then died away. The last two depth charges straddled the U-boat. The rear gunner saw the explosion close to the conning tower and then there was nothing more in the pitch blackness. The Wellington stayed near the spot for another twenty minutes and then proceeded on patrol. An hour and twenty minutes later the crew found the dinghy floating 100 miles off the Spanish coast near Cape Finisterre. It illuminated the spot, reported its position and returned to base.[47]

Forty miles WSW of Cape Spartel at the mouth of the Gibraltar Strait in the early minutes of 1 November U-340 was damaged in a bombing attack by Leigh-Light Wellington piloted by Flying Officer Arthur H. Ellis DFC on 179 Squadron. Ellis dropped six depth charges but an engine malfunction forced Ellis to abort. Later in the day RN destroyers HMS *Active* and HMS *Witherington* and sloop *Fleetwood* found the U-340 with sonar and attacked with depth charges. The U-boat, which had left St Nazaire on its third war cruise on 17 October, was abandoned by its commander, 28-year old Hans-Joachim Klaus, after passing through the Straits due to extensive damage. Forty-eight hands were rescued by Spanish fishermen but were then taken off by HMS *Fleetwood* and taken into captivity.[48] In the early hours of 10 November 1943 the U-966, commanded by 25-year old Oberleutnant zur see Eckehard Wolf, which sailed from Trondheim on 5 October, was found by a Leigh Light-equipped Wellington on 612 Squadron piloted by Warrant Officer Ian D. Gunn while inbound to France via the northern Spanish coast south-east of Punta Estace. Gunn attacked U-966, dropping six depth charges, all of which fell short. After an exchange of gunfire, U-966 dived.[49]

On the night of 26 November 'H-Harry', a Leigh Light-equipped Wellington (HF146) on the Azores-based 179 Squadron piloted by Flight Sergeant Donald M. Cornish found the U-542, commanded by Oberleutnant zur see Christian-Brandt Coester north of Madeira. The boat was on its first war cruise, having left Kiel on 21 October for the Azores area. Cornish and his crew had earlier sunk U-431 in the Mediterranean east of Cartagena on 21 October[50] and three days' later forced Kapitänleutnant Hans Hornkohl to scuttle U-566 in the North Atlantic thirty miles west of Porto after a bombing attack as the steering gear failed and the screws were ruined.[51] Flying into heavy flak, Cornish dropped six depth charges that destroyed U-542, which was lost with all hands.[52]

In November 547 Squadron converted to the Liberator. On the 15th 415 'Swordfish' Squadron RCAF moved to Bircham Newton, Norfolk, for operations using Leigh Lights to illuminate targets for its Albacores to attack E-boats. The Royal Navy was also involved, as Fred Dorken, a WOp/AG on the squadron, recalls: 'The Navy would stay a few miles beyond the convoy route in their MTB and MGBs and when the E-boats were within range, working singly we would drop flares and illuminate them for the Navy. The E-boats had impressive armament and we longed for bombs instead of flares. We flew eight-hour patrols against enemy convoys and several ships were destroyed. (We carried 500lb bombs on these trips.) All told, it was hours of boredom and every once in a while, wild excitement. 'The North Sea in wartime is a cruel place and a goodly number of crews just disappeared.'

Derek Bielby, a Coastal Command pilot recalled the experience of a Polish crew on 304 Squadron at Chivenor near Barnstaple in north Devon, one black night in the Bay of Biscay in the winter of 1943. It proved again the rugged durability of the Wellington aircraft.

'The night-aircraft of Coastal Command were navigated, in those days, by dead reckoning. The method depended on the constant measuring of drift[53] by taking back bearings on flame floats dropped overboard. These devices ignited on contact with the sea. As drift-taking took place with monotonous frequency, the sea was often dotted far and wide with the flame-float pattern of other aircraft of 19 Group flying parallel courses in the saturation search for surfaced U-boats. Indeed, on a moonless night with a heavy overcast, it appeared as though the heavens and the sea had changed places.'

Flying one night in such conditions, the captain of one of 304's Wellingtons was suddenly puzzled to see four glowing red dots just in front of him. Equally suddenly the apparition vanished and the aircraft shuddered with the stupefying shock of hard contact. Baffled by the swiftness of the phenomenon, the captain realized that there had been a collision of some sort and though the aircraft vibrated uncharacteristically, it was manageable and still flew. As the patrol was reaching its limit, the pilot at once turned for home and the long, lonely haul over six hundred miles of hostile sea. It was only after the aircraft had been safely parked and the engines shut down that the ground crew discovered that the Wellington's fin and rudder were missing. And when a Coastal Command Liberator returned to its 19 Group base the same morning after an all-night Biscay sortie, minus the outer part of a wing, the realization of what had actually happened gradually dawned. The patrolling Polish pilot had seen the red-hot exhausts of the four-engined Liberator as it closed on a collision course. Inches only must have averted the sudden and total loss of both aircrews and aircraft. Chance had, yet again, played a fateful hand.... [54]

1944 brought fresh hopes of improving the U-boat kill ratio, although the early success of Leigh Light operations was now very much reduced due to U-boats being fitted with Schnorkel equipment enabling them to re-charge their batteries at periscope height. After getting through Gibraltar Strait, late in the evening of 8 January 1944, a Wellington on 179 Squadron piloted by Flying Officer W. F. M. Davidson, found U-343 south of Sardinia by radar and a full moon. Attacking into heavy flak, Davidson dropped six depth charges on the U-boat, which was commanded by Oberleutnant zur see Wolfgang Rahn. Riddled by flak, the Wellington crashed into the sea, throwing Davidson clear, but the rest of the airmen perished. Davidson found a raft, climbed in and was later rescued by Allied forces.[55]

North-east of the Azores on the night of 13 January the U-231 commanded by 33-year-old Kapitänleutnant Wolfgang Wenzel was located by aircraft from the aircraft carrier USS *Block Island* which brought up Wellington HF168 'L-London' on 172 Squadron piloted by a Canadian, Pilot Officer W. N. Armstrong DFC who was on a night escort patrol over a convoy. In two runs into flak, 420 miles northeast of the Azores, Armstrong dropped six depth charges that wrecked the U-231 beyond saving. ''There was a brilliant blue flash after my depth charges had gone down' recalled Armstrong 'and I think one of them must have hit the sub. We stooged around for a while and then saw him again. It looked as if he was too damaged to dive and my gunners opened up immediately, raking the sub from end to end. This time, however, he was ready for us and gave us everything he had. The flak was terrifying and it's a near-miracle we weren't hit then.

'I came round for my third attack run. The U-boat was clearly silhouetted in the moon-light and I could see that the hull aft of the conning tower was under water, with the bows clear of the sea. My own gunners kept up so effective a barrage that the Jerry gunners only got off one shot before ducking for cover, but it was an unlucky shot for us. It hit our rear turret, smashing it and exploding right in front of the gunner, Flying Officer H. B. W. Heard. I didn't know about this at the time and only first learned what had happened when I asked over the intercom what the rear gunner had seen of our attack. Back came the answer, 'Sorry, but I'm afraid I must come out. I've been hit.' He showed amazing courage and managed to lever himself out of the turret with his arms - he'd been hit badly in the legs. Despite his pain, he insisted on writing up his own report during the return journey - just in case he didn't make it, as he said - and was laughing and joking. At base, as soon as we landed, they rushed him to hospital where he underwent amputation, but he lived.'

With his boat flooding heavily aft, Wenzel ordered abandon ship. An American intelligence reported that: 'Sometime during the abandoning of his boat, Wenzel, probably in a fit of despondence, attempted suicide by firing a revolver bullet into his mouth.' The bullet 'lodged harmlessly...in the back of the neck and most crew members were unaware of the event.' All fifty men on U-231 escaped from the sinking boat in rafts and dinghies, but seven soon died of exposure. About thirteen hours later, on 14 January, two aircraft found the survivors and two American destroyers, the USS *Parrott* and the USS *Bulmer* picked up the forty-three Germans and transferred them to the *Block Island*, which arrived in Norfolk on 3 February. A doctor on *Block Island* removed the bullet in Wenzel's neck.[56] Flying Officer Heard and Armstrong were each awarded a DFC.

Identification and confirmation of claims for kills were still posing problems. West of Bordeaux on 31 January 1944 Wellington MP813/K flown by Flight Sergeant L. D. Richards on 172 Squadron using a Leigh Light for a night attack, was thought to result in the destruction of U-364 but it was actually directed against U-608, inflicting no damage. The Wimpy was shot down in the attack without being able to drop its depth charges.[57] Identification and confirmation of claims for kills were still posing problems. West of Bordeaux on 31 January 1944 Wellington MP813/K flown by Flight Sergeant L. D. Richards on 172 Squadron using a Leigh Light for a night attack, was thought to result in the destruction of U-364 but it was actually directed against U-608, inflicting no damage. The Wimpy was shot down in the attack without being able to drop its depth charges.[58]

On occasion identification was easier. In the North Atlantic 180 miles south-west of the Faeroes on 11 February, U-283, which was on its first war cruise, having left Kiel on 13 January, was bombed in a night attack by Wellington

MP578 'C-Charlie' flown by Flying Officer P. W. Heron DFC on 407 'Demon' Squadron. The night before, U-283 had shot down a Wellington on 612 Squadron. Heron dropped six depth charges on the boat which was lost with all 49 hands including the commander, 21-year old Günther Ney, the youngest officer yet to command a U-boat at sea.

In the Bay of Biscay on 3 March while U-525 was homebound to Lorient, another Leigh Light-equipped Wellington on 172 Squadron, piloted by J. W. Tweddle, bombed and severely damaged the U-boat, which was skippered by 35-year old Kapitänleutnant Hans-Joachim Drewitz. U-525 limped into Lorient, escorted by two Junkers Ju 88s and several small vessels. The boat was out of action until April.[59]

On 10 March 380 miles west of the mouth of the River Shannon the gunners on U-625 and U-741 shot down Wellington HF311 on 407 'Demon' Squadron RCAF flown by Pilot Officer E. M. O'Donnell. Sunderland EK591/U on 422 Squadron RCAF flown by Warrant Officer W. F. Morton, who was on his first operational sortie as captain and Flight Lieutenant Sidney W. Butler DFC along as check pilot spotted U-625, which commanded by 25-year old Siegfried Straub This submarine was a standard 517 tonner without the forward gun and carried two twin 20mm mountings on the upper platform and one on the lower, the latter being well shielded. Butler, who was at the controls at the time, avoided flak by frequent alterations of height and dropped six depth charges. U-625 sank by the stern and all 53 hands perished.

Next day a Leigh Light-equipped Wellington 'H-Harry' flown by Flying Officer H. C. Sorley on 407 'Demon' Squadron RCAF found and attacked the U-256 and U-741, which ran into difficulties while racing to locate and rescue shipwrecked Germans. U-256 suffered 'severe' damage. British and Canadian sources state that U-256 shot down 'H-Harry' but Oberleutnant zur see Wilhelm Brauel the U-boat commander, reported that the aircraft 'crashed 1500 metres off before own fire opened up.' Oberleutnant zur see Gerhard Palmgren in the outbound U-741 also reported an air attack. When he later surfaced, he said, he was attacked again, this time by 'four carrier aircraft and three destroyers,' which pursued him for hours, but inflicted only 'slight' damage. U-256 reached Brest on 22 March;[60] the U-741 continued her patrol. Meanwhile, the U-629, commanded by 27-year old Oberleutnant zur see Hans-Hellmuth Bugs, which sailed from Brest on 4 March was damaged the following day by DCs dropped by a Wellington on 304 Squadron which forced him to return to Brest on 7 March.[61] After repairs Bugs re-sailed on the 9th, but in the early hours of 12 March, 'C-Charlie', a Leigh Light-equipped Wellington on 612 Squadron piloted by D. Bretherton attacked into heavy flak and dropped four depth charges. These inflicted so much damage that Bugs was compelled to abort to Brest a second time, arriving on 15 March. The boat did not re-sail until 8 June when Bugs put to sea on a war cruise bound for the Plymouth area.[62]

In the North Atlantic in the early hours of 13 March U-575 commanded by Oberleutnant zur zee Wolfgang Boehmer was attacked into heavy flak by Leigh-Light Wellington HF183/B piloted by Flying Officer John P. Finnessey DFC on 172 Squadron. Finnessey attacked with depth charges, dropped float flares, gave the alarm and broadcast beacon signals. At dawn Fortress FA700/R flown by Flight Lieutenant A. David Beaty DFC on 206 Squadron arrived on the scene and attacked into heavy flak and dropped four close depth charges. When the automatic feed of the U-boat's 37mm gun failed and it had to be loaded by hand. Boehmer decided to submerge. Overhead it looked to Beaty that U-575 went down stern first with her bow sticking up at a steep angle. Beaty climbed, broadcast an alarm and circled the position for five hours, sending beacons. Fortress 'J' piloted by Flying Officer Wilfred R. Travell DFC on 220 Squadron soon arrived. Seeing a large oil slick, Travell dived and dropped two depth charges into its middle. He then climbed and broadcast homing signals for the benefit of an American hunter-killer group which included the 'jeep' carrier USS *Bogue* with Grumman Avengers of VC-95 on board. One of the Avengers piloted by John F. Adams came on the scene that morning; found the oil slick and dropped sonobuoys. A hunt was commenced by USN destroyers *Haverfield* and *Hobson* and RCN frigate HMCS *Prince Rupert* escorting Convoy Outbound North 227, backed by aircraft on the *Bogue* led to depth charge and 'Hedgehog' (forward-firing depth charge) attacks which finally forced U-575 to the surface. All three warships opened fire with main guns and an Avenger piloted by Donald A. Pattie attacked with rockets and bombs. These finally destroyed U-575 which sank with the loss of sixteen hands. Fourteen survivors were rescued and taken prisoner by *Prince Rupert* and took them to Newfoundland and 24, including the commander, were picked up by USS *Hobson,* which took them to Casablanca for eventual transfer to the United States.[63]

In the Bay in the early hours of 28 April 1944 the Admiralty believed that U-193, captained by Oberleutnant zur see Dr. Ulrich Abel, which had sailed from Lorient on 23 April to report weather and to serve as a provisional refueller if needed, came under air attack by 'W-William', a Leigh Light-equipped Wellington on 612 Squadron piloted by the Australian, Flying Officer C. G. 'Max' Punter, a veteran of the U-boat wars. Punter reportedly picked up U-193 on radar and from wave-top level, dropped a salvo of depth charges that destroyed the boat west of Nantes. Punter reported 'about ten small bluish lights in the water,' evidently illuminants on the life jackets of the German survivors.[64]

In bright moonlight in the North Atlantic north of Cape Ortegal on 4 May Flight Lieutenant L. J. Bateman DFC RCAF on 407 'Demon' Squadron RCAF piloting a Leigh-Light equipped Wellington (HF134/M) bombed U-846. The U-boat, which was on its second war cruise, having left Lorient on 29 April, was commanded by 35-year old Oberleutnant zur see Berthold Hashagen. Attacking into heavy flak, Bateman released six depth charges. Nothing more was ever heard from the boat, which presumably was sunk at this time and with the loss of all hands.[65] It was sweet revenge. U-846 had shot down Halifax HR741/H on 58 Squadron into the sea two days' earlier, on 2 May, with no survivors on Flight Lieutenant D. E. Taylor's crew.

By June Coastal Command operations had reached a peak, with priority task of keeping the English Channel free of German shipping in preparation for the imminent invasion of Europe. Included in Coastal Command's Order of Battle were seven Wellington squadrons: 172, 304 (Polish), 407 'Demon' Squadron RCAF and 612 AAF at Chivenor while 179, returned from Gibraltar were at Predannack. 415 RCAF and 524 were at Davidstow Moor, a few miles from the coast and a thousand feet high, between the hills, were the remaining two squadrons.

In Biscay on the early hours of 7 June, several aircraft of 19 Group attacked U-989 commanded by 26-year old Kapitänleutnant Hardo Rodler von Roithberg. Coastal Command gave credit for the damage to a Leigh Light-equipped Wellington on 179 Squadron piloted by W. J. Hill. A Liberator and a flight of Mosquitoes also participated in the attack. Wounded in the thigh by Mosquito gunfire, von Roithberg aborted to Brest for medical attention. [66]

On the night of 6/7 June - the night of D-Day - Coastal Command reported the loss of a Wellington on 407 'Demon' Squadron RCAF flown by Squadron Leader Farrell and three Liberators, but it is not known which U-boats made which kills. On the night of 8 June Flight Lieutenant J. Antoniewicz, captain of Wellington HF331 'A-Able' on 304 (Polish) Squadron claimed to have destroyed U-441 40 miles north of Ushant.[67] Flight-Lieutenant Antoniewicz was from Bilystok. He served a year in the Polish Army, before the war and then joined the Air Force. He was still a cadet when the war began and he was posted to a station as an engineer. When Warsaw fell, he escaped to Romania where he was held in a concentration camp for three and a half months. He escaped at night, reached the coast of the Black-Sea and found a friendly Romanian who helped him to board a ship and cross the Aegean. He ended up in Syria whither so many Poles had hastened. But Antoniewicz's eyes were on France so he made his way as far as Marseilles and served four months with the Preach. His dream was to become a pilot so he began his training just before the French capitulated. Then he had to move on once more; to carry his undying faith to still another country. He went to Oran, to Casablanca and then took ship for Liverpool. He completed his training as a pilot in the RAF and during that time he had attacked three U-boats.

The story of his navigator, George Moller, is equally exciting. He was born in Poznan, forty miles from the German: frontier. He was a qualified pilot cadet, stationed near Warsaw when the war began. His school was bombed and he tried to escape in one of the aircraft, flying it to Lublin, It crashed a few miles from the aerodrome and Moller had to walk back. He then hitch hiked into Hungary where he became very ill. A family of Hungarian Jews sheltered him; they were kind, feeding him on oranges until he was well enough to escape to Greece, by way of Yugoslavia. Then to Marseilles, which had become the vague, unknown goal for so many Poles who were trying to find their way across Europe. From Marseilles Moller went to an aerodrome at Lyons, where he was twice bombed. He too was forced to escape when France fell. He went to the Atlantic coast and found a ship which brought him to Liverpool. It was the *Arandora Star,* which was sunk, four days' later. Moller joined the RAF as a navigator and has flown four years.

Antoniewicz and Moller were about to alter course to investigate a U-boat sighting when they saw the conning tower of a second U-boat surfacing in another position. Antoniewicz turned to starboard to bring this U-boat on the port side and then turned to get on to an attacking course. When he was a mile away from the target he saw the first U-boat only one and a half miles away. The Wellington kept on its course and dropped six depth charges on the second U-boat. The first two hit the water to starboard of the target, the second one falling about ten yards from the hull. The U-boat was obscured by the explosions but the crew saw a long pole-like object blown 100 feet into the air. When the plumes subsided only the conning tower could be seen. The other U-boat had submerged.

Antoniewicz tracked over the scene of the attack and his crew saw a spreading, bubbling, patch of oil, two dark cylindrical objects, each thirty feet long and a considerable quantity of smaller wreckage. They made a second run and saw oil gushing to the surface and spreading out into a big circle with a fluorescent edge. The third run over revealed the oil patch had spread to 500 feet in width and on the last run, they saw both the oil and the wreckage again. U-441 veteran boat's commander, 31-year old Kapitänleutnant Klaus Hartmann and all hands were thought to have perished.[68] Antoniewitcz's attack however, had probably been directed against U-988 commanded by 24-year old Oberleutnant zur see Eric Dobberstein which was lost with all fifty hands.[69]

There were several Wimpy losses at sea during June. On the night of 12/13 June Wellington 'K' on 179 Squadron flown by Flight Lieutenant Walmsley was lost over the Channel and all the crew perished. On 13 June a Liberator on 53 Squadron hit the U-270 commanded by Kapitänleutnant Paul-Friedrich Otto. The German gunners, who had earlier destroyed a Fortress on 206 Squadron, shot down this aircraft as well. On the same day 'Y-Yorker', a Leigh Light-equipped Wellington on 172 Squadron piloted by L. Harris, hit U-270 and caused such damage that Otto aborted to Lorient.[70] A 415 Squadron Wellington with Pilot Officer G. H. Krahn and crew went missing from Ostend.

On 10 August Hector Bolitho drove along the coast from Davidstow Moor into Devon. 'The only sign of war was a splendid convoy of ships, moving over the blue satin ocean. I was to spend the day with Poles and South Africans who were flying in the British squadrons at Chivenor. After lunch with Group Captain Dicken I met the only South African crew fighting with Coastal Command in this country. It was a curious change, after talking to Poles, to listen to the lusty South Africans who laugh more easily, treating war as an adventure for the young rather than as a grim necessity vomited up by centuries of trouble. The South African captain was B. D. Miller from Johannesburg. The navigator was W. T. Wilkins from Zululand and the radar operator, R. C. Naude. I asked Naude whence he came and he said, 'East London.' As I was writing it down he added, 'Please add South Africa or they will think I come from the East End of London.' Miller and Naude were not wholly pleased with the results of their last attack and they said they would not be satisfied until they had seen some 'nice German dinghies with lots of Germans in them.' They made the attack on 11th July when they got what Naude described as 'a nice small contact to port,' about 3.40 in the morning. They had switched on the Leigh Light, swept the sea with its beam and saw the schnörkel and periscope of a U-boat, while they were flying at 50 feet. They were not in a position for attacking so they went in again. They switched on the light once more but there was too much haze for them to see the target so they decided to run in again before attacking, without the Leigh light. The depth charges were dropped and the rear gunner saw them explode and straddle the target ahead of the wake. When the crew searched the area there was no sign of victory, but the U-boat had at least been forced to submerge and had probably been damaged.'

'On 12 August some idea of the panic among ships was revealed by a sighting about 1115 in the morning when a 1,500-ton merchant vessel was seen at sea with branches of trees still tied to the sides and rigging. This is a well-known camouflage trick of the Germans when in port but, as one of the pilots said, 'It seemed a bit odd to see a coppice moving over the water.' A Halifax of 502 also had a fruitful afternoon. About a quarter to two, eighteen vessels were seen, including a Sperrbrecher. There was an escort group with the Halifax and they shelled the Sperrbrecher which died in an immense orange explosion, no doubt from the magazine or from ready ammunition on the deck. The story of the day is just a succession of sightings and attacks. A 5,000-ton merchant ship was caught by aircraft of 404 and 236 Squadrons west of La Rochelle. It was carrying a deck cargo of timber and a small tug was heading it out to sea. Both were hit and the smoke from the big vessel rose to 500 feet, with reddish flames emerging just forward of the poop deck. Both ships were enveloped in smoke as the aircraft flew away. Another Halifax on 58 Squadron bombed a Sperrbrecher about 2.15 in the afternoon and claimed a hit. Black smoke came from amidships and the Halifax watched the results until two unidentified aircraft appeared on the scene. Two more minesweepers and a merchant vessel were attacked by Halifaxes about one o'clock in the morning and five more unidentified vessels were attacked at a quarter to five in the morning, near Ile de Croix. The U-boats were equally unlucky and a Wellington on 172 Squadron dropped depth charges on one which it sighted at half-past two yesterday afternoon, obtaining a straddle across the stern. The U-boat dived a few minutes after. A Halifax made a daring attack on another U-boat about seven in the morning, in face of concerted flak from no less than three U-boats and from the shore. It is possible that the depth charges overshot the U-boat, but the attack was made through exceptionally intense flak. The same group of U-boats were seen by a Halifax on 502 Squadron, at the same time and the rear gunner was seriously wounded by flak. The results of this action could not be judged but the U-boats were at least held up on their way.[71]

'One U-boat after another has joined the ghosts of the Spanish galleons on the ocean bed and those that have escaped are creeping out of Brest for the uncertain haven of ports in the south. And the ships, fussing like ants, are trying to save themselves. Doenitz's feathers are being plucked, one by one.'

Early in September 1944 Arthur Rawlings joined 179 Squadron at Predannack. He recalls: 'My position was that of wireless operator-air gunner in Squadron Leader E. E. M. Angell's crew. Most of our operations in the Wellington Mk XIV were night sorties, using radar search and homing procedures, descending to fifty feet (using radio altimeter to inspect suspect contacts. The Leigh Light was switched on at about a quarter mile range.'

Squadron Leader Angell himself recalls: 'With overload tanks and carrying six depth charges, we used to patrol at about 1,500 feet for up to ten hours. We were given set areas to patrol from Predannack in the Bay of Biscay and from Benbecula and Limavady in the North Western Approaches. On making a radar contact the drill was to home in going down to sixty feet on the radio altimeter and illuminating with the Leigh Light at three quarters of a mile. In preparing to attack, the bomb doors would be opened and the depth charges armed. The Leigh Light would be lowered and lined up with the target in accordance with radar reports by the second pilot who had remote controls in the nose. He would switch on and search for the target on the instruction, 'Leigh Lights on!' from the captain. The front guns would be manned by the navigator sitting astride the second pilot and he would open fire if the submarine was surfaced. The pilot would release the DCs by eye, spacing them 60 to 100 feet apart. The rear gunner would be ready to fire at the submarine after the aircraft had passed over it. The wireless operator would already have sent a sighting report before the attack and would be preparing to send an attack report. Like so many aircrew on anti-submarine operations, I never actually saw a U-boat.'

Shortly after midnight on Tuesday 26 September 1944 a Wellington XIV crew on 407 'Demon' Squadron RCAF at Wick in Scotland were briefed for a routine patrol off the coast of Norway. The 'Demon' Squadron was one of the few all-Canadian squadrons at serving in Coastal Command. At around 12.45 am Flying Officer Gord A. Biddle and his all-RCAF crew took off for what was to be an eventful operation. Flight Sergeant Harvey Firestone, one of the wireless-operator-air gunners, recalls.

'We feared that the trip would be cancelled because of persistent bad weather. A few days earlier we had missed an operation when Biddle had come down with a very high fever. We did not want to miss two trips in a row, so we hurried to board 'S-Sugar', a Leigh Light-equipped Wellington. Despite the wild and stormy weather we were given the green light to take off. With visibility down to about a quarter of a mile and with a fifty-knot wind from the west, we managed to become airborne at 0050 hours. We headed out over the North Sea and proceeded to our patrol area. We were about thirty miles out from the Norwegian coast on a course roughly parallel to it, when suddenly, at 0452 hours, our starboard engine coughed and spluttered but commenced running smoothly again. Biddle climbed hurriedly to 3,000 feet. A short time later it coughed once and a large fireball gushed out of the exhaust. Biddle throttled back immediately. Flying Officer George Deeth, the second pilot, feathered the propeller and pushed the automatic fire extinguisher on. He switched the engine off and closed the fuel cocks and gills. Warrant Officer George Grandy, at the wireless set, sent out a QDM-5 (SOS) signal to Group. Fortunately, radio reception was good but Group informed us that the headwind we faced was not expected to abate but rather increase. They suggested we should try to reach the Shetlands and told us to continue sending signals so they could plot our course and attempt to monitor our position.

'Everything that we could do without was thrown out of the aircraft to maintain height and reduce strain on the one engine. Deeth and Neil threw the batteries that powered the Leigh Light out of the forward hatch. Pilot Officer Ken Graham threw out the radar equipment. Even the Leigh Light went, after quite a struggle for Graham and me. We rid ourselves of the ammunition through the opening where the Leigh Light had been. The parachutes went too. Meanwhile, Flight Lieutenant Maurice Neil and Deeth got rid of the ammunition for the single nose gun. Biddle, who had turned for home, had jettisoned the depth charges but we were still losing altitude.

'At 1,000 feet Biddle decided, after consulting with Neil and Deeth, that as we had about 5,000lb of petrol still in the wing tanks, we could jettison about three quarters of it and still reach the Shetlands. The jettison valve was open for about twenty seconds, then closed but Graham, watching from the astrodome, reported that petrol was gushing from the wing outlet even after the jettison valve had been closed. Biddle and Deeth tried several times to stem the flow but the meter finally showed no petrol in the wing tanks. We could no longer hope to reach the Shetlands against the fifty-knot head-wind. We had only 92 gallons of petrol in our reserve tanks. We were over 100 miles from Sumburgh, the nearest British base and less than that from the Norwegian coast. Group ruled out an ASR operation for many hours and that to attempt to ditch in the raging sea would be suicidal. We all agreed, very reluctantly, that our only hope would be to turn round and head for Norway. Group were advised. They acknowledged and wished us luck. Our ground speed picked up considerably with the wind at our back and at the break of dawn we sighted the mountainous coastline of Norway. We heard Ken Graham softly praying over the intercom as we neared land.

'We could see nothing but mountains with low hanging clouds obscuring the tops. Biddle spotted an entrance to a fjord and headed towards it. We could see some ships escorting a submarine. We had little choice but to fly over the small convoy as our petrol at this time was just about all gone. As we neared the ships we were met by heavy machine-gun fire. Biddle took what little evasive action he could. I fired off a Very cartridge in the hope that we would confuse the gunners into thinking that we were a friendly plane. They stopped firing momentarily but started to fire again when they realised our deception. I fired off another but fooled no-one. Tracers entered just beside Graham in the astrodome. Our good engine had also been hit. Biddle and Deeth searched for a place to put the plane down as we had lost all power. They told me to tell Grandy and Graham to take crash positions. Grandy sent a final message and tied down the key. He strapped himself in at the wireless set. Neil was on the navigator's table. Biddle was in the pilot's position. Deeth, after first pumping down the flaps and opening the top hatch, took up his place behind the door. Graham and I braced ourselves on the floor behind the main spar. Silently, we turned to each other, shook hands and waited, wondering if we were going to make it.

'Biddle swung the plane around into the wind and without power, at over 100 knots per hour, attempted a wheels up landing on what appeared to be the only spot possible. We hit some trees with our port wing, shearing some branches about four feet from the ground. Biddle brought the tail down first to slow us up and then jammed the nose in. We slewed around and came to a very sudden stop, having landed in just about 65 feet. Grandy and the radio fell on top of Deeth, Neil was thrown from his table and had a gash in his head and a cut on his hand. Biddle was jolted but not hurt physically. The astro hatch, which had been removed in order for us to leave the plane and which had been thrown to the rear of the aircraft, came plummeting forward toward Graham and me. I instinctively ducked and when we hit the second time, I hit my head on the main spar, dazing myself momentarily. Graham and I fully expected to see water come pouring into the aircraft but we had made it safely to land. As we jumped to the ground I saw that we had attracted a small crowd of people.'

Biddle's crew had crash-landed at Haughland on the Bjørne fjord, ten kilometres south-west of Os (Osoyra) and twenty-five or so kilometres south of Bergen. They destroyed their maps and detonated the IFF equipment. Having thrown all their parachutes, harnesses and bags into the sea they set fire to the aircraft and then talked to one of the Norwegians who had gathered around the crash. Magnus Askvik informed them that there was a German garrison at Os and another at Bergen. Askvik advised the six Canadian airmen to cross a neighbouring mountain to the settlement at Bjørnen. Cautiously, Neil approached one of a group of four houses while the rest of his crew watched from a safe vantage point. They saw Neil being greeted by a Norwegian who then pointed him to another house. There the lady of the house, Ingeborg Bjørnen, already knew of the crash. Getting her cousin to hide the men on the mountain she went off to see what could be done about getting them back to Britain by fishing boat. She was back at noon with some milk and with the news that her father would be making further enquiries that night. She returned at around 8 pm, this time with Einar Evensen, who took them to a small cove where two Norwegians were waiting for them in a rowing boat. They thereupon rowed the airmen to a small island, where three more Norwegians were waiting in a second boat. Three to a boat, the airmen were rowed to the small island of Strøno, almost due west of where they crashed.

The airmen spent the night of 26/27 September in the upper storey of a boat-house, but were off before dawn to the hills. The Norwegians brought food and civilian clothing and told them to shave off their moustaches. At around 10 am on the morning of 1 October they were picked up by a motorboat and taken to another boat-house five kilometres north of Hattvik, where there was a U-boat training base from which the airmen saw three submarines operating. Avoiding the Germans the Canadians were taken to a nearby farmhouse where they met the head of the local 2nd Company of the Milorg Resistance and were fed and given dry clothing: At the farmhouse there were eight other members of the underground movement. The chief sent a message to the UK saying that the Canadian crew were safe.

Before dawn on 2 October the airmen were off once more, this time to a small cabin hidden away in the mountains. There they stayed with a Norwegian who cooked for them and looked after them. On 6 October the Canadians witnessed at first hand the first all-Canadian daylight bomber raid, on U-boat bases at Bergen and Hattvik. Though there were plenty of weapons to be had - three Sten guns and pistols (one a Colt; another a German Luger) -

the airmen never had the opportunity to use them. On 8 October the Resistance leader took them to another farmhouse, from which, at 3 am on 9 October, they stealthily made their way to a boat-house barely one and a half kilometres north of Hattvik, where they transferred to another fishing boat. This boat took them to a small island almost due west of Austervoll and north of Selbjorn fjord, where they stayed, in a fisherman's hut, with a Norwegian merchant seaman. On the night of 11 October, they were picked up in a motor launch and taken to a waiting Norwegian naval vessel, one of the three former US Navy submarine chasers that had been made available in August 1943 to the Royal Norwegian Navy and which were then based at Scalloway. These boats, named *Hitra, Hessa* and *Vigra* after islands off the west coast of Norway, were 100 feet long and powered by two 1,200hp General Motors engines, which gave them a cruising speed of 17 knots and a top speed of 22 knots. They were so well armed that German aircraft kept their distance and their speed was sufficient to get them quickly out of trouble. Each boat had a crew of twenty-six men, three of whom were officers and were skippered by Fetter Saelen, Ingvald Eidsheim and Leif Larsen DSC COM, DSM*. As a measure of the speed and seaworthiness of these boats the record crossing to the Norwegian coast and back by Ingvald Eidsheim on the *Hitra* took just twenty-five hours.

Using the very boats that had carried refugees to Shetland, agents, radio sets, arms and ammunition were landed and they returned with yet more refugees. From November 1943 until the end of the war they carried out 114 missions to Norway. In the foreword to his book *The Shetland Bus* David Howarth wrote: 'During the German occupation of Norway from 1940 to 1945 every Norwegian knew that small boats were constantly sailing from the Shetland Isles to Norway to land weapons and supplies and to rescue refugees. The Norwegians who stayed in Norway and struggled there against the invaders were fortified by this knowledge and gave the small boats the familiar name which is used for the title of this book: 'to take the Shetland Bus' became a synonym in Norway for escape when danger was overwhelming.'

On 12 October the six Canadian airmen and the Norwegian sailor were ferried back to Scalloway in the Shetland Islands aboard the Vigra, captained by Leif Larsen, a distance as the seagull flies of 220 miles. The Vigra had departed Scalloway only the day before. The remarkable recovery of the Canadians had taken just seventeen days.[72] Next day the BBC broadcast 'Coconuts on holiday' to tell their Norwegian friends that the Canadians had reached England safely.

The war continued for other crews in Coastal Command. On 21 October 1944 Squadron Leader E. E. M. Angell's crew was posted to 172 Squadron at Limavady, Northern Ireland and on 14 November Angell was posted to command a Halifax squadron. Flying Officer Chambers took over as pilot. Arthur Rawlings recalls: 'We had only one sighting of a U-boat just before the end of the war. We saw a periscope which was immediately submerged when we turned to attack. This was in the area of the Mull of Kintyre and the coast of Northern Ireland. At this time the enemy was increasingly entering the vicinity of the Clyde and North Channel in a last ditch effort against our shipping. Although Liberators and Sunderlands did most of the convoy escort duties we once did an escort for the *Queen Elizabeth* on one of her troop carrying trips. She was too fast for the convoy system and both she and the *Queen Mary* were always independently routed. Of course, we had to keep a respectful distance but we could see the decks covered with thousands of GIs.'

Apart from enemy action, changing weather was a constant source of anxiety to Wellington crews on long, over water patrols. Icing could cause severe problems, as Gordon Haddock, a WOp/AG on 36 Squadron recalls:

With radar being somewhat primitive it was deemed one man should not have to gawk at the screen for more than 1½ hours at a time. So, by having three people in the same category, one could play musical chairs every hour or so from being radar operator, to the wireless operator, to the rear gunner. Invariably, we would toss a coin as to who would choose the position for take-off. While on an anti-U-boat course at RNAS *Maydown*, Northern Ireland, on 26 December, I was lucky in winning the toss and choosing to start the trip as rear gunner. In flight the carbs iced up and we crashed into Way Moors Wood in Devon. The radar operator was killed and the wireless operator was facially burned. Neither he nor the captain ever flew again.'

On 30 December 26 miles south of Portland Bill, NB855/L a Leigh-Light equipped Wellington on 407 'Demon' Squadron RCAF flown by Squadron Leader C. J. W. Taylor spotted U-772 'on the calm sea in the moonlight' and straddled the submarine with six depth-charges. The U-boat, which was commanded by 27-year old Oberleutnant zur see Ewald Rademacher and was on its second war cruise having left Trondheim on 19 November, sank with the loss of all 48 hands.

On the last day of January 1945 the new U-927, commanded by 28-year old Kapitänleutnant Jürgen Ebert, sailed from Kristiansand to the English Channel. Off the Lizard on the evening of 24 February, 'K-King', a Leigh Light-equipped Warwick on 179 Squadron piloted by Flight Lieutenant Antony G. Brownsill, got a radar contact on U-927's snorkel. He attacked from an altitude of seventy feet, dropping six depth charges at the snort in a perfect straddle. Nothing further was heard from U-927. Brownsill was later awarded the DFC.[73] The successes of the Leigh Light Wellingtons were to continue until the final victory in Europe in May 1945; with the final confirmed U-boat sinking by a Wimpy occurring on 2 April 1945 when southwest of Ireland, Warrant Officer R. Marczak piloting Wellington 'Y-Yorker' on 304 (Polish) Squadron sank the U-321. Oberleutnant zur see Fritz Berends and 41 crew perished.[74]

Arthur Rawlings concludes, 'We had the pleasure of escorting in a surrendering U-boat off the west of Ireland a few days after hostilities ended on 4 May.' Then Coastal Command was quickly run down. During June, 14, 36 and 407 RCAF Squadrons disbanded at Chivenor while 172 disbanded at Limavady in Northern Ireland. On 14 June 304 (Polish) Squadron was posted to Transport Command. By 7 July 524 and 612 AAF Squadrons had disbanded at Langham, Norfolk.

Footnotes

23 Wellingtons so equipped included the GR VIII, GR XI, GR XII and GR XIII variants and were known as 'Sticklebacks' or, on Malta, as 'Goofingtons'. Aircraft equipped with ASV Mk.II proved so successful at detecting submarines that in August 1942 the Germans introduced the 'Metox' receiver to warn of approaching aircraft equipped with ASV. In late 1942 the Mk.III centimetric radar appeared. Comparable with the H2S navigation radar used by Bomber Command, in calm seas it was even capable of detecting a 'schnorkel' device from a submerged U-boat. The 'Stickleback' and Yagi antennae were replaced by a single rotating scanner housed in a radome beneath the nose of the aircraft, which in turn necessitated the replacement of the front gun turret with a Perspex cupola. It was not until the closing months of the war that the Germans introduced 'Naxos', a warning receiver operating on centimetric wavelengths. Even so, Naxos had a maximum range of just 5,000 metres or less than one minute's warning of an attack.

24 Very early in the war Coastal Command had realised that its anti-submarine aircraft would need something more reliable than the quickly consumed flares they were using at night to illuminate U-boats during the last mile of the approach when ASV metre-wavelength radar was blind. As a result, in 1940 Squadron Leader Humphrey de Verde Leigh a personnel officer in Coastal Command was encouraged by the then Chief of Coastal Command, ACM Bowhill to develop the idea of an airborne searchlight. A pilot in WWI, Leigh had flown many anti-submarine patrols and had experienced the frustrations of searching for the elusive underwater craft. Locating the U-boat had become considerably easier since the introduction of ASV radar; nevertheless, the difficulties of the last mile or two of the approach remained. The target simply dropped off the radar screen, leaving the aircrew literally in the dark. Despite early difficulties, Leigh had his prototype installation ready by January 1941. The Leigh Light went into production but eighteen crucial months had elapsed between Leigh's original suggestion and the first use of the device on operations.

25 In 1942 detachments form the Lancaster and Halifax squadrons of Bomber Command were temporarily transferred to Coastal Command. 51 and 77 Squadrons sent detachments to Chivenor in Devon to operate with 19 Group during 7 May to October. They were replaced on 24 October by Halifax aircraft and crews on 158 (five B.Mk.IIs) and 405 Squadron RCAF (15 Halifaxes) which operated from Beaulieu under the command of HQ Coastal Command. In addition to anti-U-boat patrols the Halifaxes were also responsible for convoy escort and anti-shipping strikes in open sea and in harbours along the enemy-held coast. *Handley Page Halifax: From Hell to Victory and Beyond* by K. A. Merrick (Chevron Publishing 2009).

26 (Henry) Hector Bolitho (28.5.1897-12.9.1974) was born in Auckland, New Zealand the son of Henry and Ethelred Frances Bolitho. A prolific author, novelist and biographer, in total, he had 59 books published. He travelled in the South Sea Islands in 1919 and then through New Zealand with the Prince of Wales in 1920, and Africa, Australia, Canada, America and Germany in 1923-1924, finally settling in Britain. He worked as a freelance journalist. At the start of WWII he joined the RAFVR as an intelligence officer with the rank of squadron leader, editing the RAF Weekly Bulletin, which in 1941 became the RAF Journal. In 1942 he was appointed editor of the Coastal Command Intelligence Review. Bolitho undertook several lecture tours of America, in 1938-39 and 1947-1949. The playright, Terrence Rattigan was posted to 422 Squadron RCAF as a Flying Officer WOp/AG and was later to be involved in the prperation of the squadron's badge and motto.

27 *Submarine: An anthology of first-hand accounts of the war under the sea, 1939-1945* edited by Jean Hood (Conway Maritime 2007).

28 On 5 June the *Luigi Torelli* was hastily repaired and left Aviles the next day. Sunderlands on 10 Squadron RAAF found the U-boat and after circling it realized that the Italian commander was unable to submerge. A total of 15 depth charges were dropped on the submarine by the two Sunderlands and they hounded the boat into Santander. A month later the *Luigi Torelli* 'escaped internment' at Santander and limped into Bordeaux. In 1943 the *Luigi Torelli* went to the Far East, was taken over by the Kriegsmarine after Italy's surrender and retitled UIT-25. After Germany surrendered in May 1945 UIT-25 was used by the Japanese who titled her RO-504. Four months later she fell into American hands and was finally scuttled in 1946.

29 See *In Great Waters: The Epic Story of the Battle of the Atlantic 1939-45* by Spencer Dunmore (Pimlico 2001). U-159 was bombed by a Martin Mariner of VP-32 210 miles ESE of Jamaica on 12 July 1943 and

was lost with all 53 hands. *U-boat Fact File* by Peter Sharpe (Midland Publishing Ltd 1998).

30   They were formerly credited with the destruction of U-578, which was outbound on its fifth war cruise, having left St Nazaire on 6 August, for an operation in the North Atlantic. During 1942 the U-578 had sent five ships to the bottom of the sea. U-578 was lost with all 49 hands and including 40-year old Korvettenkapitän (Lieutenant Commander) Ernst-August Rehwinkel. When U-578 failed repeatedly to report its position, it was posted as missing in the Bay of Biscay effective 11 August 1942. However, research by Axel Niestlé (*German U-boat Losses During WWII*, Greenhill Books 1998) states that the attack was actually directed against U-135 commanded by Kapitänleutnant Friedrich-Hermann Praetorious, inflicting minor damage. U-135 was sunk in a Royal Naval action on 15 July 1943 when it was depth charged by the sloop HMS Rochester and corvettes HMS *Balsam* and HMS *Mignonette* escorting Convoy OS.51 between the Canaries and Africa. Five of U-135's crew were killed; 41 survived and were taken prisoner. See *U-boat Fact File* by Peter Sharpe (Midland Publishing Ltd 1998). The Chief Petty Officer, describing his feelings to interrogators, said 'We felt as if we were being led to the slaughter house'.

31   Miroslav Vild, *Flying With Fate* by Alois Siska quoted in Thanks For The Memory: Unforgettable characters in *Air Warfare 1939-45* by Laddie Lucas (Stanley Paul and Co Ltd 1989). In June 1943 311 were re-equipped with four-engined B-24 Liberators, altogether more formidable aircraft for the long Atlantic or northern waters patrols. On 24 June 1944 Flying Officer J. Vella DFC and crew attacked the U-971 which crash-dived and hit the seabed and then surfaced out of control during a depth charge attack by two TN destroyers. U-971 was scuttled and all except one of the crewmen were taken prisoner. When Miroslav Vild and the crew flew their 30th operation on 1 November 1944, their tour was over; for the radio and radar-operator it was his 106th mission. Siska was shot down three times, the third into the North Sea in midwinter while piloting a 311 Squadron Wellington. The ditching, on 28/29 December 1941 and six days in an open dinghy in arctic weather, had left him with but two companions as they were finally blown into captivity on the Dutch coast. Frostbite and gangrene had forced the German surgeons' decision to amputate his legs. A heart attack stopped the operation as he was about to be wheeled to the theatre. Other treatment brought limited recovery. Three years later, Siska was taken by the Gestapo from Colditz to Prague, there to face trial by court-martial for 'treason and espionage' against the Third Reich. Only liberation by US forces thwarted the inevitable death by firing squad.

32   Wellington 'E-for-Ela' had sustained almost 40 bullet or cannon strikes, the starboard petrol tank had a six-inch square hole; the auxiliary oil tank was damaged; a jagged three feet by six feet hole had been ripped out in the wing fabric; wing ribs were damaged; airscrew spinners, engine nacelles, astro-dome, aerial and the length of the fuselage all bore strikes and ruptures. Exactly one month later, on 16 October 1942, Flying Officer Stanislas Targowski set off in high spirits on yet another trip over the notorious Biscay. That morning he had received his first letter from his wife, still in Poland - his first since 1939 - while only two hours after he left the squadron received notification of an award of the DFC for Targowski and immediately set about preparing a celebration party for his return. The squadron waited in vain - somewhere over the Bay that day Targowski and his crew, including four of 'E-Ela's crew on 16 September, were shot into the sea by the Luftwaffe.

33   In February the squadron handed its Wellingtons over to 172 and 179 Squadrons and reverted to the Whitley, which it flew until April 1943 when it was re-equipped with Wellingtons again.

34   Axel Niestlé: *German U-boat Losses During WWII* (Greenhill Books 1998)/*U-boat Fact File* by Peter Sharpe (Midland Publishing Ltd 1998). On 3 March 1943 Flying Officer Lundon and crew were shot down by U-333 during an attack.

35   U-333 was sunk on 31 July 1944. Hitler's U-boat War: *The Hunted, 1942-1945* by Clay Blair (Random House 1998). *Another 172 Squadron Wellington attack* by 'G-George' on 22 March 1943, formerly credited with the destruction of U-665 commanded by Kapitänleutnant Adolf Dumrese, was actually directed against U-448 commanded by Oberleutnant zur see Helmut Dauter, inflicting no damage. U-448 was sunk during a naval action on 14 April 1944. Axel Niestlé: *German U-boat Losses During WWII* (Greenhill Books 1998).

36   West of St Nazaire on 2 May 1943 Flight Lieutenant E. C. Smith on 461 Squadron RAAF piloting a Sunderland, attacked U-465 commanded by 35-year old Korvettenkapitän Heinz Wolf, which was bound for the Atlantic. The conning tower was sighted and a flame float was dropped, followed by an aluminium sea marker and marine marker. At 1124 Smith sighted the U-boat on

the surface and attacked with six depth charges. U-465 sank horizontally and then the stern emerged and disappeared vertically. Of the 48 crew, fifteen or more were seen to abandon ship but none were rescued. U-boat Fact File by Peter Sharpe (Midland Publishing Ltd 1998).

37   Axel Niestlé; *German U-boat Losses During WWII* (Greenhill Books 1998).

38   *U-boat Fact File* by Peter Sharpe (Midland Publishing Ltd 1998)/*Hitler's U-boat War: The Hunted, 1942-1945* by Clay Blair (Random House 1998).

39   *Hitler's U-boat War: The Hunted, 1942-1945* by Clay Blair (Random House 1998).

40   Ibid.

41   *Conflict Over the Bay.*

42   *Hitler's U-boat War: The Hunted, 1942-1945* by Clay Blair (Random House 1998). U-134 was lost with all 48 hands. *U-boat Fact File* by Peter Sharpe (Midland Publishing Ltd 1998).

43   *U-boat Fact File* by Peter Sharpe (Midland Publishing Ltd 1998).

44   After research by Axel Niestlé (*German U-boat Losses During WWII*, Greenhill Books 1998) who attributes the loss of U-669 to unknown causes. When U-669 repeatedly failed to report its position after sailing, it was posted as missing effective 8 September 1943. U-584 was lost with all 53 hands on 31 October 1943 when it was sunk by American Avenger torpedo bombers.

45   After dawn on 11 September, swarms of Hudsons and Swordfish of 48, 233, 833 and 886 (based at Gibraltar) located the abandoned hulk of U-617 and attacked with bombs and rockets. HMS *Hyacinth*, a corvette; British trawler *Haarlem* and Australian minesweeper *Woollongong* then arrived to destroy U-617 with shellfire. Hodgkinson, the Canadian who originally found and disabled U-617, was awarded the DFC. *Hitler's U-boat War: The Hunted, 1942-1945* by Clay Blair (Random House 1998).

46   Brandi was later given command of U-380. *Hitler's U-boat War: The Hunted, 1942-1945* by Clay Blair (Random House 1998).

47   See *RAAF Over Europe* edited by Frank Johnson (Eyre & Spottiswoode, London, November 1946).

48   *Hitler's U-boat War: The Hunted, 1942-1945* by Clay Blair (Random House 1998)/*U-boat Fact File* by Peter Sharpe (Midland Publishing Ltd 1998).

49   Later that morning, a US Navy PBY4-1 Liberator of VB 103, piloted by Lieutenant Kenneth L. Wright, found U-966 near El Ferrol. Wright made two attacks, dropping six depth charges and killing some Germans by gunfire. A PBY4-1 of VB 105 piloted by Leonard E. Harmon joined the attack. Soon there arrived yet another PBY4-1 of VB 110 piloted by Lieutenant J. A. Parrish, who dropped six close depth charges in spite of the heavy flak. Lastly, a Liberator on 311 Czech Squadron piloted by Flight Sergeant Otakar Zanta attacked U-966 with rockets about 3 miles off the Spanish coast. These attacks killed eight Germans and wrecked the boat. Wolf ran her aground off Punta Estaca and then blew her up. He and 41 other Germans reached shore in dinghies. *Hitler's U-boat War: The Hunted, 1942-1945* by Clay Blair (Random House 1998).

50   Cornish was flying Wellington MP741 'Z-Zebra' when he attacked the U-boat in the Mediterranean east of Gibraltar. All 52 hands including the commander, Oberleutnant zur see Dietrich Schöneboom perished. *U-boat Fact File* by Peter Sharpe (Midland Publishing Ltd 1998).

51   The crew were rescued by the Spanish fishing boat Fina and landed in Spain for return to France. *U-boat Fact File* by Peter Sharpe (Midland Publishing Ltd 1998).

52   It was previously believed that U-542 was sunk on 28 November 1943 by Wellington 'L-London' on 179 Squadron. The original assessment was changed in September 1990 following research by Axel Niestlé (*German U-boat Losses During WWII*, Greenhill Books 1998).

53   The variation in an aircraft's intended track over land and sea due to winds.

54   Quoted in *Out of the Blue: The Role of Luck in Air Warfare 1917-1966*, edited by Laddie Lucas (Hutchinson & Co Publishers Ltd 1985).

55   On 10 March 1944 U-343 was sunk in a naval action

56   *Hitler's U-boat War: The Hunted, 1942-1945* by Clay Blair (Random House 1998)/ *U-boat Fact File* by Peter Sharpe (Midland Publishing Ltd 1998).

57   Axel Niestlé; *German U-boat Losses During WWII* (Greenhill Books 1998). When the U-boat failed repeatedly to show up or to signal its position, it was posted as missing, effective 31 January 1944. All 49 hands perished.

58   *U-boat Fact File* by Peter Sharpe (Midland Publishing Ltd 1998).

59   U-525 was sunk with all 54 hands on 11 August by a Wildcat-Avenger team from the carrier USS Card. *Hitler's U-boat War: The Hunted, 1942-1945* by Clay Blair (Random House 1998).

60   On 23 October 1944 U-256 was decommissioned at Bergen and cannibalised. In May 1945 the boat was captured by British forces.

61   U-629 had been damaged in an attack on 4 January 1944 by Wellington 'C-Charlie' on 304 Squadron. *U-boat Fact File* by Peter Sharpe (Midland Publishing Ltd 1998).

62   At 2214 hours on 7 June Flight Lieutenant Kenneth Owen 'Kayo' Moore, a Liberator pilot on 224 Squadron, took off in 'G-George' and at 0211 hours on the 8th a radar contact was made dead ahead at twelve miles. At three miles a U-boat was sighted on the surface in the moonlight. Moore did not need to switch on his Leigh Light and he attacked from about 50 feet with six depth charges, which straddled the conning tower. U-629 disappeared leaving wreckage and oil on the sea. It was lost with all 51 hands.

63   *U-boat Fact File* by Peter Sharpe (Midland Publishing Ltd 1998)/*Hitler's U-boat War: The Hunted, 1942-1945* by Clay Blair (Random House 1998).

64   According to Axel Niestlé; *German U-boat Losses During WWII* (Greenhill Books 1998) it was subsequently thought that the attack by Punter was directed against U-802, inflicting no damage. U-193 failed to report its position after sailing from Lorient and it was posted as missing in the Bay of Biscay after 6 May 1944 with the loss of all 59 hands. U-802, which was presumed lost in October 1944, surfaced and surrendered on 9 May 1945. *U-boat Fact File* by Peter Sharpe (Midland Publishing Ltd 1998).

65   *Hitler's U-boat War: The Hunted, 1942-1945* by Clay Blair (Random House 1998)

66   *Hitler's U-boat War: The Hunted, 1942-1945* by Clay Blair (Random House 1998). U-989 was lost in a naval action north of the Shetland Islands on 14 February 1945. All 47 hands perished. Axel Niestlé; German U-boat Losses During WWII (Greenhill Books 1998).

67   U-441 was a Type VII, the first of eight 'Flak boats' or 'flak traps' armed with two quad 20mms on bandstands fore and aft of the conning tower and a rapid fire 37mm flak gun on a second, lower bandstand aft, plus nests of machine guns on the bridge and a team of highly trained gunners, to lure and destroy anti-submarine aircraft. Their first success had come on 24 May 1943 when they shot down Sunderland EJ139/L on 228 Squadron flown by Flying Officer H. J. Debden, who also damaged the U-boat's bow area by depth charges. None of the flying-boat crew survived. On 12 July 1943 U-441 came off worse in a gun battle with three Beaufighters on 248 Squadron who demolished its superstructure, killed ten crewmen and wounded thirteen. On 12 June 1944 U-441 was damaged by Liberator 'S' on 224 Squadron which was shot down. Flight Lieutenant J. E. 'Jimmy' Jenkinson RNZAF and crew were all killed. He sent a signal about three in the morning to say that he was attacking a U-boat west of Ushant. A Wellington returned and reported having seen a Liberator attack two U-boats and another reported seeing flak and an explosion. The 'quiet and very nice New Zealander' was engaged to the Jenkins' daughter who lived in a house near his base.

68   Antoniewicz's Wellington had a complete breakdown in its radar-search equipment and was merely relying on the 'Eyeball Mk l' for the completion of its patrol in the bright moonlight. Antoniewicz had been about to alter course to investigate a thin trail of vaporous grey smoke on the sea when he sighted at three miles distant, a black object which he identified almost immediately as the conning tower of a surfacing U-boat. He turned to port to get on an attacking course. At the same time he lost height. When one mile away, the 2nd pilot and radar operator in the astrodome sighted another U-boat, which had apparently just surfaced 1½ miles away. Antoniewicz kept on his course to attack first U-boat, which then started to submerge slowly. At 2257 hours six depth charges were dropped from 100 feet, spaced sixty feet and set to 14-18 feet. The rear gunner distinctly saw the first two hitting the water to starboard quarter of the U-boat about ten yards from hull and the remainder across the U-boat and on its port bow. Then he saw them explode and the explosions and plumes completely obscured the U-boat. He also saw a long black pipe-like object blown about 100 feet into the air with the depth charge explosion. When the explosion plumes subsided there was no sign of the U-Boat and the conning tower was only just visible when the DCs were dropped.

69   *U-boat Fact File* by Peter Sharpe (Midland Publishing Ltd 1998) which also states that U-988 was previously believed to have been sunk on 28 June 1944 off Start Point. Axel Niestlé (*German U-boat Losses During WWII*, Greenhill Books 1998) claims the 'U-boat' that Antoniewicz sank was probably 'a whale'! The Admiralty later credited a Liberator on 224 Squadron piloted by Flight Lieutenant Kenneth Owen 'Kayo' Moore with the sinking of U-441. *Hitler's U-boat War: The Hunted, 1942-1945* by Clay Blair (Random House 1998).

70 *Hitler's U-boat War: The Hunted, 1942-1945* by Clay Blair (Random House 1998).

71 U-981 had left Lorient on 7 August, transiting to La Pallice in company with U-309. The two boats were approaching the rendezvous point with their escort, south-west of La Pallice when U-981 hit a mine. Unable to dive and with both engines out of action, her captain, Oberleutnant zur See Günther Keller called for an immediate escort - but Flying Officer J. Capey's ASV operator had found the two stationary boats and the Halifax swept in and dropped flares. At that moment U-981's engineers managed to get the electric motors restarted and the U-boat moved off slowly. Capey brought the Halifax in again and this time dropped an anti-submarine bomb at exactly the same moment that the U-boat struck a second mine. Capey then attacked again with more anti-submarine bombs and twenty minutes later Keller ordered his crew to abandon ship and as the U-981 sank, U-309 reappeared to pick up the forty survivors. One officer and eleven crewmen were lost. *Handley Page Halifax: From Hell to Victory and Beyond* by K. A. Merrick (Chevron Publishing 2009).

72 See *RAF Evaders: The Comprehensive Story of thousands of escapers and their escape lines, Western Europe, 1940-1945* by Oliver Clutton-Brock. (Grub Street, London 2009).

73 *Hitler's U-boat War: The Hunted, 1942-1945* by Clay Blair (Random House 1998). U-927 was lost with all hands.

74 In total 304 Squadron flew 2,451 sorties, attacking 34 U-boats and sighting nine others, had 31 combats with German fighters and lost 106 aircrew men killed or missing. Two U-boats were claimed destroyed and a third seriously damaged.

Chapter 3

Bombers Against the German Navy

It was a bleak station with absolutely no cover or protection at all. The pilot's room was small and there was a good deal of badinage as the pilots started to don their flying kit. Hanging on the matchboard walls were maps and designs of German aircraft along with a blackboard on which were chalked flying times and the names of officers. In one corner was a green Willesden canvas camp bed with kit dumped all over it, in another stood a simple table with a couple of hard-wood chairs and pens and ink for anyone who wanted to make notes. Two camp chairs occupied so much of the remaining floor space that it needed only half a dozen pilots to pack the place. In one chair sat a tall pilot pulling over his trousers some thick socks similar to those worn by divers; another zipped up a pair of sheepskin trousers which differed from a cowboy's inasmuch as these had the wool inside; having donned his trousers, he struggled into the upper half of his suit and zipped it up with zest, glad to complete the job. Then he went to get something from his locker.
'Damn!' said he, starting to unzip himself, 'I've left the key in my trousers pocket!'
A pilot on the telephone, who was making sure that certain adjustments had been carried out on the Beaufort which he was about to take over the sea, looked up as a messenger entered and handed him a letter. He read it and scratched his signature on it with a pen.
'Here you are fellows, you must all read this and sign it,' he remarked.
'What is it?' another asked.
'About icing and frost on wings - all right getting those instructions when you are a hundred miles over the North Sea!'
'Yes, you get out with a broom and sweep it off,' came the quip from another. 'Not a bad effort of the sergeant's,' he added, nodding at a blackboard on which was chalked the following lines:-
'Hallo, Toffs, here's some good advice.
You chaps get paid for flying.
Make sure your planes are free of ice,
Dame fortune uses loaded dice.
Don't hope, make sure you're men, not mice –
It's easier far than dying.[75]

The prototype Beaufort first flew on 15 October 1938 and a production contract for 78 aircraft followed in August 1936. The Beaufort was an improvement on the Avro Anson but it was not very fast and not well armed. Faced with the much faster Bf 109, the Beaufort's defensive machine guns could put up an estimated 11 ounces of .303 calibre bullets as compared with the Messerschmitts 12 lbs of cannon and machine gun fire in the same amount of time. Coastal Command's standard torpedo-bomber from 1940 to

1943, Bristol Beauforts first entered service with 22 Squadron at Thorney Island in November 1939. The Beauforts, along with the Swordfish of the Fleet Air Arm flew out in secret, deposited their mines in the dark and flew away again without knowing whether their work would prove fruitful or futile. Such work called for strength of spirit and purpose to sustain men for any length of time. The mine-layers laid dozens of minefields on all the coasts from the northern coast of Norway right down the French coast to Bayonne on the border of Spain and German rivers and ports and even in the Kiel Canal itself. On the night of 15/16 April 1940 22 Squadron's Beauforts carried out Coastal Command's first mine-laying sortie, in the mouth of the River Jade and on 7 May 1940 dropped the first 2,000lb bomb. Beauforts saw action over the North Sea, the English Channel, the Atlantic and the Mediterranean. Beauforts also took part in the attack on the German pocket battleships which escaped through the Channel early in 1942.

It was in the ultimate issue just an odd trick of chance which led Group Captain Finlay Crerar to make history on the night of 10/11 June 1940, by intercepting the first ship which Italy lost in the war. The wireless told him at 6 o'clock in the evening that Mussolini had declared war as from midnight and while he sat at dinner in the mess he learned that one of the afternoon patrols over the North Sea had sighted the big Italian steamer Marzocco making full speed to the east. It would, he thought, be a pity to let that ship get back into Italian hands and he accordingly requested permission to go out to try to intercept her. Permission was not at once forthcoming. There were conferences in which the naval authorities joined, but at length his request was granted. There was still a little daylight left when he climbed into his aircraft with his navigator and took off. The navigator had worked out the course and estimated the position in which the Italian steamer should be picked up and along this course Group Captain Crerar flew. The weather could hardly have been worse. The cloud was practically down to the surface of the sea. To attempt to intercept a ship on such a night seemed quite hopeless - but not to Group Captain Crerar. Finding it was impossible to fly below the clouds because they were down so low, he went up and flew above them at 2,000 feet. Speeding to the area in which he expected to find the steamer, he dived down to try to get under the clouds to search the surface. He could not do it and was forced to climb. Flying a little further, he dived once more to try to get below the blanketing clouds, but was driven again to climb.

Nature seemed to be conspiring to help the *Marzocco* to escape. But the Scottish pilot was a tenacious man. He refused to give up and dived down for the third time to try to get under the clouds. For the third time he was defeated. There seemed nothing more he could do. No human power could overcome that handicap of the clouds. He was cruising round above the carpet of cloud, loath to return with his mission unaccomplished, when he saw a dark smudge on a cloud ahead. Gazing at it carefully as he flew in that direction, he was astonished to see a small black puff rise through the cloud. To his expert eye that black puff could only be one thing - smoke and immediately he concluded it must be smoke from the funnel of the *Marzocco*. He was right. The master of the Italian steamer must have heard the engines of the aircraft and in his anxiety to escape made his crew stoke up the furnaces more than ever, with the result that instead of getting away, he merely gave away his position by the big clouds of smoke emitted from the funnels. Diving for the fourth time down into the cloud, Group Captain Crerar discovered that by some strange fluke the base of the cloud had risen to fifty feet above the surface so that he was able to fly without endangering his aircraft.

'I had just been on the point of turning for home bitterly disappointed at having failed and you can imagine my surprise and pleasure at seeing the quarry in front of me,' he reported. 'She was steaming as fast as possible due east. I signalled her in international code to stop immediately, turn and make for Aberdeen, but no notice was taken of my signals. This was tried three times. Then I decided to open up my front gun as a warning and flying low across her bows I gave her a good burst, did a steep turn and repeated the manoeuvre from the other beam. Immediately there-afterwards the ship hove to and, after some exchange of signal, turned round on a course for Kinnaird's Head. We escorted her although it was dark until lack of petrol forced us to leave.'

Returning to their base, they refuelled and went off again to pick up the *Marzocco* and escort her to port. But the weather was so bad that they were quite unable to find the ship, which the navigator thought must have turned eastward to try to escape. The pilot, however, thought otherwise and felt sure that she was continuing on her course to land. His judgment was confirmed. At his request a destroyer was sent out. But eventually the Italian master cheated his captors, for he opened the sea-cocks and scuttled his ship. As she was sinking, a tug managed to take her in tow and get her as far as the entrance to Peterhead harbour where she touched bottom and was beached. Had it not been for that smudge of smoke arising from the frantic endeavours of the master to elude capture there is no doubt that the *Marzocco* would have escaped.

One of the objects of Coastal Command in attacking fringe targets was to prevent, if it could, German sailors and airmen who were taking an active part in the Battle of the Atlantic from obtaining the rest they needed. Another was to harass the German troops in occupied countries. Finse in Norway was a well-known winter sports centre. It consisted of a small railway station with a hotel nearby and a few mountain huts and chalets. The railway passing through it was protected from avalanches by a number of snow-sheds, which were wooden tunnels hundreds of yards in length. It was known that the hotel contained a large number of German officers and Norwegian quislings enjoying a skiing holiday. There were thus two objectives: to destroy or damage the sheds, which would interrupt communications of great importance almost certainly for the whole of the winter and to put out of action a number of the enemy and of the traitors helping them. Three attacks were made - on 18, 20 and 22 December 1940. So that the crews taking part in them should have as clear an idea as possible of the nature and look of the place, they had been shown a pre-war travel film containing excellent shots of the station, the hotel and the surrounding slopes of snow. The first attack was only in part successful, for despite the film which they had seen and the special maps which they carried, several of the crews did not find the target. Two nights later it was repeated and Beauforts scored direct hits on the snow-sheds and the railway line. A train in the station took refuge in a shed from which it did not emerge. In the third attack the hotel was hit. It was subsequently discovered that two mechanical snow-ploughs had been destroyed in the railway station and that the line was, in consequence, blocked for many weeks. The leader of the first attack, carried out by Hudsons, flew up and down above the target with his navigation lights on, in order to show the way to the rest.

Coastal Command, while not exclusively equipped for bombing, made 682 attacks on land targets between 21 June 1940 and the end of December 1941. Excluding aerodromes, which the Command attacked 130 times in France, 30 times in the Low Countries, 44 times in Norway and thrice in Germany, there were during that period 28 attacks on French fuel dumps and electrical power plants, 36 attacks on Dutch oil installations and eight on Norwegian. There were also 69 attacks on other miscellaneous targets. The bulk of the effort, however, was naturally directed against docks and harbours and the shipping in them. Brest headed the list with 62 attacks; Boulogne followed with 50. Then came Lorient with 30, Cherbourg with 28, St. Nazaire with 21; Le Havre with 16, Calais with 13 and Nantes with five. The raids were made mostly at night. They were harassing operations designed to destroy valuable stores and necessities for the prosecution of the battle and to interfere as much as possible with the lives of men on garrison duty in foreign and hostile lands. After the fall of France, the effort made by Coastal Command was directed against shipping. One squadron alone made 28 attacks on French ports, involving 136 individual sorties, in six weeks. In the early days even Ansons, too, played a part before they were relegated to training Groups. On Monday 23rd September 1940 six Ansons on 217 Squadron carried out an attack on Brest between 0115 and 0415 hours, dropping their 360lb bomb loads from heights as low as low as 2,000 feet and then diving to 500 feet to shoot out searchlights. On later raids the Ansons were often accompanied by Fairey Albacores of 826 Squadron of the Royal Navy awaiting the completion of the aircraft carrier HMS *Formidable* which was to be their home. Lorient, too, came to be important, for it was soon made one of the main bases for German submarines. The primary target was at first the power station and later on the submarine moorings. Blenheims attacked both on 8th, 13th and 17th October and again on 7 and 8 November, being accompanied on these last two raids by Beauforts and Swordfish. The attack on shipping at Flushing on the 13th by six Blenheims caused large fires. In December German submarines were discovered further South in the Gironde, near Bordeaux. They were attacked by Beauforts carrying land-mines on 8 and 13 December. Large explosions and fires followed.

Inevitably as time went on attacks became concentrated on Brest, especially after the last week in March 1941, when the *Scharnhorst* and the *Gneisenau* or 'Salmon and Gluckstein' (a famous London store) as they were known throughout the Royal Air Force, took refuge in that naval base on their return from commerce-raiding in the Atlantic. Coastal Command attacked them, either alone or as part of an operation by Bomber Command, 63 times in 1941, including an attack on the *Scharnhorst* on 23 July when she had sought temporary refuge at La Pallice. The defences of Brest, always formidable grew stronger and stronger. On one occasion a Blenheim was forced by the failure of both engines to glide through them. It circled slowly round above the harbour while the pilot still tried to get into a good position from which to drop his bombs. 'It looked as though we should come down in enemy territory,' he said, 'so I thought we might as well drop our bombs in the best place possible.' The first attempt did not succeed and before releasing its load the Blenheim glided three times round the docks, each time going lower and lower. At last a good target came into the bomb-sight and the bombs were dropped at the very 'moment when both the engines picked up simultaneously. The Blenheim reached base unscathed.

22 Squadron of the Coastal Command was not only the first to be equipped with Beauforts, but among the first to take part in the mine-laying operations. Under the command of Wing Commander M. H. St. G. Braithwaite, it also carried out many torpedo attacks on the shipping in the invasion ports. Its losses in the early days were sometimes due to enemy action, sometimes to circumstances over which the pilots had no control. For a period the squadron suffered heavily, which robbed the Royal Air Force of some of its most highly-trained specialist pilots. Among them was Flight Lieutenant A. R. H. 'Dicky' Beauman who carried out thirty operations in all sorts of weather, with many torpedo attacks on ships by day and by night. On 5 December 1940 he was last seen off Wilhelmshaven going in to torpedo a big ship in the face of terrific anti-aircraft fire, but whether he hit the ship before he was hit himself remains unknown. 'Dicky' Beauman was one of the most popular members of the mess and no finer pilot or braver man ever sat in the cockpit of an aircraft.

On the moonlight night of 17 September 1940 six Beauforts on 22 Squadron in two flights of three led by Squadron Leader Rex Mack DFC were detached from North Coates to Thorney Island and detailed to attack shipping in Cherbourg Harbour at 2300 hours. At that time it was probably the best defended of all the Channel ports.

'I decided,' said Squadron Leader Mack 'that I would enter by the Western entrance of Cherbourg harbour. I took this decision because there was a great deal of wind and I thought that if I were to approach the Germans with the gale in my face they might not hear me. That indeed proved to be the case, because when I entered the harbour no one fired at me. I had hardly got in, flying at about 50 feet, when the Germans opened fire. I was so close that I could actually see them and I watched a German gunner, one of a crew of three manning a Bofors gun, trying to depress the barrel, which moved slowly downwards as he turned the handles. He could not get it sufficiently depressed and the flak passed above our heads. It was bright red tracer and most of it hit the fort at the end of the other breakwater on the farther side of the entrance. At the same moment I saw a large ship winking with red lights, from which I judged that there were troops on board firing at us with machine-guns and rifles.

'I dropped the torpedo in perfect conditions, for I was flying at the right speed and at the right height. Half a second after I had dropped it five searchlights opened up and caught me in their beams. I pulled back the stick and put on a lot of left rudder and cleared out. The trouble about a torpedo attack is that when you have released the torpedo you have to fly on the same course for a short time to make quite sure that it has, in fact, left the aircraft. I remember counting one and two and three and forcing myself not to count too fast. Then we were away.'

Another Beaufort coming in immediately afterwards seemed 'to be surrounded by coloured lights,' and a third, flown by a sergeant pilot, hit a destroyer and at the same time lost half its tail from a well-aimed burst of anti-aircraft fire. It got safely back, however. All the pilots reported that the opposition was the fiercest they had ever experienced. In this gallant affair one Beaufort was lost.

Sergeant Norman Hearn-Phillips (later Squadron Leader Hearn-Phillips AFC DFM) was one of the pilots detailed but although he had completed twenty operations on Beauforts, he had only dropped torpedoes in practice. He had joined the RAF in 1936 as a Direct Entry Sergeant pilot and had trained on Hawker Harts and Audax. The attack was to be a combined attack with eight Blenheims on 59 Squadron, who were to drop bombs and flares to light the way for the Beauforts. The moon was at the full and the Blenheims were bombing the docks when the first flight of Beauforts were led into Cherbourg at no more than ten feet above the surface. They flew so low that the gun in the fort at the entrance could not be depressed sufficiently and its tracers were seen bouncing off the other breakwater. Squadron Leader Mack got his torpedo away at a steamer of over 5,000 tons just as five searchlights picked him up. The fire from the breakwater and harbour and ships was so intense that the tracer bullets cannoned off ships and walls in all directions. Flight Lieutenant Francis hit a destroyer. Sergeant Norman Hearn-Phillips brought his Beaufort down to sea-level and headed for the target at 80 feet and 140 knots. As he released his torpedo at a vessel of over 5,000 tons, the flak was intense and the aircraft was hot as he turned away. The port elevator had been shot away and the rudder and hydraulics damaged. Despite this Hearn-Phillips nursed his crippled aircraft back to Thorney Island where he carried out a successful belly-landing. One of the Beauforts was lost, but it was a wonder that any escaped at all in such a heavy barrage of fire.

Soon afterwards, at the beginning of an autumn afternoon on Friday 4th October, a roving patrol of two Beauforts on 42 Squadron found two enemy destroyers and six escort vessels off the Dutch coast near Ijmuiden. These they did not attack, but carrying on soon found a 2,000-ton mine-layer surrounded by four flak-ships all at anchor in the harbour. They attacked, but the torpedoes were swept from their course by the tide. The Beauforts were intercepted by four Bf 109s and L4488 was shot down by Oberleutnant Ulrich Steinhilper of 3./JG 52. All the crew were taken prisoner. During the engagement Beaufort L4505 was hit and the elevator controls severed. The pilot, however, succeeded in flying his aircraft safely home by juggling with the throttle and elevator trimmer. Surprisingly enough the elevator had a marked effect on the aircraft's trim despite the fact that the fore and aft controls were severed. On reaching base in very bad weather, with clouds down to 50 feet, he was seen to pass over the aerodrome, but he could not turn the aircraft in its crippled condition enough to regain it. He followed the coast and after jettisoning his torpedo in Thorney Creek, although the flaps of the Beaufort were out of action, made a successful landing at Thorney Island with most of his crew wounded.

Some weeks later, on 8 November three Beauforts launched their torpedoes at a steamer and not one of them hit the mark. Nevertheless the master of the steamer swung her about so frantically to avoid them that he ran aground and his ship became a total loss, so the Beaufort accomplished their purpose of destroying the ship, although all their torpedoes missed. Two days later, Wing Commander Braithwaite was about to make a torpedo attack on a steamer which was steaming at five knots. Circling round, he swept in and got his torpedo away. It ran perfectly straight for the steamer which was palpably doomed - or so it seemed. Then, quite unexpectedly, before the torpedo reached the target, there was a gigantic explosion and a great column of water shot up in the air. It was very hard luck for Wing Commander Braithwaite that it happened to be low tide and the torpedo hit the top of a sandbank which lay in its path. At high tide the torpedo would have sped over the top of the sandbank and the steamer would have gone to the bottom.

Apart from the torpedo Coastal Command made use of two other chief weapons dropped from the air in its operations against enemy shipping - the mine and the bomb. The task of laying mines in enemy waters was shared with Bomber Command. Each Command has been allotted certain areas along the coasts of the enemy and of the occupied countries off which mines are laid. The aircraft used for the purpose were originally Swordfish, of which the open cockpit added considerably to the discomfort suffered by the crews in winter, though in other respects it was an advantage, for the pilot could see the surface more easily. As soon as Beauforts became available they were pressed into service. The method used is as follows: The aircraft sets out flying at a height between 1,500 and 2,000 feet. When it approaches near to the place chosen - a shipping channel, the entrance to a port, the mouth of a fjord, or wherever it may be - it comes down low in order to pin-point its position. This is done by picking up some prominent landmark, such as a building, a headland, a lighthouse, a small island. Arrived there, the navigator sights the landmark through the bomb-sight and, at the exact moment at which the Beaufort passes over it, presses a stop-watch, at the same time telling the pilot to fly a course at a certain speed at a certain height for a certain time. During this, the run-up, the aircraft must be kept on an absolutely level keel. At the end of the period, calculated in seconds and fractions of seconds by means of the stop-watch, the observer releases the mine and the operation is over.

Very rarely did the crew even see the splash when the mine hit the water. The operation was dull, difficult and dangerous. 'Creeping like a cat into a crypt' is how one pilot has described it. The Germans did their best to cover all likely landmarks with anti-aircraft fire. More than once the crews of Coastal Command had seen little lights moving, like strange fire-flies, along the edges of cliffs. They came from the pocket-torches held in the hands of German gunners as they ran to man their guns.

Little was heard of these mining operations. Only an occasional reference was made to them in official communiqués. But they went on night after night and the crews who carried them out ran risks as great as those who achieved a result by the use of a more spectacular weapon - the bomb or the torpedo. Over a period of six months in 1941 seventy per cent of the mines laid by Coastal Command were placed in the position chosen for them. It was impossible to do more than estimate the damage they caused. Certain successes were known to have been achieved. In February 1941 a German vessel of about 3,000 tons was damaged near Haugesund and beached to prevent her sinking. A German trawler struck another mine on the same day and sank. The area was closed to traffic for some time. Later that month a German ship was mined off Lorient and many corpses were washed ashore on the Quiberon Peninsula. An aircraft of Coastal Command had dropped a mine in that area a night or two before. In September of that year two cargo vessels were mined and sunk in the roadsteads of La Pallice and La Rochelle. In October a 4,000-ton ship was mined and sunk in the channel leading to Haugesund and the entrance to the port was blocked for some time.

The more direct method of attack was to bomb the ships of the enemy wherever they may be found. Coastal Command began early. The first enemy ship to be bombed was a tanker attacked by a London flying boat on 10 April 1940, forty miles from the Faroe Islands. The limited resources of the Command did not permit it, in those early days, to make attacks on a large scale. Nevertheless, its achievements are not to be ignored. Between 10 April and 31 December 1940 223 attacks were made on merchant vessels and supply ships and 81 on enemy ships of war. They took place along the Norwegian coast, the Dutch, Belgian and French coasts and also in the Heligoland Bight and off the North-West coasts of Germany. The sinking of a merchant vessel off Haugesund by a Lockheed Hudson on 22 June and the hitting and sinking of twelve merchant vessels, one of which was of 14,000 tons and a tanker of 10,000 tons in July must be mentioned.

The attacks in August 1940 were not very successful, but in September two E-boats were sunk by a Blenheim 18 miles off Dieppe on the 10th and hits obtained on ten merchant vessels, one of which was certainly sunk. In October 1940 three merchant vessels were hit. The attacks fell off in November, but in December no less than 45 were made on merchant vessels and one on enemy destroyers. So ended the year 1940. The attacks had been mostly carried out by single aircraft, a Blenheim, a Hudson, or a Beaufort, though sometimes the attackers flew in formation of two or three. They were in the nature of an experiment. The crews taking part in them were gaining experience of which they were to make good use in 1941. It was not a quick process. To attack and hit a ship, especially when it is protected by its own fire and that of flak-ships, is not only dangerous but difficult. The technique was worked out and improvements made through that winter and spring. During this period much work was done to determine the correct fuse-setting of the bombs. It was very necessary to do so. On 30 March an enemy ship loaded with depth charges, probably an anti-submarine vessel, was found off La Rochelle and hit by a 250lb bomb dropped from 400 feet without a delay fuse. The bomb detonated all the depth charges and blew the ship to pieces. The aircraft returned 'riddled with bits of its target.' As a result of this and other attacks of the same kind it has become the general practice to use delayed-action bombs.

When vessels carrying ammunition, however, are hit, the explosion is naturally so formidable that the aircraft runs a great risk of suffering damage. On one occasion a Hudson belonging to a Dutch Squadron dropped a salvo of bombs on a ship near the Norwegian coast. 'Nothing happened at first,' reported the Dutch pilot. 'The rear gunner started swearing because he didn't see anything. Then he said he saw the crew frantically lowering a boat. Then came a tremendous explosion and we thought our bombs had hung up and gone off underneath our aircraft till we saw the ship in small pieces.'

The pilots who carried out attacks on German occupied ports were only slightly less laconic than the official reports. 'The bombs caused an enormous explosion,' said one of them who flew a Beaufort in an attack on Brest on 13 January 1941, 'which shook the aircraft so violently that the crew thought they had received a direct hit from anti-aircraft fire. Showers of sparks accompanied the explosion, which sent up a column of smoke to the height at which the aircraft was flying - 10,000 feet.' During a raid on St. Nazaire a Blenheim looped the loop when an anti-aircraft shell exploded immediately beneath its fuselage. 'The concussion stunned the second pilot, knocked out the rear gunner and left the pilot dazed.' When they recovered consciousness the Blenheim was in a dive from which the pilot was unable to pull out until 500 feet from the ground. On regaining a level keel it was found that all the instruments were out of order and that everything loose on the navigator's table, including his charts, had disappeared, flung out of a hatch which had been forced open. The pilot succeeded in climbing up to 8,000 feet. 'The Blenheim was see-sawing up and down like a switchback and we thought we should have to bail out.' He was able, however, to keep control until a patrolling Beaufighter was sighted off the English coast in the dawn. The Beaufighter escorted the Blenheim to an aerodrome where it made a safe landing.

Sometimes attacks were made by day. On one occasion a Beaufort was off La Pallice at 9,000 feet. 'Alongside the wharf,' says the observer, 'we could see a ship of about 7,000 tons discharging cargo. The crew were busy on the deck and workmen were coming and going about the wharf. The pilot pointed to the ship and said: 'Shall we bomb it?' I nodded, thinking he meant to do a little high-level bombing. The next thing I knew was that I was flat on my back. The pilot had put the nose right down in the steepest dive I have ever been in. We dropped from 9,000 to 100 feet. At the bottom we let go the bombs and then began to pull out, dodging between the cranes on the wharf. For a moment we were actually flying under the German flag, for as we beat it over the dock I saw out of the corner of my eye a swastika flag hanging from a staff about fifty feet above us. The ship's stern was wreathed in smoke as we left.'

Bomber Command took a prominent part in the attacks on shipping. To press home an attack on a well-camouflaged warship protected by fighters, balloons and one of the heaviest concentrations of anti-aircraft guns in Europe and to know that as it was in dry dock not even the best-aimed bombs could sink it, demanded the very highest qualities of morale. But the demand, as in every other task set to the crews of the Royal Air Force, was met to the full. Something of what these young men were called upon to face may be glimpsed from an account by Sergeant J. S. Boucher, a navigator on 144 Squadron. The squadron, still equipped with Hampdens, was required to find three crews for a daylight raid under cloud cover: 'Three crews', writes Boucher, 'were drawn out of the hat' and you can imagine our annoyance on being awakened by an orderly at 1.30 am on Christmas Eve to be told that we were to report to the Briefing Room at 2.30 am - especially after a 'stand down' evening at such a festive time of the year. Our annoyance was only exceeded by our surprise when the CO, Group Captain 'Gus' Walker, explained the hazardous mission which we were to undertake in a few hours' time.[76]The general opinion amongst the crews was that this was not a job for an obsolescent aircraft like the Hampden with its cruising speed of 140 mph and its very poor defensive armament. We kept these opinions to ourselves, however...'

In this frame of mind the crews climbed into their aircraft. Boucher's machine, piloted by Sergeant P. A. C. McDermott, took off soon after 0600 and made its way to a point west of Ushant: 'Cloud was 10/10ths with base at 1,000 feet and everyone felt relatively safe during this part of the journey. When it was time to turn eastwards for the target the pilot broke cloud at about 900 feet and we could see Ushant right in front of us. Neither of us had had much experience of operating in daylight and having experienced the fierceness of this target at 12,000 feet at night we both felt a little apprehensive, to say the least - but we did not share our thoughts openly.

'The pilot climbed into cloud again and headed south-east. A few minutes later he turned north-east and broke cloud again. The enemy coast was very close and we nipped into cloud again. These zigzag tactics were continued and accompanied by violent' jinking' as soon as the coast was crossed. Everyone was strangely silent - apart from my curt navigational directions-until the rear gunner, who was experiencing his first operational flight, asked what the 'tapping noise' was. The wireless-operator told him that it was only 'light flak' bursting as it hit the wings and the fuselage ... We broke cloud again for a few seconds, just long enough to enable me to give McDermott a course which would bring us over the docks. The flak grew more and more intense and although flying in cloud the aircraft was repeatedly hit. We could see the criss-cross of red tracer shells through the cloud haze a few yards in front of us. It seemed that all the anti-aircraft defences of the docks - as well as those of the battle cruisers - were directed against this one aircraft; and this was most probably the case.

The Hampden broke cloud again at 900 feet above sea-level and I picked out the target about half-a-mile ahead. To make a proper run up under such conditions would have been impossible if one was to survive to complete the task. I leaned over my bomb-sight and pressed the 'tit'. For a few fleeting moments I could see the German gunners frantically firing at us. They seemed so close that I felt myself to be before a firing squad. The pilot opened the throttle and we roared up into cloud again at 180 mph, too soon even to see our bombs burst, The sudden upward movement threw me back into my seat and a second later there was a yellow flash as a shell exploded, shattering the perspex nose of my cabin and driving me backwards under the floor of the pilot's cockpit. Stunned for a moment, I tried to open my eyes, but the pain was too great. I felt the wet blood on my face. The cold blast of air now passing through the gaping hole in the nose, had blown all my maps and my log through the pilot's cockpit window. I crawled back through the fuselage to where the wireless-operator was sitting and plugged in his intercom gear. We were relatively safe now that we were in cloud again and leaving the coast behind us. A rough mental calculation enabled me to give the pilot a course for the Lizard ...'

Damage, wounds and lack of maps did not prevent the crew bringing their aircraft back to England. Of the other two machines, one lost half its tail plane to a balloon cable over Brest, but still struggled home; the other failed to return.

In March 1941 meanwhile, Coastal Command aircraft made nine attacks and eight in the following month, on enemy ships of war at sea, in addition to a large number of attacks on the *Scharnhorst* and *Gneisenau* in harbour at Brest. They also hit for certain fifteen merchant vessels during the same period and probably many more. One attack on a convoy of eight merchant vessels off Stavanger on 18 April was pressed home with great determination. Two merchant vessels were hit and left sinking for the loss of two Blenheims; a second attack made on the convoy encountered heavy opposition from Me 110s which shot down three Blenheims after one of them had scored a hit on another vessel.

The attacks continued on much the same scale throughout the summer. On 11 June Blenheims scored seven direct hits on a large tanker discovered between Ostend and Dunkirk. On 5 July Blenheims, again escorted by fighters, discovered an enemy convoy near Zuydcote. Some of the aircraft attacked from a high level and drew the fire of the convoy and its escorting vessels. The remainder went in low and scored two direct hits on one merchant vessel and another on a second. One of the Blenheims, hit by anti-aircraft fire, struck the water, bending both propellers, but got back to base. By then the Blenheims and Beauforts operating over the English Channel had been so successful that it was practically denied to enemy shipping. After July attention became more concentrated on the Dutch and Norwegian coasts. By the end of that month Continental business men were complaining of the heavy losses incurred by them in shipping goods from Dutch ports.

On 23 July 1941 the captain of a Hudson bade farewell to the convoy he had been 'escorting' for several hours and was about to turn for home when a naval corvette below flashed a signal to him, 'Suspicious aircraft to starboard'. Knowing the tendency of all Royal Navy vessels to regard any aircraft as 'suspicious', the Hudson skipper at first thought the corvette had merely spotted the Hudson's due relief Wellington and, indeed, when first sighting the distant machine also believed it to be his relief on the convoy escort:

'I flew over to have a look at her anyway and pulled down my front gun sight purely for practice. As we neared the aircraft, however, my Irish second pilot suddenly swore and then shouted, 'It's a Kondor!' Automatically I increased speed while he ran aft to man one of the beam guns, the wireless operator manned the other side gun and the mid-upper gunner swung his turret round. There, about 1,000 feet above the sea and running in towards our convoy, was one of the large Focke Wulf 200s. We overhauled him fast and at 400 yards I opened the proceedings with about five short bursts from my front guns, though I don't think I hit him. He returned the fire immediately from both top and bottom guns and I saw his tracers whip past the Hudson's nose in little streaks of light. He missed us and his pilot turned slightly to starboard and ran parallel to the convoy.

'I soon realised that we had the legs of him and soon caught up with him. He put up his nose, as if thinking to make a climb for cloud cover, but evidently changed his mind and decided that he was safer where he was, down close to the sea. As we drew closer my rear gunner opened up, firing forward and I could see his tracers nipping across my wing. We drew closer and closer and the Kondor began to look like the side of a house; at the end all I could see of it was part of the fuselage and two whacking great engines. My rear gunner was pumping bullets into him all the time. When we were only 40 feet away I could see two of his engines beginning to glow. I throttled back so as not to over-shoot him, or crash into him and for one brief moment my second pilot, Ernie, saw a white face appear at one of the side windows and then quickly disappear.

'Just then the Kondor began a turn, its belly exposed to us and my gunners opened up with everything. There was a wisp of smoke, a sudden belching of smoke and then flames shot out from underneath both port engines. He turned to starboard, while I made a tight port turn ready to come at him again. We came out of the turn, only to see the Kondor again flying steadily, apparently unhurt. For a moment I thought he had got away with it, but then realised that he was getting lower and lower and a minute later he went into the sea. I yelled, 'We've got him! He's in the drink! We've got him!' The upper gunner too was yelling down the intercom great exultant Yorkshire oaths.

'It was only then that we all realised just how hard and how silently we'd all been concentrating and how full the Hudson was of cordite fumes. I also saw how short of petrol we were. We flew over the Kondor - its wing tips were just awash - and Ernie took photos. Four of the crew were in the water hanging on to a rubber dinghy which was just beginning to inflate, while a fifth man was scrambling along the fuselage. We learnt later that a Met man who had been aboard had been killed by a bullet through the heart, but the others were all right. Two corvettes were rushing to pick them up and the whole crew seemed to be crowded onto the deck of the leading one, waving and shouting at us. One man was waving a shirt. Our relief Wellington and Hudson were by now circling round too and as we made off for home we could see the white puffs of steam as all the ships in the convoy sounded their sirens.'

The attacks by bombs on enemy shipping reached a momentary climax in October and November 1941. Many of them took place by night during the moon periods and the aircraft employed were Hudsons flown by RAF, Canadian and Dutch Naval Air Squadrons. The attack on the night of 29/30 October is especially noteworthy. Reconnaissance on the morning of the 29th had disclosed a concentration of German shipping in the harbour at Ålesund and the neighbouring fjords. Hudsons set out from the North of Scotland and delivered the attack. The first to arrive saw the ships lying at anchor beneath a brilliant moon lighting the harbour in its frame of mountains on which the first snows of winter had fallen. The attack can best be described in the words of one of those who took part in it:

'There was a lot of flak coming up as I came over the target. I could see one ship burning, with smoke pouring from it. The ground was covered with snow and I had the whole target in silhouette. I flew around pretty low for a bit, then climbed up to get a better view and choose my target, keeping out of range of the flak. I saw a second ship hit and it soon became an inferno of flames. We could actually see the plates red-hot. I saw four other aircraft attack shipping in the harbour. They were flying very low and the flak was streaming down on them from batteries in the hills-green, white, red, yellow. A lot of it was going straight on to the enemy's ships.

'I had by then chosen my target - the biggest ship in the harbour, about 5,000/6,000 tons. I approached from the North, about five miles away, my engines throttled right back. I came down to about 5,000 feet, by which time I was nearly over the ship and dived straight on to it. I dropped my bombs at about 2,000 feet. I did my own bomb-aiming. Directly the bombs were gone I pulled up over the town. I was then down to about 1,000 feet, still throttled back; then I opened up fully and went off. There was a lot of flak coming up at us. Some of it came pretty close, but we couldn't actually hear it. The gunner definitely silenced two flak positions.

'I flew right round the harbour and when I came back to the target I saw the ship was still there. I said to the crew: 'We must have missed it.' A moment later the gunner shouted: 'Think I can see a glow forward.' I turned round to have another look and saw she was down by the bows. I flew round again and this time I saw the bows were awash. I kept on flying round and next time I looked the water was about up to her funnel. She got lower and lower and then we saw the rudder come out of the water and about a third of her keel. Just before she went down we saw part of the stern with the flag-pole sticking up and as we watched she sank. The ship took twelve minutes to sink from the time] released the bombs. It was a most satisfying sight to see it going down.'

All the aircraft returned safely. One of them was carrying the Air Officer Commanding the Group to which the Squadron making the attack belonged. Its bombs sank one of the four ships destroyed that night. Three others were hit and very heavily damaged. In the five nights from 31 October to 5 November eighteen merchant vessels were hit, the majority, perhaps all, being sunk or burned out. On 2 November the attack switched to the Dutch coast and four ships were hit. In less than a month about 150,000 tons of enemy shipping had been sunk or severely damaged and of this about 120,000 could be claimed by Hudson Squadrons. The denial to the enemy of these ships and the loss of their cargoes undoubtedly affected his military operation against Russia. To read the reports submitted by pilots immediately after their encounters with enemy ships is to receive the impression of men so eager to get to grips with the enemy that they disregard the risks involved. This, however, is not so. A more careful perusal of them shows that the captain of a Hudson, a Beaufort or a Blenheim, while prepared to take great risks and accepting them as in the ordinary course of duty, is not at the same time heedlessly risking the lives of his crew or the safety of his aircraft.

'From mast height I laid a stick of bombs across the ship. I didn't see them drop, but the rear gunner reported: 'There's one on the deck.' At that moment both my engines spluttered and stopped. That shook me, for we were flying right between the masts. The whole sky lit up as two of the bombs burst and the ship seemed to disappear into thin air.'

Such phrases as these indicate how closely pressed home is the attack, but they are often followed by the statement that it was made from cloud cover, that evasive action followed immediately afterwards and that the aircraft regained the shelter of the clouds as soon as possible. Such actions on the part of the pilot in no way detract from the achievement. On the contrary, they enhance it. The enemy's merchant vessels, of which all are armed and most protected by flak-ships which put up a heavy barrage, are not attacked haphazard. The tactics of swift approach and swift 'get-away' have been carefully worked out and studied and though the hazard of the operation is never allowed to interfere with its execution, if the chances of a successful attack are nil it is not made. If there is even the smallest prospect of success, it is.

Single enemy vessels or vessels in convoy hug the coasts of conquered Europe. They are discovered, therefore, by visual and photographic reconnaissance or by means of patrols given a roving commission to attack any suitable shipping target which may present itself. Such patrols are called 'Rovers.' They are sent out very often at the discretion of the Officer Commanding the station, who acts under a general order from the Group and they are flown both by day and night. They were welcomed from the start by the pilots and crews as an exciting change from convoy or anti-submarine patrols. In daylight, weather is of supreme importance. Crews detailed for such patrols cannot take off unless there is a reasonable certainty that the area they are going to investigate will be covered with cloud.

'There is a feeling of unreality,' says a Wing Commander, 'in starting out on a bright, sunny day and presently flying into horrible grey weather and so finding the enemy coasts and flying along low-lying, sandy shores or an island of the Frisian group and perhaps stumbling on a ship before either she or oneself has quite realised what has happened. The whole essence of a successful shipping 'strike' is surprise... The attacking aircraft has to come in very close and very low... It is in this position, however, for only a few seconds and we rely on catching the gunner on board when he is lighting a surreptitious cigarette, talking to a pal, or perhaps blowing on cold fingers... The moonlight Rover is quite different and in some ways more fascinating... It can take place only on bright nights. There is something indescribably exhilarating about flying low over the water along a path of living flame... Surprise is nearly always achieved because it is possible to see much more looking up-moon than it is looking the other way and the marauding aircraft comes suddenly on the ship out of the ghostly murkiness of night.'

The same conditions for attack apply to the torpedo-carrying aircraft of the Command. The Squadrons engaged on them flew Beauforts, aircraft which can carry either bombs or torpedoes. The torpedo is more effective than any other against a ship, for it explodes beneath the surface of the water and the damage that it causes is therefore, in nine cases out of ten, more severe than that caused by a bomb. The torpedo is brittle in the sense that if it is dropped from too great a height or when an aircraft is travelling too fast it will break up on striking the surface and it is hard to aim, for it must enter the water at the correct angle. If it does not it will either, hit the bottom and there explode or be diverted, or move up and down as though on a switchback, 'porpoising' as it is called and then break surface. Moreover, its delicacy of construction makes it impossible to drop it if the aircraft is flying too fast. It cannot be dropped too near the target or it may pass beneath it and this means that the pilot must become very proficient in judging distance.

Pilots and crews go through a course of intensive training in which they learn as much as they can about the idiosyncrasies of the torpedo. By means of simple .and ingenious photographic machinery the pilot under instruction who has attacked a target with dummy torpedoes and the fully trained pilot who has loosed his torpedo against a ship, are enabled to discover the exact distance from the target at which they dropped them. The torpedoes are beautifully made and covered with anti-corrosive paint, which gives them a dark blue colour. This paint is very effective against the action of sea-water and torpedoes have been known to remain in the sea for as long as thirteen years and still be perfectly serviceable.

The Beauforts operated on cloudy days or, if the weather was clear, with a fighter escort and during moonlight nights. They, too, found the enemy by means of a Rover patrol or a 'strike' directed against a ship or a convoy which has previously been discovered by reconnaissance. Group Captain Guy Bolland, who commanded 217 Squadron, which in early 1941 had been re-equipped with

Beauforts, considered that daylight raids using the aircraft were suicidal and he insisted on night attacks only. When the potential menace of *Scharnhorst* and *Gneisenau* to Britain's Atlantic shipping meant that Beauforts had to attack in daylight, Bolland declared all of his squadron's aircraft unserviceable. 'There was no possible chance of any of my aircraft getting anywhere near Brest,' he later explained 'and even if they did and were lucky enough to hit the ships the damage would have been negligible.' Bolland then reported to Plymouth where he told his air marshal and an admiral that 'sending young men to their deaths on useless missions is not on.' The visit cost him his command.[77]

Here is what happened on a March day in 1941 to a Beaufort which had scored a hit on a destroyer off the Ile de Batz and had been hit by a shell which destroyed the hydraulic system, rendering all the turrets and the undercarriage unserviceable.

'On reaching base,' says the account, 'the Squadron Leader circled the aerodrome for an hour to consume all his petrol. While doing so his air gunner, a large man, succeeded in climbing out of the turret and into the tail in an effort to staunch the holes in the pipes with rags, but in this he was not successful. The pilot spoke to the ground, saying: 'We will crash-land. Keep us some tea.' To crash-land it was necessary to fly the aircraft straight on to the ground, throttle back at the last moment and then cut off the engines. This he did and the aircraft skidded 120 yards along the runway, structure and dust flying up on either side. The starboard propeller shot off and spun along in front of the aircraft on its tips like a wheel. The pilot thought at any moment that it would pierce the perspex windows of the cockpit. 'The funny thing,' he said afterwards, 'about getting out of a crashed aircraft is when you step down. You go straight on to the ground without having to climb down by means of the usual footholds.'

Much has also been said of the activity of the flak-ships. The Germans are using them in ever-increasing numbers to protect shipping, of which the value, always great, grows daily. Sometimes as many as five have been observed escorting a single merchant vessel. Their crews are not unnaturally light on the trigger. 'Just as we were right over the ship it spotted us,' reported the pilot of a Hudson who met one such vessel off Norway. 'The Germans opened up first with machine-gun fire and then the heavier guns started firing. It seemed to me at that moment that they were throwing up everything at us except the ship herself.' It was bombed and left burning.

The torpedo attacks continued, the majority being carried out during Rover patrols. On 23 October 1940 for example, a German convoy off Schiermonnikoog, made up of nine merchant vessels and three flak-ships, was attacked by two Beauforts, the largest vessel being sunk and the second largest left listing heavily to port. Here again the anti-aircraft fire was intense, but its accuracy poor, possibly because the Beauforts, when retreating after loosing their torpedoes, had the help of a 40-mph wind behind their tails. On 8 November three Beauforts attacked a merchant ship off Norderney. All torpedoes missed, but in taking avoiding action the ship ran aground and became a total loss. The next day a torpedo running strong and straight towards a vessel off Borkum hit a sandbank and exploded, doing no harm. The state of the tide had saved the enemy.

During 1941 torpedo attacks increased. They were made not only off the Dutch,

Belgian and Danish coasts, but also along the Norwegian coast. On 9 February, for example, three Beauforts attacked six destroyers off Norway and hit two of them. On 2 March a large merchant vessel was hit off the Danish coast and left on fire. On the 12th an enemy destroyer was blown up in moonlight off the Norwegian coast. Early in September a fierce action was fought near Stavanger between Beauforts seeking to torpedo a large tanker and Me 109s which came to its rescue. The tanker was hit by two torpedoes, an escort vessel by one and a Me 109 shot down. One Beaufort was lost. Another which returned safely entered cloud cover only twenty yards ahead of the German fighters. A little later in the month a cargo vessel was set on fire near the Lister Light.

In twelve months 126 attacks by torpedo were made. Between January and September 1941 87,000 tons of enemy shipping was sunk. One attack must be specially mentioned. It was made by a torpedo-carrying Beaufort of 22 Squadron at first light on 6 April 1941. Six Beauforts were given the task of torpedoing the battle-cruisers *Scharnhorst* and *Gneisenau* known to be lying alongside the quay in the Rade Abri at Brest. The port was literally ringed by hills in which hundreds of anti-aircraft guns were located, while in the harbour three flak ships added their weight of fire to the massive guns of the two battle-cruisers. The *Scharnhorst* had put into Brest harbour on 22 March to re-tube her boilers, accompanied by the *Gneisenau* and an RAF reconnaissance flight on 28 March confirmed their presence in Brest. Bomber Command immediately carried out a series of bombing attacks on Brest without any effect. However, one bomb dropped near the *Gneisenau* failed to explode and the battleship was moved out of dry dock into the open harbour to allow bomb disposal teams to defuse it. The *Scharnhorst* was already tied up to the harbour's north quay, protected by torpedo nets. On 5 April a photographic reconnaissance Spitfire photographed the harbour, revealing the vulnerable position of the *Gneisenau*, totally exposed to an aerial torpedo attack, in the inner harbour. An attack order for 6 April was quickly passed to 22 Squadron, which at this time was nominally stationed at North Coates but had moved nine of its Beauforts to the South-West of England, to St. Eval just north of Newquay in Cornwall, to be within striking distance of the ports and harbours on the Atlantic coast. The squadron commander had already dispatched three Beauforts on another operation; leaving him with only six Beauforts available. He decided to send these in two formations of three aircraft; one formation to bomb any torpedo nets surrounding the Gneisenau first and the other to carry torpedoes for the attack.

Flying Officer J. Hyde DFC, Sergeant Camp and Flying Officer Kenneth Campbell were chosen for the torpedo attack. All three were experienced and for Campbell this was to be his twentieth operational sortie. 'Ken' Campbell was born on 21 April 1917 at Saltcoats, Ayrshire, the youngest in a family of six children and had attended Sedbergh School before gaining entrance to Clare College, Cambridge, to study for a degree in chemistry. Joining the Cambridge University Air Squadron, he had been commissioned as a Pilot Officer in the RAF Volunteer Reserve on 23 August 1938 and eventually mobilised for RAF service on 25 September 1939. His three-man crew comprised Sergeant James Philip Scott, a blond Canadian from Toronto as navigator, Sergeant William Cecil Mullins, a farmer from Somerset as wireless operator and Sergeant Ralph Waiter Hillman, a chauffeur from Edmonton, London as air gunner. They were detailed to leave St Eval first and then wait on the outskirts of Brest for the bombing formation to make the first attack against any torpedo nets; after which the torpedo bombers would go in individually to make their runs.

St. Eval was rain-soaked and two of the bomber Beauforts became bogged down in the slush and mud, leaving just Sergeant Henry Menary, a Belfast-born Irishman, to actually get airborne. The three torpedo Beauforts had already left at intervals of a few minutes, between 04.30 and 05.00. Menary groped his way through the darkness and atrocious weather conditions of rain, fog and mists and soon lost his way. When daylight came he realised he was many miles away from Brest, too late for his appointed task and accordingly he dropped his bombs on a ship near Ile de Batz and turned for home. The fourth Beaufort failed to find Brest in the haze which preceded the dawn and returned with its torpedo. The fifth went in to attack a few minutes too late. 'When I arrived at Brest,' reported its pilot, 'it was full daylight. I crossed the spit of land at the South-West corner of the harbour, coming under fire from shore batteries. I then came down to a few feet above the water and flew towards the mole protecting the Rade Abri, behind which the battle-cruiser lay. I passed three flak-ships and nearly reached the mole itself. By then I was being fired at from batteries all round the harbour. Continuous streams of fire seemed to be coming from every direction. It was by far the worst flak I have ever encountered. When I was nearly up to the mole I saw that the battle-cruiser herself was completely hidden from me by a bank of haze. I therefore turned away to the East and climbed into cloud.'

Campbell had attacked a few minutes before. He had crossed the same spit of land South-West of the harbour entrance at around 300 feet and found the Gneisenau, lying alongside the quay on the North shore, where it was protected by a stone mole curving round from the West. The Beaufort dived to less than 50 feet and was at once under the fire of 270 anti-aircraft guns of varying calibres established on the rising ground behind the battle cruiser and on the two arms of land which encircled the outer harbour. To the formidable concentration of fire which these guns immediately produced was added the barrage from the guns of the warship itself and from those of the three flak-ships already mentioned. Moreover, having penetrated these formidable defences, the Beaufort, after delivering its low-level attack, would have had the greatest difficulty in avoiding the rising ground behind the harbour. All these obstacles were known to Campbell, who stuck resolutely to the task. He passed the anti-aircraft ships at less than mast height, flying into the very mouths of their guns. Skimming over the mole, a torpedo was launched point-blank at a range of 500 yards and then Campbell pulled the Beaufort in a port climbing turn, heading for cloud cover above the rapidly-approaching hills behind Brest. At that moment all the defences opened up on Campbell's aircraft, which out of control, crashed straight ahead into the harbour. Campbell, having released his torpedo, was almost immediately killed or wounded by the first predicted flak. When the aircraft was later salvaged the Germans found the body of 'Jimmy' Scott in the pilot's seat usually occupied by Campbell. All four crew members were buried by the Germans in the grave of honour in Brest cemetery. The Gneisenau was hit and damaged below the water-line. Subsequent photographs showed that she was undergoing repairs in dry dock. Eight months later the battle cruiser was still undergoing repairs and it only went to sea again in February 1942 when it made the Channel-dash with the *Scharnhorst* to German waters.

Campbell, Scott, Mullins and Hillman were of that company - *'Who wore on their hearts the fire's centre; Born of the sun they travelled a short while towards the sun and left the vivid air signed with their honour.'* On 13 March 1942 Campbell was awarded a posthumous Victoria Cross, which his parents received from King George VI at an investiture on 23 June 1943.[78]

Two more attacks must be described. On 12 June 1941 a Blenheim on reconnaissance emerging from clouds some miles South of the Lister Light saw, 1,000 feet below, four or five enemy destroyers screening a much larger vessel, coloured light grey, steaming North-West. The larger vessel was almost certainly the *Lützow* and it seems probable that she had put out with the object of raiding our commerce in the Atlantic. In addition to her destroyer escort, the pocket-battleship had an escort of Me 109 and Me 110 fighters. The Blenheim slipped back into the clouds. It was then one minute before midnight. On receipt of its message a striking force of Beauforts was sent from a Scottish aerodrome to attack with torpedoes. At 2.20 in the morning of the 13 June - it must be remembered that in those latitudes, at that time of the year, there is almost no darkness - one of the Beauforts attacked the enemy. It flew low, crossed just above one of the protecting destroyers and released its torpedo at a range of 700 yards. As the aircraft broke away the air, gunner and wireless operator both saw a column of water leap from the *Lützow* amidships and this was followed by a dense cloud of smoke. A few minutes later a second Beaufort arrived on the scene, which the destroyers were busily engaged in obscuring by means of smoke. The second torpedo was fired from 1,000 yards into this artificial haze and almost certainly hit the pocket-battleship. She was picked up again later by Blenheims of Coastal Command, which, together with Beauforts, shadowed her for many hours. By this time she and her escort had turned about and were making for the Skagerrak at reduced speed. The *Lützow* subsequently put into a North-West German base for repairs.

The part played by Coastal Command in the Combined Operations raid on Vaagsö on 27 December 1941, may be mentioned, for this operation was an attack on a fringe target carried out by the Royal Navy and the Army. It was the task of Blenheim fighters and Beaufighters of the Command to provide protection from the air while Blenheims of Bomber Command made an attack on enemy aerodromes within' range. The sky was clear and the Beaufighters, which were over the target about 1300, successfully prevented the German Air Force from interfering. Several combats took place; four He 111s were shot down for' the loss of three Beaufighters. One Blenheim returned to base with the observer and rear gunner both badly wounded. It fought two Me 109s over the ships and during this engagement the rear gunner was put out of action. It turned for home when it encountered a Me 110 very low over the water. The observer was attending the wounded rear gunner, whom he had taken from the turret. He manned the guns, but was himself wounded a moment later by a burst of fire from the Me 110. 'Just then,' reported the pilot, 'I heard a swishing noise and spray flew in from my open side-window. An engine began to cough. I had hit the water with one propeller, but fortunately, beyond bending it a bit, there was no serious damage and the engine picked up again.' Within 50 miles of base the observer succeeded in reaching the wireless set, though it took him ten minutes to cover the six feet separating him from it and sent out a distress signal. The Blenheim, with flaps and undercarriage unserviceable, made a successful belly landing. The crew survived.

This account of attacks on land targets is best ended by the story of the Beaufort raid on the docks of Nantes on the night of 26/27 October 1941. The Beauforts set out in formation and flew a hundred feet above a stormy sea.

'We were so low,' says the leader of the attack, 'that when we reached the French coast I had to pull up sharply to avoid the sand-dunes. Every time we came to a clump of trees we leapfrogged over them and then went down almost to the ground again... It grew darker as we went farther inland and then began the most surprising experience of all. It was as though the whole of that part of France were turning out to welcome us. Every village we went over became a blaze of light. People threw open their doors and came out to watch us skim their chimney-pots. In other places hamlets would suddenly light up as if the people had torn the blackout down when they heard us coming... I remember one house with a courtyard fully lit, up. I saw a woman come out of the house, look up at us, wave and then go back. She switched off the outside lights and then I saw a yellow light from inside stream out as she opened the door.'

The docks were bombed from 300 feet. Then the Beauforts turned for home just above the roof-tops of Nantes, which, in the bright moonlight, 'looked like a city of the dead.' 'Then I began to see white pin-points on the ground and one by one, lights appeared as we raced over the chimney-pots... We were at top speed, but even so we could see doors opening and people coming out. I felt that we had brought some comfort to the people of Nantes.' They were in need of it; a cordon of German troops had for some days surrounded the city and within there were fifty hostages awaiting execution as a reprisal for the killing of the German governor. These were shot the next morning. Yet the lights which were switched on that night have been seen on subsequent raids. Through them shines the indomitable spirit of the Bretons.

Attacks on land targets by Coastal Command have yielded in the last months to attacks on shipping. The work of dealing with U-boats and surface raiders in their lairs is now for the most part being performed by Bomber Command. Yet those earlier days when Blenheims, Hudsons, Beauforts and flying boats went in to the attack must not be forgotten. They harassed the enemy - 6,000 metric tons of fuel oil were destroyed in two attacks on St. Nazaire alone, sufficient to fuel a U-boat for six to eight sorties - and prevented him from developing his full strength in the Western Approaches to Great Britain.

The Beauforts' ranks were joined on 12 February 1942 by the crews of naval Swordfish which on that day attacked the *Scharnhorst, Gneisenau* and *Prinz Eugen*[79] and her consorts in the English Channel after they had broken out of Brest heading for the safety of their home bases. None of the bomber squadrons could attack before 1500 hours so the main hope was the slender force of Beaufort torpedo-bombers on 42, 86 and 217 Squadrons and the Fleet Air Arm Swordfish of 815 Squadron commanded by Lieutenant Commander Eugene Esmonde. At 1130 hours very few of these aircraft were within range of the German ships. 86 and part of 217 were at St. Eval, in Cornwall; the remainder of 217 was at Thorney

Island, near Portsmouth; and 42 was just coming in to land at Coltishall, the fighter airfield near Norwich, after flying down from Leuchars, having been delayed by snow on airfields. Only the six Swordfish at Manston and the seven Beauforts at Thorney Island were in a position to attack within the next two hours. As the Swordfish attacked the first to fall was Esmonde, a victim of the enemy fighters. The two remaining aircraft of his section survived the fighter attacks and pressed on into the storm of flak now coming up from the vessels. Repeatedly hit and with their crews wounded, the two Swordfish still headed for one of the two big ships visible through the clouds of mist and smoke. Both crews managed to launch torpedoes before their aircraft, riddled with bullets, struck the sea. Five of the six men were afterwards rescued from the sea. From the second section of Swordfish, which disappeared from view after crossing the destroyer screen, there were no survivors. Esmonde was awarded a posthumous Victoria Cross.

Seven Beauforts at Thorney Island were available at short notice when the order to attack was received. Two were armed with bombs, which had to be changed to torpedoes and a third developed a technical fault. Only four of the Beauforts thus took off at 1325 and when they did so they were twenty minutes late on planned rendezvous with their fighter cover at Manston. To make up for this delay both sets of aircraft were ordered while in the air to proceed independently to the targets but because of radio frequency problems the torpedo-bombers did not receive the message. Eventually the front section of two Beauforts set off for the French coast, found nothing and returned to Manston, where they discovered for the first time the nature of their target. Meanwhile the two rear Beauforts, which had lost touch with their leaders, had already landed at Manston, learned their target and the latest position of the ships and set off towards the Belgian coast. At 1540, about the same time as navy destroyers from the Thames estuary were making an extremely brave but ineffective attack, the two pilots sighted a large warship which they took to be the *Prinz Eugen*. Despite intense flak they turned in and launched their torpedoes from a thousand yards range but to no avail.

Aircraft of Bomber Command loaded up with semi- armour-piercing bombs, which had to be dropped from at least 7,000 feet, were ready to attack. Cloud was 8/10ths-10/10ths, with base at 700 feet. Unless cloud-gaps occurred at precisely the right place and moment, the bomb-aimers would be faced with an impossible task. But the alternative armament, the general-purpose bomb, which could be dropped effectively from lower heights, would certainly not penetrate decks plated with several inches of steel. However, GP bombs could be used to damage the superstructure of the vessels and distract the attention of their crews from the torpedo-bombers. The first wave of 73 bombers began to take off at 1420. Most of them managed to reach the target area, individually or in pairs, between 1455 and 1558, but in the thick low clouds and intermittent rainstorms only ten crews saw the German ships long enough to release their bombs. The next wave, of 134 aircraft, began to take off at 1437 and arrived in the target area between 1600 and 1706. Twenty of these are known to have delivered attacks. A third and final wave of thirty-five aircraft took off at about 1615 and was over the target from 1750 to 1815. Nine managed to attack. All told, 242 aircraft [80] of Bomber Command attempted to find the enemy during the afternoon; and of those that returned, only

39 succeeded in bombing. Fifteen aircraft were lost, mostly from flak and flying into the sea and twenty damaged. No hits were scored on the vessels.

While these attacks were in progress, the next group of torpedo-bombers was being launched against the enemy. 42 Squadron arrived at Coltishall to find no facilities for torpedo aircraft but nine of the Beauforts had flown from Leuchars with torpedoes on and these took off at 1425. The remaining five, having no torpedoes, remained on the ground. On leaving Coltishall the nine Beauforts headed south to Manston to link up with fighters and some Hudsons intended for diversionary bombing. They were then to follow the Hudsons out to sea. But when the Beauforts arrived over the airfield they were unable to form up with the other aircraft. After orbiting Manston for over half an hour, the Beaufort commander finally decided to set a course based on information of the enemy's position given him before he had left Coltishall. As he turned out to sea with his squadron, six of the Hudsons followed him. The remaining five continued to circle until almost 1600 before withdrawing to Bircham Newton. In thick cloud and heavy rain the nine Beauforts and six Hudsons now pressed on towards the Dutch coast. The two formations quickly lost touch, but after an ASV contact the Hudsons sighted the enemy and attacked through heavy flak. Two of the Hudsons were shot down and no damage was done to the ships. A few minutes later six of the nine Beauforts, flying just above sea-level, also came across the main German force - the other three had already released their torpedoes against what were possibly Royal Navy destroyers. Most of the torpedoes were seen to be running well but none found its mark.

Nine Hampden crews on 455 Squadron RAAF, the second Australian squadron formed in Britain, led by Wing Commander G. M. Lindeman DFC had to go down to 800 feet to drop their bombs and they encountered intense and accurate AA fire. Squadron Leader W. H. Cliff, commanding 42 Squadron, who led the formation, had on either side of him a Beaufort captained by an Australian - Pilot Officer E. Birchley on his left and Pilot Officer R. B. Archer on his right. Shells and bullets from the destroyers forming a protective screen around the *Scharnhorst* flew all round them. Archer saw heavy shells hitting the wave-tops and light tracer whizzing over his aircraft. His Beaufort was hit by the *Scharnhorst's* guns and his rear gunner was wounded. The gunner was receiving first aid from the navigator and wireless operator when an enemy aircraft appeared. When the gunner re-entered his turret, Archer ordered him out and his place was taken by the navigator, Sergeant D. N. Keeling RNZAF. Birchley, who had turned away in the opposite direction from Archer after dropping his torpedo, put his head out of the open window to try and see through the mist. Tracer bullets passed close to him. Both Australians thought they would never get out of the flak. Birchley flew within 100 yards of the *Scharnhorst* and his gunner had a glorious moment when he turned his machine guns on the deck. Archer was subsequently awarded the DFC.

By this time the two Beauforts on 217 Squadron which had failed to find the ships earlier in the afternoon had set off again from Manston. Operating independently both picked up the *Scharnhorst* off the Dutch coast with the aid of their ASV. But their attacks, delivered at 1710 and 1800, were as unsuccessful as all the rest.

One last chance now remained. There were still the Beauforts of 86 and 217

Squadrons at St. Eval. These had been hastily ordered to Thorney Island, which they reached at 1430. There, after adjusting torpedoes and refuelling, they took off to link up with fighters over Coltishall. The Beauforts reached Coltishall at 1700, but found no sign of the escort they were expecting. They at once headed out to sea and at 1805, in the growing dusk, with visibility less than 1,000 yards and cloud base down to 600 feet they came across four enemy mine-sweepers. One pilot caught sight of what he took to be a big ship, but by then his aircraft was so damaged that he was unable to release his torpedo. Soon darkness was upon them and at 1830 the Beauforts abandoned their search and set course back for Coltishall. Two of their number, victims of flak or the dangerous flying conditions, failed to return.

Australia's one-legged Beaufighter pilot, Flight Lieutenant Bruce Rose DFC was probably the last airman to see the Scharnhorst that day. Flying through intense flak from the destroyer screen, he completely circled the cruiser before leaving for base. It was almost dark when he left. Single aircraft of Coastal Command which had been trying to shadow the German formation since about 1600 obtained two sightings before dark and two or three ASV contacts afterwards - the last of them, against the *Scharnhorst,* as late as 0155 on 13 February. Their reports correctly indicated that the German force had split up, but were too late to be of any value. As a final effort, twelve Hampdens and nine Manchesters were sent to lay mines in the Elbe estuary during the night. Only eight aircraft laid their mines and none of these did any damage. In the course of the evening, mines laid by 5 Group Hampdens or Manchesters in the Frisian Islands during recent nights, caused some damage when the *Scharnhorst* hit two mines and *Gneisenau,* one. The *Gneisenau* managed to maintain company with the *Prinz Eugen* and reached the mouth of the Elbe at 0700 on 13 February. The *Scharnhorst* was more seriously damaged. With speed reduced to twelve knots and shipping a thousand tons of water, she nevertheless managed to limp into Wilhelmshaven. The news of the escape of the German vessels was greeted in England with widespread dismay and indignation. 'Vice-Admiral Ciliax has succeeded where the Duke of Medina Sidonia failed,' wrote The Times: 'Nothing more mortifying to the pride of sea-power in Home Waters has happened since the 17th century.'

Both the *Scharnhorst* and *Gneisenau* were located in Kiel later. The *Gneisenau* received additional damage between 25 February and 28 February, during bombing raids on the dockyards at Kiel and was never in action again. The Navy got the *Scharnhorst* in the end and she was sunk on Boxing Day, 1943, off Norway. The *Prinz Eugen* reached Germany safely, but later, when on her way to Trondheim, was attacked off Kristiansund by HM Submarine *Trident* and severely damaged. The cruiser tried to get away again early on the morning of 18 May 1942, this time from Trondheim. Twelve Coastal Command Beauforts found and attacked her. Again Australian flyers helped to pound the 10,000-ton cruiser. It was a first experience of enemy fire for at least two of them - Pilot Officer E. Mc. McKern, a Beaufort pilot and his observer, Gordon L. Duffield. They were in the first wave. Shells from the anti-aircraft guns were whistling around them as they went in. Some of them burst over the aircraft's nose and above the starboard wing, but they kept flying on. Another shell burst beneath the aircraft and shot it upwards. A Me 109 tried to stop it, but McKern's RAF gunner poured a stream of bullets into its engine and it turned away, dropping down towards the sea. At 1,000 yards the Beaufort dropped its torpedo. Then it went straight on across the bows of the *Prinz Eugen* at about sixty feet and 600 yards in front of her. The destroyer ahead fired determinedly at the Beaufort as it came on, but it escaped damage and the crew got back in the last light to claim a 'possible' hit. Duffield brought back the only photograph which showed clearly the cruiser and her four protecting destroyers. Archer and Birchley, the Australians who had participated in the Channel attack, took part, but both were shot down. Archer was killed, Birchley taken prisoner.[81]

On the night of 11/12 February the usual patrols over Brest were flown from dusk to dawn. A reconnaissance on the previous afternoon had revealed both battle-cruisers berthed at the torpedo-boat station, protected by anti-torpedo booms and the *Prinz Eugen* at the coaling wharf. Six destroyers were also in the harbour. Sometime during the night, which was pitch-black with no moon, they slipped out. On the morning of the 12th the weather was still thick and nothing was seen. A report received by Headquarters, Coastal Command, at 11.28 stated that a large enemy naval force, including the *Scharnhorst*, *Gneisenau* and *Prinz Eugen* had been sighted between Berck and Le Touquet. A Beaufort, a Whitley and two Beaufighters were at once ordered off to shadow this force, while Hudsons and Beauforts, provided with fighter escort, endeavoured to deliver bombing attacks in the early hours of the afternoon. The weather was so thick that they achieved no result and it proved very difficult for the Hudsons and Beauforts to maintain contact with the fighter escort. Beauforts carrying torpedoes delivered attacks off Holland, which were possibly more successful. 'One Squadron did so only at its second attempt. At the first the enemy was not found. At least three torpedoes were observed to be running strongly towards the targets and one crew reported that they had seen an enemy warship listing badly with smoke pouring from her bows. The Beauforts were subjected to very fierce anti-aircraft fire and to severe fighter opposition.

Most of them found the enemy by the simple process of running into heavy flak fired by unseen ships. One made three attempts to attack, but was by that time so badly damaged that its torpedo could not be released. 'I saw my leader waggle his wing,' runs the account of one pilot. 'That meant that he had seen the ships... The *Prinz Eugen* was steaming along very slowly at the head of a tremendous line of ships. Destroyers were trying to lay a smoke-screen round her... At that moment I saw two Me 109s fly across in front of me... They circled to get on our tail and the *Prinz Eugen* was in my sights.' He dropped his torpedo and then the Beaufort became involved in a heavy fight with the Messerschmitts. One of them was shot down and the other made off. 'My Beaufort was hit in twelve places... A bullet had gone through a propeller and a cannon shell had ploughed a furrow in the tail-plane. The action was fought very near to Overflakee Island off the Dutch coast. We thought the name appropriate in the circumstances.'

In this confused and unsatisfactory action the palm for courage, cold and unshaken, has rightly been awarded to the Swordfish of the Fleet Air Arm, which, operating from one of the South coast bases of Coastal Command, delivered their attacks about noon. They came in low in two flights of three in the face of tremendous and accurate anti-aircraft fire, with swarms of enemy fighters about them and all discharged their torpedoes. They were all shot down and of the eighteen members of their crews only five survived.

On the afternoon of 23 February 1942 six Beauforts on 42 Squadron left Sumburgh for a sweep against enemy shipping. They reached the Norwegian coast, but saw no vessels and on the return journey the aircraft became separated. Suddenly Beaufort M, piloted by Squadron Leader W. H. Cliff, went into an uncontrollable dive and hit the sea. Cliff and his crew, who only a fortnight before had led 42 Squadron's attack on the *Scharnhorst* and *Gneisenau*, thought that their last moment had come; but by some miracle all survived the impact and scrambled out, or were thrown clear, as the aircraft went down. Fortunately one of them was able to secure the dinghy and this all four men eventually succeeded in boarding. Very soon they were joined by one of the two pigeons carried in the aircraft. They at once captured this welcome arrival, attached to its leg a note of the approximate position of the crash and launched the bird into the air. But the creature was wet and darkness was already coming on. After performing a few perfunctory circles the pigeon merely alighted back to the dinghy; and no amount of cajoling, or beating about the head, could persuade it to resume its flight. Its fixed intention was obviously to make a fifth passenger. In disgust the crew therefore abandoned their attempts to drive it off and huddled together against the rigours of the February night.

By this time the search had begun. The last known position of the aircraft was 150 miles east of Aberdeen and throughout the night a Catalina sought in vain for the distressed crew. At first light other aircraft went out from Leuchars, Dyce and Arbroath, but several hours' search yielded no sign of the missing men. Meanwhile a pigeon had arrived back at base-not the obstinate creature of the previous evening, but its companion from the same basket. Unknown to the Beaufort crew, 'Winkie' - as the unfortunate bird was called - had made his escape from the aircraft. He of course carried no message; but this did not defeat the acute intelligences at the station. Since he could not have flown in the dark, he must obviously have found somewhere to rest; and an examination of his feathers revealed unmistakable traces of oil. Someone hazarded the guess that he had spent the night on a tanker; enquiry revealed that such a vessel had been passing off the North East Coast; and from knowledge of its course and a calculation of the time taken by the pigeon to reach base, the area of search was readjusted to fifty miles nearer shore. The next aircraft sent out, a Hudson on 320 Squadron, flew almost straight to the spot where the dinghy lay tossing on the waves. The crew wirelessed a message to base and then dropped a Thornaby Bag. Three hours later a high-speed launch arrived and the sufferings of the four bruised and frost-bitten airmen were over.

The next occasion on which the *Prinz Eugen* was attacked by Coastal Command was on 17 May 1942 when she was found off the Southern tip of Norway seaming southward. She was on her way to a German port for repairs made necessary because of the damage inflicted on her by HM Submarine *Trident*. The attack was carried out by Hudsons and torpedo-carrying Beauforts escorted by Beaufighters and Blenheims. It was pressed home with the greatest determination in the teeth of heavy anti-aircraft and fighter opposition. The Beaufighters, sweeping ahead, raked the decks of the German vessels with cannon and machine-gun fire while the Hudsons and the torpedo bombers went in to the attack. In this action the rear gunner of one of the Beauforts beat off a series of attacks by enemy fighters lasting 35 minutes, though one of his guns had jammed and he himself had been wounded in the face, hands, legs and head. Five enemy fighters were claimed shot down and nine RAF aircraft failed to return. Fighter protection was not always possible; the waters in which targets were to be found were too far off. Blenheims, Beauforts and Hudsons still had to go out into the murk of a foggy day alone and unescorted to strike at such targets, themselves the target for German fighters. Sometimes a 'strike' was a running engagement against opposition that would increase as the minutes and the hours went by.

Aircraft of Coastal Command, between 3 September 1939 and 30 September 1942 escorted 4,947 merchant convoys, attacked 587 U-boats and, if offensive operations against enemy shipping are included, flew 55 million miles.

Hampden AN149/X on 455 Squadron RAAF captained by Flight Sergeant J. S. Freeth took part in a hand in the submarine war on 30 April 1943 when U-227 suddenly appeared crossing the Hampden's course, 110 miles north of the Faroes. The boat, which was commanded by 25-year old Korvettenkapitän Jürgen Kuntze, was on its first war cruise, having left Kiel on 24 April for the North Atlantic. Freeth dived immediately and laid a stick of depth charges alongside the conning tower. U-227's stern rose ten feet out of the water and sank again. The Australians made another attack and the U-boat split into two parts with oil gushing from its sides. The German crew continued firing until the U-boat slithered under, but the Hampden, although hit; suffered no casualties. Afterwards the Australians counted thirty or forty heads bobbing in the water. One sailor shook his fist at the Hampden as it flew off to notify the Air Sea Rescue organization of the location. U-227 was lost with all 49 hands.

455 Squadron RAAF was converted from Hampden bombers to Hampden torpedo bombers in July 1942 and for a time a detachment operated from Russia. The presence of the Hampdens over the North Sea forced the enemy to provide both escort vessels and air cover for their convoys. Torpedo-bombers had to come down so low and keep such a straight course before they could launch their torpedo that sometimes they almost collided with their targets before they could pull up and away. It called for special training and outstanding skill and judgment in assessing the speed and direction of a moving ship and in launching the torpedo. Unless a torpedo was launched at the correct angle, it would dive below the surface and then come up again and do another dive, behaving just like a porpoise, instead of speeding straight to its target at the correct depth below the surface. At first the torpedo was loaded in a line parallel with the fuselage of the aircraft and the pilot had to approach the surface of the sea at the exact angle at which the torpedo should enter. Then the torpedo mounted the torpedo under the aircraft at an angle which enabled it to be correctly launched when the aircraft was flying parallel with the surface, or on an even keel!

It was the misfortune of war which led to Pilot Officer John Davidson, a young New Zealander, receiving a direct hit from a flak ship while he was seeking to bomb German E-boats off the Danish coast. Badly wounded in the thigh and leg, he hung on despite his injuries and flew his aircraft for 300 miles over the sea to his base. The aircraft itself was considerably damaged and when it arrived over the aerodrome the undercarriage was seen to be out of order. The bombs were still on board and the watchers down on the ground fully anticipated that unless the pilot could get the undercarriage to work, the aircraft and crew would be blown to pieces when he attempted to land. For half an hour the pilot flew around the aerodrome struggling to, make the undercarriage function properly, but the task was beyond him.

'Can you go out over the Wash and jettison your bombs?' asked Control.

'Yes,' he replied and flew off over the sea to drop his bombs; but owing to the damage to the aircraft there was one at the back of the rack which stuck. Unaware of this menace, he flew straight in to make a .crash landing and, as he touched, the bomb exploded and blew the tail to smithereens. The observer and the pilot tumbled out as the engine flamed up and began to run for their lives. Suddenly they thought of the rear-gunner, who was nowhere to be seen. Those who were hastening to their aid saw them turn back and rush into the flames and smoke. A few moments afterwards they emerged again, dragging Sergeant Aslett, the rear-gunner, as though he were a sack of potatoes. He was peppered with bits of nuts and bolts and scraps of metal and although he was knocked out by the explosion and would certainly have lost his life if Pilot Officer Davidson and the observer Sergeant Ross had not gone to his rescue, he recovered along with his companions, to bring their tale of high courage to a happy ending.

Footnotes:

75 *So Few; The Immortal Record of the RAF* by David Masters. From June 1942 Beauforts on 217 Squadron attacked Axis shipping from Malta and 39 Squadron operated from the Western Desert. In 1943 the Beaufort was superseded by the 'Torbeau' and the last in RAF service was retired in 1946. Total Beaufort production reached 2,129, including 700 built in Australia.

76 On the night of 8/9 December 1942 133 bombers and Path Finders including 108 Lancasters were ready to be dispatched. While bombing-up at Syerston incendiary bombs fell from the racks of a 61 Squadron Lancaster, exploded and set fire to the aircraft and the inhabitants of Newark and district were able to hear for themselves the explosion of a 4,000lb bomb. Group Captain Clive 'Gus' Walker, the Station Commander went out to the bomber on a fire tender and the Lancaster blew up killing two men and blew the Group Captain's arm off. 'Gus', who had played rugby for Yorkshire, Barbarians and England, returned and post war became AVM Sir Gus Walker CBE DFC AFC. See *Bomber Command: Reflections of War; Under Cover of Darkness 1939-May 1942* by Martin W. Bowman (Pen & Sword 2012).

77 *From Coastal Command to Captivity: The Memoir of a Second World War Airman* by W J 'Jim' Hunter (Leo Cooper, an imprint of Pen & Sword, 2003).

78 See *For Valour; The Air VCs* by Chaz Bowyer (first published by William Kimber and then Grub Street in 1992).

79 These warships were attacked by aircraft of Coastal Command on 63 occasions in 1941.

80 92 Wellingtons, 64 Hampdens, 37 Blenheims, 15 Manchesters, 13 Halifaxes, 11 Stirlings and ten Bostons. It was the largest Bomber Command daylight operation of the war to date.

81 The *Prinz Eugen* was surrendered to the Allies in Copenhagen Harbour in May 1945 and later became one of the test-ships in the Bikini Island atomic bomb test of 1946.

Chapter 4

One Way Ocean

'Bruce Sanders'

On we flew, engines running sweetly and it seemed as if - we could go on forever.'

There is one man in the world who fell out of an aeroplane flying at four thousand feet, without any parachute and lives to tell the story today. He is a young Ferry Command pilot, Harry Griffith by name. He is one of the men who spend their lives bringing supplies of bomber aircraft across what to them is the one-way ocean, the Atlantic. True, some bombers return westward, but the great mass of bombers coming off the assembly lines of the American and Canadian factories which are ear-marked for the European battlefronts are flown only one way-east. Bombers fly east because the course of battle is eastwards.

Harry Griffith, when he made his record jump, was a passenger in a Boston bomber flying over Lake Louis, in Quebec. The aircraft rolled and he fell straight through the bomb-hatch. As he went down, released like a human bomb, he made a wild grab at the edge of the hatch, got his fingers to it, held on with the prehensile strength of a marmoset and remained there dangling with his body in space and beneath him four thousand feet of uninterrupted thin air. Fortunately the pilot had throttled down and heard Griffith's cries rising from beneath the fuselage. He looked back, saw in a glance what had happened and turned down the nose of the Boston.

Lake Louis was ice-bound, for it was the depth of the Canadian winter, The Boston continued in a gentle glide until it was skimming along only ten feet above the frozen surface of the lake. The pilot turned towards a large mound of deep snow. As he approached it he cried, 'Drop!'

Griffith's numbed fingers opened and he plummeted into the snow mound, He suffered only a few minor injuries from his terrible ordeal and the final drop and in a very short time was recovering in hospital and inquiring about the next bomber he was to fly back to Britain.

That is the sort of man who flies the bombers to Britain from bases in Canada and Newfoundland. They are tough, they are strenuous and they have that essential quality found in the crews of Bomber Command and Coastal Command, the ability to hold on when the going is rough. Hold on to themselves and their aircraft.

Their job is to deliver the goods across thousands of miles of ocean. The countless American-built aircraft now darkening the skies of North-western Europe with their wings attest to how well the goods have been delivered. They cross the Northern Atlantic in good weather and foul, rain or shine, blizzard or squall. Electrical storms do not stop them, nor does ice and drifting snow piling up on the wings and forcing them lower over a wintry sea. Roving Focke-Wulf Condors cannot stay their flight, nor can Atlantic fog.

They fly by the clock. Time alone governs their take-off and true touch-down and time, we are assured, waits for no man. Not that they are oblivious to what is happening around them. Ferry Command pilots keep sharp eyes on the Atlantic's grey horizon. They observe what rises with the sun ahead and sets with the sun behind. Their observations are valuable. They have even been the means of saving lives.

Flight Lieutenant R. W. Gautrey of Peterborough, a RAF ace pilot attached to Ferry Command, once saved a whole boatload of shipwrecked mariners. He was flying to Britain at the time in one of the latest American flying-boats, which was badly needed by Coastal Command. The flying-boat was entered in his log-book as AH553. He was bringing it over the one-way Ocean with a crew of six. His job was to deliver AH553 on time; with its fully trained crew.

He flew all night. Flying conditions were good and at regular intervals he checked his position. AH553 was a Catalina flying-boat and it had begun its long journey to Britain from the workshops of the Consolidated Aircraft Corporation in San Diego, California.

Shortly before dawn broke Gautrey took a good 'fix' under exceedingly clear astronomical conditions. He found that his course tallied precisely with the earlier checks he had made. He was dead on course - and on time.

But he was meeting a fairly strong head-wind, which rose with the coming of daylight. He decided to go down to a lower altitude to avoid the full force of the wind. He turned down the nose of the Catalina and descended from the bright stars to about 6,000 feet. The descent took him below a belt of cloud.

As he went through the cloud and caught the steely light of the Atlantic dawn on the broad waters he felt a strange thrill. This day would see him arrive at an English base with the first Catalina aircraft to cross the Atlantic. Great things were expected of the Catalinas when they came into operation. Coastal Command would employ them in their U-boat hunting. And AH553 would be the first of the many that would wreak destruction and retribution among the U-boat packs congregating along the Atlantic sea-lanes.

Any man would have felt some justifiable pride in meeting that dawn as Gautrey met it. But all such personal retrospection was brushed from his mind by a large stain on the sea. He saw the wide patch of oil as his glance swept over the surface of the ocean.

'Look!' he called to his companions on the flight.

They looked.

'A ship's gone down,' one said.

For a moment or two they were all silent, reading this clue to another sea tragedy. A U-boat had struck; and an Allied merchantman had gone down right below where they were flying.

And they were a thousand miles from the nearest land.

Gautrey, staring at the oil stain, fancied he saw it sparkle in the semi-darkness of the dawn. Then he was over it and flying on. He glanced back and caught the sparkle again. The next instant he was turning off course.

What that sparkle was had suddenly come to him. It was a flash-lamp signalling. Somewhere down there in the oil-covered water was a boat with survivors. As he went lower the number of flashes increased and to his amazement, in the brightening daylight, he was at last able to make out no less than nine boatloads of people. One of the boats was towing a raft. He swooped low and saw Lascars in blue dungarees standing up and waving at the flying-boat. Gautrey told one of the Catalina's crew to signal a message to the boats, asking for the name of their ship. In reply one of the flash-lamps below began slowly Morse-coding the name of the torpedoed ship, letter by letter. But Gautrey had his own job to attend to and time was precious. While 'he waited for the name of the vessel to be completed he got his radio operator to send out a message to base giving the exact location of the boats.

Then he swooped again and His men waved farewell to the people standing in the boats waving back and flashing their lamps. 'The occupants of the boats seemed to be in good condition,' Gautrey reported, when he arrived in Britain. 'I do not think the vessel, could have been sunk more than six hours earlier, probably in the middle of the night. All the boats appeared to be full and were close together.'

Thus the first Catalina to fly the Atlantic and join the forces of the free peoples of the world made history, for on the day following his safe arrival with his flying-boat and crew Gautrey learned that his radio messages had been duly picked up and promptly acted upon; all the survivors of the torpedoed ship had been found and taken aboard a destroyer which had dashed at full speed to the rescue.

Six weeks after the story of Gautrey's flight was released another RAF officer who had been posted to duties with Ferry Command broadcast his story of how he had navigated the first of the American Liberators across the Big Pond.

'We took off,' he said, 'from our Canadian base and flew a steady thousand miles or so to Newfoundland. Everything in the aircraft behaved perfectly - just as we expected; and we landed safely. I stood at a window gazing eastwards across the snowy waste which was the aerodrome; looking over the long, wide-paved runways, kept clear of snow by snow-ploughs, which were constantly going to and fro in a plume of powdery cloud and over the hangars, over the snowdrifts and trees' to the eastern sky, where I knew lay England and home.'

He had been away from England for ten months, training under the Empire Air Training Scheme. During those ten months the blitz had changed much of the landscape of the English cities. He felt a sudden desire to be back with his kith and kin in the middle of the struggle and was glad when finally it was time to take off.

'With good wishes from all the muffled figures standing around in the zero weather,' he went on, 'we climbed in and took off into the darkness on our 2,350-mile trip. Up we climbed through the lower layer of threatening cloud into the clear sky above. Up, up, still higher, to get into the region of favourable winds and favourable weather and also to ensure that we should be able to see as much as possible the stars by which we were going to navigate.

'The flight engineer sat on my right, adjusting the throttle and mixture controls to agree with the instructions given him by the captain, who was carefully studying his cruising card. Then the captain adjusted his controls, trimmed the aircraft and switched on his automatic pilot, which we in the RAF jokingly called George, but which our American pilot called Iron Mike. On we flew, engines running sweetly and it seemed as if - we could go on forever.'

To the German High Command, a couple of years later, those last words must have sounded something of a prophecy. The pilots and crews flying the big bombers and flying-boats made the one-way crossing as much an everyday occurrence as driving a car along a city street.

The navigator directing the course of this first member of the Liberator squadrons continued: 'I was constantly kept busy checking our ground-speed and positions by astronomical observations. In spite of the fact that we were very high and the outside temperature was minus thirty-four degrees I did not feel at all uncomfortable. Of course, we were all wearing oxygen masks, but these were of a pattern which did not hamper our movements in any way. My mathematics came as easily as they would at ground-level. It was beautifully warm in the aircraft and there were moments when I felt I would like to have taken my tunic off; I was not wearing any special flying clothes except my flying-boots and I only wore them because one's feet are apt to get cold sitting still for a long time. The cabin heating was really fine and I only felt the intense cold when I occasionally opened the astro-hatch to take a shot with my sextant. And so we proceeded on, going through the night ever eastwards towards England.'

Those are personal impressions by a man coming back to England for the first time after a long absence and flying the first of a welcome new fleet of sky giants which were to reinforce the hard-pressed RAF in the great air battle centred on the British coast-line. He is enthusiastic because he is a man making a discovery. He is seeing for himself what tools America was about to put into the hard, capable hands of the RAF. But he had something to add about the men flying with him in the Liberator.

'Our captain,' he went on later, 'was with British Imperial Airways and has had years of experience flying aircraft of all types. The co-pilot, or first officer, as he is called, was an American, who has flown for years and who has now volunteered to ferry these American aircraft to Britain. Our radio officer, also of Imperial Airways, sat in a little cabin aft, surrounded by his radio equipment, which is of the very latest type that America can supply and which is for use in the Royal Air Force. And the flight engineer was an RAF sergeant fitter-air-gunner, who has been specially trained for this work.'

America, seemingly, was giving of her best and it must be borne in mind that this broadcast was made six months before Pearl Harbour brought the full responsibility of active participation in the war as a fighting ally to rest on the shoulders of the American nation.

The navigator concluded: 'Seven hours passed, the engines still purring sweetly, our course still eastwards. The stars faded out and the sun, like a ball of fire, was just lighting the eastern sky when the radio officer made contact with English stations. I again checked our position and estimated our time and place of landfall; and after seven hours thirty minutes in the air we were off the Irish coast, which I think proves the high standard of these aircraft now being supplied to us in ever-increasing numbers from our friends in America.'

That broadcast was made on 18 June 1941. Four months later to the day, on 18 October, a Ferry Command pilot said over the radio to a British listening audience: 'There is nothing very much in flying the Atlantic nowadays and RAF pilots regard Atlantic ferrying as a rest from operational flying. And so it is, for it comes as an interesting relief from routine bombing raids.'

Lindbergh and those others who made headlines by conquering the Atlantic skies had faded very far into a flying era that was becoming as remote to the modern ocean fliers as the day when Bleriot spanned the English Channel. As the number of pilots and navigators drafted to Ferry Command multiplied, so the actual crossing of the Atlantic from west to east became more of a routine job.

As one ferry pilot put it: 'The crossing takes very little time, considerably less than many routine patrols by Coastal Command and many raids over Germany and on the ferry trip you have the great advantage of being able to plan the whole affair on the lines of a civil airline passenger flight.'

The same pilot has provided an intimate picture of such a crossing.

'From Canada you fly to Newfoundland,' he explains almost nonchalantly. 'Just a hop. You get a surprise when you arrive there. A boom town has sprung up in a matter of months, where there was previously nothing but bare rock. This is where the real business starts. Pilot and navigator check up with the weather experts. These are the men who have killed the bogy of Atlantic flying. They will tell you with certainty the sort of weather you will meet right the way across. Any sudden change will be wirelessed to you. It is left to the captain of the aircraft to decide whether and when, he will take off. He's the boss.

'We check up and examine very carefully our aircraft, which is under an armed guard. You can't even approach it without a pass. Meantime the wireless operator goes to see the chief steward, to select a menu for the trip. We carry half a dozen thermos bottles and there is a wide choice of food and drink. There's soup, cocoa, coffee, pineapple juice, tomato juice and sandwiches in infinite variety. The food's grand. Then, after one last word with the weather folk, we're ready to take off. There remains a final duty for the captain to perform. He has to search the aircraft for stowaways. Then we're off. The trip lasts round ·about ten hours or so, though some pilots have done it in much less. More often than not you don't see the sea all the way across. It's freezing, of course, but you fly so high that there is no moisture in the air to ice-up wings and air-screws.

'We take a good look at the coast of Newfoundland as we say good-bye. Then as we climb up through the cloud the navigator gets busy. He waits for it to get dark, for he wants to get an astro fix, to check our position by the stars and it's extraordinary how long it takes to get dark after the sun has disappeared behind us. Then we plug in the automatic pilot and settle down for the night. The navigator is the only one with much to do - the rest of us read or talk. At last we see the dawn break. That's a grand sight. On my first trip it had just got light when I saw a great red blaze through the cloud. I thought it was a ship on fire, but it was just the sun coming up through the cloud.'

He concludes succinctly: 'Then eventually we put down on this side. It's satisfying to descend through a hole in the cloud and find yourself in exactly the right spot at the right time. It's a grand feeling. That's about all there is to it. I can tell you of no incidents I've experienced on the way over and neither can my fellow-pilots.'

Food and flight are both grand.

The same might be said of the pilots and crews and of the records they achieved. For the pilots of Ferry Command soon found a way of livening up the routine journeys. They began lopping minutes off each other's flying time.

A Boeing Flying Fortress piloted by Coastal Command's Squadron Leader Bulloch, the ace U-boat hunter, made the crossing in eight hours forty-five minutes. That was the first Fortress flown by Ferry Command. This time was equalled by a Liberator pilot. For a period both pilots held the record and shared it.

Then a former Imperial Airways and British Overseas Airways pilot, Captain O. P. Jones, rocketed a Liberator across in eight hours twenty-three minutes. He arrived in Britain on 1 December 1941. The time of crossing was taken to be the interval from take-off to touch-down.

By July 1942, seven months later, crossing the Atlantic had become monotonous for one famous Ferry Command crew, headed by Captain F. A. Dugan, of New Orleans. Dugan and his crew were employed normally in flying the west-to-east bombers, but in one week they were asked to supplement the Montreal-to-Britain return ferry service, which transports Government-sponsored passengers and urgently needed war material, carrying back ferry crews to collect still more bombers. In the one period of nine days Dugan and his men made the Atlantic crossing five times in the same aircraft, a Liberator, carrying on each journey a maximum all-up load. This record was completed without incident.

At the end of that period the crew had seventy-two hours' rest, while their Liberator was given a routine overhaul. Then they flew back to Montreal - their sixth crossing in less than two weeks.

Dugan and two of his crew had been in the service for nearly two years, since September 1940. They held the amazing ferry record of more than five hundred hours of trans-ocean flying in ninety days. In that period of special flights they flew the Atlantic, the Pacific and eight journeys to and from Australia.

On the 21st of that same month, July, the Air Officer Commanding-in-Chief, RAF Ferry Command, Air Chief Marshal Sir Frederick Bowhill GBE KCB received a telegram of congratulations from the Chief of the Air Staff, Air Chief Marshal Sir Charles Portal KCB. Sir Charles said: 'I send you all congratulations and best wishes on the first birthday of Ferry Command. You are playing a most important part in building up the strength of the RAF and we are full of admiration for your magnificent record. May your second year be as successful as your first.'

It was a Ferry Command pilot, Captain W. J. Vanderkloot, who flew Mr. Churchill home in August 1942 after his historic journey to meet Premier Stalin.

'Having flown from Africa to Montreal,' Captain Vanderkloot related subsequently, 'we were given ten hours off duty and then we were ordered to return to England to fly Mr. Churchill to Russia. We brought back to this country Lord and Lady Halifax.

'During the whole of the fourteen or fifteen thousand miles Mr. Churchill has flown with us he was certainly swell. I calculate that he has spent two-thirds of the whole time in the cockpit. He is obviously very interested in everything connected with flying and with either the second pilot or myself with one stick he often took over the other.'

Captain Vanderkloot, a Californian, had 5,000 hours in his log-book when he piloted the British Prime Minister to the Soviet Union.

Ferry Command has its moments of celebration. Such a moment arrived on 30 September 1942, at a Ferry Command terminal base in England. An aircraft from the United States was signalled in and landed. It drew up and out stepped Lieutenant-Colonel Elliot Roosevelt, son of the President of the United States, Ten seconds later a Liberator got the signal to come in. It touched down after making a 3,000-mile flight from Montreal. From it alighted the Right Honourable Clement Attlee, the Deputy Prime Minister and Mr. Malcolm MacDonald, the British High Commissioner in Canada. Twenty seconds after their arrival a third aircraft landed, to deposit Air Chief Marshal Sir Frederick Bowhill, Ferry Command's chief. As he walked across the tarmac another aircraft from Montreal got the all-clear signal to drop its undercarriage and touch-down. The passengers alighting from this plane included a special Canadian Government mission made up of the Honourable C. D. Howe, Minister of Munitions and Supply, Colonel the Honourable J. L. Ralston, Minister of Defence, Mr. Ralph Bell, Director-General of Aircraft Production and Mr. Desmond A. Clark, Director-General of Shipbuilding.

As though a magician's wand had been waved, these men met from the distant corners of the earth on the aerodrome's apron, to chat together, drink a glass of sherry and bite a welcome sandwich and then disperse. Sir Frederick Bowhill stepped into a Liberator and went on to Montreal and Lieutenant-Colonel Roosevelt left to join the American Army Air Corps in Britain.

Of course, every crossing is not of the magician's wand kind, unless one includes very unfriendly magicians. In December 1942 the North Atlantic weather turned very bad for the ferry pilots. So bad that one Catalina flying-boat took twenty-three hours and 58 minutes on the journey across - two minutes under twenty-four hours. That month one Ferry Command skipper with 37 crossings in his log-book described the journey from farther south, in Bermuda, as the worst he had ever experienced. His flying-boat was at times scudding along on its back, blown like a feather before the force of the storm.

But the Ferry Command aircraft came through. Schedules as well as masses of equipment went overboard, but the much-needed flying-boats finally made it.

Here is how one of the Catalinas that month beat the worst storms on record.

'About fifteen hundred miles out we really hit it,' the wireless operator reported. 'Something struck the kite then and for the next minute or so what happened was almost unbelievable. The skipper says we went up five hundred feet and down six hundred as nearly simultaneously as mattered. In any event, everything that was loose in the aircraft began flying around the fuselage. We began ducking our personal luggage, spare parts and everything else. We were all spattered with oil that came splashing out of every place it could splash from.'

The civilian wireless operator took up the story at that stage.

'And that wasn't all,' he added. 'I was sitting at the wireless set and suddenly blue flames started shooting out from it. I don't know whether it was static electricity or whether we were hit by lightning that our radio aerial diverted through the wireless. The same blue lights were just dancing along the top of our wing.'

The captain decided to climb above a storm he could not outpace. The crew had no oxygen equipment, but he risked climbing up to 19,000 feet and stayed at that altitude for the best part of an hour. Referring to this, the wireless operator said: 'The skipper told us all to sit down and not move around anymore than was absolutely necessary. But sometimes we had to get around. Even walking the few feet to the rear of the fuselage was a physical effort. You'd come back absolutely tired out. We sat there and watched our finger-nails slowly turning blue from lack of oxygen.'

The Catalina, not unnaturally, got badly off course, so that when land was sighted it was neutral Eire. If they touched down in Eire the RAF members and the aircraft would be interned. So, with storms still raging, they turned out to sea again, despite the fact that they were all physically exhausted and waited for dawn to make a careful landfall.

In one day, in that weather, the RAF put down four Catalinas at British bases. Whatever job they tackle, the RAF crews seem to be unstoppable. They get through; produce the necessary results - somehow.

The following April was another bad month. Icing conditions were really bad. The Ferry Command captains took their aircraft well above the 20,000-feet line to make the journey, necessitating the use of oxygen for continuous spells of seventeen and eighteen hours by the crews. For long, unbroken periods those April 1943 flights were made at times through a cold that reached an average temperature of sixty-three degrees of frost, Eighty and even ninety degrees of frost were common on some trips.

From November 1942 until that April the continuous flow of Ferry Command supplies of bombers and flying-boats went on uninterrupted in any serious way, in weather conditions not generally equalled in severity for forty-seven years.

But the fact remains that the aircraft continued to set out - and arrive.

And in May, when the weather improved, Ferry Command pilots began setting up fresh records. Record-breaking is an established pastime with Ferry Command skippers. As one laughingly told a reporter, 'No one gets hurt when we break another - except Jerry.'

Chapter 5

Queen of the Boats

*The squadron leader of a Sunderland flying-boat who was used to flying over the
ocean for fourteen hours on end remarked nonchalantly to the pilot of a Hudson:
'You don't need navigation on Hudsons - you are never out of sight of land for more
than six hours!'*

***So Few; The Immortal Record of the RAF* by David Masters**

One hundred and sixty-three tired and hungry men in dark blue uniforms
peered through the windows of a French train and stared glumly at an
approaching town half-hidden in rain. It was Christmas Eve, but real
Christmas cheer seemed far away and the war in Europe seemed very close
indeed. The year was 1939 and the Germans were on the frontiers of France.
The rain-wet town was Cherbourg and the men in blue were members of
Australia's first of eighteen Australian squadrons to serve in the European war.
It was in July 1939, about the time Germany was preparing to sign a non-
aggression pact with Moscow that British people first began to notice the
unique Royal blue of the RAAF uniform. In that month a group of seven RAAF
officers and fourteen airmen reached England to ferry back to Australia nine
Short Sunderland flying boats, bought by the Australian Government to assist
in the defence of the Commonwealth against the looming threat of war. But
within weeks of their arrival, while the Australians were still learning to fly
the thirty-ton flying boats, which the Germans called Fliegende Stachelschwein
(Flying Porcupines), war was declared and they stayed to form the nucleus of
10 Squadron RAAF.

The Australians who spent that gloomy Christmas in Cherbourg in 1939
had left Australia in November to put 10 Squadron into the fighting line. It
was the month Hitler escaped the bomb that wrecked the Munich Beer Hall,
when the first German magnetic mine appeared and when the first German
bomb fell on English soil. On the long sea journey to Marseilles (whence they
went by train to Cherbourg) the Australians had a temporary taste of U-boat
lookout, the task which, from the air, was later to occupy much of their time
in the flying boats of 10 Squadron. But they saw no tell-tale swirl of water
round a rising conning tower and on board the ship - the liner *Orontes* - the
only incident remembered vividly was the burial at sea of an English admiral,
who died on his way home to England. The RAAF men gave him his final
guard of honour. During the voyage of these pioneers, an event of great
significance in the annals of war in the air had taken place at Ottawa. There,

on 17 December, representatives of the British Commonwealth of Nations signed the Joint Air Training Plan agreement - the great plan which, through the war years, provided an enormous reservoir of Dominion flying men which the enemy could never hope to empty. Out of this pool, following in the footsteps of the first group of Australians who reviled their luck that day in Cherbourg, came many thousands of other Australians - despite the Japanese threat in the Pacific and with them men from other parts of the Empire, to play their varied parts on a stage where the United Nations rang down the last curtain in 1945. [82]

On dark December nights leading up to Christmas 1939 British families huddled around the wireless in the 'best room' and listened to the depressing war news on the BBC Home Service. The conflict was not going well for Britain but stirring tales of the RAF in action against the enemy boosted morale. On Boxing Day a Squadron Leader RAFVR regaled his audience with a story called *Christmas Day in Coastal Command*. The broadcast was about Sunderlands although the speaker deliberately fails to mention them by name. 'As you can imagine' he began, 'the Royal Air Force in Great Britain has had to be on its toes over Christmas. This has been particularly true of the crews of Coastal Command aircraft. Co-operating with the Royal Navy, they are responsible for the safety of shipping on the seas of Western Europe. For them, there could be no holiday... Enemy submarines for ever on the prowl... the possibility of German warships breaking out from their bases... watch to be kept on the great convoys of merchant vessels on their way to Britain... the traffic lanes to be searched for mines.

'Since the war began, the aircraft of the Coastal Command have flown fully four million miles, on watch and guard over the North Sea and the Atlantic. In other words, in four months, the crews of this Command have covered a distance equal to more than 165 journeys round the Equator. A substantial part of this immense air mileage has been contributed by the Royal Air Force flying boats, many of which are flying boats of the type used on the Empire routes for the carriage of passengers and mails. In outward appearance these Royal Air Force and Empire flying boats are identical. But the interior furnishings are very different. In one, as you know, there are armchair seats, tasteful dining-rooms and comfortable sleeping quarters. But the inside of an RAF flying boat is an arsenal, with batteries of guns on both decks and a ton of bombs slung from a kind of overhead railway on the roof, ready to be run out for easy dropping from the wings. I spent Christmas Day in one of these flying boats on an anti-submarine and convoy protection patrol of upwards of 1,500 miles over the Atlantic. The crews of the aircraft were aboard, as usual, before dawn and took off in the darkness so that advantage might be taken of every minute of daylight at sea.

'Before we boarded the flying boat, pilots and navigators received their instructions for their Christmas Day's work in a small hut which is the Operations Room of the Squadron. Orders were read to them in front of a big map of the Atlantic seaboard on which seven white graveyard crosses are pinned. Each cross marks the spot where a German submarine has been destroyed by a flying boat of this single squadron.

'Just before we left to embark, an orderly from the wireless station brought in a sheaf of messages. They were Christmas greetings from the pilots, crews and passengers on Empire flying boats which are still maintaining, just as in peacetime, their twice weekly, two-way services between Britain and Australia, Central Africa and South Africa. These messages of goodwill to the Royal Air Force flying boats had been sent from their sister flying boats while they were in the air over the Dutch East Indies, Singapore, Malay, Thailand, Burma, India, the Sudan, Egypt, Kenya and Uganda. Reading them in that tiny hut on the English shore of the Atlantic on Christmas morning, one could not help feeling some pride in the fact that the British Empire's Command of its civil flying routes is still completely unchallenged. There was another Christmas Day message. It came from the Australian crews of flying boats now working with the Royal Air Force from a station further north on the west coast of Britain.

'By dawn, which came in saffron splendour, we were having breakfast nearly 200 miles at sea. A FULL breakfast - grapefruit, bacon, sausages, eggs, coffee and toast, served piping hot from the galley next door. The cook reported to the young captain of the flying boat, a youth of twenty-two, that he wasn't satisfied with the behaviour of the ice-box in the galley. Why he should be worrying about an ice-box 2,000 feet over the Atlantic on a freezing Christmas morning, neither the pilot nor I could understand.

'Back in the control cabin which, like the gun turrets, was decorated with holly and mistletoe, we saw the answer to Germany's propaganda claim that the Nazi sea and air fleets are blockading Britain. In the first flush of day, scores of heavy-laden merchant ships from Australia, New Zealand, Africa and South America were riding the seas triumphantly to Britain. Every mile or two for the rest of the day we came on more ships going on their business, unaccompanied and unafraid. But our special job for Christmas Day was to find and protect a convoy which had been assembled at a rendezvous from all parts of the world and which an escort of French warships was bringing along. We knew that the convoy was about twenty hours late and that it had gone far off the course set for it because of bad weather and threatened submarine attack. We could only guess the course it was taking. The ships themselves couldn't help us to locate them. They had, of course, to keep wireless silence so that their position might not be betrayed to lurking U-boats.

'Our flying boat combed the sea for 550 miles. Then we found the convoy. Rather, it nearly found us! Cloud had become so dense and low that often we could see only the nose of the flying boat and the wing-tip floats. I heard the pilot beside me whistle sharply. 'Blimey!' he said as he lifted the boat suddenly from the height of sixty feet at which we had been flying. In the nick of time he had avoided the masthead of a ship which had appeared beneath the wing. As he climbed to starboard, we saw another mast ... then another ... then mast after mast. His anxious look gave way to a happy smile. He took his hand from the joystick and cocked his thumb. He was over the lost convoy. Through the thick mist we could see the columns of ships flashing Christmas greetings to us with their lamps. The bank of low cloud which blanketed the sea was now more than 200 miles square. We flew through it for a couple of hours and then located the British destroyers which were waiting to take over from the French warships. By lamp signals we gave them the position and course of the convoy.

'Our Christmas Day job was now half done.

'We had to fly back to the convoy and for the remaining five hours of daylight, sweep the sea ahead of it for enemy submarines. As quickly as it had fallen, the thick belt of mist vanished. Wintry sunshine filtered into the flying boat as the crew sat down, two at a time, to a quick Christmas dinner of soup, goose and plum-pudding. Until dusk we cruised for 500 miles in the path which the convoy would take to England. There were no submarines about. At least, if there were, they kept their heads down for fear of our bombs. And a U-boat submerged at sea is as useless as it would be in its base in Germany. Part of the job of the Coastal Command of the Royal Air Force is to destroy them or, failing that, to keep them submerged.

'Twice the look-out men on our flying boat gave the 'action' call to bring the crew to submarine stations. They did so by pressing a button which caused an electric hooter to scream 'DAH-DE-DIH-DI-DOH' throughout the boat. Both times a sea marker was thrown overboard by the lookout men and the pilot made the flying boat stand on its wing-tip so that the sea was like a wall in front of us, with the horizon over our heads. The pilot's fingers caressed the bomb switches. But no bombs fell. As he swept round the column of smoke rising from the sea-markers, he decided that the ripples of water among the 'white-horses' which the look-out men had seen were not the footprints of a submarine periscope, but only the foam on the trail of drifting wreckage.

'We had left the English coast in the morning black-out against air raids. Twelve hours later we came back to it -again in complete darkness, just in time for a second and more leisurely, Christmas dinner.

'Today, Boxing Day, the flying boat is out again over the Atlantic, guarding the great convoy of merchant ships on another day's safe march to England. Its crew and the crews of the other flying boats of the Squadron have asked me to offer you their good wishes.'

One of the first operational Sunderland sorties was flown on 3 September 1939; the day Britain declared war on Germany, when South African Flight Lieutenant A. S. Ainslie on 210 Squadron took off from Pembroke Dock in L2165 at 0500 on a convoy patrol sweeping ahead of seven destroyers that were patrolling the route to Milford Haven. His second pilot was Pilot Officer Ernest Reginald Baker, who before the war he was the second pilot of a Sunderland flying-boat. 'My skipper, who taught me all I know about flying-boats, would win the DFC. He was the grandest chap I've ever known - we used to call him Angel.' On patrol on 3 September they alighted at 4 o'clock in the afternoon they had no idea that war had been declared, nor had they a gun or a bomb on board.

In his book *So Few: The Immortal Record of the RAF*, published in 1941, David Masters described Baker as 'the luckiest man in the RAF' and few in the Royal Air Force or Royal Navy would disagree. 'Information concerning him, however, was so meagre that one morning I trudged through the deep snow of a distant city to travel all day in search of someone who knew him. Around that city dozens of motor cars lay abandoned in the drifts, but the train gradually carried me into a belt of country that was quite balmy and spring-like, with no snow to be seen. It was an astonishing transformation. For hours I journeyed slowly through sunny valleys over which the touch of spring already seemed to hover. It was lovely country with beauty everywhere, far removed from war. The shoulders of the mountains piling up around were covered with snow. Now and again the sun was reflected by fairy-like waterfalls which had solidified into icicles and by evening I arrived at my destination.

'Never in my life have I seen anything more beautiful than the scene which greeted me next morning. The snow on the peaks around was turned to a rosy pink by the sun, their bases were purple and blue, lovely clouds made a pattern in the sky and in the foreground were sparkling blue waters with ships falling picturesquely into place and Sunderland flying-boats at their moorings, while the buildings of the town were grouped so artistically round the waters that it was difficult to believe that this enchanted place was in the British Isles. Gazing on the scene to take in its full beauty before the changing light banished the exquisite tones, I went on to pay a call to try to find out something about the luckiest man in the Royal Air Force. He is at least 6 feet 2 inches tall, with a spare figure, very blue eyes, a small fair moustache to set off a well-cut mouth and firm chin and a natural wave in his fairish hair. Very modest, quiet of speech, with a sense of humour, Flight Lieutenant Ernest Reginald Baker DFC has wrought more havoc among the German U-boat fleet than any other man in the fighting services. He is the captain of a Sunderland flying-boat which he regards with as much affection and pride, as any owner of a shapely yacht. His flying-boat, which he christened *Queen of the Air,* has her name painted over the doorway leading into the hull and over the name are painted four white stars. Those stars are signs of high honour, for each represents a submarine which has been sunk by Flight Lieutenant Baker and his crew of the *Queen of the Air.* Happily the same boat and crew have taken part in all four triumphs.

'It is not easy for anyone outside the navy or the air force to realize the magnitude of this accomplishment. There are captains of flying-boats who have patrolled since the beginning of the war for thousands of miles, far out into the Atlantic, right up into the Arctic circle, off the Scandinavian and European coasts without catching so much as a glimpse of an enemy submarine. For twelve and fourteen hours at a stretch they have flown over the sea, searching and seeing nothing. Other pilots of the Coastal Command have also carried out many patrols in their Hudsons and Ansons and Blenheims without seeing a U-boat.'

The 210 Squadron detachment in the Shetlands flew four sorties on 4 September. Five days' later Flight Lieutenant Ainslie and Pilot Officer Baker in L2165 on 210 Squadron took off from Pembroke Dock on an ASP (Anti-Submarine Patrol) for a convoy and on this first war patrol observed the *Empress of Australia* on an evasive zigzag course. They were lucky enough to sight a U-boat on that initial trip. They at once attacked with bombs, but to their chagrin the submarine escaped. Shortly after leaving the convoy at 1310, the crew attacked a U-boat that had just crash-dived and saw a 25-yard patch of oil on the surface after the attack, but no other proof of a kill. 210 Squadron recorded four further attacks in September but all without definite result. During Ainslie's and Baker's second patrol on 14 September, they again sighted a submarine and let loose their load of bombs, but once more the enemy eluded them. On 16 September they went out for their third patrol and sighted their third submarine which was promptly bombed without avail. Three submarines sighted on three trips and not one attack successful - there is no need to touch on their feelings! [83] Hopefully they took the air again on 19 September and generous Dame Fortune gave them another chance to sink an enemy submarine, but although their bombs crashed down without delay, the U-boat got away. Thus on four successive patrols Ainslie and Baker had the unusual luck to sight four submarines and the misfortune to lose them all. The following months increased the experience of Flight Lieutenant Baker. On those long patrols which took him hundreds of miles out into the Atlantic to watch over the convoys of ships that were conveying essentials to Great Britain, his knowledge of the tricks of the weather and the sea grew with every hour that was added to his flying time. Baker then tasted the joy of being promoted to command a fine new flying-boat which to him and her crew was the *Queen of the Air* and he suffered the loss of his friend Ainslie, who was shot down by a U-boat.

On 6 September 204 Squadron had flown its first war operation when Flight Lieutenant Harrison piloted L5799 on a convoy patrol over St George's Channel in co-operation with six destroyers. The sortie was uneventful until the flying boat returned to base, when it was fired on by a shore battery. Two days' later Flight Lieutenant Hyde was on patrol in N9021 and during this sortie the crew made attacks on two U-boats, dropping four bombs on each occasion, but with no observed result. The following day Harrison bombed a 'submarine feather', an oily patch being subsequently observed near the explosion. [84] A little later, Flying Officer Phillips in N9046 attacked a submerged U-boat: The aircraft then called on three Polish destroyers to check out the area and these warships made depth charge attacks. Although there was no solid confirmation of a success, C-in-C Plymouth assessed the attacks as having been effective.

For 228 Squadron the outbreak of war saw five aircraft based at Alexandria and three at Malta. The squadron had spent a year in the Mediterranean and was ordered back to the UK, four more aircraft moving to Malta on 9 September. The following day four Sunderlands flew back to Pembroke Dock via Marignane, although one aircraft had both floats torn off when Squadron Leader Menzies had to land downwind in poor visibility. During the salvage operation the aircraft turned turtle and was eventually beached in that position. 12 September brought the unit's first war sortie, Flight Lieutenant Smith taking N9025 and Pilot Officer McKinley L5807 on an anti-submarine patrol to the west of Ireland. Flight Lieutenant Skey made 228's first U-boat sighting on 15 September, but the first attack was carried out on the 24th by Flight Lieutenant E. J. Brooks. On 16 September a new Admiralty policy decreed that aircraft be given patrol areas up to 200 miles out into the Atlantic, listening out on the merchant vessel distress frequency, the idea being to allow them greater freedom during their 10-hour patrol to adopt their own methods of finding and destroying U-boats. The first such operation was flown the following day by 204 Squadron, although the crew had nothing to report. On 18 September Flight Lieutenant Harrison piloting L6799 attacked a diving U-boat and in two attacks dropped two salvoes, each of four bombs dropped in the line of the submarine wake. A black object was observed on the surface shortly after the explosion of the second salvo, projecting momentarily from the water close to the position of the explosion. No oilier evidence of destruction was available, but the C-in-C Plymouth subsequently informed operations room Mount Batten that the submarine was considered sunk. After watching the position for 15 minutes, the aircraft returned to base. It was later revealed that this and the others already mentioned were not destroyed.

U-boats were not the only danger to Allied shipping and aircrews in the vast expanse of the Atlantic. Four days before the opening of April 1940 a very determined duel had been fought between a Sunderland and the enemy's four-engined convoy hunter, the Focke-Wulf 200 or 'Kondor' engaged in bombing a British merchantman. The enemy was first observed five miles away on the starboard quarter flying out of the sun and succeeded in delivering its first attack on the ship before the Sunderland, which, being a flying boat, was considerably slower than the Focke-Wulf, could come up. Two bombs hit the ship and the 'Kondor' then went in to make a second attack while the Sunderland was preparing to engage a Ju 88 which had arrived on the scene. This second German aircraft joined the 'Kondor' and both attacked the ship, but missed. The Sunderland was now within 800 yards of the Ju 88, which at once sheered off to port and was not seen again. The 'Kondor' however, showed more fight and closed head-on in a shallow dive, opening fire with cannon, The Sunderland replied with its front guns and then with its side guns. The result was uncertain, but the 'Kondor' disappeared into the cloud, which was now down to sea-level and was not seen again.

The Sunderlands on 10 Squadron had been on operations since 1 February 1940 and had already sunk their first U-boat. They played their part in the Battle of France by providing air cover for the feverish removal of Allied and other merchant ships from such ports as St. Nazaire, Bordeaux and Brest. Ships of all nations were moving out from these ports, some towed by others, in a long, slow procession. These protective patrols had to be done by the Sunderlands in daylight because their base at Mount Batten was so jammed with ships that night fighting on the squadron's basin was impossible. One of 10 Squadron's Sunderlands struck trouble during the unit's first reconnaissance of Bordeaux and St. Nazaire, made without escort on 12 July 1940 after the fall of France. Seeking pictures of 'invasion-of-England' barge concentrations and shipping at Bordeaux, the Sunderland was hit by AA fire, but little damage was done. The Australians' activities had apparently been annoying the enemy, for three days later, at 1.30 pm on 15 July a Junkers 88 made an attack on the flying boat station at Mount Batten. As the enemy aircraft came in from the south-west two Spitfires were seen flying beneath it, but they apparently did not notice it. The Junkers turned into the clouds until the Spitfires were out of the way and then dropped four bombs on the station. One bomb failed to explode and the others did no important damage. There were no casualties.

Warrant Officer E. I. 'Lucky' Long and a party of volunteers courageously removed the unexploded bomb from the fifteen-foot hole which it had made in the ground. The work took twelve hours with the party always in danger of the bombs exploding. Long was later officially congratulated. It was the first of many air raids on the station, including one of the heaviest made on any English port.

On Sunday 21 July Sunderland N9028 on 204 Squadron at Sullom Voe captained by Wing Commander Davis OBE DFC set out for a long range reconnaissance patrol to Trondheim, Norway. When he reached the Norwegian coast the Sunderland was intercepted and shot down by a Bf 109 flown by Oberleutnant Lorenz Weber of 8./JG77. Eight days' later, Sunderland P9602 on 10 Squadron RAAF, en route for Gibraltar, was attacked by a Dornier Do 18 and returned to base. On Wednesday 31 July Sunderland P9601 on 10 Squadron RAAF on convoy patrol engaged Ju 88s attacking the SS Moolthan. Sunderland 'B' on the Australian squadron on patrol over the Western Approaches attacked a crash-diving U-boat but saw no positive results.

Between Dunkirk and the beginning of the Battle or Britain, statesmen were preoccupied with the political tangle arising from the fall of France, particularly with reference to North Africa and it was in this connection that 10 Squadron RAAF received its third Distinguished Flying Cross on 25 June 1940, the day the Battle of France ended. The award was made to Flight Lieutenant J. A. Cohen for his courage and ingenuity in extricating Lord Gort and Mr. Duff Cooper from a difficult situation in Rabat, Morocco. Cohen had taken Lord Gort and Mr. Duff Cooper from Calshot to Rabat. From the moment he brought his Sunderland down in the narrow estuary of the river at Rabat, the port authorities created trouble. The passengers were disembarked without difficulty, but the harbour master ordered the aircraft to move fifty yards downstream to an awkward position. At 9 pm Cohen received a cypher message to warn Lord Gort that his mission might not be successful.

When the Australian called for a shore boat to take his passengers off he was ignored by the authorities, so he set out in the Sunderland's rubber dinghy. He was headed off by a police boat and when he showed signs of forcing his ray ashore a small boat with an armed crew compelled him to return to the Sunderland. But Cohen was made of tougher stuff than to be baulked by this and finally he forced his way ashore, revolver in hand, taking his first pilot with him. He was prevented from talking to the British Consul and the French authorities threatened to commandeer the Sunderland unless its captain returned to it.

Cohen pretended that his first pilot was captain of the Sunderland and sent him back while he himself went on to a hotel and delivered the warning message to Lord Gort. The party discovered then that the police would not allow them to return to the Sunderland and it was not until 3 am after much argument with the authorities that Cohen succeeded in getting Lord Gort and Mr. Duff Cooper into the aircraft. He took off in a rough sea, landed his passengers at Gibraltar and took them back to Calshot on June 27.

10 Squadron RAAF had its first combat with a Focke-Wulf 'Kondor' on the morning of 25 September 1940 when a RAF and a RAAF Sunderland on

convoy patrol sighted one heading for the convoy the flying boats were protecting. The Australian Sunderland, captained by Flight Lieutenant I. S. Podger, a later DFC recipient, raced to intercept it. The FW 200 flew straight along the lines of the convoy about a mile and a half ahead of the Sunderland and dropped a bomb just astern of a motor vessel. Then it turned to port and headed towards the Sunderland at 800 feet, 100 feet above the flying boat. As the two aircraft closed, the Sunderland turned towards the 'Kondor' and the RAAF front gunner opened fire. The Focke Wulf made a climbing turn to port and opened fire from a gun position beneath the fuselage. Podger put the Sunderland into a diving turn and at the same time his rear and mid ship gunners fired short bursts. The Sunderland followed the Focke Wulf when it made for the convoy again and as the German came within range the destroyer's anti-aircraft guns joined in the fray. The RAF Sunderland attacked and the Focke Wulf turned and disappeared towards the south-east. The whole engagement had lasted about fifteen minutes.

The three Australian squadrons in Coastal Command were credited by Admiralty with eleven submarine 'kills,' and a share in the destruction of two others, during the war. The RAAF Sunderlands scored five 'kills' each and each shared in destroying one other U-boat. One other 'kill' was credited to 455 Squadron RAAF, in April 1942, when the squadron was flying Hampdens. Many other submarines were claimed as 'probables'. Squadron Leader C. W. Pearce DFC attacked 10 Squadron's first submarine in the Atlantic on 17 June 1940. An ocean-going U-boat was reported operating 450 miles off Cape Finisterre and Pearce's flying boat set off at 3.30 am in search of it. Five hours later a feather of water revealed the submarine and Pearce dropped two anti-submarine bombs. Then he swooped again and dropped two more bombs immediately astern and two, right above the submarine. Bubbles and thick oil poured upwards for forty-eight minutes, indicating a probable 'kill.' Pearce was awarded the RAAF's first DFC on July 30 that year.

10 Squadron's first confirmed submarine 'kill' - shared with one of the convoy escorts, the new Flower-class corvette HMS *Gladiolus* - came on Monday 1 July 1940 and earned a DFC for Squadron Leader W. N. 'Hoot' Gibson. He had been ordered to carry out an anti-submarine patrol in the Atlantic and was taxiing to take off in the darkness of the early morning when he received a message that the British freighter SS *Zarian* in convoy had been torpedoed. After some hours' flying in the darkness the Sunderland sighted the *Zarian* about three miles away, just as dawn was breaking. The ship had been torpedoed aft and was slightly down by the stern. A British sloop, *Rochester*, stood nearby as the Sunderland circled the *Zarian* and then began its search for the marauder, U-26 commanded by Kapitänleutnant Heinz Scheringer. The U-26 had reached the Western Approaches in late June with serious engine problems. Despite the deficiencies, Scheringer had patrolled aggressively, sinking three freighters as well as damaging the *Zarian*.

The *Gladiolus* pounced on U-26 in favourable sonar conditions as soon as the echo grew slightly larger on the steady, green scan of the tube. Suddenly, Lieutenant Commander H. M. C. Sanders the Skipper shouted:

'Hold that echo. Range and bearing every minute.'

128

'Aye, aye sir' answered the radar operator.

There was a strident clanging of alarm bells. Range and bearing on the echo went to the bridge every minute. The gap between the submarine and the corvette narrowed fast and the little cabin rattled as the engines thrust it along at full speed. Sanders was at the voice pipe again.

'Cease reporting, Radar. We can see it now keep it on your scan as long as you are able.'

'Aye, are sir' answered the radar operator.

Depth charge crews were at the ready; the four-inch-gun's crew were on target and the machine gun crews had their weapons pointing dead ahead. Six depth-charges sailed from the deck of the *Gladiolus* and exploded with a huge hammer-crack to make a semi-circle of death in the boiling sea around the U-boat. The seconds ticked away as Sanders brought the corvette around on the proverbial three-penny-bit. The depth charges exploded with a roar that rattled teeth and huge columns of water spurted skywards. In all, *Gladiolus* dropped thirty-six of her forty-one depth charges set at 350 to 500 feet. The charges badly pounded U-26, causing leaks but not fatal damage. In the early hours of 1 July Scheringer surfaced to charge his depleted batteries and to escape in the fog. Seeing U-26 surface, Rochester commenced a high-speed run to ram. Had the U-26's diesels and motors been working properly and had Scheringer been able to charge batteries, the boat might have escaped. But with Rochester (believed to be a 'destroyer') bearing down firing her forward gun and the Sunderland overhead, he was forced under again.

About thirty miles from the torpedoed vessel Gibson's First Pilot, Flying Officer H. G. Havyatt sighted a disturbance on the water about five miles off. It looked like a round path with a wake leading up to it. Gibson correctly concluded that this was from a U-boat preparing to dive. U-26 crash-dived as the flying boat approached and Gibson's four 250lb bombs fell on the swirl, exploding very close and rocking the U-boat. The bombs did no real damage, but Scheringer had no battery charge left and the boat was still leaking in the stem as a result of the depth-charge attack from *Gladiolus*. Fearing U-26 would be fatally damaged by the approaching 'destroyer,' Scheringer surfaced, intending to scuttle. As Gibson circled, he saw the U-boat's thin steel bows break surface again at a very steep angle, apparently because all its tanks had been blown in a rush to get to the surface after the bombs exploded. It shuddered, rolled and then slowly the conning tower and stern came into view and the submarine settled sluggishly upon the water on an even keel. U-26 was completely surfaced, moving forward slowly under the impetus of her rush to the surface, when Gibson's Sunderland dropped four more depth charges at a low level but by then U-26's chief engineer had set in motion scuttling procedures and the crew was leaping into the water.

Gibson saw the submarine immediately swing round violently to starboard and stopped. The conning tower opened and the crew scrambled out and lined up on the after-deck. The U-boat's gun was on the opposite side of the conning tower and this indicated surrender. The submarine was slowly settling under its crew and when its decks were almost awash, its bow levered up at a sharp angle and it began to settle quickly by the stern. 'I saw that the submarine was settling down, first of all evenly fore and aft' recalled Gibson 'but soon, when the decks were almost awash, she adopted a sharp angle and settled down very quickly by the stern. Now, no submarine would willingly go down by the stern in the normal way of diving. So I knew that this was no trick to fool us. She was definitely sinking. The bow rose right out of the water and she sank. The whole thing only took minutes from the time of the second attack.'

The crew jumped into the water and bunched together there to await rescue. Gibson called on the *Gladiolus,* some miles distant, to complete the 'kill.' After allowing the survivors to swim a while in order to scare them into talking more freely, three-quarters of an hour later, at 7 am, HMS *Rochester* fished all forty-eight men from the water. There were no casualties, but the scare tactic did not work. The U-26 crew was one of the most reticent to be captured, British intelligence reported. The Australian Sunderland crew watched from above before turning for base, 400 miles away. [85]

On Sunday 20 October 1940 a Sunderland set out at 1700 hours from a Scottish base on a special mission. Two hours later a magnetic storm of the first magnitude developed. This put the wireless set partly out of action and gravely affected the compass. After seven and a half hours the Sunderland succeeded in making a signal saying that it was returning to base. It received none of the replies sent in return. Five hours later an SOS followed by a request for bearings was picked up at base and Group Headquarters. By then it was six in the morning but still dark. The Sunderland, its compass unserviceable, was lost and had no fuel left. The captain decided to alight. The gale was now blowing at 80 mph and the navigator judged the waves to be more than twenty feet high. Three flame-floats were dropped, but they did not burn and the direction of the wind was gauged by a parachute flare. The captain brought the flying boat down in the trough between two waves. It was lifted up by one of them, so large and powerful that it took all flying speed away from the boat, which came to a halt with both wing-tip floats intact. The crew were at once prostrated by violent sea-sickness and this endured for many hours. The wireless operators began to send out signals, not knowing if any would be received. One was and they presently picked up a message telling them that a warship would arrive in eight hours.

The Sunderland continued to drift in tumultuous seas at a speed of about 8 mph. How long she would endure the buffeting it was hard to say. The wireless set was dismantled, repaired and reassembled. The signals subsequently made were picked up by the warship, faint at first, but strong after midday. At 1420 the Sunderland signalled: 'Hurry, cracking up.' Fifteen minutes later she was sighted and the look-out on the bridge of the warship read the word 'hurry' flashed by a lamp. At that moment as the crew caught sight of the warship a wave larger than the rest struck the Sunderland head on. She began to break up and the crew - there were thirteen of them - were flung into the water. The captain of the warship manoeuvred her so as to approach the wreckage of the flying boat from the lee quarter. He took the way off his ship as the crew swept past abreast of and almost as high as his bridge. A Naval Commander and twelve ratings with lines secured to them went over the side and pulled on board nine of the crew, who had then been fifty minutes in the sea. The other four were lost. The Sunderland had remained afloat in a full gale for not quite nine hours. The name of the warship was HMAS *Australia.*

In the middle of October 1940 Flight Lieutenant Podger was patrolling in his Sunderland about 200 miles out in the Atlantic when a lifeboat full of men was sighted tossing about in the rough seas. Conditions were far too bad to allow the captain of the Sunderland to alight, so he dropped an emergency parcel of food and a first-aid outfit in a watertight container which floated close by the boat and was soon secured. Then the navigator of the Sunderland fixed the position of the boat while a message was flashed to the shipwrecked men that assistance would be sent to them. After the Sunderland flew away, the sailors trimmed the sail of the lifeboat and made what progress they could towards land. They sighted nothing next day, nor were they seen by the aircraft which sought them. During that night the seas quietened and just before dawn the shipwrecked men, some of whom were very cold and exhausted owing to the fact that they had escaped from the stokehold of the ship only half-clad, heard the sound of aircraft engines. It was the Sunderland of Flight Lieutenant Podger. At once the seamen began to flash a red lamp. A gunner in the Sunderland saw it and reported it to his captain, who was searching for the boat and the aircraft flew over and circled round for a quarter of an hour until it was sufficiently light to see whether conditions were suitable for alighting on the surface. It looked calm enough, but when he came down Flight Lieutenant Podger found there was quite a lumpy swell which made the Sunderland lurch a bit. Keeping two of the engines running, the captain of the Sunderland waited for the lifeboat to overtake him, but the ship-wrecked men, who were about four hundred yards away, were unable to do so.

Bringing the Sunderland round, the captain taxied to within fifty yards and stopped all his engines. 'Lower your mast and come up to the bow!' he ordered, being rather afraid that the mast might damage the wing of the Sunderland as the boat came alongside. Two or three sailors fended off the lifeboat while it rose and fell under the bows of the Sunderland, as their companions scrambled to safety. Some of them began to throw their kit from the lifeboat to the flying-boat. 'Sorry I can't manage your kit. It will make us too heavy to take off,' said Flight Lieutenant Podger and the shipwrecked men were obliged to leave their kit in the boat.

'What about these?' asked the captain of the sunken ship, who had a big cardboard box under his arm.

'Here are my ship's papers!'

'You can take those,' was the reply.

In about half an hour the rescue was effected. Distributing the shipwrecked men throughout the Sunderland to equalize the weight as much as possible, Podger started up the engines. 'It was a tricky take-off because of the confused swell and the additional weight,' he reported. 'We struck rather a bumpy patch in the course of our run which sent several cups scuttling off the galley table and we nipped the tops off two small swells before we were properly airborne. On the way back to base the rigger, who is our cook, gave the survivors as good a breakfast as he could on the food available, which unfortunately was not much for so many. But it was at least hot - cooked on the galley stove.' So twenty-one shipwrecked men were picked up 150 miles from land and flown back to safety.

The Sunderland had a useful galley with a two-ring pressure stove, racks for stowage of crockery and stowage for food. A typical menu for a long maritime patrol sortie might be: Breakfast: Cereal, bacon and sausage, tea, bread and butter. Lunch: Soup, half the quantity of steak carried cubed and stewed, potatoes and vegetables, dried fruit, orange. Tea: Poached or scrambled egg, bread and butter, tea. Supper: Remainder of steak fried, potatoes and vegetables, bread and butter with cheese. The crew's main wartime flying rations were tinned Maconachy's stew, disliked by many. Members of the crew turned out to be very acceptable cooks. One of their 'specials' was soya sausages and corned beef fried in thick batter and tea, coffee or cocoa were regularly available and helped to keep crew active during the long, lonely patrols. Between the four hot meals chocolate and barley sugar were eaten and cocoa, tea or other hot drinks were provided by the cook, so that the crew could eat or drink something every two hours.

On Monday 28 October Sunderland P9620/K on 204 Squadron, Oban, captained by Flight Lieutenant S. R. Gibbs became lost on a convoy patrol when the compass failed in an electrical storm. The aircraft ran out of fuel and landed on the sea 100 miles from St. Kilda. It stayed afloat in a gale for nine hours before breaking up. Nine crew members were rescued by HMS *Australia*, but four were lost and are remembered on the Runnymede Memorial. Next day Sunderland P9622/W on 201 Squadron, Sullom Voe, captained by Pilot Officer Field became lost and flew into a hill 28 miles south-west of Wick while on an Air Sea Rescue search. Field and four others were injured, two escaped injury and four men were killed.

On 3 November 1940 an Australian Sunderland was flown to Alexandria and picked up the then Commander-in-Chief Mediterranean Fleet, Admiral Sir Andrew B. Cunningham GCB DSO and other officers and took them to Cairo. It remained there for a few days and then took Mr. Anthony Eden, then Foreign Secretary and senior officers, to Malta via Crete. After refuelling, the aircraft took Mr. Eden to Gibraltar and from there to Mount Batten. Mr. Eden flew again in Sunderlands several times, although he is a bad 'air traveller.' Perhaps his worst experience of air travel was as a passenger with Sir John Dill, then Chief of the Imperial General Staff, from Plymouth to Gibraltar in November 1940 during the most severe hurricane experienced in the Bay of Biscay for eighty-seven years. The Sunderland crew, captained by Flight Lieutenant H. G. Havyatt RAAF fought through this storm with an ever-present fear that their petrol would not see them through. The weather grew worse and Havyatt said he would send back a message asking for instructions, but Mr. Eden said 'Push on,' and the Sunderland drove on. It landed with ten minutes' petrol left. A few days later 10 Squadron received a, telegram of thanks from Mr. Eden for the work of the crew.

On 21 January 1941 a Sunderland (T9049) on 201 Squadron captained by Squadron Leader Cecil-Wright flew up the Norwegian coast from Trondheim to Narvik. Twenty miles from that town German soldiers were seen on parade. They received a general purpose bomb and the rest of the load was dropped on a barracks, a motor convoy and a large ship in the harbour of Narvik. Immediately afterwards the Sunderland was hit by two bursts of AA fire, the first putting both front and rear turrets out of action, the second damaging the tail-plane. On the way home, as the flying boat was nearing Scotland, the clouds closed right down and the Sunderland ran into raging winds and blinding snow. Finally, Cecil-Wright had to ditch on the sea near an island some miles off the Scottish coast. As it touched down, the heavy seas damaged the port wing tip and float. While the pilot taxied slowly towards land, the available crew members, swept and frozen by spindrift, snow and winds lay out on the starboard wing to balance the boat. It had to be taxied up and down in the lee of a cliff for the whole night, thirty-one vain attempts being made to get the anchor to hold. The Sunderland was towed at dawn to a nearby cove and beached. The finale of this story is that the boat was buoyed with 400 herring barrels until temporary repairs could be made and some weeks later, took off for Felixstowe for refit stripped of all gear and guns. Out of the cloud loomed a Messerschmitt 110 and for the second time within weeks, the Sunderland was in peril. Fortunately, one member of the crew had brought a Tommy-gun and after firing one burst at the 110 through the empty turret, was amazed to find it had sheered off! It is recorded that from this day on this particular Sunderland, formerly known as 'O for Oscar' was always referred to as 'One-gun Oscar'.

'From time to time the trail of the enemy on the wide waters gladdened hearts and sent aircrew leaping to the attack' wrote David Masters. 'Coastal Command by the end of April 1941 were credited with 250 attacks, an average of one in every two days. Many a pilot who patrolled dozens of times without sighting a U-boat must have envied the luck of Flight Lieutenant Baker to whom Dame Fortune has been so lavish in her favours as to bring four enemy submarines under his deadly attack. He himself always points out that the credit for the third submarine is not yet settled. It transpired that a destroyer rushed up and proceeded to drop depth charges after the *Queen of the Air* had pressed home her attacks, so the decision is left open.

'At the beginning of 1941 Flight Lieutenant Baker had already done 1,000 hours of active service flying. It looked as though Dame Fortune, who had given Flight Lieutenant Baker four chances to sink enemy submarines in the first month of the war, viewed him with disfavour. Then early on 16 August 1940 he dropped into the launch at the quay to be rushed out to the Queen of the Air and by 7 o'clock he opened the throttle, taxied over the water and took off to pick up a convoy and go on anti-submarine patrol. It was a dreadful day. The rain poured down and the base of the clouds was within 400 feet of the sea. The Sunderland thrashed through it, but the weather was so bad that her captain once said that he almost decided to go home. He changed his mind, however - which was as well.

'Six hours of flying brought little improvement in the weather, but the activities going on at the primus stoves in the galley reminded the crew, whose appetites were in no way affected by weather or anything else, that lunch was ready, so they settled down to enjoy their meal and a friendly chat. The engines roared rhythmically as the flying-boat cruised over the sea with the captain at the controls. The second pilot kept a keen watch on the seas below, though the bad weather made visibility poor. Suddenly the second pilot let out a shout of 'sub!' and pointed to port. A glance revealed the U-boat to the captain who instantly sounded the warning Klaxon which made the crew drop knives and forks and jump to action stations.'

The submarine was U-51 commanded by 28-year old Korvettenkapitän Dietrich Knorr, which had left Kiel on 9 August on its fourth war cruise and was bound for French ports.

'I put my foot on everything!' was the graphic way the captain on his return explained how he unleashed all his power to get to the submarine before it could escape. 'The U-boat was on the surface when we sighted it and they must have sighted us at the same time, for they started to do a crash dive. By the time the submarine was down, I was diving low over the top of it to attack. The result was terrific. The whole of the surface of the sea seemed to shudder for yards around and then suddenly blew up. In the middle of the boiling sea, the submarine emerged with its decks awash and then sank rather like a brick. I did a steep turn and came over it again just as it was disappearing. The explosion actually blew the submarine right out of the water. There was such an enormous amount of it out of water that my rigger saw daylight under it. I turned and climbed and as the submarine heaved on its side and sank I dropped my bombs right across it. Large air bubbles came rushing up - one was over thirty feet across. Then great gobs of oil began to spread over the surface until a wide area was covered. I waited for about an hour until there was no more air or oil coming up and then I fetched a destroyer from the convoy and signalled what had happened. After carrying out an Asdic sweep and reporting no contact, the destroyer signalled to me: 'Nice work. I hope you get your reward!'

'From the moment the submarine was sighted until was [claimed] destroyed only ninety seconds elapsed. A submarine can crash dive in about forty seconds and unless the first blow is struck at it within about this time, there is a good chance of it escaping, so it will be realized that the captain and crew of a flying-boat must act instantly, without a second's hesitation, if they are to sink the U-boat. Obviously much depends on the distance at which the submarine is sighted and the time that the flying-boat takes to reach the spot. So steeply did the captain bank the *Queen of the Air* to bring her round with the least possible delay that each time he turned, members of the crew were flung about and the observer who tried to take photographs collapsed on the bottom of the boat in a heap. But it was the rear-gunner who came off worst. Sitting in the tail waiting for a chance to have a crack at something, he suddenly thought that somebody was having a crack at him, for the flying-boat was so low when she made her attack that the force of the explosion gave her tail a jolt which bounced him out of his seat hard up against the top of the turret, with the result that his souvenir of the action was a large bump on top of the head. Of course, the other members of the crew laughed - no one was in a mood to do anything else after their triumph.

'But as base was informed and the *Queen of the Air* continued to guard her convoy, memories of the grandest chap he'd ever known crept into the mind of the blue-eye a pilot sitting so quietly at the controls. 'Well, thank God, that's one back for Angel!' was his first reaction. As the rigger made a cup of tea to take to the captain, he was heard to remark: 'I'll bet those fellows in the sub are drinking salt water now instead of tea!' The Queen of the Air taxied to her moorings about 7.30 that evening, after flying for twelve and a half hours. Shortly afterwards the first white star appeared on her hull.'

U-51 however had escaped destruction, although its survival and that of its 43 hands would be all too brief because just four days' later U-51 was torpedoed by RN submarine HMS *Catchalot* in the Bay of Biscay west of Nantes.

'On 29 August, just before dawn, continued David Masters 'the *Queen of the Air* began to roar over the waters. The smoke from the adjacent city mingled with the mist to add to the difficulties of that particular base, but she got safely away and was soon heading out to sea to pick up her convoy. At dawn contact was made and thereafter for hour on hour the captain and crew of the Sunderland carried out their normal submarine patrol, circling the convoy and flying ahead to search for submarine or mines in the course of the ships. About 11 o'clock that morning the escorting destroyer signalled: 'There's a U-boat about here somewhere.' The sensitive ears of the Asdic had detected the sound of the submarine moving under the sea and the naval commander had at once invoked the eyes overhead to help to find the enemy. Diving low, the flying-boat began a creeping line-ahead search, but it was about ten minutes before the keen eyes on the aircraft saw the track of the submarine's periscope.

Instantly the captain attacked, flinging the crew about as he came round steeply to get in another attack before climbing to finish the U-boat off with bombs. He made no mistake. All that he had been taught about the distance a submarine can travel under water in a minute was in his mind as he made his three attacks along the track of the invisible enemy. Directly the Sunderland had finished attacking, the destroyer came roaring on the scene to add a few more depth charges just to make sure. The huge air bubbles which belched up to the surface and the gobs of oil which appeared and spread over the area marked the destruction of the enemy. When the destroyer carried out a sweep with the Asdic, she signalled: 'No contact. Sub destroyed.' That evening the *Queen of the Air* landed at her base at 6 o'clock with a very happy crew. If anyone had cause for complaint it was the rear-gunner who had another large bump on the top of his head to prove how the explosion had flicked the tail and jolted him hard against the top of the turret. But he was in no mood to grouse. He was quite willing to stand any number of bumps providing they got the U-boats. So, with due ceremony, the second white star was painted n the hull of the flying-boat.

'The third white star was earned on 17 October, about 300 miles away from Cape Wrath, that bleak headland in the north of Scotland, where the Atlantic pours through the Pentland Firth into the North Sea, often with such fury under the lash of the gales that the English Channel, at its worst bears no comparison. Getting away in the dark about 5.30 in the morning, the crew of the flying-boat watched the dawn gradually light up the sea beneath them. For several hundred miles they cruised on their normal routine of guarding a convoy when, about 9.30, the warning Klaxon blared through the aircraft. The front gunner sighted the submarine on the starboard side and at once signalled and opened fire. It was on the surface and travelling towards the convoy, but a smart look-out was being kept on the submarine, for it immediately did a crash dive. Quickly as it tried to escape, however, it was seconds too slow for the Sunderland, whose captain sent her diving down to attack. Round came the flying-boat, throwing her crew about, to attack again. Just before this attack, all on board felt the flying-boat stagger as a great blow hit the tail. 'There was a most colossal crack on the tail plane,' explained Flight Lieutenant Baker later. 'It gave us a big shaking.'

The rear-gunner, who received his usual bump on the head when the first attack was made, got a nastier bump still the second time round, for there was a big explosion inside the submarine and he saw pieces of wreckage flying up out of the sea and felt them hitting the tail plane. 'The tail plane has been damaged by wreckage from the sub,' he reported to the captain. They watched the surface of the sea belching great air bubbles, saw the oil gushing up and spreading wider and wider and as the sea quietened down the captain turned the flying-boat for home. 'Are you all right?' he inquired of the rear-gunner through the intercom. The rear-gunner felt his bumps. 'There is no need for you to press the buzzer in future,' he replied, 'as every time I get a crack on the head I shall know you've got a sub.' They landed safely at base, to find their tail plane fabric badly cut about in dozens of places by the wreckage hurled up from the exploding submarine. In due course the third star made its appearance on the hull of the *Queen of the Air.*

They were a happy crew who manned the *Queen of the Air;* they came to know each other so well during those long and, for the most part, monotonous patrols that in an emergency they knew exactly - what to do and did it automatically. If the skipper got a laugh at the bumps of the rear-gunner, the rear-gunner and the rest of the crew got many a laugh at the expense of the skipper. Often the Klaxon blared out to send them to action stations - where they waited tensely to attack, only to find that the skipper had dived down on some innocent basking sharks or a whale which he had mistaken for submarines. 'They used to laugh themselves silly,' the skipper once remarked.

'So at his appointed times the captain of the *Queen of the Air* continued to take her across hundreds of miles of ocean to help to bring the tall ships, the food ships and ammunition ships and tank ships and aeroplane ships, safely to the shores of England. And throughout those long patrols, keen eyes on the flying-boat searched for a sight of submarine or periscopes, while the captain was ready to let loose death and destruction upon the German outlaws of the sea.

'The weeks passed uneventfully until the beginning of December. At dawn on 6 December 1940 Baker took the *Queen of the Air* off the water and flew north to shepherd a convoy. The weather was unspeakable. The cloud base was down to 300 feet and visibility was nil. It was raining and snowing hard and the temperature was at zero. They thrashed along for hour after hour, peering out and seeing nothing, wondering where their convoy was and if the rain and flurries of snow would ever hold up. Then the miracle happened. Quite suddenly about 1 o'clock the weather broke in a perfectly straight line across the sky. 'It was the most amazing thing I have ever seen in my life. We stuck the nose of the aircraft out into clear weather while the tail was still enveloped in clouds,' the captain said afterwards when he came to explain this phenomenon. 'It took us a few seconds to grow accustomed to this bright light after flying in gloom for so long. As the second pilot and I blinked and looked ahead, we sighted a sub at the identical moment, turned our faces to each other, opened our mouths together and howled in unison 'Sub!' It was rather funny.'

'In that clear area, about a mile away a large submarine of about 3,000 tons was travelling at ten knots on the surface. The aircraft which had been flying at cruising speed suddenly accelerated as her captain went after his quarry. He could see men on the conning tower and recognized her as an Italian submarine of the Ballilla class. The men on the conning tower saw their doom approaching. Quick as they were to close the conning tower and open the valves to flood the tanks that would take them down to safety, they were too late. As the *Queen of the Air* dived, her skipper saw part of the stern of the submarine still showing. He struck home on each side and there was a big explosion as he climbed to renew the attack. The rear-gunner, rubbing the usual bump on his head, looked down excitedly. 'There's a sheet of metal about six feet by four just been hurled out of the sea. It was all torn and twisted,' he reported to the captain. The crew of the flying-boat, circling round, gazed on the waters. There was no doubt about the destruction of the Italian submarine. The air released from the shattered craft shot up like fountains for six feet above the surface. The oil gushed up and spread and spread until an area of about a square mile was covered with it.

'These Italians seem to be having a hell of a fine time in this war!' commented the wireless operator. 'They're getting it where the chink got the chopper.'

It was indeed amazing the way the weather cleared to enable them to sight and sink the submarine; it was no less amazing the way it closed down again as soon as their task was completed. The weather in fact grew so bad that the flying-boat could not make contact with her convoy, so she was obliged to return to base, where her skipper reported his fourth success and the crew with due ceremony painted the fourth star above her name. Thus by sinking four enemy submarines before the end of 1940, Flight Lieutenant E. R. Baker DFC made ample amends for missing those four U-boats in September 1939 while patrolling with his friend, the late Flight Lieutenant Ainslie DFC. As one of the crew of the *Queen of the Air* remarked: 'If we don't win this war, the crew of this aircraft will be in a devil of a mess.'

On 9 March 1941 Squadron Leader Birch flying T9047 on 10 Squadron RAAF attacked a U-boat. As it was estimated that the aircraft would only be able to escort the convoy for approximately forty minutes, the two port depth charges were hauled inboard in order to reduce fuel consumption. At 1153 hours a submarine was sighted on the surface two miles away. The aircraft immediately altered course and attacked with two depth charges from a height of 30 feet. At the instant the depth charges were released the tip of the U-boat's periscope was still visible. The first depth charge exploded 20 feet on the starboard side and level with the bow of the U-boat; the second exploded 30 feet ahead of the bow and 20 feet on the port side. A smoke float was dropped 200 yards along the U-boat's track and a second attack was made at 1155 with the port depth charges. No results were observed and a submarine marker was dropped. The Sunderland homed two destroyers to the area and they put down patterns of depth charges, still without apparent result.

On 19 May 1941 the newly completed German battleship *Bismarck* left Kiel on her maiden voyage, in company with the cruiser *Prinz Eugen* bound for British transatlantic re-supply routes. The battle cruisers *Scharnhorst* and *Gneisenau* had destroyed 115,622 tons during the cruise which finished at Brest on 22 March and the enemy plan was for the *Bismarck* to co-operate with them in the North Atlantic. The *Scharnhorst* was delayed at Brest after attacks by Coastal Command and on 21 May the *Bismarck* and the *Prinz Eugen* were anchored in Dobric Fjord, Norway prior to heading for the Atlantic. They were spotted by a PRU Spitfire near Bergen and next day a Fleet Air Arm Maryland forced its way up the Bergen fjords at very low level in 10/10ths cloud down to 200 feet and established that the two warships had left safe harbour. The weather deteriorated and the German vessels were lost. Sunderlands and Hudsons were among the aircraft that reconnoitred the Faeroes-Iceland gap in an attempt to locate the warships, the Sunderlands maintaining a patrol from 0615 to 2115 and covering 2,000 miles in a single sortie. But they encountered strong headwinds, fog, rain-squalls and heavy cloud in which severe icing conditions developed. The German warships were spotted in the early evening of 23 May by Royal Navy ships in the Denmark Straight and a Sunderland from Iceland set off in the long twilight of the far northern latitudes to search for them.

On 24 May the Sunderland (L5798) flown by Flight Lieutenant Vaughan on 201 Squadron arrived in the neighbourhood of HMS *Suffolk* and, on sighting this ship, saw at the same time a flash of gunfire well ahead. 'As we closed', said Vaughan, 'two columns, each of two ships in line ahead, were seen to be steering on parallel courses at an estimated range of 12 miles between the columns. Heavy gunfire was being exchanged and the leading ship of the port column was on fire in two places, one fire being at the base of the bridge superstructure and the other farther aft. In spite of these large conflagrations she appeared to be firing at least one turret forward and one aft.' At first Vaughan could not identify the burning ship. It was HMS *Hood*. Vaughan turned towards the starboard column and noticed that the second of the two ships composing it was making a considerable amount of smoke and that oil escaping from her was leaving a broad track upon the surface of the sea. He approached nearer and as he did so HMS *Hood*, which was on fire in the column to port blew up. Bam Martyn the first wireless operator, who was taking his turn in the rear turret of the Sunderland, had an abiding memory of the 'unbelievable flash of the explosion that killed *Hood* and the shock of the realisation that a ship had been sunk.'

A few seconds later the Sunderland came under heavy AA fire at the moment when its captain was identifying the ships in the starboard column as the *Bismarck* and *Prinz Eugen*. Vaughan was forced to take immediate cloud cover and when, five minutes later, he emerged into an open patch, the *Hood* had almost completely disappeared. When the Sunderland flew over the spot all that could be seen was an empty raft, painted red, surrounded by wreckage in the midst of a large patch of oil.

Despite the loss of the *Hood*, HMS *Prince of Wales* scored hits on the *Bismarck* which pierced the battleship's oil tanks and reduced her speed and she was forced to leave the *Prinz Eugen* and make towards France. The weather was still poor and the shadowing Royal Navy ships kept losing contact but 'Z-Zebra' a RAF Catalina piloted by Pilot Officer Douglas A. Briggs on 209 Squadron found the great warship on 26 May. 'Z-Zebra' was hit and lost contact with the battleship but another Catalina, on 240 Squadron, was soon on the scene and regained contact. Fleet Air Arm Fulmar and Swordfish crews from HMS *Victorious* carried out a series of daring torpedo attacks and three hits crippled the *Bismarck's* steering gear. On 27 May the Royal Navy force closed in and sank the *Bismarck*.

The Catalina general reconnaissance flying-boat with provision for a crew of 8-9 first entered service with patrol-bomber squadrons of the US Navy in 1936 under the designation PBY-I. With the outbreak of war Britain placed an initial order for 30 PBY-5 aircraft designated Catalina I. The first deliveries to the RAF were made early in 1941. Some of the first Catalinas entered service on 209 and 240 Squadrons of Coastal Command at Castle Archdale in Northern Ireland. Catalinas went on to serve Nos. 119, 190, 202, 210, 330, 333 and 422 in Coastal Command. The 196th and final U-boat sunk by Coastal Command was destroyed by a Catalina on 210 Squadron 120 miles North-east of Sullom Voe on 7 May 1945.[86]

On 13 June Beauforts on 42 Squadron torpedoes the *Lützow* off Norway. By now the nineteen squadrons in the Coastal Command inventory in 1939 had grown to forty and more than half the aircraft of the Command had been fitted with improved ASV radar and the introduction of the airborne searchlight or Leigh light was imminent.

On 30 June 1941 Sunderland P9600 flown by Flying Officer A. Wearne on 10 Squadron RAAF was involved in a combat with a FW 200. The Sunderland fought the heavily armed German aircraft just above the surface of the Atlantic until finally it fled, damaged, into the clouds. Then the Sunderland crew found that the port outer engine oil tank had been holed and that oil was pouring out. It would be only a matter of minutes before the engine seized. It is just possible for a small man to stretch out at full length inside the wing of a Sunderland and LAC (later Corporal) Milton Griffin, a young Sydney air gunner, volunteered to do so. Wearne agreed after some hesitation. He feared the engine might stop while Griffin was inside the wing and that if they had to come down on the water, Griffin might not be able to get out in time. The struts inside the wing were slippery with oil and when Griffin opened an inspection plate, hot oil sprayed his face. The only light to help him came through a bullet hole in the wing, but he could see that oil was still pouring from holes in the tank. He crawled back into the body of the flying boat, got some plugs and going in again, stopped up the holes. But that was still not enough. Only about a gallon of oil remained in the tank, which normally held twenty gallons. Griffin went back again into the Sunderland cockpit and collected some Plasticine - which was carried by flying boat crews to plug bullet holes - a hammer and chisel, an empty peach tin and two gallons of oil. He pushed them in front of him as he went into the wing and laboriously chiselled two holes in the upper part of the oil tank. Then he made a funnel from the Plasticine and poured in two gallons of oil with the peach tin. It was trying work. Every time the Sunderland rocked he slipped and some of the oil was spilled. At last he came out and reported that everything was safe. Sweat and oil were dripping from him, but still he was not satisfied. He smoked a cigarette, then wriggled back into the wing and put two more gallons of oil into the tank. The Sunderland got home without further trouble. 10 Squadron's first DFM was awarded to Corporal Milton Griffin on 9 July.[87]

The story of one encounter between a Hudson and a Focke-Wulf 'Kondor' on 23 July 1941 can be told in the words of the Hudson's pilot. The Hudson had just taken leave of a convoy which it had been protecting throughout the morning. The usual farewell signals had been exchanged, when a naval corvette was seen flashing a signal with its lamp. 'Suspicious aircraft to starboard,' it read. The captain of the Hudson thought that in all probability the corvette had mistaken for an enemy a Wellington of Coastal Command known to be in the neighbourhood. When he himself caught sight of it he made the same error. 'I flew over,' he said, 'to have a look at her, pulling down my front gun sights just for practice. In fact I was just remarking to Ernie (the navigator and second pilot) that we were in a lovely position and that I had the Wellington beautifully in the sights, when he suddenly let out a wild Irish oath - Ernie was from Ulster - and shouted: ' It's a Kondor!' 'Automatically I increased speed and he ran back to man one of the side guns. The wireless operator grabbed another. The rear gunner swung his turret round and trained his twin Brownings. Flying towards the convoy, at about a hundred feet above the sea, was one of the big Focke-Wulf Kondors. We were overhauling him fast. Whether he saw us or not I don't know, but at four hundred yards I opened up with about five bursts from my front guns. I don't think I hit him. He returned the fire at once from his top and bottom guns and I could see his tracer bullets whipping past the nose of the Hudson in little streaks or light. But he missed and his pilot turned slightly to starboard and ran for it parallel to the course of the convoy.

'We had the legs of him all right. We were overhauling him very fast. Once he put his nose up a trifle, as though meditating a run for the clouds. He must have decided he couldn't make it and was safer where he was, right down on the sea. As we drew closer in, my rear gunner opened fire. He was firing forward and I could see his tracer nipping over my wing. Ernie watched it flash straight past him as he waited with his side gun pointing through the window.

'We drew closer and closer. The Kondor began to look like the side or a house. At the end all I could see of it was part of the fuselage and two whacking big engines. My rear gunner was pumping bullets into him all the time. When we were separated by only forty feet I could see two of his engines beginning to glow. I throttled back a bit so as not to over-shoot him or, what was more likely, crash into him. For one short moment Ernie saw a white face appear at one of the windows in the Kondor's side. Then it disappeared.

'Just then the Kondor began to turn away. His belly was exposed to us and Ernie opened fire with the side gun, the rear gunner keeping up his stream of bullets all the time. There was a wisp of smoke, a sudden belching of smoke and then flames shot out from beneath his two port engines. He turned away to starboard and I made a tight turn to port ready to come round at him again. I remember vividly thinking that I must keep up, we were so close to the sea. We came out of the turn and I could see the Kondor again flying steadily away, seemingly unhurt. I was wild with disappointment. I thought he had got away with it. Then I saw he was getting lower and lower and next minute he hit the sea. I found myself yelling: 'We've got him! He's in the sea. Ernie, we've got him!' The gunner was yelling down the intercom, too, great, strange, exultant Yorkshire oaths.

'It was only then that we realised how hard and how silently we had all been concentrating and how full the Hudson was of cordite fumes and how short of petrol we were getting. We flew over the Kondor - its wing-tips were just awash - and Ernie photographed him. Four of the crew were in the water, hanging on to their rubber dinghy, which was just inflating. A fifth man was scrambling along the fuselage. We learnt afterwards that a Met man who had been aboard was .shot through the heart. The others were all right. Two corvettes were rushing to pick them up and the whole crew seemed to be crowded on the deck of the leading one, waving and shouting to us. One man was waving his shirt. Another was in pyjamas. Our relief Hudson and the Wellington on U-boat search were circling round too and as we made off for home we could see the white puffs of steam as all the ships in convoy sounded their sirens.'

Though U-boats were frequently sighted and attacked, the work more often than not is of great monotony. To keep an unblinking and vigilant look-out from the turrets and side-windows of a Sunderland or from the blisters of a Catalina flying over what seems an illimitable stretch of sea demands physical and mental-endurance of a high order. Sometimes a fishing vessel, British, Spanish, French, Norwegian, Icelandic, is seen; sometimes a raft, more rarely a periscope with a spume of foam about it. When that is sighted or when the submarine is seen on the surface, the klaxon sounds and the crew get ready for immediate action. Both bombs and depth charges are used to destroy the enemy. Many attacks were made. One, carried out by a Catalina, well illustrates the fortunes of war. Its pilot saw a U-boat on the surface. He dived towards it, but hardly had he put the nose down when he saw another on the surface also but closer at hand. He diverted his attack to this second U-boat and as he was delivering it, came under machine-gun fire from his original quarry. He carried on, got into a good position, but when he pressed the button his bombs hung up. Both submarines submerged. On landing at base it was found that the Catalina had been hit by one bullet only. It had severed the electrical connections of the bomb-release gear. This was but an incident in four days of intensive and successful attacks.

A Sunderland attacked an enemy submarine in a position 2850 Cape

Finisterre 210 miles. Bombs were dropped within twenty feet when the submarine was at periscope depth and a large oil patch with air bubbles was observed. Later more bubbles appeared in the centre of the patch. After twenty minutes the oil patch extended with bubbles continuing to rise. The aircraft remained in the vicinity for three and a half hours.' ...'Two 100lb high-explosive bombs were dropped which fell a few yards from the periscope. It is considered that the submarine was hit. Two large brown patches and a pale blue patch appeared on the surface about seven minutes afterwards.' ...'One Sunderland reported attacking an enemy submarine U-26 in a position 2400 Bishop's Rock 204 miles; forcing the enemy submarine to the surface. ...Bombs were dropped, one of which obtained a direct hit on the stern, causing the submarine to sink. Forty-one survivors were being picked up by a naval unit when the aircraft left.' ...'A Lerwick on convoy escort attacked an enemy submarine and claims a direct hit on the conning-tower. Oil and air bubbles were seen after the attack.' Passages such as these are to be found in plenty in the reports prepared by the Air Ministry War Room.

The Battle of the Atlantic was fought over more than ten and a half million square miles of sea, North to a line of latitude beyond the Arctic Circle and South to the Equator, to the East the coasts of Western Europe and of part of Western Africa, to the West the Eastern coasts of Canada, Newfoundland, the USA, the Central and certain of the South American States. It was realised that Scottish and Northern Irish bases alone would not be sufficient. Others had to be found from which to cover the North Atlantic. Coastal Command reached out and established itself in Iceland. That island, larger than Ireland, was occupied by British troops on 10 May 1940. It was not, however, until 27th August that half a squadron of Battles landed near a little fishing village on its South-Western shores.

The other half arrived on 14 September. Their flight, though uneventful, was none the less remarkable, if the limited endurance of this type of aircraft is remembered. It had been necessary to wait several weeks for favourable weather, for the endurance of a Battle would not permit it to cross the 700 odd miles of sea separating Scotland from Iceland unless there was a tail wind or no wind at all. They flew in two groups of nine preceded and followed by a Sunderland to ensure that there would be no navigational difficulties. Before the eyes of the pilots as they drew near stretched a line of black hills bearing no trace of trees or vegetation save for an irregular pattern inscribed upon their dark flanks in streaks of yellowish-green moss. Beyond, some sixty miles away, the shapes of high mountains and the foot of a glacier a hundred miles long were to be perceived, now dim and hesitant, now clear cut and bold against a sky whose colour and texture were in constant movement.

On this land of savage yet delicate beauty the Battles alighted by the mouth of a river flowing through a desolate marsh of lava and grey tussocky grass which divides the dark hills from the sullen sea. They began at once to take their part in the fight, a part subsequently played by aircraft more suited to the purpose. Thus by September 1940 the Northern bases had been increased and reinforced. By August 1941 aircraft using them were finding and attacking U-boats at the rate of one every other day in addition to maintaining patrols off Brest and the other French ports on the Atlantic seaboard to watch for any surface raider seeking to break out. Coastal Command presently moved much further south, a two days flight from England and in the first months of 1941 established a base on the West coast of Africa with a port of call at Gibraltar, which had been an outpost for flying boats since October 1939. Here, in the mouth of a wide river fringed with mangrove swamps and palm scrub, Sunderlands were stationed. Conditions in the North, which touched the Arctic Circle, differed appreciably from those in the South where it touches the Equator. At one station in Iceland the average temperature in December was 30 degrees Fahrenheit, falling sometimes to as low as minus 6 degrees, while at another in West Africa the average during the same month is 81 degrees in the shade, rising on occasions to 95 degrees. Yet the operational problem was the same at any point along this front of 3,540 miles. Iceland was of vital importance in the battle. It was, to quote the Admiral in command there, 'the Clapham Junction of the North Atlantic.' As such it is heavily garrisoned by American and British troops and protected by units of the Navy and Air Force of both Allies. It is a strange country, warm and inviting in summer, at all other times stark and inscrutable. Within the whole circle of its coasts there is hardly a tree. In summer almost without darkness, in winter almost without light, it guards the secret of its sombre mountains, its still active volcanoes, its geysers and its glaciers, silent and aloof under the Northern Lights.

Aerodromes had been built in the lava swamps on which the Battles landed in August 1940 and elsewhere. The runways were made of concrete and lava dust laid on a bed of stones. The aircraft were protected from the fierce and sudden winds by 'breaks' fifteen feet high built in the Icelandic fashion of lava faced with sods of turf. The crews and ground staff lived in Nissen huts, their chief enemy in autumn and winter being mud, in summer lava dust which spread over everything, caused sore throats and severely shortened the life of clothing and boots. The roads, of the consistency of a hard tennis court after heavy rain, were vile. Yet vehicles contrived to average a thousand miles a month. Major repairs - the driver of a car and the officer with him once removed a broken back axle and fitted a new one, dropped from the air by parachute, with the aid of a hammer, chisel and three spanners - had often to be carried out by the roadside.

For recreation in the South of the island there was salmon and trout fishing, shooting in the marshes, duck, mallard and snipe for the most part and hacking on sturdy Icelandic ponies, the most robust of the robust natives of the island. In the North such amenities were rare. Football and other games were played, one strongly contested match which took place in winter lasting from dawn to dusk, a period of little more than an hour. The Army and the RAF exchange concert parties and in the long, dark evenings of the Icelandic winter the men carved bracelets and rings from the perspex fittings of crashed aircraft. Officers and men did their own washing and darning and all available packing-cases were turned into furniture for the huts.

In June 1941 Fairey Battles in Iceland were replaced by Lockheed Hudsons for anti-submarine and convoy patrol. Their task and that of Sunderland and Catalina flying boats, Northrop float-planes, Wellingtons and Whitleys was not easy, for weather conditions in and around Iceland are among the most variable in the world. It is almost possible to see the depressions off Iceland, in peace time so prominent and disheartening a feature of the daily Press. Fog is frequent and clouds will move down upon an aerodrome faster than a galloping horse. Above all there are the winds. These can reach more than gale force in a matter of minutes. At one aerodrome the wind once began to blow at 62 mph. An hour later it was blowing at 76 mph and an hour after that at 89 mph. The maximum velocity of the gusts reached 133 mph. This hurricane turned the Guard Room on its side, took the roof off the Flying Control Headquarters and caused six Whitleys to move along the runway from their dispersal point, each dragging with it six 300 lb concrete blocks. 'A Nissen hut took off at 10.00 hours,' says the report' and reached an estimated height of sixty feet before crash-landing on an adjacent runway.

At another aerodrome near by the anemometer broke down after recording a velocity of 90 mph... The propellers of Hudsons were seen to be turning although the engines were completely cold.' No aircraft was lost or damaged. Despite the hostility of the climate the average number of hours spent each month in flying has been high. To ease the strain the time of patrols was reduced when possible. Other difficulties concerned the behaviour of compasses, which vary often by as much as 11 degrees and of wireless installation, which not infrequently faded out entirely. It was, moreover, difficult to divert aircraft if their bases were obscured by fog or ten-tenths cloud, for landing grounds were few and far between. Once a Hudson was diverted to an emergency ground near the shore and it was ten days before it could take off again. During that time the crew consumed ninety-two tins of meat and vegetable ration and on their return regarded bully-beef and biscuits with much the same feelings as the Israelites displayed towards the fleshpots of Egypt.

On 27 August 1941 a Hudson crew on 269 Squadron at Kildadarnes on Iceland prepared for a patrol which was to make war history. 'From all reports there are U-boats in packets of ten all over the wicket,' said the Intelligence Officer brightly to his audience of four airmen. 'The last reported sighting was here,' he added, tapping a wall chart of the Atlantic which bristled with tiny flags. 'A square search?' Squadron Leader James H. Thompson, Hudson pilot, a Yorkshireman who was nearing his thirty-second birthday, asked his second pilot and navigator, Flying Officer William John O. Coleman. 'Fair enough,' was 'Jack' Coleman's reply. Thompson and Coleman, together with Flight Sergeants Frederick J. Drake, the gunner and 'Duggie' Strode, wireless operator went out to 'S for Sugar' in the mud and mists of Kildadarnes airfield and at 0840 hours in near gale conditions set off on patrol. Three hundred feet above the wind-whipped wave-tops 80 miles south of Iceland the Hudson charged through a series of blinding squalls. 'What chance of a sighting in this weather?' thought the crew? 'A million to one against. Million to one against. Million to one against.'

The twin engines seemed to chant the mocking odds. Thompson was thinking along similar lines. One of the oldest pilots flying with Coastal Command, he was old enough, he reflected, to have more sense than to flog a

Hudson across the Atlantic in half a gale, seeking a ghost. And precisely at the moment that this cautionary thought crossed Thompson's mind a U-Boat slowly and almost sedately surfaced 1,200 yards ahead! In the nose of 'S for Sugar' Coleman roared the alert a split second after Thompson had muttered 'My God' under his breath. The sight was almost unbelievable. Their aircraft had barely reached the spot from which, according to the Intelligence Officer, the last sighting of a U-Boat had been reported. And now a German submarine was rising from the sea mists right into their range of vision. It was fully surfaced and steering smack into the perfect position for a first-time attack from the air. Thompson throttled back into a shallow dive as Coleman bounded up the steps to his side, automatically opening the bomb doors as he climbed. And at that moment 32-year old Kapitänleutnant Hans-Joachim Rahmlow, Commander of U-570, which was on its first war cruise, came through the hatch on to the slippery bridge of the submarine. After a 'rousing farewell party in Trondheim, where much beer and wine had been consumed, U-570 sailed at 0800 hours on 24 August but she was not as sea-worthy as she might have been and when the boat reached open seas, a large proportion of the crew became desperately seasick.'[88]

Rahmlow had just spent fifteen uncomfortable minutes at the eye-piece of the search periscope after the hydroplane operator had reported there were no surface echoes in the vicinity. Check and double check! He remembered the warning he had received from German Naval Chief Dönitz, 'In the time it takes a U-boat to submerge, an aircraft can travel 6000 metres.' It seemed reasonably clear and so Rahmlow had squeezed through the hatch. His eyes automatically went upwards towards the skies and to his horror he saw a fat little shape coming straight at him from the clouds. It was the Hudson. He shrieked the order to dive, but he knew that his boat was already doomed. When the U-boat surfaced, the Hudson crew picked her up on ASV radar. Presently, Thompson sighted 'the swirl and wake of a U-boat' about 800 yards ahead: It was then a little after 6.30am. 'No actual part of the U-boat was seen,' reported Thompson 'and vision was very limited owing to rain-squall. Marked position with smoke floats ... and made a submarine sighting report to base.'

The Hudson cruised round for a little less than an hour, when it again sighted U-570, this time on the surface a mile away on the port bow. Thompson reached U-570 before she got under. 'Let me know when to drop, Jack.' His thumb stabbed the release button just as Coleman said quietly, 'Now!' In the rear turret of the Hudson, Drake saw the wind-flick of the 250lb depth charges set to detonate at fifty feet, as per the new procedure and then the ocean bulged up in four great, towering water pillars. Thompson opened the throttle and banked in a sharp turn to port after he had inwardly counted one-two-three-four. 'The U-Boat was completely enveloped by the detonations,' he recalled later 'and I lost sight of the enemy as I turned away, getting into position for another pass. I had no depth-charges left, but we had any amount of three-o-three bullets.'

Coleman saw two charges straddle the bow as the submarine dived. U-570 was completely enveloped by the explosions and shortly afterwards submerged completely. Coleman jumped back to join Strode at the guns in the waist. All four men in the Hudson stared ahead. Thompson claimed later that he felt no excitement until his quarry foamed to the surface again, streaming green water. 'It was rather disconcerting in some respects. I had hoped to see much more visible sign of damage.' He did not realise then that he had scored a perfect straddle on the enemy, two depth-charges exploded on either side of the pressure hull. But Rahmlow and his men knew it only too well and U-570 had screwed herself almost upside down in the sudden eerie darkness after the blast. First came the preliminary shudder. Then the ear-drum shattering embrace of the two explosions to starboard which blew all lights. Then the roll, over and over. Over and down into emptiness. A man screamed in terror. Somebody else moaned through his teeth in fear. The man who screamed did so because his arm had been trapped in flailing machinery above his head - machinery which should have been underfoot. Somebody near the bank of batteries began coughing. Another engine-room rating retched helplessly. The wheezing and spluttering reached Rahmlow in the control-room, above the noise of the hissing escaping air which dominated the silence after the detonations. The boat seemed to be filling with deadly chlorine gas. 'Up! Up! he urged, adding his weight to that of the man wrestling with the big wheel of the hydroplanes. 'All hands on deck...when I call.' The boat was bow-heavy, but they were rising. Slowly, like a mortally wounded killer whale. Oberleutnant Bernhard Berndt the first watch officer sprayed his torch across the depth gauges, of the needles quivered, raced back, settled at zero. 'I'll chance it. Close the hatch behind me.'

Rahmlow deliberately trapped himself in the kiosk, his light wavering upwards like the doubt in his mind. He had left his crew below in temporary security. What lay beyond the top hatch was any man's guess. The depth gauges could have knocked out by the shock wave he reasoned. There might be several fathoms of Atlantic pressing against the six butterfly nuts he was unscrewing, but there was no time to risk a try with the periscope, even if the housing was undamaged. Sweat blinded him and made the last bolt the worst of all. His breath gusted in relief as air, not tons of water, gushed down over his head and shoulders. He dropped back td first hatch and banged with his heels. 'All out! All out! Get them out Berndt.' He allowed half a dozen crew to clamber past him, stopped the next man and went up the steel ladder to take command on the upper bridge.

At that moment, Thompson, boring the Hudson back for the second calculated run, shouted over the intercommunication system, 'Look out! They're going for the gun.' All four men in the aircraft, from different vantage points, saw the menace of water swirling away from the mounting on the casing. Coleman, who rarely swore, yelled, 'Let the bastards have it!' Thompson, thumbing the buttons for the front guns, ordered 'Open fire on a target bearing. Points of aim...gun and conning tower.' Then, with a word over his shoulder - 'Drake, don't let them get near that gun as we pass.' In his controlled urgency, he was annoyed at the seemingly lazy way in which the red tracer was clawing over the bridge of the enemy. He could see jagged white rents in the innocent green which heaved up and down in the lee of the submarine, but no holes in harsh metal. He saw the men in the yellow life-jackets break like a wave on the casing and flow back to the shelter of the bridge. There they were swamped by the second group scrambling from the hatch, in a welter of arms, heads and legs.

Thompson skidded his sweaty thumbs from the firing buttons and yanked the Hudson around in a tighter turn. Young Drake, in the rear turret, nursing his twin Brownings between his knees, flicked a tongue around a back tooth which had been bothering him and decided, in his diffident way, that his captain's words made sense. He hated pain. Even less did he like the thought of inflicting pain upon others. This was impersonal enough. He sprayed the forward leading edge of the bridge in his turn until the range opened and then he felt naked at the realisation of what a vulnerable rump the banking Hudson must be presenting to the enemy below. They were round quickly enough and now roaring for the third attack. The 3.5-inch gun was still mute in the fore-and-aft position, but more and more Germans were crowding into the oval-shaped conning tower. 'There was no indication of the enemy's intentions and some of the Huns were getting very close to that ugly brute on the casing. We kept squirting, to sort-of keep their heads down.'

Coming down on the fourth pass, Thompson saw the white board of surrender was held aloft by Rahmlow. 'Hold your fire,' shouted Thompson. He eased himself back in the bucket seat and mechanically, he checked the instrument panel. Something might have been missed in the last half-hour of concentrated destruction. Half-hour? He looked at the wrist watch his wife had given him. Ten bleeding minutes! It was almost beyond belief. He shifted weight to peer down as he banked. A white flag was seen to be waved ... the crew also brought out what appeared to be a white board and held this up on the deck.' The white flag was subsequently found to be the captain's shirt. It was lightly starched and had frills down the front.

'What do we do now, Jack? Tow the basket back to Iceland?'

'We must whistle up the Navy - and quick!' he observed as he put his aircraft into a series of spirals to gain altitude. Coleman had been studying the behaviour of U-570 for some minutes. 'Don't want to add to our worries, Tommy,' he said rather too airily, 'but the weather is definitely worsening and our pal is beginning to look a bit nose-heavy.' 'It is, as they say, going to blow a bastard,' was the answer.

While the gunners kept their machine guns trained on U-570's bridge, 'Duggie' Strode broke radio silence and requested help. Another Hudson on 269 Squadron, piloted by Hugh Eccles en route from Scotland to Iceland, picked up the message and headed to the scene, as did a Catalina (AH565) of Coastal Command's 209 Squadron, piloted by Flying Officer Edward Jewiss, who had sunk U-452 two days earlier.[89]. Freddie Drake told his hut mates later: 'I went back to the astrodome. It was weird. We were really beginning to take a beating from the weather. When I looked at the poor slobs in the submarine tossing around. I began to feel sea-sick for the first time in my life. That big, ugly Catalina winging through the clouds looked like some angel of mercy.'

Thompson saw the Catalina at the same instant as his look-out shouted. He altered course and headed the larger aircraft away from the submarine, just in case the other pilot had not been briefed. They blinked recognition signals at each other. Thompson chuckled and passed a verbal message to Coleman. 'Make him look after our sub - repeat, our sub - who has shown the white flag.' Within fifteen minutes three more aircraft were over the area. 'Worse than Piccadilly Circus in the rush hour,' grumbled Thompson but he smiled as he said it. Hugh Eccles took photographs and served as a radio-relay station; Jewiss, fully armed with depth charges, circled, prepared to attack U-570 at the slightest sign that she was diving. Throughout the rest of the day the Hudsons and Catalinas took turns in guarding the prize, being over it for about eleven hours and a half. Then, low on fuel the Hudson had to leave. 'Time we went home' said Thompson. Fuel is getting low, anyway. Give me a course for base, Jack.'

When he flew over Kildadarnes, Thompson saw to his amazement that the station had turned out to the last man to cheer him in. The crowds even covered part of the runway. They were cleared just in time for the landing, but Thompson part of his attention undoubtedly absorbed by the crowds, was caught in a squall on landing and 'S for Sugar' ended its historic patrol ignominiously nose first in the mud alongside the runway. No one was hurt.

When it was realised that the U-boat might still have secret Enigma coding apparatus other secret gear and papers on board the fleet was alerted. Two four-stack ex-American destroyers, *Durwell* and *Niagara*, HMS *Burwell* and the *Canadian Niagara*; and four RNNS trawlers, *Kingston Agathe*, *Northern Chief*, *Wastwater* and *Windermere* were ordered to intervene and prevent the U-boat from being scuttled. The nearest vessel was the naval trawler Northern Chief, commanded by Lieutenant N. L. Knight, about sixty miles to the southeast, an eight- or nine-hour run in the heavy seas.

After having been airborne about sixteen hours (about thirteen of them circling U-570), Jewiss's Catalina departed for Iceland to be replaced by Catalina piloted by Flight Lieutenant B. Lewin on 209 Squadron. Dusk began to fall and no vessel had yet arrived. 'If it appears surface craft unable to reach position before dark,' said an order issued at sunset, 'after giving due warning you should sink U-boat.' It was found possible, however, to arrange for aircraft to remain in relays over the submarine all night and to keep it in view by dropping flares. Its crew were to be ordered to remain on deck and to show a light throughout the hours of darkness under penalty of destruction if they did not comply. Before this order could be executed the *Northern Chief* arrived at about 22:00 in the gathered dusk and sought in heavy seas to take the U-boat in tow. A single-engine Northrop float plane manned by a Norwegian crew on 330 Squadron from Iceland suddenly appeared overhead and dropped two small bombs near U-570, then mistakenly attacked the *Northern Chief*, which returned fire. Contact was established with the Norwegians by radio, calmly explained the situation and refused their request to make a second attack on U-570. Presently a search for the Enigma and other intelligence documents proved unsuccessful.

At dawn on 28 August the *Kingston Agathe* and HMS *Durwell* and HMS *Niagara* arrived and the crew were taken off so that U-570 could be towed to Iceland, escorted all the way by aircraft [90] U-570 was almost certainly one of a large concentration discovered in Icelandic waters. Every serviceable aircraft of Coastal Command based in Iceland and the North of Scotland was dispatched in a series of sweeps maintained from first to last light. On 26 August 50 sorties were made, on 27th 34, on 28th 84 and on 29th 56; a total of 224 in four days.

U-570 was almost certainly one of a large concentration discovered in Icelandic waters. Every serviceable aircraft of Coastal Command based in Iceland and the North of Scotland was dispatched in a series of sweeps maintained from first to last light. On 26 August 50 sorties were made, on 27th 34, on 28th 84 and on 29th 56; a total of 224 in four days.

Both Thompson and Coleman were soon wearing the ribbons of the DFC for their part in the action and just when it seemed that the Navy had forgotten who had made the capture, there was a ceremony at which Thompson was presented with the Swastika battle emblem from U-570 and, as a personal souvenir, the commander's binoculars.[91]

On Christmas Eve 1941 there occurred the first attack by flying boats on an enemy merchant vessel at sea. Two Sunderlands on 10 Squadron RAAF took part with three RAF Sunderlands and two RAF Catalinas which had been sent out on a wide sweep for U-boats. In the Bay of Biscay, 100 miles off Cape Finisterre, soon after first light, the grey hull of a heavily laden tanker of 12,000 tons was sighted - a U-boat 'mother ship.' When the flying boats came in sight, the tanker immediately altered course. In reply to signals, the tanker said her name was Belinda. This was wirelessed back to base, which gave orders to attack. First to attack was Sunderland 'K' on 10 Squadron, captained by Flight Lieutenant A. V. 'Vic' Hodgkinson, one of the original Sunderland pilots on 10 Squadron in 1939 who would later serve in the South Pacific on Catalinas. The Sunderland approached the tanker down-sun at 1,000 feet and the ship immediately opened up a concentrated fire from near the bridge with machine guns and two heavier guns, badly damaging the Sunderland and wounding an airman. The Sunderland's front gunner replied, scoring hits on the bridge, while the other gunners raked the tanker's deck. A stick of depth charges and two anti-submarine bombs were dropped. They straddled the tanker and tall columns of water hid the ship. When the water subsided, billows of smoke were seen and the ship was listing and had slowed to about four knots, with a wide oil streak astern.

The attack was renewed next day by Flight Lieutenant J. Costello in Sunderland 'S.' As 'S' manoeuvred to attack, a Ju 88 came in on the Sunderland's port beam and both aircraft opened fire at each other. Sunderland 'S' drove off the Ju 88 and dropped six depth charges and two bombs around the ship. At 09.30 the Royal Navy destroyer Vanoc was sighted and was given the tanker's position and the Australians returned - to shadow the damaged ship. At 10.15 the Australians saw an explosion near the destroyer and seconds later it signalled that the same or another Ju 88 had attacked it. One Sunderland sped to the destroyer, circled it and then turned to meet the enemy aircraft head-on. The Sunderland passed over the Ju 88 firing with front and rear guns and her incendiaries ripped into the enemy's fuselage and main plane, beneath which - so close were the two aircraft - the Australians could see the rows of bombs. The Ju 88's speed slackened suddenly and it made off into cloud.

On 9 January 1942 Squadron Leader Garside on 230 Squadron flying Sunderland W3987/X bombed U-577 north-west of Mersa Matruh. The boat, which had left St Nazaire on its second war cruise under the command of Herbert Schauenburg on 16 December entered the Mediterranean two days before Christmas. The boat was lost with all 43 hands.

During the last quarter of 1941 Coastal Command had sunk fifteen ships for the loss of forty-six aircraft, but in the first four months of 1942 it sank only six for the loss of fifty-five aircraft. This was largely a 'seasonal decline'. Better weather, coupled with increased resources in the form of four Hampden squadrons converted to torpedo bombers, soon gave rise to renewed hopes. By May the Command was attacking more fiercely and more frequently than ever before. Much the larger part of this work against enemy shipping fell to the Hudsons. With the help of the Hampdens, those of 18 Group (48 and 608 Squadrons) were responsible for strikes off Norway; those of 16 Group (53, 59, 320 (Dutch) Squadrons and 407 'Demon' Squadron RCAF) concentrated on the traffic between the estuary of the Elbe and the Hook of Holland. With iron determination the pilots of these squadrons dived through the flak and released their bombs from mast-height - or so near it that damage from impact with ship or sea was distressingly frequent. On 28 May, for instance, 59 Squadron recorded that one of its aircraft 'struck the sea with port prop-badly bent and homed on one engine at 60 mph'. The next day 407 Squadron reported. 'For the second time in two nights Pilot Officer O'Connell successfully bombed enemy shipping. After this last episode he is seriously thinking of taking up paper-hanging after the war. He went in so low to attack that he struck a mast and hung one of the bomb-doors thereon'. As material for an impressive 'line' this was probably surpassed only by an incident two years later, when a pilot on 455 Squadron RAAF returned from a shipping attack near the Dutch coast with several feet of mast attached to his aircraft.

During May Coastal Command claimed twelve ships, ten of which were confirmed and many others were damaged but attacks at so low a level also involved severe losses; forty-three aircraft in May. The war diarist on 407 Squadron, wrote: 'Since this squadron became operational again on 1 April we have lost twelve crews, in all fifty persons either missing or killed. During the past month six crews have been designated missing or killed on operations with the loss of twenty-seven lives. This does not take into consideration the fact that after every major operation of this nature at least two or three aircraft are so very badly damaged that they are of no use to this, or any other, squadron '.

By the end of June 1942 it was recorded that during the previous three months, out of every four Coastal Command aircraft attempting to attack, one had been shot down. The Germans were arming their merchantmen more and more heavily, surrounding them with more and more escorts-sometimes they now employed as many as four or five warships for a single merchant vessel. With his resources stretched to the utmost Joubert could not afford losses of anything like this order. In July he instructed his crews to abandon the low attack and to bomb from medium level. The resulting fall in casualties was equalled only by the decline in sinkings. The ineffectiveness of medium-level attack arose partly from the lack of a good bomb-sight for the type of work, partly from the drain of experienced crews - including two of the four Beaufort Squadrons - to the Middle East. The Hampdens, too, were not fast enough for work against the more powerfully escorted convoys. 'There was', records a member on 455 Squadron RAAF, 'a very keen type who earned himself the nickname 'Hacksaw', because whenever he had the opportunity he sawed off some of the many appendages the old Hampden acquired, to try and squeeze the extra half-knot out of her'.

On 5 June during an attack on Convoy HG.84 in the Bay of Biscay, Sunderland W3986/U on 10 Squadron RAAF piloted by Flight Lieutenant S. R. C. Wood, picked up a contact on radar. A wake was then seen through binoculars, Wood dived towards it and he found a U-boat making 10 knots. It was the veteran U-71, commanded by 33-year old Korvettenkapitän Walter Flachsenberg. An attack was made from 50 feet at a speed of 205 knots, 25 seconds by stop-watch after U-71 had disappeared. Wood released eight shallow-set Torpex depth charges from the starboard quarter. The centre of the stick was aimed to explode at the presumed position of the conning tower, 130 yards ahead of the swirl and is believed to have exploded there; the depth charges straddled the line of advance. A minute later U-71 surfaced bows first, at a steep angle, an air bubble 25 feet in diameter appeared to port alongside the conning tower and oil bubbles rose in the wake, just ahead of the explosion mark. Then the bows dipped as the stem came high out of the water and gradually U-71 steadied, with its bows awash and listing to port. It was still moving ahead on the motors. In the next ten minutes the aircraft raked the U-boat with 2,000 rounds of machine-gun fire from the nose, port and tail guns in to the hull, upper deck and bridge structure, killing one of the crew. U-71 moved slowly in figures of eight, finally getting under way on the Diesels. Two men appeared in the conning tower but vanished when the tail gun opened up on them.

At 1635 some of the crew seized an opportunity, when the Sunderland had ceased firing to conserve ammunition and manned both the anti-aircraft gun, on the after end of the bridge and the main gun forward of the conning tower. They opened fire and hit the flying-boat several times but caused no casualties. Ten minutes later U-71 increased speed to 8-10 knots. At 1731 it reduced speed and submerged. A large oily patch remained in the position of diving and an oil streak continued to extend along the course. The aircraft sent a message to base at 1819, when the oil streak was moving at one knot and at 1924 established wireless contact with relieving aircraft. The Sunderland left at 1939 when the oil track was fading and was immediately attacked by a Focke-Wulf 'Kondor'. The enemy made four attacks, all from abaft, beam or astern, in the course of an hour and five minutes. In the first three the Sunderland was several times hit by cannon fire and had the rear turret disabled; it was kept in action by hand.

The last attack was made from close range and the Sunderland then sustained five large and eighty small holes, the R/T aerial was shot away and both flaps were damaged. It returned fire from all guns that would bear, throttling back to reduce the range. The Focke-Wulf overshot and was hit repeatedly; it yawed at right angles, broke off the attack and disappeared eastward, flying low over the sea; probably it failed to reach its base. The Sunderland returned uneventfully though other enemy aircraft had come near the coast to intercept it. Some of the bullet-holes were beneath the water line, but arrangements were made to plug them as soon as it moored and it was quickly beached.

Wood recalled: 'We had been so busy with the submarine that we had forgotten to eat and one of the crew was just preparing a meal when the Kurier appeared. We took evasive action making a diving turn to port, which brought a strong protest from the cook. His flour basin was upset and fish heads - it was fish and chips for tea - were thrown about and slithering all over the galley floor. We were busy with the Focke-Wulf for about an hour and the cook apologized for the meal being a little cold when we finally got down to it. We carried out an improvised repair to the rear-turret by putting surgical sticking plaster over a hole in an oil-pipe. The only casualty in the crew was a slight scratch on one man's leg but the Sunderland had half a dozen holes big enough to put your head in, as well as something like a hundred little ones. As some of the damage was below the waterline we had rush her up to the slipway when we landed in case she sank. The ground crew were on her like a lot of ants and had her safe on her beaching chassis almost before we stopped moving.' German PT boats raced out to escort U-71 into La Pallice. Repaired quickly, the boat re-sailed a week later, on 11 June.

On 6 June 1942 a Spanish radio report asserted that an Italian submarine [the *Luigi Torelli* of the 1,200-ton Marconi class commanded by Capitano di Corvetta (Lieutenant Commander) Augusto Migliorini] had been beached near Santander. The foreign radio reports that continued to mention the beaching added that two Sunderland flying-boats of Coastal Command, which had attacked the U-boat, had been forced down. The foreign radio reports were misleading. The Sunderlands were back at base. The episode involving the Italian submarine had all started on the night of 3/4 June. Air Marshal Sir Philip Joubert, knowing that only a successful operational demonstration of the capabilities of Leigh Light Wellingtons would carry the day had thrown caution to the wind and despatched four of the five Wellingtons on 172 Squadron into the Bay of Biscay. The *Luigi Torelli* was damaged by Squadron Leader Jeff H. Greswell and the crew on a Wellington on 172 Squadron (one of five Wimpys fitted with the Leigh Light) picked up an ASV contact. His target was outbound from Bordeaux to the West Indies. Greswell homed on the *Luigi Torelli* by radar and then switched on the Leigh Light but owing to a faulty setting in his altimeter, his approach was too high and he saw no sign of the submarine. However, Migliorini, mistaking the Wellington for a German aircraft, fired recognition flares, precisely pinpointing his boat. On a second approach with the Leigh Light, Greswell got the *Luigi Torelli* squarely in the brilliant beam and straddled the Italian boat with four shallow-set 300lb Torpex depth charges from an altitude of fifty feet.[92]

Unsurprisingly, the blasts to *Luigi Torelli* forced Migliorini to abort and he headed to Aviles, Spain.

On 5 June the *Luigi Torelli* was hastily repaired and left Aviles the next day.

Two Sunderlands on 10 Squadron RAAF, W4019/R flown by Flight Lieutenant Edwin St. Clare Yeoman from Victoria and W3994/X, flown by Pilot Officer Thomas A. Edgerton from Melbourne operating from Gibraltar found the submarine and after circling it realized that the Italian commander was unable to submerge. At 0358 hours Yeoman's Sunderland received a contact three miles on the port beam. Visibility was 500 yards, with the aid of a young moon. The aircraft circled and homed and finally sighted a submarine making 12 knots. An attack with eight 250lb depth charges was made from 100 feet at an angle of 30 degrees to the track and the centre of the stick was thought to have been about 30 yards from the port beam. The submarine was then still fully surfaced and firing light flak, which hit the aircraft several times. As the aircraft broke away, the submarine opened up with heavy flak, hitting the starboard outer engine and holing the starboard float. The aircraft began to vibrate and Yeoman therefore set course for base, after firing about 1,075 rounds. No results could be observed in the darkness. A total of 15 depth charges were dropped on the submarine by the two Sunderlands and they hounded the boat into Santander.[93]

At 0834 on 11 June Sunderland W3993/W on 10 Squadron RAAF flown by Flight Lieutenant E. Martin flying at 2,000 feet, in cloud and rain (using the beam aerials) saw a U-boat five miles ahead, in a patch of better visibility. It was U-105 commanded by 26-year old Kapitänleutnant Jürgen Nissen and it was making 8 knots. U-105 was still on the surface when six depth charges were dropped up the track from 30-50 feet (250lbs torpex, set to 25 feet, actual spacing 40 feet). They exploded all round it and on their subsidence it was seen to be lying almost stationary in the centre of the disturbed area, with a list to starboard. It porpoised slowly (first bows up, then stem up), turned sluggishly to port and eventually gradually submerged, three or four minutes after the attack. A minute later U-105 reappeared and opened fire with cannon. The Sunderland, returning fire, immediately attacked up the track from 600 feet, dropping an anti-submarine bomb, but it fell short. Another was then released and this exploded alongside. A great patch of oil then appeared; in spite of a rough sea which rapidly broke up the patch, it maintained a width of at least 50 yards. The Sunderland remained for 3½ hours keeping contact by Special Equipment in bad visibility, while U-105 remained on the surface, moving slowly; its speed now varied between two and four knots and occasionally it stopped, while its course was erratic, with a variation of 20 degrees. In all 700 rounds were fired from the aircraft, which was itself hit in the port wing. U-105 was damaged and Nissen put into El Ferrol in Spain where it remained until 28 June. A year later, on 2 June 1943, U-105 was sunk off Dakar by Antares, a Free French Potez flying-boat of 141 Escadrille. The U-boat was lost with all 53 hands.[94]

On 28 July, with the gunner working feverishly to repair a jammed front turret, Sunderland 'C' on 10 Squadron RAAF deliberately circled for half an hour within range of enemy land-based fighters in the Bay of Biscay in order to attack an enemy convoy and its escort of two armed trawlers between Cape Higuer and Cape Machichaco. When the flying boat, captained by Flight Lieutenant R. W. Marks, prepared to attack, the front turret jammed. Since a successful attack depended largely on the front gunner's ability to silence the convoy's AA fire as the Sunderland closed, the captain decided to circle the ships and let the gunner repair the turret, although he knew that the trawlers would almost certainly SOS for land-based fighter protection. Half an hour later the damage had been repaired and the pilot began the run-up. As the ships opened fire a Messerschmitt Bf 109 appeared. Marks left it to his gunners while he took slight evasive action against the flak from the ships. In the first attack the Me 109 overshot, but it came in again on the starboard side and opened up with cannon and machine gun fire. The Sunderland's midships and rear gunners poured tracer bullets in as it closed and the front gunner let it have a final burst as it flew across just below the flying boat's nose. The Me 109 went past in a gradual dive. A wisp of smoke came from its fuselage and a moment later it burst into flames and crashed into the sea. At that moment a heavy shell smashed into the Sunderland's hull. A fragment flew diagonally upwards, snipped a piece of the control column and whipped past the captain's face and out through the port hole beside him. He felt the wind of it. Another splinter set fire to a marine distress flare. The cockpit was instantly filled with smoke.

The Sunderland's navigator, whose aim the shell had disturbed at the last moment and caused his bombs to miss the trawlers, picked the flare up and threw it overboard. The pilot could not see his instrument panel for smoke, but he banked away and began the long flight home. Both inner engines of the Sunderland began to give trouble and soon the port inner stopped. The pilot had to 'hold' the aircraft in the air all the way home while the crew threw out the anchor and other movable equipment to lighten it. The Sunderland got home safely and soon the ground crew were making her ready for another sortie.

Several Hampden squadrons were converted to torpedo carriers in mid-1942 and the margin of safety for German supply shipping along the Norwegian coast was considerably reduced. When the German convoys reached Bergen on their way to the northern garrisons with vital stores, they had considered themselves safe from further air attack. Bergen was practically the limit of the effective range of Coastal Command's Beauforts and Hudsons; beyond that point the ships had to contend only with British submarines. But the Hampdens, with their greater powers of endurance, could range much farther afield in search of their prey and fjords and anchorages north of Bergen, which were once looked upon by German seamen as 'reception areas,' now came within the danger zone.

10 Squadron RAAF was well on the way to having flown 3,000,000 nautical miles when 461, the second RAAF Sunderland squadron in Britain, had come into being, at Pembroke Dock, also the home of its sister squadron, on Anzac Day, 25 April 1942. Using Consolidated Catalinas originally. 461 soon took its own Sunderlands on strength, under the command of Squadron Leader R. B. Burrage OBE DFC. Part of 19 Group, Coastal Command 461 Squadron began working-up soon after formation and its first two boats were ready for operations on 1 July. By the end of that month, the squadron was at full strength as regards personnel and aircraft and now commanded by Wing

Commander G. A. R. Halliday RAF. Determined to surpass the efforts of their already famous sister squadron, the crews of 461 were inexperienced initially; using the call-signs for the day, an Australian skipper called base on return from patrol to enquire, 'Randy One, this is Randy Two - have you a buoy for me?' It took some time for the pilot to live this one down! Backed up by depth charges, the Leigh light, radar and Torpex explosives which made up part of their Sunderlands' equipment, the Aussies were ready to tackle the task. On 30 July, while on patrol off Ushant, the Sunderland on 461 Squadron skippered by Pilot Officer F. V. Manger drew first blood for the unit by destroying an Arado Ar196, one of three hostile aircraft which attacked the formidable flying boat in broad daylight. There was nearly a catastrophe on 9 August when a 461 Squadron Sunderland attacked a submarine vigorously, but happily no damage was done when the captain and crew realised that this particular vessel belonged to the Royal Navy. Mount Batten, where the unit was now based, was becoming so cluttered with the aircraft of the two Australian squadrons that 461 temporarily detached some of its elements to Poole, returning when the situation had eased.

On 17 July 1942 north-west of Cape Ortegal Whitley 'H-Harry' on 502 Squadron at St. Eval flown by Pilot Officer A. R. A. Hunt DFC who was from Oxford, spotted a U-boat on the surface. It was U-751 captained by 33-year old Korvettenkapitän Gerhard Bigalk who three days' earlier had left St. Nazaire for the Americas to lay TMB (magnetic) minefields at Charleston, South Carolina. Bigalk had been awarded the Ritterkreuz for sinking the 'jeep' carrier Audacity in December 1941. Attacking from an altitude of fifty feet, Hunt dropped six 250lb Mark VII depth charges with Torpex warheads set for 25 feet. The close straddle literally lifted U-751 out of the water but Hunt decided to make a second attack with ASW bombs and machine guns. U-751 survived these attacks and Bigalk dived. Two hours later when he returned to the surface, a Lancaster (R5724/F) of Bomber Command on 61 Squadron on loan to Coastal Command and piloted by Flight Lieutenant Peter R. Casement DSO DFC, an Irishman from County Antrim, was orbiting overhead. U-751 was drifting helplessly on the fringe of an oil patch larger than a football field. Just before two o'clock in the afternoon, as Casement ran in to attack, U-751 returned fire with all her guns. At two o'clock, according to his log, he bombed the submarine again. The Lancaster dropped ten close Mark VIII depth charges and then a string of ASW bombs. The U-boat was now so low in the water that at times it disappeared in the wash of the bombs. At a minute past two the submarine's crew jumped to the deck gun and fired at the Lancaster. A minute later the aircraft replied. Two minutes afterwards Casement bombed again. After another six minutes U-751 began to slide stern first beneath the sea and the crew threw themselves overboard 'some of them shaking fists in defiance' reported the Lancaster crew. The bow of the U-boat rose vertically and she sank. Three minutes afterwards the sea was undisturbed save for the bobbing heads of the German crew. No attempt was made to rescue the crew, all 48 hands being lost.

On 3 August 423 Squadron RCAF flew its first Sunderland operation since being formed at Oban in May when Flying Officer John Musgrave carried out an anti-submarine search. During August the Canadian squadron recorded eleven U-boat sightings and made six attacks on enemy boats. 461 Squadron recorded three sightings and one attack on 10 August when at 1413, E/461 flying at 2,500 feet sighted a U-boat on the surface five miles away on port quarter. The U-boat left a definite oil streak about 10 yards wide and 1½ miles long. Musgrave turned towards the U-boat, which submerged when 2½ miles away, but when the aircraft was about 600 yards from the swirl the conning tower and stern re-appeared for a short time. The Sunderland attacked from the U-boat's port beam at right angles to its track and released six torpex depth charges (set to 25 feet, spaced at 35 feet) from 50 feet, 12 seconds after the second disappearance of the conning tower. The DCs straddled the line of advance at the point of aim, about 60 yards ahead of the swirl, which should have been the actual position of the conning tower. Five minutes after the attack an oil bubble 60 x 25 yards and two large air bubbles were seen 200 yards ahead of the explosion mark. This well executed attack certainly shook the crew severely and probably caused a certain amount of damage.

By September 1942 the average of U-boat kills from air attacks had fallen to 6 per cent per month despite improved tactics of search and final approach which, coupled with the gradually increasing number of aircraft devoted to anti-U-boat work.

On 1 September 461 Squadron's first Sunderland was lost in a combat with two Junkers Ju 88s, all eleven crew members perishing. That morning A/461 and R/10 and U/10 were engaged on an anti-shipping patrol in the Bay of Biscay. While proceeding to the patrol area, U/10 got a Special Equipment contact twelve miles on the port beam and on homing sighted, at a range of five miles, a vessel that was emitting so much smoke that it was thought to be a merchantman. Approaching up sun and making use of cloud cover, the aircraft finally identified it as a large Italian submarine, travelling at six knots. It was the *Reginaldo Guiliani,* which was returning from a war cruise off Brazil. The submarine opened fire with light flak from the after end of the bridge, but at 1028 hours the aircraft pressed home the attack from SAP bombs while the submarine was still fully surfaced. Only one bomb was seen to explode and this about thirty yards to port of the submarine, but yellow smoke immediately issued from its port quarter and continued for about half a minute. At this point, R/10 came on the scene, having obtained simultaneous Special Equipment and visual contacts at ten miles' range and carried out two machine-gun attacks on the *Reginaldo Guiliani* from stern to bow, diving from 1,500 feet to 500 feet and firing from nose and tail guns. The submarine replied from all gun positions, the cannon fire being intense.

A few minutes later, R/10 sighted A/461 one mile away. Meanwhile, U/10 had turned to port in a wide sweep and now attacked again from the starboard bow but, owing to an error, the bomb did not release. Eight minutes later R/10 attacked from the submarine's starboard beam with two 250lb SAP bombs, turning to repeat the same manoeuvre with one more bomb. None of the bombs fell sufficiently near the submarine to do appreciable damage. After R/10's second bomb attack the submarine ceased fire and did not fire again owing to casualties caused by the aircraft's tail guns. R/10 sustained several hits but suffered no casualties. Throughout the action a large volume of bluish-brown smoke came from the submarine's diesel exhausts, clouds of it trailed astern for half a mile. The three aircraft on the scene then contacted each other by R/T and from 1035 to 1055 circled the position, arranging a concerted attack, but before this could be put into effect, orders were received from base to continue with the anti-shipping patrol. The *Reginaldo Guiliani* could consider itself lucky that the aircraft were carrying anti-shipping armament and had a major objective which precluded the use of every bomb.

On the last day of the month Pilot Officer H. G. Cooke on 461 Squadron heavily damaged a blockade-running U-boat 700 miles west of La Pallice, forcing the enemy vessel to limp home for lengthy repairs. That same day 10 Squadron took part in a submarine attack when Sunderland W3983 captained by Flight Lieutenant H. G. 'Graham' Pockley of Randwick, New South Wales attacked the *Reginaldo Guiliani,* which had been attacked on 1 September by 10 Squadron RAAF. The Sunderland was on patrol over the Bay of Biscay when the submarine was sighted on the surface. Pockley dived, firing as he descended. As he rose to circle the submarine another 10 Squadron Sunderland (W3986), captained by Flight Lieutenant S. R. C. Wood DFC of Sydney, who, in 1936, rowed number four for Oxford, arrived and went in to attack, dropping a stick of bombs. Pockley followed in with another stick and then he swept down in two more gun attacks. During the battle an uncyphered message in Italian was picked up from the submarine: 'Am being attacked by Sunderland. Captain killed and casualties among crew. Require immediate air protection. Viva. First Lieutenant.'

In Pockley's last attack the submarine's guns were silent. His gunner pumped in 1,000 rounds at point blank range and watched the bullets ricocheting off the conning tower. The 461 Squadron Sunderland, captained by Pilot Officer B. L. Buls had arrived during the attack and was circling the submarine when all three Australian Sunderlands were called to another target, leaving the submarine to be finished off by another Allied aircraft. Pockley was awarded the DFC and in November 1942 after further successes, added a Bar to his decoration. [95]

On 9 September R/10 was again flying in the Bay, at a height of 3,500 feet, when a weak Special Equipment blip was received at 18 miles on the port bow. At ten miles the contact grew strong. R/10 continued to home just above the thin layer of cloud at 2,000 feet and at five miles' range descended through it to sight a dark grey U-boat right ahead. The pilot climbed back into cloud and again broke through at 3 miles' range, then dived at 195 knots, turning slightly through the 3/10ths cloud. Finally breaking cloud at 400 feet the U-boat was seen 1½ miles away on the surface, travelling at 8 knots. The aircraft turned slightly to starboard, observing men on the bridge and one man running along the upper deck and circled astern at a range of one mile, when it climbed to 900 feet, waiting for the U-boat to submerge. When the submarine was one mile on the starboard beam, the U-boat began to dive and the aircraft turned and attacked from its starboard bow, releasing six torpex depth charges with spoiler nose and tails (set to 25 feet, spaced at 21 feet) from 50 feet, while the top of the conning tower and the stern were still above water. The stick straddled the U-boat's bow abaft the stern, three DCs on either side; they should have exploded just before the conning tower. The explosions were particularly heavy and two minutes later large air bubbles effervesced for five minutes over an area 50 feet across, 50 yards from the inside edge of the explosion mark and continued for a quarter of an hour, when the aircraft left to adopt baiting tactics. Nothing new was observed when it returned 40 minutes later. This model attack undoubtedly inflicted severe damage to the U-boat.

On 14 September Sunderland W6002/R on 202 Squadron at Gibraltar flown by Flying Officer E. P. Walshe was off the coast of Algeria, flying at 800 feet, when at 1430 hours an object was sighted five miles away. At 2 miles' distance this was identified as a submarine painted grey and green. It was the Italian submarine, *Alabastro*. The aircraft approached from astern so that the enemy's main gun could not be brought to bear, but there was some light flak, which ceased when the aircraft's front gun opened up. An attack was made from 50 feet and five torpex depth charges were released while the submarine was still fully surfaced. One hung up and of those which dropped, one took the fuzing link with it. Two DCs fell on the starboard side, just forward of the conning tower and the other two along the port bow. Immediately the *Alabastro* lost all way and oil gushed out all round it. It then steamed slowly round in circles, keeping the gun trained and firing at the aircraft, until 35 seconds after the attack, when it gradually sank bow first. About forty survivors were left floating in the water or on their dinghy.

In October 1942 Halifax 209, a large fast convoy Europe-bound was successfully guarded from the attentions of a U-pack, which trailed the ships for four days, starting on 2 October. The Royal Navy, Coastal Command and the US Naval Air Arm co-operated in making things difficult for the submarine commanders. When the pack was reported, Catalinas of VP-73 swept down from Iceland to provide an air umbrella for the convoy. The pack held off. The next day the danger area was reached. Coastal Command Flying Fortresses, Liberators and Hudsons and a Catalina on a Norwegian Squadron of Coastal Command joined the Americans. Two U-boats partly surfaced. According to a contemporary account 'American Catalinas pounced upon them like cats on unwary mice'.[96] The U-boats had to dive without being able to attack. Oil patches marked the scene of their diving. The same afternoon a submarine dived before a Liberator could reach it and afterwards the same aircraft forced another U-boat down before it could fire its torpedoes. In less than an hour this same Liberator attacked a third submarine with bombs and machine-guns.

Some miles away a Hudson on 269 Squadron piloted by Flying Officer J. A Markham stormed at a submarine with all guns firing. It was U-619, commanded by 26-year old Oberleutnant zur see Kurt Makowski. Markham then bombed the boat and in a few seconds masses of oil and exploding air bubbles festooned the sea surface. Ten minutes later wreckage floated up. U-619 was lost with all 44 hands. A Fortress spotted two U-boats, attacked one and caused the other to slink away into the ocean depths. When evening came on the night of the 5th/6th the American Catalinas had another chance to hit at the underwater buccaneers. They attacked two and one of them was credited with sinking U-582. The next day the crisis was over. Only two U-boats were sighted. A Hudson got to one (U-257 commanded by Kapitänleutnant Heinz Rahe) and attacked with depth charges which damaged the boat and forced Rahe to abort to France where battle-damage repairs required weeks;[97] the other chose discretion rather than valour. Another watchful twenty-four hours passed and then the giant convoy was in British waters, the danger past.

In the Mediterranean on 13 November 1942 Flying Officer Mike Ensor piloting Hudson 'S-Sugar' on 500 Squadron, attacked and so severely damaged U-458 that it was unable to dive. The U-boat was forced to return to La Spezia. Ensor was born on a sheep station in New Zealand and his horizon was within the hills of Canterbury. He had arrived in England in April 1941 when he was twenty, to fight with the RAF. In January of the following year, he was seeking for enemy shipping near Heligoland. He flew down to mast height and bombed a German ship. He then flew his aircraft towards the mouth of the Elbe but was blinded by searchlights and the aircraft hit land in the dark. There was a crash and the aircraft bounced. The propellers of the starboard engine were bent over the cowling, the motor was so damaged that 'Mike' had to switch it off and the airspeed indicator and the wireless were both out of action. He climbed to 1,000 feet and set course for home but the aircraft was 180 degrees out of course and Ensor found himself flying in darkness over Holland. The Germans fired at them so that they had to fly inland and escape by hedge hopping. The observer came up beside Ensor and told him when to climb so that he would miss the trees and buildings. The flak was coming at them all the time, but they escaped over the sea. They flew through a heavy snowstorm in the pitch black night. 'It was dark as the inside of a horse,' Ensor said. With the help of Very cartridges he landed in a field in which posts had been erected, to prevent enemy aircraft from landing. The aircraft hit two of the posts but Ensor brought it to rest, with no mishaps to the crew except a black eye and one tooth knocked out, for the observer.

For this Ensor was given the DFC. When he went to Africa with a Hudson, to help to cover the 'Torch' landings, he was twenty-one. He had already attacked three U-boats and had been awarded a bar to his DFC. In the Mediterranean he attacked his fourth. The U-boat was raked by gun fire and several of the crew were killed. On 15 November, 35 miles north of Algiers, he attacked his fifth U-boat - U-259 commanded by 26-year old Kapitänleutnant Klaus Köpke - also in the Mediterranean, with four depth charges, one of which fell directly on the top side deck and caused a violent secondary explosion that threw the deck gun and entire conning tower skyward. U-259 then sank very quickly with all 48 hands. One of the explosions and the flying debris hit the Hudson, throwing the aircraft up to 500 feet. Ensor was unconscious for a few moments. When he came to, he found the perspex in a broken heap on his knees. The aircraft was diving steeply towards the sea and, just in time, he jammed forward the throttles so that the nose came up to meet the horizon. Six feet of the port wing tip were bent almost at a right angle. The starboard wing was also broken and bent. The aircraft was then at about 1,000 feet and the controls were almost useless. The only way Ensor could turn her on course for Algiers was by alternating the speed of the engines. He was able to make the aircraft climb to 3,000 feet and he ordered the crew to check their parachutes. Then the nose dipped and the aircraft descended to 200 feet and levelled out again.

The Hudson limped along at 100 miles an hour; little more than stalling speed. A few moments after, when the altimeter was registering 1,000 feet, Ensor saw Algiers in the distance. Then one of the motors cut out; the Hudson began to go into a spin and about twenty miles north of Algiers the crew had to bail out quickly. Two of the crew perished. The others were picked up by a sloop and brought to shore. Ensor learned later that the U-boat had been sunk. He was still twenty-one when a DSO was added to his DFC and bar. For some months after this Mike Ensor was on the Air Staff at Coastal Headquarters. But he was stubborn and embarrassed by files and he asked to be sent back to operational flying. Now, at twenty-two, he is leader of his flight, responsible for organizing, under the wing commander, a big slice of operational patrols, in addition to being captain of his own aircraft which takes its turn in patrolling the South-Western Approaches.[98]

Two days later, in the same area, Squadron Leader Ian C. Patterson in another Hudson on Squadron 500 found and attacked the veteran U-331, commanded by 29-year old Kapitänleutnant Hans-Dietrich Freiherr von Tiesenhausen, who had sunk the battleship HMS *Barham* in the Mediterranean on 25 November 1941. Three depth charges and one ASW bomb wrecked the boat and blew open the torpedo-loading hatch in the bow compartment, flooding that space. Two other Hudsons on 500 Squadron, flown by Andrew W. Barwood and Sergeant Young joined Patterson and carried out depth-charge and strafing attacks, which killed and wounded some Germans who had come up on deck. Von Tiesenhausen ran up a white flag. The Hudson airmen cheered this second surrender (after U-570) of a U-boat to RAF aircraft. But the celebration was short-lived. A Fleet Air Arm Martlet fighter suddenly appeared on the scene and strafed the boat, killing more Germans and wounding von Tiesenhausen and others. Then an Albacore torpedo-bomber on 820 Squadron on the carrier HMS *Formidable* appeared from nowhere and sank U-331 with a torpedo, killing many Germans who were still below decks. The destroyer HMS *Wilton*, racing from Algiers to assist in the capture and a Walrus amphibian pulled von Tiesenhausen and sixteen other Germans out of the water.[99]

A typical Sunderland sortie is described by Flight Lieutenant Jack Sumner, skipper of a 423 Squadron RCAF Sunderland crew at Castle Archdale in late 1942: 'The time, 0030. The batman taps the sleeping skipper on the shoulder. 'Time to get up, sir, briefing's at one-thirty, take-off three-thirty.' (Batmen could seldom tell the time in Service officialise). A few hours before, the weather had looked anything but promising. The sky was heavy with a low overcast and rain was pelting down - real 'scrub' weather. Bed felt especially comfortable and warm as the batman shuffled off to wake the other officers. Nonetheless...

'Sleepy-eyed aircrew stumble through a drenching downpour to their Messes. Breakfast consists of porridge, bacon and egg, tea or coffee and 'lashings of toast and marmalade'. 'Looks like a really long stooge this time', some pre-informed flight engineer remarks. Engineers had a talent for ferreting out the gen about forthcoming ops before anyone else. 'Almost seven hundred miles out! They'd better have those petrol tanks good and full or there'll be a lot of us in the drink waiting for the air-sea rescue types.' 'By briefing time the clouds have gone and the sky is a mass of stars. A strong wind has picked up, which means head-winds on the way out. Covering one wall of the briefing room is an Atlantic area map which itself looks as big as an ocean. Lines of ribbon run out from British ports to code-lettered sea positions that represent the latest reported positions of convoys in-bound from America. Just beyond 25 degrees west is a miniature submarine. 'That's where you're going,' announces the Operations Officer, pointing to the U-boat marker. 'Americans patrolling that area yesterday came on a pack of subs. They attacked them but we don't know what the results were. As you can see from the chart, there's a convoy in the vicinity, but your job is those submarines. You'll get the weather conditions from the met man.'

'The weather-merchant is far from happy. Only the urgency of the situation, he admits, permits the operation in the first place. The weather overhead is purely a local condition. Information from the Atlantic is so vague that he cannot predict with any accuracy. There are several fronts out there, but their movements are indefinite. 'If you're lucky you may return under conditions just as they are now' - and he adds, 'or it may get thick.'

'After a few words from the squadron commander (Wing Commander F. J. Rump), the air crews leave the briefing room. Sumner's navigator, Warrant Officer Harry Parliament, is loaded down with maps and charts. The second pilot, Pilot Officer George Holley, carries two orange-coloured metal boxes housing Gertie and George, homing pigeons which will be released if the Sunderland is forced down at sea. At the docks crews board motor boats which take them to their flying yachts moored well out in the lake. There the rest of the crew of 'J' awaits them - Pilot Officer Art Mountford, Sergeants Jack Kelly, Hal Hutchinson, Phil Marshall, J. B. Horsburgh and A. J. Lunn. They have been in the aircraft all night, having slept aboard. Mountford is busy making tea in the galley. There is still time before take-off and the crew sit around the table in the wardroom, chatting the minutes away.

'Suddenly the skipper looks at his watch, heaves himself to his feet and gives the order to douse cigarettes and the oil heater. It's time to start up. In quick succession four Pegasus power-plants kick to life and then merge into an unsynchronised roar. The big 'boat moves towards the flare path - a row of lights bobbing on the water - guided by a dinghy-borne airman flashing an Aldis lamp. Both pilots make their pre-take-off checks, the crew get into their take-off positions and presently the ship is trimmed and ready to go. Then, throttles opening wide in an angry crescendo, the Sunderland gathers momentum, pulls itself up on to the step and is soon moving over the lake at express train speed. Sumner brings back the control column in one smooth movement, with a slight jerk and 'J-Jig' gets airborne.

'But the operation isn't yet under way. Before reaching its patrol area 'Jig' is re-called because of threatening weather at base. It returns to the mooring place and the crew awaits another order to go. This comes sooner than

Aerial reconnaissance photo taken by a PR Mosquito of the harbour at Gdynia on 5 October 1942 showing the *Gneisenau* moored at its jetty (arrow top centre) for repairs and the German aircraft carrier *Graf Zeppelin* (bottom arrow).

Short Sunderland I on 204 Squadron being brought ashore at Mount Batten. The Sunderland carried four .303 inch Browning machine guns in each of the power-operated nose and tail turrets (the first British flying boat to do so). The aircraft's considerable armament prompted the nickname 'Flying Porcupine' being bestowed on it by the Germans.

Handley Page Halifax GR.II JP165 'D-Dog' on 58 Squadron in all-white finish off the Welsh coast near St. David's in 1944. The aircraft is powered by four Merlin XX engines and armed with a mid upper turret and a single Vickers Gas Operated .303 inch machine gun (later replaced by a Browning .5 inch gun) in the nose. On 9 April 1945 this aircraft was lost in a fatal crash in mountains five miles SW of Tarbet on the Isle of Harris.

Crew of 'S-Sugar', 407 'Demon' Squadron RCAF at Wick in Scotland: standing left to right, Warrant Officer George Grandy, wireless operator; Flying Officer Gord A. Biddle, pilot; Pilot Officer Ken Graham; seated, Flight Lieutenant Maurice Neil and Flight Sergeant Harvey Firestone, one of the wireless-operator-air gunners. Flying Officer George Deeth, the second pilot, remained in England and is missing from this photo. (Firestone)

Air Marshal Sir John Slessor CB DSO MC who commanded Coastal Command from February 1943 to January 1944.

A Sunderland skipper and his second pilot who is using an Aldis lamp for signalling.

A Sunderland navigator plots his charts during a long sea patrol in the North Atlantic.

Right: Sunderland crew members at work.

Below: Off Trondheim on 21 May Pilot Officer E. T. King on 4 OTU RCAF flying Sunderland 'S-Sugar' dropped six depth charges and hit and damaged U-995 which was three days out from Bergen on passage to Trondheim on its first war cruise to commence Arctic operations. The depth charges damaged the boat and four crewmen were wounded when King strafed the submarine. In May 1945 U-995 surrendered to the Allies at Trondheim.

Sunderland beam gunners at their stations with drum-fed (800 rounds per gun) Vickers Gas Operated .303 inch machine guns (later replaced with two manually-operated belt-fed .50 inch Brownings). Some aircraft were armed with four fixed remotely-controlled .303 inch Browning machine guns in bows.

On 10 March 1944 Sunderland EK59J/U on 422 Squadron RCAF flown by Warrant Officer W. F. Morton, who was on his first operational sortie as captain and Flight Lieutenant Sidney W. Butler DFC along as check pilot, spotted U-625. Butler, who was at the controls at the time, avoided flak by frequent alterations of height and dropped six depth charges. U-625 sank by the stern and all 53 hands perished.

A 201 Squadron Sunderland skipper using binoculars to look for a U-boat target.

Sunderland I L5798 DA-A on 210 Squadron taking off from Pembroke Dock.

A Sunderland pilot flashes a recognition signal with an Aldis lamp as soon as the aircraft makes contact with the convoy.

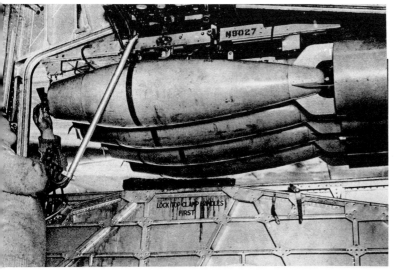

Four 250lb Mk.VIII anti-submarine bombs being loaded into the wing of a Sunderland. This bomb was the standard offensive weapon used by Sunderlands in the early part of the war but its killing power proved quite inadequate and led to the development of the depth charge, which proved the most effective weapon in the anti-U-boat armoury.

Following service as a flight sergeant on 50 Squadron on Bomber Command, during which he was shot down on the 1,000 bomber raid on Cologne on 30/31 May 1942 and his subsequent evasion, Flight Lieutenant Leslie 'Beve' Baveystock DSO DFC DFM served on 201 Squadron in Coastal Command as a Sunderland pilot. The award of the DFC followed the award of the DFM, on 25 January 1944 and he received a bar to his DFC on 25 August.

On 7 June 1944 Flight Lieutenant Baveystock sank U-955 (pictured) in the Bay of Biscay north of Spain and on 18 August he sank U-107 in the Bay of Biscay south-west of St. Nazaire. Baveystock was awarded the DSO on 13 October 1944.

Squadron Leader Terence 'Hawkeyes' M. Bulloch (centre front row) became the most highly decorated pilot in RAF Coastal Command, credited with sinking more U-boats than any other.

Flight Lieutenant Dudley 'Dud' Marrows DSO DFC RAAF, born in Bendigo in 1917 and an accountant when the war began in Europe. He served on Sunderlands on 461 Squadron RAAF and on 30 July 1943 he took part in the 'Greatest air/U-boat battle of WWII' when three U-boats were sunk. Marrows accounted for U-461. On 16 September 1943 his Sunderland was attacked by six Ju 88s, after having battled them for more than an hour, shooting one down and losing three engines in the process, he force landed on the Bay of Biscay in a 15 foot swell. His Sunderland, riddled with bullet holes subsequently sank with all crew surviving to be rescued by the Royal Navy. Marrows then captained one of six Sunderlands to Australia for service on 40 Squadron RAAF.

On 10 March 1944 Sunderland EK59l DG-U-Uncle on 422 Squadron RCAF flown by Warrant Officer W. F. Morton, who was on his first operational sortie as captain and Flight Lieutenant Sidney W. Butler DFC along as check pilot, spotted U-625. Butler, who was at the controls at the time, avoided flak by frequent alterations of height and dropped six depth charges. U-625 sank by the stern and all 53 hands perished.

Depth charges from a Sunderland flying boat on 10 Squadron RAAF captained by Flying Officer William Boris Tilley straddle a U-boat in an attack on 8 July 1944 while the flying crew's rear guns strafe the submarine.

U-243 under attack and sinking by Sunderlands W4030 and JM684 on 10 Squadron RAAF on 8 July 1944.

Survivors of U-243 in the Bay of Biscay on 8 July after the submarine had been attacked by Flying Officer Tilley DFC RAAF. U-243 was scuttled by the engineer, who went down with the boat, leaving the commander, 26-year old Kapitänleutnant Hans Märtens and 37 of his crew in the water. Later two Mosquitoes circled until the arrival of the rescue ships seven hours after the U-243 sank.

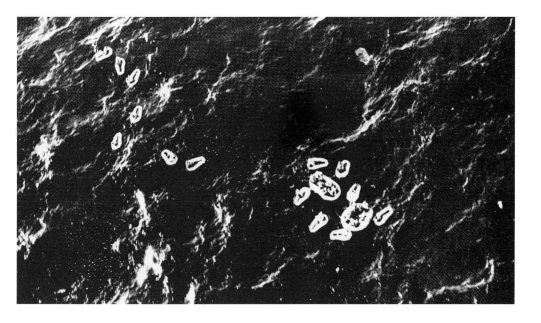

Wellington XIV 'H-Harry' on 458 Squadron RAAF takes off from Gibraltar with 'X-X-Ray' in the foreground in February 1945 on an anti-submarine patrol.

Wellington GR XIV on 304 (Polish) Squadron. (IWM)

Wing Commander John Barrett DFC and his crew on Sunderland ML778 'Z-Zebra' on 201 Squadron on the final war patrol on 3/4 June 1945 over a convoy. At one minute after midnight on 4 June, when 500 miles southwest of Ireland 'Zebra' received the order to 'Cease patrol'. (IWM)

U-224 blowing tanks and flying the black surrender 'flag' photographed from 150 feet by a Liberator on 13 May 1945.

A Schnörkel-equipped U-boat surfaces at Londonderry during the surrender in May 1945.

expected and the routine begins all over again. This time it's a convoy escort. The briefing is much like the previous one, except that one of the U-boats has been definitely sunk and another two probably destroyed by escort surface vessels. But a pack of them are still shadowing the convoy and it must have aerial protection - it's that simple.

'Taking off again in darkness the Sunderland, soon after first light, reaches the area where it is to pick up the convoy. Sumner and Holley scan the ocean for sign of a ship. Mountford is glued to his wireless set, Parliament checks and rechecks his navigation. Kelly swings his mid-upper turret slowly back and forth. The wireless operator calls the captain on the intercom and gives him a radio bearing on the convoy. A course alteration is made to starboard and soon the long lines of ships are in sight. The Sunderland begins to circle the convoy just within visual range. The armament of those ships carried quite a sting and it was considered unwise to venture too close to them until they'd sent out a recognition signal. It wasn't unusual for such ships to shoot first and ask questions afterwards

The message of recognition is received, followed by a second message giving a bearing on a suspected submarine well to starboard of the convoy. Everybody aboard the Sunderland perks up. Even if they don't see one, at least they'll have the satisfaction of knowing that their presence is keeping one of the foe out of striking range. The circling goes on and on... A welcome break in the monotony comes with the call to lunch. The crew retires in shifts to the wardroom to partake of thick steaks with potatoes and turnips and a 'dessert' of bread and jam. The next meal, tea, will feature fried egg sandwiches. Time passes - slowly - the monotony grows. Everyone is wishing the patrol would hurry up and end.

'As if in deference to their wishes the alarm siren shrieks and red warning lights flash. 'The skip's spotted something!' Hutchinson shouts as he heads towards the bomb racks. As he and another crew man pull down the side flaps of the bomb bay and press the button that moves the depth charges out on a track to their position on the lower surface of the wing, Sumner banks as tightly as possible and dives at full throttle in the direction of something long and black in the distance. The thing - it's a sub all right - appears to be five miles away, but distances are deceptive over water. Uppermost in each man's mind is the question, 'Will it see us and submerge before we can attack?' The answer comes only seconds later, when the alarmed enemy crash-dives to safety. The vicinity around the sub's vanishing act is carefully scrutinised, but any attempt to depth-charge now would be nothing but the wildest stab in the dark - the raider may have beetled-off in any direction. 'Bring in the bombs', orders the skipper and the load of high explosive returns to its stowage in the fuselage. Now the circling begins anew, but the patrol period is soon over. A signal to that effect is sent to one of the escort destroyers. The Sunderland turns for home...'

Although 19 Group Coastal Command was always on the hunt for U-boats it was not averse to making attacks on other vessels like speedy blockade-runners whose captains were well versed in all the arts of maritime deception. Almost invariably these were picked up as they approached the Bay of Biscay.

In January 1943 the Rhakotis was spotted by a Hampden on 502 Squadron and shadowed by a Sunderland on 10 Squadron RAAF. She was finished off by a cruiser which 'homed' on to the flying boat. This single stroke deprived Germany not only of useful quantities of fats, vegetable oils, quinine bark, tea, tin, rice and wolfram, but also of 4,000 tons of rubber -enough to supply four armoured divisions for a year. And the fate of the Rhakotis was by no means untypical; in the first four months of 1943 only one blockade-runner out of seven reached the French coast. After that, until the end of the year, the Germans gave up even trying.

During mid-1943 an unprecedented number of submarine sightings and attacks kept the plotters at Coastal Command busier than ever before but out of 52 U-boats sighted in the bay of Biscay, 28 were attacked but only one (U-332) was sunk, on 29 April, although two were so badly damaged that they had to return to France for repairs. In a combined attack Flying Officer R. deV. Gipps on 461 Squadron forced a surfaced U-boat to dive in his first attack, dropping a marker flare on the spot. Flying Officer N. C. Gerrard next came in to attack, just as U-119 had surfaced and was bringing its anti-aircraft guns to bear on the huge, airborne target. Dropping depth charges around the now zigzagging submarine, the crews of both Sunderlands saw the apparently stricken vessel draw to a stop in a flurry of foam, and returned to base to claim it as sunk. U-119 however, managed to return home for repairs, but was subsequently sunk on 24 June by HMS *Starling* when it was caught on mine-laying operations off the coast of the USA.

In May 1943 the number of U-boats sighted rose to 98, the number attacked to 64 and the number destroyed to seven. On 1 May Admiral Dönitz[100] issued his 'Fight Back' order to the U-boats, whereby the submarine should engage the attacking aircraft rather than risk an emergency dive which would leave it vulnerable to depth charge attack. The U-boat was an uneasy anti-aircraft platform even in calm sea. Air Chief Marshal Sir John Slessor KCB DSO MC, commanding Coastal Command had the greatest confidence in his crews and averred would not be deterred by casualties from attacking U-boats at low level. Events would prove him right. 'It is up to us to take the fullest advantage of the good opportunities afforded before the buzz goes round in the Biscay ports that fighting back is an expensive and unprofitable pastime' he wrote. At the same time he did everything possible to give anti-submarine aircraft protection against anti-aircraft fire. Additional forward-firing guns were mounted and the gunners ordered to use them to the fullest possible extent during the run up to attack.

The Australian Sunderland squadrons claimed five submarines and a share in the destruction of two others between 29 April and 2 August 1943 and during that year each squadron received fourteen decorations for gallantry. On 29 April in the Bay of Biscay attacks were made by 'F' on 10 Squadron RAAF and 'P' on 461 Squadron. The 10 Squadron aircraft was first to attack. At 1102 hours a smoke float was sighted; the aircraft investigated and then sighted the periscope of a U-boat in the act of surfacing. It was U-332 commanded by 24-year old Oberleutnant zur see Eberhard Hüttemann, which was bound for the North Atlantic on its sixth war cruise. U-332 opened fire and the Sunderland attacked from the port quarter, releasing six Mk.VIII Torpex depth charges, Mk XVI pistol, set to shallow depth, spaced slightly less than 100 feet, while U-332 was still on the surface. Immediately after the depth charge explosions, an oil streak was seen and then blue and black smoke. At this point Sunderland 'P' flown by Flight Lieutenant E. Smith appeared and carried out an attack, its depth charges being accurately placed, although no success was credited. Credit for the kill went to Flight Lieutenant A. Russell Laughland DFC, a Liberator pilot on 224 Squadron. U-332 was lost with all 45 hands. Two days later Flight Lieutenant E. C. Smith was airborne in DV968/M and in an attack on U-415 damaged the boat. Later that day a Whitley on 612 Squadron piloted by Norman Earnshaw found the U-boat and dropped six depth charges at the swirl but they fell wide. He made a second attack and dropped his last two depth charges and these caused 'heavy damage'. However, U-415 could still dive and was able to limp into Brest.[101]

U-boat losses (to all causes) peaked in May, forty-one being lost. Taking off at 1331 hours on 2 May M/461, at the start of a busy afternoon, Flight Lieutenant E. C. Smith later spotted a U-boat on the surface well out in the Bay west of St Nazaire. It was U-465 commanded by 28-year old Kapitänleutnant Heinz Wolf, which was bound for the Atlantic. The conning tower was sighted and a flame float was dropped, followed by an aluminium sea marker and marine marker. Smith sighted the U-boat on the surface and turned in to attack from four miles astern with six depth charges. Diving through broken cumulus cloud, he was at a low altitude, a mile astern, when the U-boat's gunners opened fire, Smith's nose gunner retaliating. Straddling his quarry with four depth charges, the pilot saw four enemy gunners hurled into the sea by the blast and circled to attack again. By now, U-465 had begun to turn in tight circles, its rudders probably out of action and the stricken submarine began to founder. During the Sunderland's next attack, several of the crew members counted fifteen men from the 48 crew jumping into the sea just as the conning tower slid under in a turmoil of foam, accompanied by much wreckage and a huge pool of oil. U-465 sank horizontally and then the stern emerged and disappeared vertically. None of the fifteen or more men who were seen to abandon ship were rescued.

On 7 May in the Bay of Biscay Flight Lieutenant Geoffrey G. Rossiter on 10 Squadron RAAF piloting Sunderland W3993 'W-William' on Derange patrol, spotted U-663 on the surface and straddled the submarine with six 250lb depth charges. Nothing further was ever heard from the commander 28-year old Kapitänleutnant Heinrich Schmid and his crew, who had left Brest on only their second war cruise on 10 March. The boat was lost with all 49 hands. North-west of Cape Ortegal at 0931 on 11 May, U-528 inbound from the North Atlantic was bombed by Halifax BB268 'D-Dog' on 58 Squadron flown by Pilot Officer J. B. Stark DFC after the submarine had been damaged in an attack by a USN Catalina south-west of Iceland. U-258, which was heading back to Kiel on the surface, submerged but was depth charged to the surface by the sloop HMS *Fleetwood* and the corvette HMS *Mignonette* escorting Convoy OS.47. It was abandoned under gunfire with eleven crewmen killed. The commander, Kapitänleutnant Georg von Rabenau and 44 hands were rescued and taken into captivity.

During the morning of 12 May U-456 commanded by 27-year old Kapitänleutnant Max-Martin Teichert damaged the straggling 7,138-ton SS Fort Concord, which was loaded with a full cargo of grain and a deck cargo of military supplies. The U-456 was on its eleventh war cruise having left Brest on 24 April and had sunk six ships during patrols in the Arctic and North Atlantic. On the night of 12/13 May, 600 miles NNE of the Azores, U-456 was attacked by a Liberator on 86 Squadron and was badly damaged. On the following morning on the surface attempting repairs U-456 was discovered by Sunderland 'G-George' flown by Flight Lieutenant John Musgrave on 423 Squadron RCAF. U-456 was unfit to dive but Teichert did so anyway and he was depth charged by the destroyer HMS *Opportune*. The U-boat sank with the loss of 49 hands.[102] Teichert was awarded a 'Ritterkreuz' posthumously. Five hundred miles north-east of the Azores Flight Lieutenant John Musgrave attacked U-753 commanded by 34-year old Korvettenkapitän Alfred Manhardt von Mannstein with depth charges in the face of heavy 20mm flak. The destroyer HMS *Pathfinder*, frigate HMS *Lagan* and corvette HMCS *Drumheller*, which were escorting Convoy HX.237 were called up by the Sunderland and they finished off the submarine with 'Hedgehog' attacks. U-753 was lost with all 47 hands.

On 24 May Dönitz suspended attacks on convoys in the North Atlantic. So successful had the campaign against U-boats become in 1943 that U-boats had to seek new counter moves against air attack. More Junkers 88s came out to protect the submarines and the German crews themselves began to show a preference for remaining fully surfaced to fight it out with AA guns, where previously they had quickly submerged on the approach of aircraft. Type VII 'Flak boats' or 'flak traps' were introduced to lure and destroy anti-submarine aircraft. Their first success came on 24 May when west of Gibraltar, the veteran U-441, the first of eight such boats, which was armed with two quad 20mms on bandstands fore and aft of the conning tower and a rapid fire 37mm flak gun on a second, lower bandstand aft, plus nests of machine guns on the bridge and a team of highly trained gunners, shot down Sunderland EJ139/L on 228 Squadron flown by Flying Officer H. J. Debden, who also damaged the U-boat's bow area by depth charges. None of the flying-boat crew survived. U-594 also laid claim to the same Sunderland. But mainly the only result of the new German tactics was the sinking of more U-boats.[103]

On 31 May U-563 commanded by 26-year old Oberleutnant zur see Gustav Borchardt, was bound for the North Atlantic having left Brest on 29 May on its eighth war cruise, when it was attacked by Halifax HR774/R piloted by Wing Commander Wilfred E. Oulton DSO DFC on 58 Squadron.[104] At 1550 hours Oulton's flight engineer sighted an indistinct wake six miles distant. Oulton, who had just taken over the controls from Flying Officer Anthony J. W. Birch the second pilot, confirmed the sighting with binoculars as being a surfaced U-boat travelling at 12 knots. He began stalking the submarine, turning the Halifax to starboard, using the 5/10ths cloud clover to bring the aircraft into a position for an attack before finally breaking cloud at 3,000 feet, four miles from the target.

It was only then that a second U-boat was sighted dead ahead, but within seconds it had crash-dived. Oulton never hesitated and he went straight for U-563, his navigator opening fire with the nose gun at 1,000 yards and recording strikes on the conning tower with a second burst from 600 yards seen to penetrate it. With the U-boat now yawing, Oulton swung to starboard making his final run in at an angle of 30° to the U-boat's track and dropping six depth charges across it. As the spray subsided, Oulton brought the Halifax in again from dead astern, the navigator again laying down concentrated fire from the nose position as three more depth-charges were dropped. As the spray plumes from the depth charge explosions subsided, the U-boat was seen to be lying beam-on to the sea surrounded by a large oil slick and a great deal of wreckage.

As Oulton circled the U-boat weaving and varying height, Borchardt's gun crew fired back at the Halifax with flak guns. Oulton's gunners raked U-563 with machine gun fire, cutting down members of the crew manning a cannon mounted just abaft of the conning tower. By now, U-563 was moving slowly in small circles with a heavy list to starboard. Twice more the Halifax gunners raked the submarine with machine gun fire but it was still obstinately afloat when Oulton received the recall order 70 minutes after he had sighted it. As he turned for home Halifax DT636/J on 58 Squadron piloted by Pilot Officer Eric L. Hartley appeared and dived to attack the crippled U-boat. Though Oulton tried to warn him to take his time he was unable to make contact. Hartley carried out two almost identical attacks, dropping nine depth charges but they fell short. Although they produced a fresh gout of oil and white vapour U-563 still refused to sink.[105]

Two Sunderlands now took a hand. Flight Lieutenant Maxwell S. Mainprize DFC on 10 Squadron RAAF recalled: 'The U-boat, which had been trailing oil and manoeuvring freely, stopped. I circled and made a second attack with four depth charges, two minutes later, from the starboard beam. After the second attack the U-boat was down by the bows, stern clear of the water. It appeared to be sinking slowly.' Flying Officer William M. French DFC on 228 Squadron also carried out two attacks, both of which straddled the U-boat and it sank. More than thirty survivors were seen in the water wearing life jackets but none of the 49 hands were rescued. A search on the following day by Ju 88s carrying life rafts also proved futile. The kill was shared between the Halifax and the two Sunderlands. [106]

That same day Flight Lieutenant Douglas M. Gall DFC piloting DD835/R on 201 Squadron attacked U-440 in the Bay of Biscay. The U-boat, which was commanded by 27-year old Kapitänleutnant Werner Schwaff who had been born in Peking in 1915, was bound for the North Atlantic on its fifth war cruise. Gall attacked in the face of heavy flak from U-440 and dropped four depth charges in a good straddle near the U-boat's stern. The explosion must have badly holed the submarine aft because her bow raised vertically and she sank stern first. The U-boat was lost with all 46 hands.[107]

An epic air battle occurred on 2 June when Sunderland 'N for Nan' on 461 Squadron piloted by Flight Lieutenant C. G. Walker, who was on anti-submarine patrol in the Bay of Biscay at 2,000 feet was sighted by eight Junkers

88s six miles distant which immediately gave chase. Flight Sergeant R. M. Goode the tail gunner reported that the enemy aircraft were closing fast. Crew members manned their posts, several standing by guns mounted in the galley hatches - a special, unofficial modification peculiar to at least several machines on 461. The Ju 88s were flying at 3,000 feet in three formations, one of four and two of two behind. Walker opened full throttle and made for what cloud cover there was 3/10ths at 3,000 feet. The Ju 88s gave chase and took up attacking positions three on each beam, 1,500 yards distant and 1,500 feet above and one on each quarter at the same height and distance. The Sunderland jettisoned its depth charges and prepared to meet the attack. The Ju 88s peeled off to attack in pairs, one from each bow. The first attack hit the port outer engine, setting it on fire and also resulted in an incendiary bullet entering the P4 compass, setting alight to the alcohol. The engine fire was extinguished by means of the Graviner switch, but the engine became unserviceable. The alcohol fire, which had set the captain's clothing alight, was also put out with the fire extinguisher. Walker and Pilot Officer W. J. Dowling, his first pilot, were both slightly burned. Dowling took control and continued with the evasive action. During the attack, one of the Ju 88s attacking from starboard broke away, exposing his belly to the midships gunner at point blank range. The midships gunner fired and the Ju 88 burst into flames and crashed into the sea, disintegrating immediately. The next attack, by the second pair of Ju 88s, severed the hydraulics of the tail turret, shot away the elevator and rudder trimming wires, the rudder and elevators were peppered and dozens of holes appeared in the helm. However, the midships and nose gunners made the enemy pay for his success.

Flight Sergeant Goode had been knocked unconscious when the tail was hit, but he came to and he and Flight Sergeant Fuller, one of the mid-ship gunners, opened heavy fire on another Ju 88 which came in on the port quarter - Goode, owing to hydraulic failure, depressing the sears with his fingers in short bursts. It broke away, bounced vertically and crashed nose first into the sea - leaving five Ju 88s to attack the badly damaged Sunderland. Simultaneously another Ju 88 came in on the starboard quarter and his burst wounded the starboard galley gunner. He died twenty minutes later. Meanwhile the port galley gunner drove off another of the enemy with his fire. Conditions now became chaotic. A shell hit the Sunderland's wireless and the navigator, Flying Officer K. Simpson, was wounded in the leg by shrapnel. The intercom and the radio were shot away, the ASI ceased to work and evasive action was controlled by hand signals from the navigator to the second pilot and thence to the captain. Owing to the unserviceable engine and the damaged controls it required both pilots to carry out evasive action. A Ju 88 cut in from the starboard bow to meet the fire of the nose gunner who got in a good burst. The Ju 88's port engine burst into flames and smoke billowed from its cockpit. The combat continued for forty-five minutes in all and the remaining Junkers stood off for a few minutes and then turned away at last.

The crew of the Sunderland estimated that every Ju 88 had been hit, with three shot down. Taking stock of the situation, the Sunderland crew now found that the hull was so strained that all doors had now jammed; the radio and instrument panels had been shot away, added to which there were some 500 holes in the aircraft, mainly in the hull. Despite his injuries and the damage to the aircraft, Walker nursed the Sunderland over nearly 300 miles of sea with one member of the crew killed and another injured and he just managed to reach the Cornish coast where he was able to carry out a landing in the surf. Preparing to abandon what was left of his charge, he noted that the beach itself was not far off, gunned the remaining serviceable Bristol Pegasus engines and beached the Sunderland just as it was about to sink. The crew were sent a message of congratulations by the Secretary of State for Air, Sir Archibald Sinclair and in forwarding this message the Air Officer Commanding-in-Chief added: 'Congratulations were never better earned.' It had been one of the war's really outstanding combats against overwhelming odds. It brought the immediate award of the DSO to Walker and a DFC for the navigator, Flying Officer K. Simpson and a DFM for Flight Sergeant Goode. Simpson and Goode were presumed to have been killed flying with another captain not long afterwards.

On 13 June a surfaced U-boat group consisting of U-564, U-185, U-415, U-634 and U-159 were attacked by Sunderland DV967/U flown by Flying Officer L. B. Lee on 228 Squadron who was shot down by return fire from U-415 with loss of the whole crew.[108] U-564, which was commanded by 28-year old Kapitänleutnant Hans Fielder, sent a signal to base reporting that it was badly damaged and the German Admiralty at once ordered U-185 which was nearby, to go to the help of U-564. At the same time two German destroyers were ordered to sea from La Verdon to meet and escort the submarine into port. On 14 June in the Bay of Biscay at 1439 hours U-564 and its escort, U-185, were found by Whitley BD220/G flown by Sergeant A. J. Benson DFM on 10 OTU. Benson asked for instructions. Base replied: 'carry out homing procedure for aircraft in the vicinity'. This involved shadowing the U-boats and summoning other aircraft with sufficient endurance to the spot. At 1757 hours while still pursuing a lone course Benson signalled to base 'have attacked with depth charges; hydraulic u/s'. After the attack and when struggling homeward the lone Whitley fell in with a number of Ju 88s which had also been sent to the assistance of the U-boats and Benson was forced down into the sea. U-564 however was sunk with the loss of 28 hands. Fielder and eighteen men were rescued by U-185.[109]

Next day another 228 Squadron Sunderland (JM678) flown by Flying Officer S. White attacked three U-boats, dropping four depth charges in an indeterminate attack before the flying-boat was engaged by Ju 88s but escaped into cloud. On 17 June Flight Lieutenant S. Butler pilot of Sunderland W6031 on 422 Squadron was on a Sea Slug 3 patrol when he sighted three U-boats on the surface. While attempting to close, his aircraft was engaged by the main guns and 20mm fire from all three submarines and all he could do was circle the area while his rear gunner sprayed the boats with machine gun fire while the wireless operator vainly attempted to fix his broken transmitter so that he could summon other aircraft and ships to the scene but the three U-boats disappeared into the haze.

On 27 June 1943 Flying Officer Brian E. H. Layne, a New Zealander, on

Sunderland W6005/P on 201 Squadron operating from Castle Archdale claimed a U-boat destroyed when he attacked U-518, which had landed a secret agent in the Gulf of St. Lawrence on 9 November after leaving Kiel on its first war cruise on 26 September 1942. However, the submarine, which was commanded by 27-year old Kapitänleutnant Freidrich-Wilhelm Wissmann, was only seriously damaged and Wissmann was forced to put about for France but on 30 June a Sunderland on 10 Squadron RAAF piloted by Flight Lieutenant H. W. Skinner, hit the U-518 again. Skinner came in at 150 feet in the face of heavy gunfire. Six depth charges went down, one exploding twenty yards from the submarine's port beam but the others overshot. Fire from the Sunderland appeared to hit at least three sailors on the conning tower but the German gunners also scored hits as the flying boat went over. The rear turret, port elevator, both wings and the rear section of the hull were all hit and the tear gunner, Flight Sergeant J. S. Burnham, not yet 21 years old, was mortally wounded. With his aircraft severely damaged, tail gun out of action and a seriously wounded crewman, Skinner broke off the action. Wissmann made it to Bordeaux on 3 July and after repairs, put to sea again on 18 August. The submarine was only finally sunk on 22 April 1945 on her seventh war cruise when it was depth-charged by two USN destroyers and was lost with all 56 hands.[110]

'The Sunderland was probably the most spacious of all RAF operational aircraft' recalled James Kernahan, a front-gunner on 228 Squadron; 'plenty of room to move around on the long 10 to 12 hour flights we made on anti-sub or convoy patrols. There were two pilots, a navigator, flight engineer and assistant and also a wireless operator and assistant, the mechanics and was doubling as gunners. We would spend two hours in a turret and have four hours off. When you were relieved you'd go into the bomb bay where there were bunks. Even though the two engines were roaring away each side, it was only a matter of a few minutes before you were asleep; the noise was no obstacle. The Sunderland had a nice galley at the rear and we ate well, especially while flying out of West Africa when we had steaks, oranges, bananas, sweets and all those things that were never seen by the general public in the UK. The worst thing was the boredom, continually searching the ocean with your eyes until you'd lose the horizon as sea and sky became one. Even so, there was no chance of becoming disorientated as the turret had to be rotated to and fro all the time, the two bolted doors behind your back rattling away every time you turned them into the slipstream. To try and overcome the boredom I'd have a crafty smoke - which one was not supposed to do in the turret - or scribble notes with my name and address on bits of paper, forcing them out of the rear turret. Watching them flutter away I probably hoped some girl would find them and write me. None ever did!'

Sunderland 'M for Mother' on 228 Squadron captained by Flight Lieutenant Charles Gordon Drake Lancaster, left Pembroke Dock in the early evening of 6 July 1943 for a 12-hour anti-submarine patrol over the Bay of Biscay.

'It was uneventful until the sun started to brighten the sky in the east' recalled James Kernahan. 'I saw something on the sea ahead and excitedly told our Skipper that I could see a submarine. Before we could get within effective range the sub had disappeared but the Skipper decided he would conduct a square search of the area. As we were on the last leg I again caught sight of the submarine on the surface. The skipper called out 'Tally Ho!' and we charged in. Sitting in the front turret I opened up with the single Vickers .303 and saw the bullets curving into the conning tower. This fire was only intended to dissuade the crew from getting to their anti-aircraft guns. While I was firing, Lancaster had run the bombs out on their trollies and released them, but the rear-turret gunner reported only splashes and no detonations. Disappointed, we finished our patrol and flew back to Wales. We were greeted by the Intelligence Officer who produced a manual of submarines and asked me to identify the type. I selected what I thought was similar but he said: 'No, you're wrong, you attacked a British one like this' and pointed to another picture. This was a demoralizing blow but happily the Navy lads had not taken any harm through either they or us being in the wrong place at the wrong time. Had we been able to find out who the crew were, it was our intention to stand them a dinner.'

On 12 July during a Biscay patrol, Sunderland DV977/Y on 228 Squadron flown by Sergeant R. Codd failed to return when the aircraft was shot down by Ju 88s with the loss of all except one of the eleven crew. After eight and a half hours in the sea the flight engineer, Sergeant E. Davidson, who was operating the mid-upper turret, was picked up by a Royal Navy sloop.[111] Next day three surfaced U-boats - U-445, U-607 and U-613 travelling together and heading out for a patrol in the Central Atlantic - were spotted nine miles distant by Flying Officer A. R. Burns, the second pilot on the Halifax crew captained by Flying Officer A. R. D. Clutterbuck[112] on 58 Squadron. Clutterbuck and Flying Officer Reader D. 'Hank' Hanbury, captain of Sunderland JM708/N on 228 Squadron, who was on a Musketry patrol in the Bay of Biscay, circled the U-boats, which made no attempt to dive. Clutterbuck attacked U-445, which was commanded by 22-year old Oberleutnant zur see Rupprecht Fischler Graf von Treuberg but this submarine and U-613 dived in time to avoid being damaged.[113] After some time Hanbury, a former Imperial Airways pilot, managed to separate U-607 from the formation. This boat was bound for Jamaica on its fourth war cruise from St. Nazaire and was commanded by 24-year old Oberleutnant zur see Wolf Jeschonnek, half brother of the late Generaloberst Hans Jeschonnek the Luftwaffe Chief of Staff. Hanbury dropped seven Mk XI Torpex depth charges, set to shallow depth, spaced at sixty feet, from fifty feet. Evidence states that three charges fell close to the port side aft, one on the conning tower and three close to the starboard side forward. The attack was made under heavy flak and the pilot had to jink over the conning tower after release. The tail gunner and at least one other member of the crew saw the conning tower blown into the air. A large part of the bow moved forward, stood on end, went over the vertical and slid under the surface. Of the 52 crewmen, 25 were seen in the water after U-607 sank but only seven were rescued by HMS *Wren.*

On 15 July U-558 commanded by 29-year old Kapitänleutnant Günther Krech, in company with U-221 commanded by Kapitänleutnant Hans Krojer was moving independently towards the coast of Portugal; where they were to patrol when a Wellington on 179 Squadron attacked U-558 off Cape Rocaby. The submarine gunners drove off the attack and U-558 escaped by diving. Two days' later the submarine was attacked again and damaged by a Liberator on 224 Squadron. On 20 July U-558 was sunk north-north-west of Cape Ortegal by depth charges dropped from Halifax DT642/E piloted by Flight Lieutenant G. Satwell DFC on 58 Squadron and those from a USAAF Liberator of the 19th Anti-Submarine Squadron piloted by 1st Lieutenant Charles F. Gallimeir from Fort Wayne, Indiana. U-558 was lost with 45 hands. Two officers and three crewmen were taken into captivity.

During the great battle with U-boats in the Bay of Biscay on Friday 30 July 1943 - subsequently officially described as 'the greatest single victory of the war against U-boats' - a formation of two 'milch cow' tanker submarines U-461 and U-462 with U-504, was annihilated by aircraft of Coastal Command and the US Navy and by sloops of the Royal Navy in a six-hour engagement. In an earlier engagement, on 21 June U-462 was damaged in an attack by Mosquito aircraft on 151 Squadron and 456 Squadron and sustained several causalities. On 2 July the submarine had been damaged again, this time by a Liberator on 224 Squadron.[114]

Thirty-two-year old Korvettenkapitän Wolf Stiebler commanding U-461, recalled, 'I received the order as the senior commander to escort U-462 and U-504 in convoy through the Bay of Biscay. We travelled in formation at various depths and surfaced only for charging the batteries. The signal to surface was given by me. On the third day, [30 July] U-462 did not surface and with batteries drained, it was necessary for the three of us to remain on the surface while U-462's batteries were charged. Half an hour later the first plane was spotted and it wasn't long before several were above us. On the horizon, three more destroyers (sic) appeared.'

The first sighting of the U-boats was credited to Liberator BZ730 'O for Orange' on 53 Squadron piloted by Flying Officer W. J. Irving at 0945 hours when three large U-boats in V-formation were sighted on the surface moving at full speed. Irving did not attempt to attack, but climbed and transmitted his sighting report and began homing procedure. While a Catalina guided a group of naval sloops steaming at full speed towards the U-boat formation, first to arrive in response to the message was Sunderland JM679 'R for Robert' on 228 Squadron from Pembroke Dock captained by Flying Officer Stan White who recalled circling out of range of the light AA fire from the U-bats. He sent an accurate sighting report giving the position and commenced homing procedure but was attacked by a Ju 88 thundering in from the east. White climbed hard for cloud but could not climb hard enough and to get away he had to jettison his depth charges. That was enough for the Junkers and it broke away. It had knocked the Sunderland out of the fight as effectively as shooting it down but other aircraft were heading towards the U-boat.

A PBY-4 Liberator of 19 Anti-Submarine Squadron, US Navy and soon afterwards Sunderland W6077 'U-Uncle' on 461 Squadron and two Halifaxes on 502 Squadron piloted by Flying Officer A. van Rossum DFC - a Dutchman - and Flight Lieutenant Jenson and Flying Officer W. S. Biggar, arrived on the scene. W6077 was being flown by Flight Lieutenant Dudley 'Dud' Marrows

DFC RAAF, born in Bendigo in 1917 and an accountant when the war began in Europe. 'U-Uncle' had been well south on patrol when the crew received a signal to divert to a position where a U-boat had been sighted. Marrows was more than interested in the U-boats below - firstly because he had never seen a U-boat before and secondly because the submarine on the port side of the formation was numbered 'U-461'.

'From wireless traffic' Marrows recalled 'it was obvious that aircraft were already there and reporting three subs. Pilot Officer Jimmy Leight, first pilot, sighted them through binoculars - three in tight formation. We were at the end of our outward endurance. When we got within 'attack' range aircraft were circling, the U-boats manoeuvring in formation, keeping bows-on to the aircraft and putting up a formidable barrage of cannon and machine-gun fire. From our height of 1,000 feet the RN sloops were not visible.'

The U-boats had made no attempt to submerge, but maintained close order, manoeuvring in tight S turns and keeping up extremely heavy and accurate AA fire. Jenson attacked first, taking his Halifax down to 1,600 feet and braving the cannon fire. On the run-up his Halifax was holed in the starboard elevator and its bombs overshot the target, but the front gunner saw his bullets straddle the enemy's decks. A few minutes later van Rossum attacked the starboard U-boat (U-462, commanded by 23-year old Kapitänleutnant Bruno Vöwe) from dead astern, coming out of the sun. The Dutchman took his Halifax in low for a straight bomb run and then deliberately made three more runs from 3,000 feet; releasing one of his three special 600lb anti-submarine bombs on each of the latter runs. The 600lb depth bombs could be dropped at higher altitude than the depth charges and with the aid of the normal bomb sight. One of van Rossum's bombs found its mark, close to U-462's stern, crippling the submarine and causing it finally to stop. Dark smoke streamed from the conning tower as it broke out of the explosion plume and began circling slowly to starboard. Wolf Stiebler saw 'people' from U-462 'jumping into the water.' One crewman was killed, the remainder of the crew being rescued by the Royal Navy. Stiebler was shocked. 'Now it was more difficult as planes were flying from various directions. Two machines approached from different angles. I had only the quadruple guns and shot at a machine; the volley struck well as I saw the strikes using glasses.' U-462 was the first U-boat to be sunk with the 600lb depth bomb.

Almost at the same time 'Dud' Marrows dropped one wing-tip and turned his Sunderland towards the U-boats. 'A U-boat damaged isn't a U-boat sunk' he said. 'Let's see what we can do with it.' But 'his' U-boat was still firing. It was just as hard as the others. Marrows roared in at 1,000 feet; only to quickly realise that the flak was just too fierce to offer any real chance of success this way. 'Too hot' he said and meant it like he had never meant anything before. He swung out of his run and circuited again, pondering how best to slip through the curtain of fire. Just then the American PBY-4 pilot came through to him on the R/T. 'This stuff's too thick for one aircraft. What we've got to do is divide the flak. Coming in with me?' Both aircraft, 400 yards apart, started their attack runs. Undulating down towards the sea but again the U-boats promptly swung beam-on and put up yet another devastating hail of fire as hard as a brick wall. It was too much. Both pilots pulled away steeply and throttled back in the circuit to think again. It was now two and a quarter hours since the action first began and not one airctraft had penetrated the flak at low level. Now someone would have to attempt a head-on attack and then tackle the impossible - out-turn the U-boats - and, having failed to achieve the impossible, face alone the full flak from the U-boats' beams.

This time Flying Officer W. J. Irving at the controls of 'O for Orange' led the attack, followed closely by the PBY-4 Liberator. Irving dived straight and true right down towards the sea and the U-boats, with smooth precision, again swung beam-on, as Irving had known that they would and hurled up their barrage round him and in front of him. He did not pull out; just continued his dive firing every gun he could bring to bear, while shells and shrapnel tore his aircraft to pieces. As he circled above Marrows watched and knew that the Englishman had given him a chance he would never get again. He rammed his four throttles against the gate and headed for U-461. The engines howled as he ran straight in. He got in to 1,000 yards without facing a bullet or a shell because the U-boat had been concentrating on the Liberator, which was so seriously damaged by flak that Irving had to break off the action and head for Portugal. At point blank range Marrows flew straight into the enemy fire, thundering down to the very surface of the sea itself. As the U-boat turned its guns on the Sunderland, Pearce in the flying boat's nose turret suddenly got the line and the range and opened fire, killing the two loaders on the quad 20mm and severely wounding two officers. Marrows brought his aircraft down to fifty feet; so low that he almost hit the conning tower with his float and let go a stick of seven shallow-set depth charges in a line across and just forward of the U-boat's superstructure. Then he ran straight through the fire of the other U-boat's guns. A cannon shell hit the flying boat in the starboard wing, but, pulling back on his control column with every fibre of his being Marrows jinked and screwed his way up and out of the murderous crossfire, seeking calmer air. Behind him an immense eruption engulfed U-461 and as the plumes of water from the depth charges subsided, the U-boat surged forward and disappeared. He heard the voice of Jock Holland his second pilot say, 'You got him'.

The PBY4 swung in on the far left side and now all the flak that was left switched to the Liberator. A shell burst in his bomb bay and the American crew should have been blasted out of the sky. The PBY4 streaked in, its gunners sweeping the decks clean but when the pilot tried to release his depth charges they would not drop. They stayed firmly stuck in their racks because the mechanism had been shot away.

Marrows, still wholly intent on his 'kill', reached height, turned as tightly as possible and headed back towards his chosen target. Tracers and shells still flaked around him, but below, he could see a brilliant red-orange pool of oil, wreckage and scum, with U-461's surviving crew members dazedly, frantically trying to grab anything which floated. Fifty-three hands were lost when Stiebler's U-boat went down. Marrows took in the whole scene in a second and then swept over the survivors fast and low. They took photographs and dropped a dinghy near to the struggling sailors the crew could now see swimming in the water. One of them was Wolf Stiebler. He stated that there was 'an almighty explosion, after which I thought the boat, had been blown apart. I was dragged into the depths and then there was a jerk and I shot to the surface. We were drifting; on my command we tried to stay together. The depth charges of the destroyer against the surfaced U-504 were hellish torture. After a short time a dinghy was thrown to us by Dudley Marrows. There were still eleven of us; the injured got into the dinghy, the others held on tightly outside. Later the Woodpecker took us on. I was put in an officer's cabin and treated very well; a guard in front of the door watched over me. Before leaving I was able to thank the English commander for taking us on board.'[115]

U-504 commanded by 35-year old Wilhelm Luis, the only surviving U-boat, still undamaged, was now heading for the open Atlantic, so Marrows turned towards it, intent on using his last shot as effectively as possible. North-west of Cape Ortegal the sky around him suddenly filled with flak; thick, almost impenetrable. Marrows couldn't believe that one U-boat could throw up so much flak and then he realised that he was in the middle of a sea battle. The 2nd Escort Group, summoned by the Catalina, had arrived on the scene and the sloops Woodpecker, Kite, Wren and Wild Goose were pouring shells at the U-502, which was lost with all 53 hands. Marrows abandoned his intended attack and climbed into clear air. He watched L/461 (W6050), another Sunderland on the scene later, which returned to base after 13 hours aloft, with Flying Officer J. B. Nicholls the captain and Flight Sergeant R. E. Pollock, 2nd wireless operator, having both counted 50 U-boat survivors in the water as a result of this black day for the German Navy. W6050 put down marine markers on the locations of the wreckage of the two sunken U-boats and then flew over the RN Escort Group, signalling the news of the sinkings and the positions of the surviving German crew members.

'Next stop, home', Marrows said cheerfully to his crew, only to receive the calm voice of his engineer, 'We haven't enough petrol to reach home, skipper.'

With little alternative, Marrows set course for the Scilly Isles, the southernmost tip of the British Isles. Then Marrows almost jumped in his seat as the voice of his nose gunner yelled, 'U-boat on starboard bow!'

'Forty degrees starboard, one and a half miles!'

Marrows couldn't believe it; a year without sighting a single U-boat, they had now seen four on a single patrol! 'I'm going straight in! Get that depth charge out!' he announced.

Diving straight down from 2,000 feet, Marrows closed on the U-boat at 1,000 yards and the front guns opened up, spraying the submarine's decks. The German crew manned the flak guns on deck and began pumping shells at the Sunderland as it loomed large.

A shell burst near the wing root and the bomb rack began to burn. Marrows prepared to set his controls for a fast pull-out once over his target as the flying-boat continued downwards with Marrows fighting the controls, his feet against the dials, exerting every ounce of muscle power in his attempt to bring the Sunderland out of its dive. The Sunderland's nose inched up, reluctantly and swept over the U-boat so low that the German gunners ducked their heads.

Pushing the bomb release button, Marrows got no response - the bomb gear traversing motor had seized and was on fire. As the engineer dowsed the small fire Marrows and Jimmy Leight his first pilot fought to get their aircraft into a climb and finally succeeded. It was the last straw for Marrows. With dud bomb gear, little petrol and now (apparently) flak-damaged controls, he decided that it was time to go home. As he checked around his cockpit he then realised that he had accidentally engaged 'George', the automatic pilot, his sleeve operating the lever, during the hasty action against his last target. With a sigh of relief, he returned the controls to 'manual' and finally, he landed in the channel outside St Mary's in the Scillies. The petrol tanks were to all intents dry by the time he cut the engines. Survivors from two of the U-boats were taken prisoner and brought back to England. Flight Lieutenant Marrows was awarded the DFC.

On 1 August another Australian 'kill' was recorded; again it was an instance of a daring attack made through heavy fire. Sunderland W4020 'B for Baker' on 10 Squadron captained by Flying Officer Lieutenant K. G. Fry was on patrol above the Bay of Biscay flying at 1,700 feet over tumultuous seas beneath a cloudy sky. About 1630 hours her look-outs saw five sloops and a Catalina engaged in a U-boat hunt'. Fry decided to take a hand and had just altered course to do so when he sighted a U-boat two miles away on the starboard bow. The submarine - it was U-454 commanded by 33-year old Kapitänleutnant Burkhard Hackländer - was six miles from the nearest sloop and was moving on the surface at a speed of about ten knots. By coincidence, Flight Lieutenant J. B. Jewell DFC RAAF, 10 Squadron's navigation officer, was on exchange duty with the naval vessels engaged in the battle and watched from the pitching, deck of a sloop as the Sunderland from his squadron dived to the attack. Jewell was spending fourteen days' exchange duty on HMS *Wren* (Lieutenant-Commander R. M. Aubury RN). He recalled:

'About 8.30 the fun really started. What a terrific day! A Sunderland and a Catalina were around and they signalled that no less than three U-boats were on the surface about ten miles away ahead. The Senior Naval Officer on *Kite* made the signal 'General Chase'. Off we went at full speed, line abreast - a grand sight - smooth blue sea and blue sky - all ratings and officers at action stations. Soon we saw the aircraft circling low and diving to drop depth charges. Two of the U-boats were visible by this time and the Sunderland dropped a couple of depth charges plumb on either side of the conning tower of one of them. That broke the U-boat's back and he disappeared pretty quickly, leaving some survivors and a raft in the water. Simultaneously, all our ships had opened fire with 4-inch on the second U-boat. He, too, left survivors who had to wait until U-boat No.3 had been located and dealt with. Not unnaturally, No.3 dived in some haste and we were now set the task of finding him beneath the surface. It was like great cats stalking an oversized mouse. *Kite* found him first and dropped a pattern of depth charges. Then *Woodpecker* set about him and dropped depth charges. *Kite* got a 'fix' and with his direction we proceeded to lay a 'plaster', which is rather what the name denotes. *Wild Goose* repeated the dose, but while she was doing so the first patches of oil were observed and soon it was coming up in great quantities - the sea stank of it. Wood and other wreckage came up too. This was about 3.30 pm. We recovered various things. Wren found some German clothing. The evidence was decisive and the ships (which had been shielding one another during the action) reformed and made off to pick up survivors. We picked up seventeen, including the captain and 1st officer. The other ships picked up a further fifty or so altogether. Ours were in or clinging to a rubber float, shaped like a big rubber ring. Some were injured. One had a bullet in his stomach and a broken ankle. They were mostly shaking with cold and/or reaction from their experience. Several of them were truculent. Some had never been in a U-boat before - possibly never to sea before.'

'B for Baker' made a tight turn and attacked from the U-boat's starboard quarter at an angle of sixty degrees from her track. During the run in, that most perilous of moments - for if the depth charges were to be accurately dropped it was necessary to fly straight and level - Fry came under heavy fire from the 20-mm cannon on the bridge. The enemy fire was returned by the Sunderland's forward gunner, but soon the flying boat was in trouble. First the aircraft's inner engine was hit and then, when the Sunderland was about 400 yards away, a hit in the starboard main fuel tank caused petrol to pour into the cockpit in which sat the captain and his two co-pilots, all three of whom were by then seriously wounded. Despite the petrol and the pain, they flew on and from a height of fifty feet dropped six depth charges set to shallow depth and spaced at 60 feet of which three fell on one side and three on the other of the target. The foam and spray of the explosions had scarcely melted when the rear gunner 'saw the U-boat lift out of the water and then sink by the bows'. 'B for Baker' was also mortally wounded. Fry maintained course for the sloops but after about six miles, he turned 180 degrees to port and set the Sunderland down before he reached them. Jewell and other watchers saw the Sunderland alight on fifteen-foot waves, bounce from one wave to another and then dive into the water and then begin to settle. The sloops sped for the scene. When the Wren arrived, all that still floated was a stump of the mainplane. Five of the crew were on it, others were in the water. One was swimming with a broken ankle about 400 yards away from the wreckage. It was too rough to launch a lifeboat, although oil was pumped on to the water to calm it and the captain had to use a lifebelt to pick up the injured swimmer and then manoeuvre alongside the wreckage to enable the other survivors to climb aboard - 'my if it isn't Johnny Jewell!' said one of the survivors as he came aboard. Only at this moment did Jewell realize the Sunderland was from his own squadron. Six Australians lost their lives in the crash. U-454 was lost with 32 hands. Hackländer and twelve other survivors were rescued by HMS *Kite*.

On 1 August also Flying Officer S. White DFC on 228 Squadron flying JM678/V departed at 1450 on a Musketry patrol and while tasked to search for a dinghy came across a U-boat west of Brest. It was U-383 commanded by 36-year old Korvettenkapitän Horst Kremser, which was on its fourth war cruise, having left Brest on 27 July. At 2013 hours JM678/V lost height and began an attack from up sun. U-383 put up very rapid fire and the aircraft took violent evasive action and thus failed to track over the target. During the approach the gunners opened up accurate return fire and two of the German crew were seen to fall. The Sunderland then turned to port and ceased fire.

When the flying-boat was 600 yards away the enemy again opened very accurate fire which carried away the starboard float and put the starboard aileron out of action. The hull was holed in several places and a shell exploded in the port mainplane. There were, however, no casualties on the Sunderland. The attack was delivered from U-383's starboard quarter at 15 degrees to track; seven depth charges, set to shallow depth, spaced at 60 feet, were dropped from 75 feet. The depth charges straddled the target just abaft the conning tower and U-383 was completely enveloped in spray. When the plumes subsided U-383 had a bad list to port and was turning sharply. The Sunderland left the scene immediately, as the damage to the lateral control prevented it from turning. U-383 transmitted a distress signal to which three torpedo boats responded. The U-boat must have foundered during the night with the loss of all 52 hands and the torpedo boats rescued survivors from U-106 who they found nearby.[116]

U-106, commanded by 24-year old Oberleutnant zur see Wolf-Dietrich Wolf Dietrich Damerow, sailed from Lorient in company with U-107, which planted a minefield in American waters. On the fifth day out, 1 August, Damerow reported that he had repelled an aircraft, but that it or another was shadowing the boat, doubtless calling in other planes. The shadower was a Wellington on 407 'Demon' Squadron RCAF piloted by a RAF officer, J. C. Archer who had dropped six depth charges and had indeed given the alarm.

In company with N/228 of 228 Squadron, he found U-106 surfaced at 2015 hours,

It says much for the stamina of airmen and aircraft alike, when it is realised that many such operations covered in excess of 13 hours airborne by day and night, most of this over the lonely expanses of the Bay of Biscay and the Atlantic. Rescue, in the event of being forced down, was a remote possibility. Mostly the air war at sea was a dull, monotonous life, seeking out U-boats which seldom appeared; being on the alert for the one chance in a hundred when all the months of training could be put to good use in a hectic few moments of battle. The moment for Flight Lieutenant Irwin A. F. 'Chick' Clarke DFC piloting Sunderland DV968/M on 461 Squadron RAAF came on 2 August. Clarke engaged three German destroyers, having shadowed the ships until just after 2000 hours. Then, at 20.05 hours northwest of Ortegal he was startled by a frantic message from the first pilot: 'Captain, there is a U-boat 1½ miles, 10 degrees starboard and it's a whopper.' It was U-106; a 740-tonner, painted light grey, spick and span, new and full of power. It was on the surface and moving fast. The sea was calm with a moderate swell. Clarke grasped for his throttles and dropped like a brick. He went down as steeply as he could manage in a tight circular dive, rushed his depth charges out and selected seven and fused them.

Another Sunderland, JM708/N on 228 Squadron captained by Flying Officer 'Hank' Hanbury, who had been awarded the DFC for sinking U-607 on 15 July, came in from the south-west and swung in behind Clarke. The two Sunderlands raced round the circuit, just outside the bursting flak and then, while Clarke turned in for his first attack, Hanbury covered him with his guns. U-106 took violent evasive action and tried to keep the Sunderland on her beam. Considerable flak was experienced but the Sunderland's front gun kept spraying the enemy's decks and the hapless Germans lay on the decks like felled skittles and slid over the sides and into the sea. They floated on the surface like dead goldfish in a film of blood. Most of them were disintegrated, or pulped out of human shape. Some, who must have been on edge of the explosion, were split open from chin to crutch as neatly gutted as any herring. Just before the depth charges attack the aircraft's front gun fire was so accurate that it prevented the relief crew from manning U-106's guns. Clarke delivered his attack from the U-boat's port bow at 80 degrees to the track while the U-boat was still on the surface and turning to starboard. The depth charges straddled the target, the centre of the explosions being just abaft the conning tower. At the moment of the attack the U-boat was still turning to starboard and in doing so she presented her starboard quarter to the waiting N/228.

Before the plumes of the first attack had subsided, Hanbury ran in and dropped another seven depth charges. This attack was made only 30 seconds after the first and also resulted in a straddle. The U-boat vanished within a gigantic eruption of foam and spray and thundering noise, but it came through, long nose thrusting out of it in a sea of boiling scum, shedding its crew man by man as they hastened up through the hatch and sprang overboard. After the attacks U-106 stopped and began to settle by the stern. Black smoke, white smoke and oil were pouring from her. The crew rushed out of the conning tower and began to jump into the sea. Some, however, attempted to man the guns again, but were mowed down by the concentrated fire from the two Sunderlands. Forty minutes later U-106 blew up as the demolition charges went off. The middle of the boat was punched ruight out of it and water and smoke shot skywards like a depth charge plume. The stern vanished, the bows stood up straight and then, foot by foot, passed down into the sea with 25 hands. Thirty-seven men were rescued by the torpedo boats searching for the survivors of U-383. Wolf Dietrich Damerow died of his wounds on 21 May 1945.

South of Iceland on 3 August Hudson 'J' on 269 Squadron flown by E. L. J. Brame found U-489, commanded by 33-year old Korvettenkapitän Adelbert Schmandt which was on its first war cruise, having left Kiel on 22 July. Brame carried out two attacks with 100lb ASW bombs as the U-boat returned fire from its quad 20mm and other flak guns. The first bomb missed, but the second fell close. When a B-17 and a Catalina appeared Schmandt dived 656 feet and escaped but the single bomb had caused a leak of seawater into the after battery, posing the possibility of chlorine gas. Schmandt surfaced and the leak was fixed, but patrolling warships closed in on the submarine and dropped depth charges. Though none fell close Schmandt was forced to remain submerged until her batteries were exhausted.[117]

U-489 was forced to surface the next morning when Sunderland DD859/G captained by Flying Officer A. A. Bishop on 423 Squadron RCAF, who was on patrol in the North-West Passage sighted the hated grey hull of the surfaced U-boat. Bishop, son of the Canadian World War I ace, Billy Bishop, immediately lost height to deliver an attack. He had closed to within one mile when it became apparent that U-489 was not attempting to dive. Bishop therefore decided to manoeuvre for position in order to deliver an attack from dead ahead, but U-489 circled in such a way as always to present her stern to the aircraft. Smoke puffs were seen coming from the U-boat's guns but no bursts were seen and no hits felt on the aircraft. When Bishop decided that he could not outmanoeuvre the U-boat, he flew to a position about one mile up sun of it and turned in to attack at about 300 feet. Fire was opened at the correct time - 1,200 yards with the 0.5 in guns in the nose - and an undulating approach made. The bullets were seen falling very close to the conning tower after the first few rounds. At 500 yards the flying-boat levelled out at 50 feet and flew straight in, opening up with the 0.303 guns in the front turret. At that moment the aircraft began to be hit by U-489's flak. At 300 yards the Sunderland was seriously hit near the port wing root by a lucky shot from the U-boat's 4.7 inch gun. Although this damaged the aircraft's controls and the flak increased in intensity, Bishop pressed home the attack and released six accurate shallow-set depth charges. By this time a violent fire was raging in the wing root and the galley of the Sunderland and the ailerons and trimming-tab controls had become useless. The outer engine controls were also out of action, so Bishop switched off those engines and made a forced alighting. The aircraft bounced three times and the port wing dropped. The wing tip hit the water caused the aircraft to swerve violently to port and nose in. Six of the eleven members of the crew managed to get clear of the aircraft, which was then burning furiously. After about four minutes it sank.

When three British destroyers, including HMS *Castleton* and HMS *Orwell*, appeared, Schmandt ordered his crew to abandon ship and scuttle. U-489 approached the scene of the crashed Sunderland and after fifteen minutes was within 200 yards. The crew were standing on the forward deck taking to their raft. U-489 continued to sink. Scuttling charges were then fired and the U-boat disappeared. Twenty minutes later the *Castleton* picked up Schmandt and the other fifty-three members of the crew, including the chief engineer, who later died aboard the *Castleton*, plus three Luftwaffe airmen who had been shot down by a Beaufighter on 29 July and had been rescued by U-489. The *Castleton* then picked up Bishop and five of his aircrew who were less than one hundred yards away, swimming in the water. Bishop later was awarded the DFC.

A fortnight after his DFC was gazetted Flight Lieutenant 'Dud' Marrows was awarded the DSO for a gallant fight with six Ju 88s in the approaches to the Bay. It was a dramatic story. It happened during a patrol on 16 September 1943 on what was to have been Marrows' ultimate operational sortie on 461 Squadron prior to being returned to Australia. Soon after 3pm, P. T. Jensen the tail gunner reported six enemy aircraft approaching on the starboard quarter about fifteen miles away. Marrows headed for the nearest cloud cover thirty miles away, but the enemy aircraft came up too fast. They formed up for attack, four of them in a stepped-up echelon-on the starboard bow and two on the port quarter. The Sunderland jettisoned its depth charges and prepared to fight. The leading Ju 88 took little part in the combat, which its pilot apparently directed. The second Ju 88 on the starboard bow opened the combat. The Sunderland began corkscrewing as the other aircraft attacked simultaneously from port and starboard. During the attack the tail turret hydraulics were severed and only one gun in the mid-upper turret was left in action. The enemy re-formed and made a second combined attack, then a third from a different quarter. Half the formation attacked from one beam and broke away whenever the Australian aircraft returned the fire, while the other half attacked from the other beam. The Sunderland's port engines were hit, the tail turret hydraulics were severed and only one gun in the mid-upper turret remained in action. When the enemy realized that the tail turret was out of action - although Jensen courageously tried to operate it by hand in the face of intense fire - they concentrated on attacks from astern and from the quarters.

A. N. Pearce amidships and P. R. Criddle in the nose continued to fire and one Junkers was hit. It retired from the fray with its starboard motor smoking and the gunners saw their bullets hit at least three other enemy aircraft. Then a burst of cannon fire disabled the Sunderland's starboard outer motor and with only one engine still working Marrows had to put the Sunderland down in the sea. There the Sunderland crew launched three dinghies, stowing as much equipment as possible into them. The aircraft was abandoned, taking in water rapidly through numerous holes in its hull. Soon after leaving the aircraft two of the dinghies burst. Apparently they had been hit and the entire crew of eleven, together with what equipment could be saved, huddled into the remaining one. The crew decided that as rescue might be delayed they would conserve their emergency rations by going without food for the first forty-eight hours afloat and they set about making themselves comfortable for the night.

At three o'clock next morning they heard an aircraft overhead and they fired a Very cartridge and lit torches. The aircraft circled and made a run-up, turning its landing lights on the men in the dinghy. The aircraft, a Leigh Light Catalina, circled above the men dropping marker flares to maintain position until, just after dawn, it signalled: 'I go - help coming-good luck.' Scarcely five minutes' later a Liberator - and naval sloops appeared and the men were picked up. It was the same 2nd Destroyer Group which had finished off the action of 30 July and its commander Captain Frederick J. 'Johnny' Walker CB DSO presented Dudley Marrows with the life-jacket and escape gear worn by Korvettenkapitän Stiebler, commander of Marrow's victim, U-461. Several weeks later Flight Lieutenant Dudley Marrows DSO DFC RAAF went back to Australia, saw further service on 40 Squadron RAAF and survived the war.

October 1943 was a comparatively quiet month for the aircrews of Nos 10 and 461 Squadrons. Despite a collective total of 1,058 hours flown over the Bay of Biscay, no enemy sightings were reported by either unit. On 28 October on D/461 (EK577) Flying Officer J. B. Nicholls DFC the captain and Flight Sergeant R. E. Pollock, 2nd wireless operator had an unhappy time, together with the rest of the crew, when the port outer engine of 'D-Dog' went unserviceable during an antisubmarine patrol. Adding to the excitement, the navigator made a slight miscalculation in his DR, so that the Sunderland crossed the French coast at Brest! Amazingly, they returned to Pembroke Dock without further event. However, on 8 October Flying Officer Alfred H. Russell DFC on 423 Squadron RCAF flying Sunderland DD863 'J-Johnnie' on convoy escort 480 miles SSW of Iceland had attacked U-610 commanded by 27-year old Kapitänleutnant Walter von Freyberg-Eisenberg-Allmendingen who earlier had sank the Polish destroyer Orlan. In his initial attack Russell toggled four depth charges but only three fell. These closely straddled the U-boat near the conning tower, which, Russell said 'lifted fifteen to twenty feet'. When the foam and swirl of the explosions subsided, Russell saw 'fifteen' Germans in the water swimming amid oil and wreckage. All 51 hands perished.[118]

On 9 November Flying Officer J. S. B. Dobson's Sunderland on 461 Squadron was attacked by four Ju 88s a total of nine times without result. Sunderlands on 461 Squadron were also fitted with armour plating by now, making the 'flying porcupine' an even tougher proposition for the Luftwaffe and in this instance the added protection probably helped to save the day. Flight Lieutenant C. C. Clark had been on patrol for nine hours on 30 November when his boat came under a determined attack from six Ju 88s. Attacking from an almost cloudless sky, the enemy attackers wounded the Australian pilot and two of his gunners, shot away three of the throttle linkages and caused other damage, obliging Clark to head for a friendly cloud bank 20 miles distant for some form of cover. In the 20 minutes it took him to reach this haven, the Ju88s attacked repeatedly, but two of their number were damaged in the process. Wounded, and with his fuel supply dwindling rapidly, the pilot struggled to keep his machine airborne as he headed for home, finally alighting on the water a few miles short of base to travel the remaining distance under tow to Plymouth. It was almost a squadron tradition that if a Sunderland could be kept aloft or afloat by any means, it would be brought back to fight another day; even under tow!

Bad weather prevailed for the remainder of 1943, particularly over the Bay of Biscay, hampering Sunderland operations to a great extent. Bombing and gunnery practices, air-to-air firing and local flying became almost the daily norm, with one successful operation helping to round off the year, in spite of the elements. During the course of an Atlantic patrol which lasted for 13 hours 40 minutes on 28 December D/461 (EK577), now flown by Flight Lieutenant J. Newton, was attacked by a Focke-Wulf 200K, the action being broken off in cloud. A message was flashed from the Sunderland, giving the enemy aircraft's height, speed and course and based on this, the FW 200 was soon intercepted and shot down by an RAF Mosquito. Opening the squadron's account for 1944, Newton took off from Pembroke Dock on New Year's Day in Y/461 (JM686) for a lengthy antisubmarine patrol over the Bay of Biscay, spending nine hours 30 minutes airborne by day and a further six hours 10 minutes at night on the one mission. Attacked by an aircraft which was initially unidentified, the Sunderland's gunners returned the fire promptly. In a second pass they poured a withering hail of lead into what had now been clearly identified as being a Ju 88. Acting on information received, the operations room later credited the gunners of Y/461 with having probably destroyed this Junkers - a conservative credit since the lone Ju88 was crippled well out to sea.

A modest little ceremony marked the close of the fourth year of war for the submarine hunters of 10 Squadron. 'Eleven officers and men' was the toast of the evening; they were the remaining eleven of those 163 'originals' who, on

Christmas Eve 1939 steamed gloomily into Cherbourg Station on their way to Britain. The Australian Sunderlands went on to destroy five U-boats - and their last - in the first eight months of 1944. 10 Squadron sank one on 8 January (Flying Officer J. P. Roberts captained the aircraft) and another on 8 July (Flying Officer William Boris Tilley). 461 Squadron's 'kills' were on 28 January (Flight Lieutenant Richard D. Lucas), 11 August (Pilot Officer Ivan F. Southall) and 13 August (Flying Officer Donald A. Little). All the captains were awarded DFCs.

Late in 1943 the Sunderland squadrons endured possible replacement by the Martin Mariner but by December four of these aircraft which had been delivered to 524 Squadron at Oban for evaluation were gone and the squadron disbanded. It had been decided that the Mariner was inferior in endurance and carrying capacity to the Sunderland. As 1944 approached, the Air Ministry called for more trained crews to fly Sunderlands. In January 228 Squadron lost three Sunderlands in the Bay of Biscay. On 8 January Flying Officer J. P. Roberts on 10 Squadron RAAF at Mount Batten flying Sunderland EK586/U sank U-426 commanded by Christian Reich which was on only its second war cruise, having left Brest on 3 January for operations in the North Atlantic. Roberts released six depth charges and the forward machine guns opened at 1,200 yards, strafing the U-boat and killing or wounding all the German gunners before the U-boat was destroyed 'at leisure'. Approximately forty survivors were seen in the water but none of the 51 man crew were rescued. The Australian squadron was the first to fit four additional .303 inch machine guns in the noses of their Sunderlands and other squadrons soon followed suit.

It was on 8 January that U-571 commanded by 26-year old Gustav Lüssow left La Pallice on its tenth war cruise and headed for the North Atlantic. On 28 January, while escorting Slow Convoy 151 and Outbound North 221 180 miles west of the mouth of the River Shannon, U-571 was bombed by Flight Lieutenant Richard D. Lucas flying Sunderland EK557/D on 461 Squadron RAAF airborne from Pembroke Dock. At 3,000 yards range the U-boat opened fire with cannon and machine-guns. During violent evasive action Colin Bremner the navigator fell over and was knocked out. At 1,000 yards Flight Sergeant Simmonds in the nose position opened fire with his two .303 Brownings effectively knocking out the U-boat's gunners. In two runs into heavy flak, Lucas dropped two salvoes of depth-charges. In the first attack Lucas and Flying Officer Prentice in the 2nd pilot's seat released four DCs. U-571 turned sharply to port and the nearest DC fell thirty yards abeam. In the second attack two DCs released straddled the U-boat and while the Sunderland circled, Bremner recovered enough to use his camera in the port galley hatch. At the instant he released the shutter; U-571 blew up in a 'huge explosion'. In a signal to base Lucas reported seeing thirty-seven crewmen swimming. The Sunderland crew surveyed the scene and realising the enemy was without dinghies, released one of their own. Another Sunderland on 461 Squadron reached the area (the U-boat sank about 300 miles south-west of Fastnet) and also dropped a dinghy but none of the 52 hands could save themselves.[119] Lucas was awarded the DFC and later served with Qantas Airways. The RAF front gunner, Flight Sergeant Simmonds, was awarded the DFM.

U-546 commanded by Paul Just had left Kiel on a mission to report the weather on 22 January and on 16 February it was attacked by an unidentified Sunderland which killed a gunner and caused diesel-engine damage. Just was able to effect his own repairs and he continued with the mission. Before returning to Lorient on 23 April his gunners shot down Halifax 'H-Harry' on 53 Squadron and also survived three more air attacks on the 17th when his gunners claimed a Mosquito shot down.[120]

Tales of the Sunderland's ability to survive against enemy aircraft attacks are legion. On 15 February 1944 Flight Lieutenant J. McCulloch on 10 Squadron RAAF was on patrol in Sunderland EK574/Q over the Bay of Biscay at 1,500 feet when a formation of twelve Ju 88s was spotted about five miles distant. McCulloch at once turned 180 degrees to port to reach cloud cover seven miles away. When he came out of this turn he saw two other formations of four Ju 88s each, one of these formations, however, did not join in the attack. The twelve Ju 88s, now on 'Q's' port bow, split into three sections of four and the individual aircraft formed line abreast while the formation of four on the starboard side went in to line astern. All the enemy aircraft were then flying at the same height as the Sunderland, which increased speed and held course until the enemy opened fire. The large formation attacked from 70 degrees on the port bow; at least eight of them and possibly the whole twelve began firing simultaneously at 500 yards and persisted to within 100 yards. McCulloch immediately made a climbing turn to port and passed over the formation, which had apparently expected the Sunderland to dive as most of their fire went low. At the same time the four Ju 88s attacked from the starboard quarter, but were balked by the others and did not score any hits. During the attack the nose gunner fired at one of the aircraft in the leading formation and saw tracer enter the cockpit; he also got in a burst at the leading Ju 88 of the first section and estimated hits. Only very slight damage was done to the Sunderland, but a stray bullet killed Flight Sergeant G. S. Mills the tail gunner outright. McCulloch turned to starboard again and reached cloud cover before a new attack could develop. Quick action on the part of the captain and good training all round undoubtedly saved the Sunderland and her crew from destruction by overwhelming odds. McCulloch later went to London with his navigator to record a broadcast for Australia.

Between January and March 1944 of 3,360 merchant ships in 105 convoys only three had been sunk, whereas 29 U-boats had been lost and six more damaged. En route to its patrol area on 10 March to escort Convoy SC.154, 380 miles west of the mouth of the River Shannon, Sunderland EK591/U on 422 Squadron RCAF flown by Warrant Officer W. F. Morton, who was on his first operational sortie as captain, spotted a U-boat on the surface. It was U-625 commanded by 25-year old Siegfried Straub. This submarine was a standard 517-tonner without the forward gun and carried two twin 20mm mountings on the upper platform and one on the lower, the latter being well shielded. The gunners of U-625 and U-741 had just shot down Wellington HF311 flown by Pilot Officer E. M. O'Donnell on 407 'Demon' Squadron RCAF.[121] Flight Lieutenant Sidney W. Butler DFC, who was along as check pilot, was at the controls at the time. He immediately manoeuvred to attack U-625, reducing height to 400 feet and the range to one mile. U-625, however, sighted the flying-boat as it turned and the German crew opened fire at about five miles. Not unnaturally the fire was well short and it dropped about half way between the aircraft and the enemy submarine. U-625 also began to zigzag hard, but when the Sunderland was about a mile away Straub turned sharply to port and circled in order to keep stern on to the aircraft.

Meanwhile, the Sunderland avoided flak by frequent alterations of height and course and circled in an attempt to attack from the bow. It was soon evident that this was impossible and when the Sunderland was 1,000 yards away on U-625's starboard beam, Butler dived in to attack from the quarter. The last 400 yards of the run-in was made at 50 feet and the enemy put up intense flak, one shell hitting the Sunderland's hull below the waterline. The flying-boat's front guns replied to such effect that in the end only one enemy gunner appeared to be serviceable. The attack was made from the U-boat's starboard quarter and six depth charges spaced at 60 feet were released while U-625 was still surfaced. The depth charges straddled the conning tower, one being seen to enter the water on the starboard side and three to port just abaft the conning tower. Three minutes after the attack U-625 submerged but re-surfaced after another three minutes. She was then moving very slowly leaving a heavy oil trace and turning to starboard. An hour and a half later Straub signalled by V/S 'Fine bombfish' and the crew abandoned ship. Ten minutes later U-625 sank by the stern leaving her crew in numerous small dinghies and one big one but none were rescued and all 53 hands perished. The Sunderland crew were able to repair their damaged hull and the aircraft alighted safely at its base.

From March onwards U-boats would never pose any serious threat to the passage of convoys across the Atlantic again. Luftwaffe aircraft however, were still a serious proposition. On 23 March two Sunderlands on 461 Squadron were attacked by Luftwaffe aircraft while on patrol over the Bay of Biscay. Sunderland 'M' captained by F. H. 'Tim' Bunce was engaged by nine Ju 88s, the enemy tactics being a similar series of attacks by pairs of aircraft, although in this case the genuine attacks came in from the starboard side. In a series of attacks various hits were made on the Sunderland and as the aircraft was getting ready to meet yet another attack the fire controller called that one of the port fuel tanks was on fire: Bunce decided that he would have to ditch and ordered everyone to take up ditching stations. All the turrets except one were vacated, but D. W. Duke the mid-upper gunner continued to fire at the enemy until 'M' actually touched the water. Bunce tried to land across wind along the swell, but there was too much drift. He therefore turned into wind and at the last moment turned back along the swell, thus cutting out most of the drift. The aircraft was thrown off the crest of the first wave, went down into the trough and bounced again. Bunce tried to gain a little more speed, but the port inner motor had become unserviceable and, through lack of flying speed, the Sunderland hit the next wave half way up. The tail turret was knocked off and the aircraft sank within two minutes. One member of the crew went down with the aircraft and four of the others drowned. The first pilot, O. L. I. Howard and the second pilot were last seen clinging to the starboard inner propeller before a wave of great violence smashed over the mainplane and swept the two men overboard. They vanished in the swirl. Not a man saw a sign of them again. The other two jumped into the water, but owing to the heavy seas and strong wind it was impossible to reach them with the dinghies and they were not seen again. Bunce, M. G. J. Fuller, navigator, R. N. Thompson, rear gunner, D. W. Duke and the three other men got away in two dinghies and were picked up fifty hours later by the RN destroyer HMS *Saladin*. During the hours of daylight on the 24th and 25th, aircraft kept constant cover over the dinghies. [122]

Further west Sunderland 'F' captained by H. M. Godsall had intercepted the radio flash from Bunce's aircraft but the wireless operator confused his codes and transmitted a U-boat sighting report. Godsall turned in and increased speed to investigate. He came in on a due easterly heading through a clear blue sky. He was just as naked in a cloudless world as Bunce had been and flew straight into four Ju 88s which were first sighted three to four miles away on the port bow at 2,000 feet. Godsall jettisoned its depth charges and lost height to 1,000 feet. The 88s turned towards the Sunderland and flew up abreast, two on either side. Both aircraft on the port beam closed to 200 yards, turned in to attack and opened fire. The Sunderland turned sharply to port to meet this attack and began to corkscrew. The 88s broke off at 600 yards and about 800 feet above the Sunderland, the tail gunner of which fired a long burst at one of them as it passed astern. The two aircraft on the starboard side did not attack, so the fire controller instructed Godsall to cease corkscrewing and resume course. The second attack opened in much the same way as the first, two 88s taking station on each beam. The starboard pair made a dummy attack but broke off at about 1,000 feet above the Sunderland. Fortunately, the controller was not drawn by this manoeuvre and the genuine attack from the port side was countered by a steep diving turn to port. By then the starboard outer engine had stopped, as a fuel supply line had been cut during the first attack. The Germans made four more similar attacks before they finally gave up the battle. Godsall took the same evasive action every time, ignoring the dummy attacks from starboard and countering the real attacks from port with steep diving turns into each attack. Only the first attack did any damage to 'F'. The Sunderland was hit and damaged in the first assault and fought most of the action on three engines. Excellent team work was chiefly responsible for the safe return of the aircraft from this combat. The navigator, who acted as fire controller, was always ready with the right instructions and Godsall handled the aircraft skilfully and the gunners kept the enemy at a distance with accurate shooting. Godsall did not know that Bunce and his crew were missing until he returned to base. [123]

Now led by Wing Commander J. MacL. Hampshire DFC, brother of the famous ace and leader of 456 Fighter Squadron, 461 Squadron began to use Mk VI radar equipment during 1944, adding 1.7 inch flares to the inventory for use in night attacks. As the war progressed, so did the unit's equipment, in the never-ending battle against the U-boat menace.

Shortly after midnight on 24 April a Leigh Light-equipped Liberator on 120 Squadron piloted by L. T. Taylor found U-672 on radar in the Bay of

Biscay. The boat, which was commanded by 27-year old Oberleutnant zur see Ulf Lawaetz, was planting 'Thetis' radar decoys at the time. Taylor attacked using the Leigh Light, dropping six depth charges that fell wide.

About twelve hours later, during the afternoon, at 1530, Flight Lieutenant F. G. Fellows RCAF, the captain on Sunderland DD862/A on 423 Squadron was engaged in a creeping-line-ahead search for U-boats. Visibility, for a change, was unlimited and Fellows spotted what he thought was a wake. Increasing speed to 140 knots, while his second pilot trained his binoculars on the spot and confirmed that it was a U-boat, Fellows soon made out the definite shape of a surfaced submarine about 16 miles dead ahead. They had picked up the U-672. The U-boat's conning tower had two bandstands both of which contained guns. Fellows held his course and height for about eight miles and manoeuvred until he was five miles on the U-boat's beam. At five miles range the U-boat evidently spotted Fellows' Sunderland and, instead of crash-diving, began evasive manoeuvring attempting to keep its stern towards the approaching flying boat and meanwhile bringing into play its flak guns. U-672 turned hard to starboard in order to keep stern on to the aircraft and opened fire with medium flak which exploded with white puffs. The fire was accurate for line but fell short by three miles. The rate of fire and the fact that the bursts were in clusters of six or seven suggest that the enemy was using a gun of the Bofors type.

Following each manoeuvre of the U-boat, Fellows eventually got to a position up-sun and when the U-boat slackened her rate of turn the Sunderland bore in on a straight attack run. At 1,200 yards the Sunderland opened fire with the four fixed nose guns and the two front turret guns with such effect that for the last 300 yards of the run the enemy's gunners did not reply. Up to this point the aircraft had been repeatedly hit but Fellows pressed home his attack taking only the minimum of evasive action. He attacked from the U-boat's port bow and from 50 feet released six depth charges spaced at 60 feet intervals. As the rear gunner with his guns fully depressed saw the sub enter his sights, he pressed the firing controls - and there was a violent explosion. The blast appeared to have been No 4 depth charge detonating prematurely on striking the U-boat's hull and the effect of this on the aircraft and crew prevented them from seeing the explosions of the rest of the depth charges. As the rear gunner got the forward part of U-672 in his sights there was a violent explosion which threw up everything movable in the aircraft - floorboards, IFF set and crockery; these, together with some eggs and the crew, formed a new variety of omelette on the edge of which the rear gunner lay unconscious. The wireless operator was thrown from his perch in the astrodome, all the electrical circuits became unserviceable, the R/T cable was cut, seams in the wings were opened and the port flaps were put out of action while the rear-facing camera's leads were severed. Apart from damage to the rear turret, the whole airframe was twisted and the elevators almost put out of function. It took all the strength and skill of the captain and second pilot to overcome this.

Now extremely tail-heavy the aircraft began to climb and even with full nose trim Fellows had to put pressure on the controls. Eventually all the crew were brought forward of the main spar in order to help maintain trim. When the aircraft was 300 yards away the front gunner saw a brownish pool with blue smoke hanging over it 70-100 feet astern of U-672. While the Sunderland was being brought under control, the rear gunner, who had regained consciousness, saw the U-boat down by the stern and listing. It took three minutes for Fellows to regain reasonable control of his aircraft. He climbed to 600 feet and once more in control of the Sunderland, turned back over the target area and for a second attack. In that interval the U-boat disappeared from view, leaving just a spreading patch of oil but no wreckage. Searching the sea carefully Fellows found no further evidence of results except a patch of oil.[124] Fellows' Sunderland was so badly damaged that he was forced to return home. Lawaetz dived U-672 and escaped, returning to St Nazaire on 12 May. [125]

On 16 May, 70 miles north-west of Stadlandet, Norway, Sunderland JM667/V on 330 Norwegian Squadron piloted by Sub Lieutenant C. T. Johnsen, is thought to have attacked U-240 commanded by 26-year old Oberleutnant zur see Günter Link who had left Bergen on 13 May and was en route for Narvik. The Sunderland approached and opened fire at 1,000 yards, the U-boat replying and hitting the aircraft on the bottom of the hull. At 800 yards the front gunner opened fire and scored hits on the conning tower and gun crews, sweeping them away in the hail of bullets. Both sides took evasive action, the aircraft jinking and the U-boat zigzagging and then turning violently to port. The aircraft ran in over the enemy's port quarter at 50 feet and attempted to release four depth charges, but all of them hung up. As the aircraft passed over the submarine the rear gunner fired into the conning tower and several of the German gunners were seen to fall overboard. During the run-in the enemy's flak was very concentrated but after the aircraft had turned to port to attack again the flak was much lighter, only one gun being seen in action. The U-boat continued to circle to port while Johnsen came in again from the port quarter. During this second attack the front gunner was killed, the third pilot and flight engineer wounded and Johnsen temporarily blinded by bursts of cannon fire in the cockpit as well as flames and oil from the front turret. Nevertheless, Johnsen pressed home his attack and released four depth charges from 40 feet while the U-boat was still on the surface. Three of the depth charge explosions were seen, the nearest being 15 feet away from the U-boat's port quarter. Several of the Sunderland's crew saw the plume of this depth charge wash over the U-boat's stern. Meanwhile the aircraft had been hit again in the starboard outer engine, which stopped; at the same time the starboard inner engine began to vibrate violently. Immediately after the second attack, when the explosion plumes had subsided, the bow submerged and then lifted clear out of the water at an angle of about 30 degrees. About three minutes after the attack the U-boat submerged stern first. The Sunderland, owing to its extensive damage and casualties, set course for base immediately. Johnsen had great difficulty in maintaining height and the crew were sent to ditching stations. After jettisoning 1,000 gallons of petrol, all spare ammunition, practice bombs and smoke floats, Johnsen was able to gain height and returned to base on three engines. U-240 was lost with all 50 hands.[126]

Off Trondheim on 21 May Pilot Officer E. T. King RCAF on 4 OTU flying Sunderland 'S-Sugar' dropped six depth charges and hit and damaged U-995 which was three days out from Bergen on passage to Trondheim on its first war cruise to commence Arctic operations. The depth charges damaged the boat and four crewmen were wounded when King strafed the submarine. The submarine aborted to Trondheim for repairs.[127] Three days' later, off Namsos, Flight Lieutenant R. H. Nesbitt on 423 Squadron RCAF and Sunderland DV990/R on 422 Squadron RCAF flown by Flying Officer George E. Holley attacked and damaged U-921 commanded by 26-year old Wolfgang Leu, who was en route to search for survivors of the lost U-476 which was sunk by a Catalina on 210 Squadron that same day. Holley's aircraft was shot down. When U-921's 37mm flak gun failed, Leu, who was wounded on the bridge, dived the submarine but he could not get below and he perished. After repairs in Norway U-921 joined the Arctic force. [128]

West of Ålesund on 24 May, a Sunderland on 4 OTU piloted by an Australian, Flying Officer T. F. Peter Frizell DFC, an instructor, attacked the new U-675, commanded by 25-year old Karl-Heinz Sammler and which was on its third war cruise, having left Narvik on 17 April. Frizell dropped five depth charges, one of which hit and bounced off the forward deck and exploded. Frizell reported that bodies and wreckage ('oil drums and planking') rose to the surface. All 51 hands perished.[129]

On 5 June, the day before D-Day, Flight Lieutenant Bowrie on 228 Squadron piloting Sunderland ML763 obtained two SE contacts and sighting a fully surfaced U-boat. The Sunderland tracked over the submarine at 75 feet but the bomb doors failed to open. Having dropped a marker, the Sunderland positioned for a second attack but the U-boat was not re-sighted. Two days' later, on the night of 7 June, two Sunderland captains claimed two more U-boats. One of them was credited to Flight Lieutenant Leslie 'Beve' Baveystock DFC DFM on 201 Squadron at Pembroke Dock who was piloting ML740/S. Baveystock was born in Finchley in 1914 and enlisted in 1940, undertaking flying training in Canada before flying Manchesters on 50 Squadron at Skellingthorpe. [130]

In May he had been asked to leave his own crew to be captained by his second pilot and to himself captain the crew of an injured pilot. Up to 6 June he had made eleven trips with them. '...we knew that the invasion was about to begin for while flying over the Irish Sea we saw the huge armada of battle-wagons on its way south to soften up the German defences. I awoke on 6 June to find the whole station alive with the news that the invasion had commenced. At the flight office I found I was scheduled to fly that night on a special trip down off Gijon in Spain, to find and attack a known U-boat which had been harried for two days without success. It had been attacked on the night of the 5th and remained submerged throughout the daylight hours.'

Shortly before midnight Baveystock was flying at 450 feet just below 10/10ths cloud North of Cape Ortegal when a radar contact was obtained bearing Red 106 degrees, range 9 miles. Baveystock recalled that 'We felt sure it was our quarry as the size of the blip was the same as we normally got from our tame sub we practiced with.'

Height was reduced from 450 feet to 250 feet as he homed and the contact was down to half a mile, when the blip disappeared. The Sunderland was then at 100 feet and began to drop flares. Immediately afterwards the crew saw an unmistakable swirl and the second pilot saw bubbles rising to the surface. One minute later another Sunderland, N/461, dropped flares in the same area. Baveystock recalled: 'Unknown to us the other Sunderland had picked up my sighting report that I sent and turned round to join us. We were now climbing to a safe height when suddenly the whole area lit up and the 461 Squadron Sunderland dived in to make an attack on us. He had picked up our blip on his radar and mistaken it for the U-boat; we were approaching it at about 300 mph but they passed directly beneath us, neither pilot having time to take avoiding action.' (N/461 left at its PLE - Prudent Limit of Endurance - at 0240 hours). We now started baiting tactics flying for two minutes, about four miles north of the flame-float and then turning south, crossing the float again and going four miles south, back again, four miles to the east and then four miles to west. Knowing his batteries would be very low, after being kept under all day, we reckoned he would only be doing a few knots. Also, as it would be dawn at about 0500 hours, we estimated that he would need to resurface at the latest by 0300 hours to get two hours necessary for a recharge.'

At sixteen minutes before that hour, flying at 400 feet, the Sunderland crew obtained a firm contact bearing Red 70 degrees, range 11 miles. Baveystock immediately homed, the radar operator holding the contact throughout the run and giving faultless homing instructions. When the range was half a mile flak appeared dead ahead, but the tracer passed high and to port of the Sunderland. The aircraft turned slightly to starboard, dived and began dropping 1.7 inch flares which illuminated a U-boat 600 yards fine on the port bow. It was U-955 commanded by 29-year old Korvettenkapitän Hans-Heinrich Baden and was steering due east at ten knots to Lorient from a 54 day weather patrol.

'We must have been silhouetted against the faint light of the clouds' continued Baveystock. 'We immediately started dropping flares and our U-boat was fully lit up a little too port and turning sharply to his starboard. As he came broadside on, his four 20mm cannon opened up with tracer streams all around us. I turned the aircraft into attack and opened up with my four fixed guns as the front gunner fired with his twin Brownings; the whole area was a criss-cross of tracer bullets and shells but when 200 yards away, all return fire stopped for we had smothered the guns with continuous fire from our six Brownings.'

Baveystock attacked over the enemy's port quarter at 75 feet and released six depth charges spaced at 60 feet while the target was fully illuminated by fifteen flares. 'Our DCs had an underwater travel of 36 feet forward and 20 feet down' said Baveystock 'so it appeared as if No.4 DC had gone off directly under the centre of the hull but with No.5 making a direct hit on the superstructure and exploding prematurely alongside.'

The rear gunner saw the U-boat's silhouette completely blotted out by plumes. Three or four seconds after the depth charges had been released and just before the explosions were seen, there was a heavy thud in the aircraft as if it had been hit. Throughout the attack flares were dropped and continuous radar watch was kept. The blip was held all through the run in but it disappeared immediately after the actual attack and was not picked up again. In spite of an hour's search the crew saw nothing more of the target. U-955 was lost with all 50 hands. [131]

The story has a sad end. When Baveystock landed he went to London because his father had died the day before. Baveystock received a bar to his DFC and two of the crew were awarded the DFM but they were unable to receive their decoration. On their next sortie Baveystock's crew flew with the Flight Commander, Squadron Leader W. D. B. Ruth DFC and the aircraft did not return.

On 9 June Hector Bolitho put pen to paper and recorded that 'The weather has become unkind and although eight U-boats were sighted in the past twenty-four hours, sorties flown fell from 142 yesterday to 79 to-day. This means a fall in flying hours from 1,040, to 587. Nevertheless six U-boats were attacked and not one has yet penetrated into the Channel. During yesterday afternoon three U-boats were sighted by United States Navy Liberators flying from Dunkeswell. One of the captains saw the conning tower of a U-boat just after three o'clock and attacked. Liberators of 15 Group, operating from Northern Ireland, joined in the patrols during the night and two of them made attacks. One, from 120 Squadron, was patrolling west of Brest when the navigator, Sergeant Cheslin, sighted the U-boat some miles away. The aircraft dived in to attack, releasing the depth charges twenty-odd yards ahead of the swirl, a few seconds after the U-boat dived. The centre plumes came up dirty grey in colour and oil' patches swelled up to the surface and spread until they covered an area three miles long.

'Another aircraft from the same squadron was carrying out a sweep on the French side of the Channel, at almost half-past one in the morning. A U-boat was contacted, the Leigh Light was switched on and the Germans replied immediately with red tracer. The nose gunner fired a short burst into the source of the tracer and then his gun jammed. But the navigator saw the U-boat, too late to change course. The depth charges straddled the U-boat track about fifty feet astern. A marker was dropped and surface vessels were homed to the spot to continue the hunt.

'The Australians also came into their own to-day, for one of their squadrons, 461, made two good attacks. Flying Officer Sheehan, of Sydney, was flying his Sunderland at 800 feet when he contacted a U-boat. As they approached they saw a light, probably the glow from below as the Germans were coming up to the conning tower. Flares were launched at one mile and the U-boat was disclosed, almost dead ahead. The sea was jet black, the U-boat pale grey, with a shining white wash astern. Fire was exchanged and the aircraft tracked over the U-boat's bows and released depth charges. The rear gunner saw them enter the water but he was blinded by the flares and unable to see how near they had fallen. The mid-upper gunner saw the plumes, over 270 feet high, rise above the tail plane. Forty minutes later Sheehan flew over the spot and saw a dark object in the sea and nine hours afterwards another aircraft flew over the scene and saw oil streaks, converging towards one spot and debris in the water.

'Fifteen minutes later the second Australian Sunderland made its attack and damaged another U-boat. The captain was Flying Officer Livermore, from Melbourne. The radar contact was obtained at eight minutes to one o'clock and thirty-five flares were dropped, illuminating a U-boat on the surface. The U-boat opened fire and red tracer enveloped the aircraft without doing any damage. But the fire of the aircraft was more successful and a hit was scored on the conning tower. Six depth charges were dropped and the tail gunner gave the U-boat 250 rounds. Again the flares blinded the crew so that they could not see the depth charges enter the water, but both the tail and midship gunners saw at least two explosions close to the hull, abaft the conning tower. Two other aircraft flying within fifteen miles of the position at one-thirty this afternoon saw considerable wreckage in the water, including a rectangular metal box.'

On patrol in the Bay of Biscay on 10 June Sunderland ML762 flown by Flight Lieutenant Hewitt failed to return. Another Sunderland, on 10 Squadron RAAF, piloted by H. A. McGregor, hit the U-333, commanded by 32-year old Ritterkreuz holder Korvettenkapitän Peter-Erich Cremer. The U-boat's 37mm jammed after the first round, but the German 20mm gunners repelled the Sunderland. Even so, the boat incurred heavy damage. On the following night, 11/12 June, Sunderland ML880/U on 228 Squadron piloted by a Canadian, Flight Lieutenant M. C. Slaughter, hit U-333. Cremer's gunners shot down this Sunderland with the loss of all hands, but U-333 was so badly damaged that Cremer had to abort to La Pallice. [132] On 19 June Flight Lieutenant F. H. 'Tim' Bunce on 461 Squadron was patrolling through very bad weather when his radar picked up a surfaced U-boat some 90 miles west-southwest of the Scilly Isles, obtaining a visual at 1500 hours. Thundering down through the muck, the Sunderland was still four miles away from its target when it crash-dived. Pressing on, Bunce released two of his depth charges ahead of the surface swirl created by his quarry, but under such limited conditions, he could only report 'doubtful results'.

A Sunderland on 228 Squadron had a fierce gun battle with a U-boat at three o'clock on the afternoon of the 22nd. The aircraft was hit but the crew had the satisfaction of seeing seven of the U-boat's gun crew fall under their fire. The Sunderland dropped six depth charges, while still under heavy fire. It made a second attack with two more depth charges and then an aircraft of 502 Squadron arrived on the scene and dropped three of the big anti-submarine bombs, one falling twenty-five yards from the target. The flak was then heavy but inaccurate and both aircraft returned to base after seeing the U-boat submerge, leaving a patch of oil on the surface. [133]

Sunderland ML877/R on 228 Squadron captained by Flight Lieutenant Charles Gordon Drake Lancaster, left Pembroke Dock in the early evening of 7 July for a twelve-hour moonlight patrol in the Bay of Biscay. Shortly before midnight between Brest and Bordeaux and about 150 miles out to sea the radar operator picked up a weak contact at 15 miles to starboard. There was a full moon but there were patches of black cloud. Lancaster, who a year earlier had attacked a RN submarine in error, dropped his flares at half a mile and revealed the U-boat's bearing and position. This time there was no doubt about the identity of the submarine. It was U-970, captained by 26-year old Korvettenkapitän Hans-Heinrich Ketels, which had left La Pallice on D-Day and was steering west of Bordeaux at 10-12 knots. Lancaster immediately altered course towards the enemy who, as soon as the first flare ignited, began firing wildly well to port of the aircraft. The Sunderland replied with the fixed guns and front turret which temporarily silenced the U-boat gunners; at 200 yards, however, they again opened fire, this time accurately and hit the aircraft in eight places.

Flight Lieutenant O. T. Brown the second pilot of the Sunderland had every reason for being excited. He had joined the Squadron the day before, never having been on operations and never having been in a Sunderland. Brown said, 'I was in the second pilot's seat when the Captain said, 'Look chaps, we've really got something.' He took over the controls, the bombs were run out and the men in the galley dropped the flares when we were half a mile away. I saw the U-boat clearly, just as one expected it would look. But the flares were so blinding - they were like a flickering bonfire behind us - I could not see whether there were any Germans on the deck. The U-boat opened fire and the tracer came past us like red and blue needles, but well to port of the aircraft. Then our skipper replied with his four fixed guns, but I was much too young at the game to know which was which. Then came complete silence. At 200 yards they opened fire again and hit us in eight places. We came in and dropped six depth charges at 55 feet using the low-level bombsight. I heard the four thuds as we passed over. We circled round and they fired at us again but I did not see the result of the attack from where I was sitting. The bomb-aimer estimated that the centre of the stick overshot slightly but it was the mid upper gunner, who was in the best position to see the results as he was not blinded by the flares, who gave evidence of the straddle. He saw one small explosion plume subsiding on the enemy's starboard side and a big plume on the port side just abaft the conning tower. The stern of the U-boat seemed to lift out of the water and she heeled to starboard. Then a big patch of oil appeared, 200 feet across, with a thin oily wake, 400 feet long, leading to the U-boat, which lay either stationary or stopping.'

U-970's gunners fired six rounds of tracer vertically in the air nowhere near the aircraft. The Sunderland stayed in the area for another two hours and twenty minutes but saw nothing more. U-970 was lost with 38 hands.[133] In November 1944 Flight Lieutenant Lancaster was killed flying Air Chief Marshal Sir Trafford Leigh-Mallory to the Far East when their Avro York crashed in France.

On the afternoon of 8 July Sunderland W4030/H on 10 Squadron RAAF at Mount Batten piloted by Flying Officer William Boris Tilley DFC found U-243 on the surface west of Nantes and about ninety miles from Brest. Hector Bolitho arrived at Mount Batten the next day and found Tilley who pointed beyond where the *Golden Hind* once lay at anchor and where a flock of white

Sunderlands was resting on the water, to a shining green slope. 'That's where Drake played his game of bowls,' he said. 'I play there myself sometimes on warm evenings.' Then he added, 'It's an old man's game in this country, but back in Australia the young ones play it as well.'

'Tilley was a reluctant talker at first. When he began to trust me he sat back and told his tale, through the clouds of smoke from an American cigarette. 'Before I went on patrol,' he said, 'I saw my room-mate, Johnny Mabbett, who comes from South Melbourne. I come from Port Melbourne, the adjoining town. Next time I saw him was towards the end of my patrol. It was still early in the afternoon and I was only about ten minutes from base when I saw a streak on the water which might have been from a periscope. I called Johnny over the R/T and told him I had seen a suspicious looking object. He circled, saw nothing and answered, 'You're up a tree, Joe. I'm going back on patrol.' I persisted and said, 'I think we've got something. I'll stick around.'

'Mabbett flew away and after I had flown over the spot again and seen nothing, we cut across the area of our patrol to pick up time. We had been flying along the line for about two or three minutes when the second pilot, Roy Felan - he's our Australian junior tennis champion - said, 'What do you make of that over there?' He was doing his hourly stretch in the captain's seat. I looked and then jumped right up and got into the captain's seat as I said, 'It's a bloody U-boat. I sounded the U-boat warning and the crew went to action stations. I had done 550 hours operational flying since I arrived in England and it was the first U-boat I had ever seen so I was a bit excited. We turned in immediately to attack but before I finished the turn, the U-boat must have seen us because it opened fire. The flak was pretty thick. We went straight for them, using fairly violent evasive action until we were 2,000 yards away. We expected to be hit at any minute so I opened up with my four fixed nose guns. I could see by the splashes in the sea that our fire was falling short so I ceased, opening up again when we were 1,500 yards away. This time I could see the spray coming up a little to port of the U-boat. It wasn't difficult then to keep the fire on the conning tower. We had ceased our evasive action while I concentrated on the guns and as the flak was coming up pretty thick, I kept saying to myself, 'We're going to cop it.' Just before my guns ceased firing, there was an explosion in our bow compartment. I thought that we had collected a shell but later we found a round had exploded in the breech block of one of our own guns.

'The U-boat made no attempt to submerge and I kept saying to myself, 'When are we going to get to the bloody thing?' The gun fire appeared to cease at 400 yards and we could see the U-boat, nice and grey and sleek, on the water. The Germans ceased fire at 400 yards and our guns ceased at 300 yards. We were flying then at 140 knots, at 75 feet above the sea. Then I dropped our DCs. Crew drill was perfect and the only break in the silence over the intercom was the navigator, Flight Lieutenant Ive Wood, giving his calm, running commentary and his instructions to the wireless operator regarding the signals to be sent (to base). After we had passed over we evaded in case they re-manned their guns. Then pandemonium broke out over our intercom. The tail gunner had given the U-boat a final burst as we ran over and he saw the results of our bombs. He shouted, 'You beaut, you've got him.'

'I then said, 'We've forgotten our marker so we'll have to go in again,' but the port waist gunner said, 'OK sir, marker's been dropped.' It was part of the perfect crew drill which was maintained all through. We then circled at a quarter of a mile to see the results of our handiwork. The U-boat was low by the stern, but one gun kept popping at us. Felan had been out of it up to then and he said to me, 'What will I do?' So I sent him downstairs to get the hand-held camera. He took photographs all the time from then, out of one of the hatches, as the U-boat was slowly sinking. Then a United States Liberator [of VB-105 piloted by Aurelian H. Cooledge] arrived on the scene and made two runs over the U-boat, firing at it but dropping no depth charges. We also kept circling. Then another Sunderland [JM684/K] came along - one from our squadron, with [Flight Lieutenant] Dick Cargeeg, a West Australian, as Captain. He dropped depth charges but the U-boat had ceased to move. White smoke was coming from the conning tower and some of the Germans climbed out. Cargeeg's depth charges fell 30 yards ahead and slightly on the port bow. He had allowed for the U-boat still making way. But he got some good photographs showing the Germans lined up on the deck, with about fifteen yellow dinghies. They were abandoning ship. These photographs proved afterwards that we had got it so I felt bloody pleased.

'The US Liberator made another attack and dropped eight depth charges near the sinking U-boat. The blokes were in the water at this time and they must have been fairly shaken up by the depth charges. I then tested my own nose guns but we had fired the lot during the attack. The U-boat was sinking fast and it went down tail first, almost vertically. I've never been as thrilled in all my life. The survivors were in the water and I made a run over them with the camera. There were two big dinghies and fifteen one-man dinghies. One of the men I could see had a red and black-stripped pullover on. The dinghies looked very yellow in the water. I kept running over out of curiosity and they were waving to us and we were waving back. I felt a bit sorry for them so I dropped one of our dinghies and a Bircham barrel and a food pack. By this time the Liberator and the other Sunderland had stooged off, but we stayed over the sinking U-boat as long as we could and then flew back to base with only ten minutes petrol to spare. For some unknown reason the Sunderland went back to the patrol line where I had talked to Mabbett; where I had thought that I saw the first U-boat. I must have been right because the Sunderland sighted a periscope in the same position, just under his port main plane. It was impossible for him to get down too attack it, but it proved that something was there. We stayed over the sinking U-boat as long as we could and then flew back to base with ten minutes' petrol left. At eight o'clock that night the Germans were picked up by a Canadian destroyer, the Restigouche [of hunter-killer Support Group 14]. We had killed fourteen of them with our guns and thirty-seven of them were brought back to England alive. The Germans talked to the crew of the Canadian destroyer and said that the captain of the U-boat exposed himself on the conning tower as we were firing and his head had been chopped off. It just fell on the deck.'

U-243 was scuttled by the engineer, who went down with the boat, leaving the commander, 26-year old Kapitänleutnant Hans Märtens and 37 of his crew in the water. Later two Mosquitoes circled until the arrival of the rescue ships seven hours after the U-243 sank.[135] In the interrogation his crew related their view of the attack:

'We were making for Brest when at about 1420 hours on 8 July we came to the surface to fix our position. Immediately we surfaced we sighted two Sunderlands. The commanding officer decided to fight it out and we opened fire with the 37mm gun. One of the Sunderlands came in to attack from the starboard bow with cannon fire and dropped six depth charges. The last of these was a direct hit on the after part of the boat. As the aircraft flew off the rear gunner fired at us and put both the 37mm and the port twin 20mm guns out of action. The second Sunderland ran in from the port beam straight over the bridge, circled round the bows and came in again from the port bow firing cannon. Everyone on the bridge, including the commanding officer, was killed, except one petty officer and the second lieutenant, who was wounded. Others told me that this Sunderland dropped depth charges but everything was in such confusion that nobody knew just where they exploded. In the meantime the direct hit from the first aircraft had caused chaos below. The motors were on fire, the propeller shafts, propellers, hydroplanes and rudders were smashed, the diesels were torn from their mountings and everything in the engine rooms was badly knocked about. A diving tank was damaged and the W/T transformer was put out of action. The galley hatch was also forced open. Moreover, we had used up all the flak ammunition and it was therefore decided to abandon ship. Two seven-man rubber boats were cleared for taking off the ship's company but one was hit before it could be used. [136]

Flight Lieutenant L. F. B. 'Wally' Walters DFC* and crew on 201 Squadron also made a good Sunderland attack on 11 July. Walters' pilgrimage through the RAF had been long and he had certainly gone the hard way. Fifteen years earlier he joined the Service as an apprentice Wireless Operator Mechanic, destined it seemed, to serve on the ground: Promotion was slow in those days and three years passed before he was an LAC. His attitude towards the Service at that time probably explained why he had gone so far. He was sent to Upavon for eighteen months and, much against his desire, because the flying bug had bitten him, he serviced the R/T equipment on a single seater fighter squadron. 'Don't imagine I did this well,' he said, 'but with such a grand crowd of officers and NCOs one couldn't but give one's best.'

Then Walters went to Transjordan, a school of experience for which many older RAF pilots were grateful as it gave them a peacetime taste of active service. The motto of his squadron, No. 14 was I spread my wings and keep my promise. Walters did both in time. He was posted to 6 Squadron which patrolled the desert, escorting trains and road convoys and rounding up political truants, shooting up belligerent Arabs and being shot at by them. He came to know the shape of the country until it was as familiar to him as his village green. He says that he ended up 'with a wholesale respect for John

Arab, mingled with a sneaking sympathy.'

Seven years had passed since Walters watched the aircraft take off at Cranwell, while he spun his dream of becoming a pilot. The dream came true and he returned to England for training. Next came flying in Egypt, the encouragement of promotion; and return to England as a sergeant, 'heady with stripes.'! He did a four months' navigation course and then he went on to flying-boats.

'The aircrews of flying-boats in Coastal' wrote Hector Bolitho 'look upon the rest of the Command rather as Boston looks on the rest of America, or as the Grenadier Guards look upon Boy Scouts. Walters had at last become one of the elect. He said, 'I went to 204 Squadron which had just returned from the centenary celebrations in Australia.' In June 1939 the squadron was equipped with Sunderlands and one of Walters' first jobs was to deliver an aircraft to Singapore. He was slowly conquering the world. War came and after making fifteen operational sorties Walters crashed at night while landing in Plymouth Sound. He was out of the picture for a month. He then went back to operations and flew 98 sorties and 1,160 operational hours before he had first rest. He says of this first tour, 'The thing that shook me most was the risks we took with the elements. We operated from advanced bases, like the Shetlands and Iceland, with very few modern aids, in weather which makes me think it was a miracle that made us survive. The enemy showed up occasionally and-I remember two scraps, one with a Dornier 17 and one with a Dornier 18. We fought the latter for twenty minutes and although we did not kill him, we had the moral victory of seeing him turn and make for home. The U-boats usually saw us first and submerged before we could attack them, but we kept them down'

'During one month in the summer of 1940 Walters spent almost seven days airborne. Then came rest during which he trained the young. He said, 'it took nineteen whole months and considerable belly-aching to get back to Ops and during that time I circuited and bumped my pupils around for a total of 550 hours.' The belly-aching worked at last and in March 1943 Walters went to 201 Squadron, to begin his second tour. His crew sighted a fully surfaced U-boat at dawn on the second day, but 700 dreary hours of vigilance were to pass before he saw his second one. These 700 hours took him over waters as far flung as Reykjavik and Gibraltar.'

This long story led at last to success on 11 July when Flight Lieutenant 'Wally' Walters DFC* and his crew were successful west of La Rochelle. They were flying ML881/P, one of a full complement of Sunderland IIIAs which had been received by the end of June. Among the IIIA's improvements were a fourteen gun armament, ASV III and 'Gee' II. The aircraft was on patrol in good weather when the second pilot 'poked his binoculars in the right direction' and sighted a wake about eight and a half miles away on the starboard bow. No initial radar contact was made and the set was switched off 30 seconds but the crew clearly identified the periscope and raised schnörkel of the U-boat. The Sunderland closed in rapidly and Walters dived towards the wake. The white belly of the flying boat was well hidden in a layer of woolly strato-cumulus clouds and, as Walters said 'we had tons of time to prepare for attack.' The U-boat - it was U-1222 commanded by 27-year old Kapitänleutnant Heinz Bielfeld, which was returning from the Canadian coast at the end of its first war cruise, at first held its course but as Walters said, 'at about three miles we were flying at 500 feet, silhouetted against the horizon, when the blighter saw us and stopped. This rather foxed me for a moment as I couldn't make out which way he was heading. But he solved the problem for us. When we were about half a mile away his stern came up to the surface as he was trying to crash dive. He was in that position when I straddled him from 50 feet with five depth charges spaced at 60 feet, blowing his stern out of the water.' When the Sunderland returned to the scene of the attack the crew saw nothing but a few pieces of wood and whitish froth on the surface of the sea. Waters saw wooden slats in the sea and a pigeon; then he resumed patrol. About four hours later a 461 Squadron Sunderland scoured the scene and noticed a fresh red patch on the surface of the sea, about 50 yards in diameter. Photograph evidence was used to assess that the No. 2 Depth Charge had proved lethal. U-1222 was lost with all 56 hands.[137]

Hector Bolitho saw Walters a few days later, 'trying to accustom his restless feet to a desk at Group Headquarters'. He had completed 149 sorties and 1,906 operational hours and was being forced to rest, 'but he was a little embarrassed by the placid tempo of the office and he darted about like the first wasp of summer. I suppose it is not easy for a man who has flown between Singapore and Iceland to squeeze his horizon down to the space between an ink pot and a telephone.'

In July 1944 sixty sightings were made in the waters round the British Isles and 45 attacks were carried out.[138] Early in August 1944 anti-submarine squadrons flew patrols at the western end of the Channel as a blockade to prevent U-boats from reaching resupply convoys crossing from England to the Normandy the invasion area around Cherbourg but once this threat diminished, patrols were flown west of Brest. When the submarine bases on the French Atlantic coast were no longer available to the U-boats, operations focused on an area nearer Bordeaux, just west of the Gironde.

'An excellent and unusual attack was made by a Sunderland of 228 Squadron on the 9th' wrote Hector Bolitho. 'The captain of the aircraft was Flying Officer Bunting. It is just one more of those perfect attacks which show how the training before D-Day has eaten into the minds of the crews. Bunting was flying at 1,000 feet about half-past six in the evening when he saw a U-boat surfacing some two and a half miles away. The aircraft lost height and two depth charges were dropped forty-five seconds after the U-boat had submerged. As a U-boat moves ten feet a second this means that it was 450 feet ahead and under water when the depth charges were dropped. A black mass of debris appeared at the edge of the disturbance caused by the depth charges. Normally, this attack would have driven the U-boat deep, but ten minutes later it appeared again with its periscope above surface. It must have been damaged by the first attack; otherwise it would have sought the safety of the lower regions. Bunting flew in again and dropped six more depth charges from eighty feet. When the aircraft was about three-quarters of a mile away the rear gunner saw big globules of heavy black oil welling up to the surface. Then the crew saw a violent disturbance about a mile and a half from the position of the attack. This continued for some time and it is certain that the U-boat was damaged: possible that it was killed. Naval vessels were ordered to the scene of the attack and there is every hope 'of later news that the U-boat was destroyed.'

On 10 August Pilot Officer Ivan F. Southall piloting ML741/P, a Leigh-Light Sunderland on 461 Squadron, attacked a U-boat west of La Rochelle. It was U-385 commanded by 25-year old Hans-Guido Valentiner, which was bound for the English Channel having sailed from St. Nazaire on 9 August on its second war cruise. Upon activation of the snort, it malfunctioned and filled the boat with exhaust gases, felling Valentiner and many crewmen. At about dusk on 10 August Valentiner surfaced the boat, just 7,000 yards from the sloop, HMS *Starling*, commanded by N. A. Duck. Starling opened fire, drawing counter fire from U-385's flak guns. After about a half hour, Valentiner dived and attempted to escape submerged. When he resurfaced three and a half hours' later, in the early hours of 11 August Southall's Sunderland picked up the U-boat on radar.[139] Southall turned away until the range had opened to eight miles and then turned back towards the target, which had been held all the time by radar. He made a series of S turns to get the U-boat in the moon-path, eventually sighting her again at a range of six miles. At four miles he lost height to 500 feet and at two miles he dived to attack, releasing from 100 feet six depth charges spaced at 55 feet. He used no illuminant, as he could see the target up moon in perfect visibility. The depth charges were dropped across the U-boat's beam and are stated to have straddled her amidships, four entering the water to starboard and two to port. The explosion plumes completely obliterated the target. Immediately before the attack the U-boat fired a few shots and what may have been a red recognition cartridge. At the moment of the depth charge explosions a bluish-white flash was seen from the U-boat.

After the plumes had subsided U-385 was still on the surface, but was stationary. Southall turned to port after the attack and flew past the enemy's stern at a range of 1,000 yards. The German gunners opened up with about six guns, but their fire, though fairly heavy, was most inaccurate. At two miles range the U-boat disappeared from view and two minutes later the blip also disappeared. The Sunderland flew off to make contact with an Escort Group, which was then nine miles SE of the position of the attack and led the ships back to the area. On returning to the marker the crew found a patch of oil 100 yards wide. Later they picked up a radar contact at three miles on the U-boat's original track about two miles ahead of her last position. After three attempts this was illuminated with flares and identified as a radar decoy balloon. The Sunderland reported the position to the ships and continued to stand by. About two and a half hours after the attack the radar operator picked up another contact, but it disappeared when the aircraft was a mile away. This was also reported to the ships, which began to sweep towards the new contact. After about an hour they reported having found an empty dinghy. After having stayed in the area for three and a half hours the Sunderland reached PLE (Prudent Limit of Endurance) and Southall set course for base. At 0636 on 12 August U-385 was depth-charged to the surfaced by HMS *Starling* and from 3,000 yards ahead was heavily engaged and hit by gunfire. U-385 sank five minutes later. [140] The sloop *Wren*, which had the survivors of U-608 on board, rescued 41 Germans, including Valentiner.

On 12 August 461 Squadron was again successful when Flying Officer Donald A. Little and crew on ML735 returned victorious. U-270, which was unfit for combat and had sailed with a scratch crew commanded by 27-year old Heinrich Schreiber from Lorient on 10 August bound for La Pallice with an escort of three M-class minesweepers to evacuate personnel. Unfortunately for U-270, the escort was recalled late on 10 August. The submarine was steering 110 degrees at 15 knots when Little arrived on the scene. The U-boat looked very big and had a high conning tower with two bandstands aft. About ten men were seen in the conning tower or manning the guns aft of it. These gunners promptly opened fire with light and medium tracer which came up in four streams from points abaft the conning tower. The Sunderland replied with 120 rounds from the nose gun and 380 from the fixed guns. This fire discouraged the U-boat's gunners so effectively that the last 400 yards of the Sunderland's approach was unopposed. Little attacked from abaft the U-boat's starboard beam and from 300 feet released six depth charges spaced at 55 feet. The aircrew did not see the points of entry of the depth charges and saw only two of the explosions, the nearer being about 15 feet from the port side of the conning tower. (While none of the depth charges hit the U-boat they caused damage to the pressure hull near the No. 5 diving tank. The vessel attempted to continue on the surface but water was entering and she was in danger of sinking). At two miles' range the contact disappeared and when the Sunderland returned to the position ten minutes later, intending to attack again, the crew neither saw the U-boat nor picked up any contact. However, about an hour after the attack, they saw many small lights in the water, two of which were flashing SOS. (When a Wellington flew over the U-boat the crew abandoned ship before an attack was delivered). About 0130 hours some escort vessels arrived in response to the Sunderland's homing signals and 20 minutes later the SNO reported by R/T that the U-boat had been sunk and that Streiber and 70 other survivors rescued. Ten hands perished.

On 18 August Flight Lieutenant Leslie Baveystock DFC* DFM, flying Sunderland EJ150, was credited with the destruction of his second U-boat. Having lost his original crew when they went down with Squadron Leader Ruth DFC, Baveystock had taken over another crew. 'I took over the crew of Flight Lieutenant Eddie Bent, a Canadian, who had just finished his tour. My 2nd pilot was Brian Landers, my navigator Flying Officer Ian Riddell, a New Zealander. We carried a third pilot - a Canadian, Flying Officer McGregor. We had been briefed to look for U-boats which were being used by the Germans to ferry senior officers from the Brest peninsular which had been cut off from the main German forces by the advancing American army and it was believed that they were being taken down to Bordeaux. Our search was south-west of Belle Ile of the French coast.'

Landers was flying the aircraft while Baveystock was in the cubicle under the second pilot's seat on the lower deck. Baveystock was just buttoning up his trousers when he heard the alarm. 'When I got to the bridge they said, 'hey, look, there's a periscope' and I looked and there was a periscope.' It was U-107 commanded by 23-year old Korvettenkapitän Karl-Heinz Fritz which was on its 13th war cruise from Lorient during which it had sunk 38 ships and damaged four more since going to sea in 1941. The U-boat was earmarked for evacuation to Norway, thence to Germany and retirement.[141] Landers ran out the DCs while both he and Baveystock made the settings of the controls for the attack.

'A signal was sent by W/T' continues Baveystock 'and when Landers brought the aircraft round, the wake from the periscope was clearly visible. I then took over and flew the aircraft from the second pilot's seat and delivered a normal attack such as we had practiced many times. I had tightened the stick of six DCs before taking the 2nd pilot's seat so that the DCs would releases at 50 feet intervals instead of the normal 60 feet. The stick fell with three on each side slightly ahead of the periscope which was still visible. No.3 DC must have exploded directly alongside the hull for the effect was devastating. A huge mass of white surging froth of air, oil and wreckage came to the surface covering an area of about 100 feet in diameter. This massive eruption of air continued for about 15-20 minutes before subsiding but with bubbles coming up from two adjacent points. We believed that the U-boat had broken in half.'

A few minutes after the attack oil came to the surface and an hour and a half later the slick had grown to a length of two miles. Miscellaneous wreckage also appeared, including pieces of wood and sheets of white paper which turned out to be charts and a round wooden wheel. An escort group and two Wellingtons were homed to the area before the Sunderland left. The surface vessels picked up some of the wreckage and the aircraft confirmed that the debris and patches of oil were in the same position. U-107 was lost with all 58 hands. Baveystock was awarded an immediate DSO for this action. The citation said: 'Flight Lieutenant Baveystock continues to set the highest example of skill and leadership. His record as captain of aircraft is one of consistent efficiency and devotion to duty and his work has contributed much to the success of operations against the enemy surface and underwater craft.' Baveystock commented: 'My second pilot and the crew did it all for me. I just sat in the second pilot's seat and pressed the tit. It was easy; I'm going to do the rest of my ops blindfold!' More seriously, he reflected much later 'I often wonder how many men I sent to their death but in those days we did not think of U-boats as containing men like ourselves. We just thought of the U-boats as vicious killers of our shipping...'

Coastal Command crews were now of the opinion that as far as the South-Western Approaches were concerned, there was little more to fear from the remnants of Dönitz's forces. In their own language, they said they had 'had it'

Anti-submarine operations continued in the English Channel and inshore waters in late 1944-early 1945 and patrols were also flown over the Irish Sea. Squadrons recorded many attacks on possible targets but few of these were proved to be definite U-boats. On 9 September U-484 was depth charged by the Royal Canadian Navy frigate *Dunver* and corvette *Hespeler* supported by a Sunderland on 423 Squadron RCAF 18 miles south of Barra Head and was lost with all 52 hands. [142]

On 6 December Flight Lieutenant D. R. Hatton on 201 Squadron which had moved from Pembroke Dock to Castle Archdale in Northern Ireland in November, attacked U-297, which was commanded by 28-year old Korvettenkapitän Wolfgang Aldegarmann. This U-boat was on its first war cruise, from Horten in Oslo fiord. Hatton was on a CLA (Creeping-Line-Ahead, a navigational search) patrol at the controls of NS-Y having taken off at 0710 hours. Three and a half hours later Hatton received a signal to co-operate with escort vessels in a U-boat search. By 1053 hours he had reached that area to sight a sinking escort vessel which had been torpedoed. This was the frigate HMS *Bullen,* which had been claimed by U-775. Hatton circled the life rafts on which there were survivors. For the whole of the day Hatton saw only other escort vessels throwing patterns of depth charges. Just after sunset, in fading light, while flying at 400 feet the Sunderland crew sighted white smoke at five miles distance. At one mile range a wake 1,100 feet long with its source moving at 11-12 knots was observed. An attack was attempted from 50 feet but the DCs failed to release. In a second attempt with six DCs, three fell along the wake spaced at 60 feet. Both wake and smoked disappeared. Five minutes later an oil patch spread over the surface for a half mile, when PLE was reached, Hatton returned to Castle Archdale. The Admiralty assessment at the time was a probable kill but post-war the submarine was credited as sunk by depth charges dropped by Royal Navy frigates *Goodall* and *Loch Irish* 18 miles ENE of Cape Wrath. U-297 was lost with all fifty hands. Hatton never learned of the re-assessment because on 14 March 1945 he was airborne in NS-A at 0203 hours and 27 minutes later the Sunderland crashed in the hills northwest of Killybegs, County Donegal. The aircraft caught fire and was completely destroyed. There were no survivors. [143]

In January 1945, a determined U-boat pack penetrated into the Irish Sea and patrols were immediately mounted by Nos. 10 and 461 Australian Sunderland squadrons, but, lamentably, without success. The weather was less than kind again, with the added, disastrous result that three of the Sunderlands were lost on 18 January in a gale at Pembroke Dock, causing the boats to slip their moorings and be dashed to pieces to sink in the harbour. One aircraft was manned in time and practically 'flown' on the water into the teeth of the gale in order to save it, but the others could not be reached in time.

In the early part of 1945 ASV VI-equipped Sunderland Vs promised better results but U-boat kills by Sunderlands were now few and far between. When Flight Lieutenant K. H. 'Ken' Foster and crew on ML783/H on 201 Squadron at Pembroke Dock shared in the destruction of a U-boat on 30 April it the last kill of the war. At about 0800 hours while flying at 1,000 feet over the

Irish Sea, the 1st pilot and front gunner sighted a cloud of white smoke issuing from the sea. It was from a grey object 1½ feet in diameter and projecting about two feet and moving at 12-15 knots. During and attempted attack the Sunderland's port bomb rack jammed against the bomb door and could not be freed. The aircraft's crew fired at the schnörkel which submerged. Sonobuoys were released to detect any U-boat but only water noises were heard. A frigate nearby was informed and a square search was carried out. At 1133 hours the 2nd pilot sighted spray and white smoke 2½ miles away and when the Sunderland was flying at 500 feet. The port bomb rack was wound out manually and six DCs were released from 70 feet. Foster said later:

'After we got the contact at 0810, the bomb doors failed to open and we had to attack with the fixed and turret machine-guns. We signalled Group that contact was lost - nothing. At 0915 we asked for instructions - again nothing. At 1000 we sent 'resuming patrol'. When we regained the contact at 1135 we hand-lowered the bomb racks and straddled the target's course with our attack. We sent further signals to Group and again asked for instructions with again no reply. At 1235 we got the message 'comply with my 1135'. What flaming signal? I think it turned out that my WOP just received that signal as we were banging out a sighting report at 1135, put it under his folder and forgot about it. When we got home it was rockets all round, not a word of congratulations for the first two submarine attacks for months, although the Navy were very good and sent us a note and a copy of the ASDIC trace.' [144]

Three frigates were led to the area and after obtaining a bottom contact they attacked at 1900 hours. Diesel, oil, wood and German tins surfaced. The Admiralty credited the sinking of the U-boat to the Sunderland and the 14th Escort Group, determining that it was destroyed as a result of the attack delivered by Hesperus and Havelock. The Air Staff of HQ Coastal Command did not rule out the possibility of lethal damage to the U-boat by a depth charge rereleased from the Sunderland. At first it was thought that the victim was U-242 which was claimed destroyed off Holyhead but which had disappeared with all 44 hands after hitting a British mine on 5 April. It seems that Foster's and the 14th Escort Group's victim was U-246, commanded by 38-year old Ernst Raabe which was on its second war cruise having left Bergen on 21 February and it went down in the Irish Sea with all 48 hands.[145]

On the morning of 10 May one of the first U-boats to surrender to the Allies was sighted and escorted by Sunderland 'N' on 461 Squadron captained by Flight Lieutenant R. C. Allardyce. The first pilot, Pilot Officer F. Robinson DFM, sighted the fully surfaced U-boat fifteen miles on the starboard bow in the Bay of Biscay and Allardyce prepared for an attack if the U-boat commander disregarded Allied orders and opened fire. The Sunderland drew closer and circled the U-boat and the crew distinguished two flags, the swastika and the black flag of unconditional surrender. On the bridge and along the foredeck about twenty Germans stood rigidly to attention as the flying boat passed over. Fifteen minutes later the RAAF flying boat was joined by an RAF Sunderland and the two flying boats remained with the U-boat until two destroyers arrived to take it to port. Two days later, K/461 was also on patrol when yet another U-boat was sighted, but the appropriate symbol of surrender was not in evidence, so the captain of the aircraft, Squadron Leader R. R. Alexander DFC immediately began to make a long, shallow bombing run on the submarine. With his crew at action stations, ready for what appeared to be an imminent outcome, the Australian skipper called it off and climbed for height when the U-boat raised its small, black flag at the last possible moment. Alexander maintained height, circling the submarine until ships of the Royal Navy appeared and escorted the reluctant U-1010 to port in Scotland. This was the last operation for 461 Squadron, which was formally disbanded on 20 June.

Meanwhile, on 3 June, a Sunderland crew made Coastal Command's last air escort of the war in Europe. ML778/NS-Z - by coincidence the identification letter of the war's last air escort was the last in the alphabet - flown by Wing Commander J. Barrett DFC was airborne at 1643 hours to escort convoy HX358 of 51 merchant and escort vessels. 'Z for Zebra' was met at 2121 hours and escorted until 0019 hours on 4 June. She was at that moment the only aircraft airborne in the whole command. In the crew of thirteen were two Australians, Flying Officer L. F. Williams, second wireless operator and Flight Sergeant R. J. L. Armstrong, a Canadian and a New Zealander. The patrol ended when 'Z for Zebra' alighted on Lough Erne in Northern Ireland, in the early hours of 4 June. The Admiralty signalled Coastal Command that no further escort for shipping would be needed after midnight that night. [146]

Footnotes

82   *RAAF Over Europe*, edited by Frank Johnson (Eyre & Spottiswoode, London, 1946).
83   A Sunderland was lost on 17 September, Flight Lieutenant Davies in L2165 having become lost over the Irish Sea and running out of fuel when almost back to safety, the aircraft crashing near Milford Haven with the loss of all on board
84   Flight Lieutenant Harrison was killed on 7 April 1940 when he failed to return from a reconnaissance patrol off the coast of off Norway.
85   See *Hitler's U-Boat War; The Hunters, 1939-1942* by Clay Blair (Random House, New York 1996).
86   Thetford.
87   On 24 October Flight Lieutenant Wearne's aircraft (P9605) having been hit by fire from an 'unknown vessel', was hit again. After an investigation LAC Hunter the second fitter reported that there were two large holes in the port outer tank. AC1 King the first fitter and LAC Hunter then crawled out to the port engine with some tools and plugged the holes. Hunter returned to the cabin

for a five gallon drum of oil and a hatchet while the first fitter kept watch on the engine. A hole was cut in the top of the tank and the tank was refilled from the spare drum of oil. Both Fitters then returned to the cabin. While Hunter kept watch on the pressure and oil gauges, King returned to the port outer engine with a jug. He remained there for the next two hours and kept the engine running smoothly by collecting the oil from the nacelle of the engine and pouring it back into the tank.

88   *Hitler's U-Boat War; The Hunters, 1939-1942* by Clay Blair (Random House, New York 1996).

89   *Hitler's U-Boat War; The Hunters, 1939-1942* by Clay Blair (Random House, New York 1996).

90   After capture U-570 was re-commissioned on 19 September 1941 as HM Submarine Graph and used operationally before reverting to training duties. It was wrecked on Islay on 20 March 1944 when on passage to the Clyde from Chatham for extensive refitting. Salved and scrapped in 1961. Oberleutnant Bernhard Berndt, was held accountable in a German PoW 'court of honour' for the capture of the boat (the commander was beyond their reach for 'trial') and escaped in an attempt to scuttle the boat and regain his standing in the eyes of fellow prisoners. He was shot dead by British soldiers on 19 October 1941 whilst on the run. *U-Boat Fact File* by Peter Sharpe (Midland Publishing Ltd 1998).

91   See *U-Boat Capture!* by John Drummond writing in *RAF Flying Review*, August 1958.

92   See *Submarine: An anthology of first-hand accounts of the war under the sea, 1939-1945* edited by Jean Hood (Conway Maritime 2007).

93   A month later the *Luigi Torelli* 'escaped' 'internment' at Santander and limped into Bordeaux. In 1943 the *Luigi Torelli* went to the Far East, was taken over by the Kriegsmarine after Italy's surrender and retitled UIT-25. After Germany surrendered in May 1945 UIT-25 was used by the Japanese who titled her RO-504. Four months later she fell into American hands and was finally scuttled in 1946.

94   *U-Boat Fact File* by Peter Sharpe (Midland Publishing Ltd 1998).

95   Squadron Leader H. G. 'Graham' Pockley DFC* was posted home to Australia and in early 1945 he took command of 200 Flight RAAF, a Special Duties (SD) unit formed at Leyburn airfield near Toowoomba, on 20 February 1945 using Liberators to deliver agents and supplies of the Australian Army's 'Z Special Operations Unit by parachute into enemy territory. Once 200 Flight was fully operational, it had six Liberators and nine eleven-man crews with about 450 ground staff. In the middle of March 1945, two Liberators, one (A72-191) captained by Pockley , left for McGuire Field on Mindoro Island in the Philippines for their first mission. Two days later they took off to drop some 'Z' Special 'Semut 1' agents into Borneo. The mission was aborted due to low cloud. A second attempt on 21 March also failed due to bad weather. Finally on 24 March they were able to drop men into Borneo. A72-191 and Pockley's crew did not return from this mission. It is believed that it may have been shot down by a vessel that it was seen to be attacking.

96   'Bruce Sanders'.

97   *Hitler's U-Boat War; The Hunters, 1939-1942* by Clay Blair (Random House, New York 1996).

98   *Task For Coastal Command/Hitler's U-Boat War; The Hunters, 1939-1942* by Clay Blair (Random House, New York 1996). Ensor would later take command of 224 Squadron.

99   *Hitler's U-Boat War; The Hunters, 1939-1942* by Clay Blair (Random House, New York 1996) and *U-Boat Fact File* by Peter Sharpe (Midland Publishing Ltd 1998).

100   Kapitän zur See Karl Dönitz, a former World War I submarine commander, was appointed Commanding Officer for U-boats in September 1935. His primary task was to develop fighting tactics for his craft. One of the first post-1918 German commanders to believe that Germany's future enemy would be Britain, Dönitz, remembering his own experiences during the war, was sure that in the event of a war the Royal Navy would again institute merchant shipping convoys as the best method of protection for Britain's vital sea routes. Accordingly, he aimed from the beginning to introduce groups of U-boats - wolf packs - for offensive operations against such massed ship formations as a prime tactic.

101   *U-Boat Fact File* by Peter Sharpe (Midland Publishing Ltd 1998).

102   U-Boat Fact File by Peter Sharpe (Midland Publishing Ltd 1998).

103   U-441 was lost with all 51 hands in June 1944. On 4 June 1943 U-594 was attacked west of Gibraltar by a rocket-firing Hudson flown by Flying Officer H. C. Bailey DFC DFM on 48 Squadron and was lost with all fifty hands.

104   Wing Commander Oulton had sunk U-266 north of the Azores on the night of 14/15 May while escorting Convoy SC.129. 'We had a lengthy patrol in Halifax HR746/M and were feeling

pretty brassed off. We had dived down several times to investigate suspicious-looking objects on the sea, all of which turned out to be small trawlers. Then we saw yet another wake. 'Another trawler' we thought, as I pushed the control column forward, 'but we'd better have a look anyway'. I had my lunch on my knees at the time and was munching bread and butter and tomatoes. At four miles' range I suddenly realised it was no trawler but a U-boat. I tensed and sat up straight without a thought to my lunch; the plate flew off my knees and spilled all over the cockpit floor. As we ran in to starboard I saw the U-boat ploughing through rough seas, which were occasionally breaking over the conning tower. There seemed to be no one on the deck or conning tower - I think no one could have stood that rolling without being pitched over-board. Probably the crew were keeping dry below deck and maintaining only a periscope watch. When we passed over the sub just for'ard of the conning tower, the bomb aimer let go the depth charges. For a few seconds I thought we'd overshot and felt like swearing hard. Then the rear gunner's voice came over the intercom, 'Right against her port side, sir. Good show.' I started to turn, with the gunner burbling comments into the microphone, 'Her bow's lifting...the whole fore-part is out of the water... she's going down!' A few seconds later I saw it for myself. It was an astonishing sight. Straight up in the air stuck the bows of the U-boat, some 50 feet of them. It looked just like Cleopatra's Needle. Then, as though a giant hand was slowly pushing it down, the bow - still vertical - started to sink in the water. Soon only 20 feet of it were left and in about three minutes it had disappeared. We saw no survivors at all and I believe Jerry must have been caught flat-footed. The depth charges must have torn his hull open at the stern before he even knew he was being attacked and the rush of water into the rear compartments pulled the stern straight down. They must have all died like rats in a trap.' Quoted in Coastal Command At War by Chaz Bowyer (Ian Allan Ltd 1979) / U-Boat Fact File by Peter Sharpe (Midland Publishing Ltd 1998). U-266, which was commanded by Kapitänleutnant Ralf von Jesson, was lost with all 47 hands.

On 16 May Flying Officer Anthony J. W. Birch sank U-463 commanded by 47-year old Korvettenkapitän Leo Wolfbauer off Cape Ortegal. The Type XIV tanker had left Le Verdon on 10 May on its fifth war cruise. Approaching out of the sun, Birch swung HR746/M around to starboard and began his run-in from 1,000 yards while the navigator opened fire with the 0.5-inch nose gun. Six Mk XI Torpex depth charges were dropped and the Halifax's gunners raked the U-boat with machine gun fire. The depth charges were well-placed and as the spray subsided, the U-boat suddenly jerked upwards and the whole forepart rose vertically out of the sea as a large light blue oil patch appeared ahead of the bow of the stricken submarine. Two minutes later U-463 slid beneath the waves with all 56 hands. The next day HR774/R intercepted and sank the Italian submarine Tazzoli. Handley Page Halifax: From Hell to Victory and Beyond by K. A. Merrick (Chevron Publishing 2009) and U-Boat Fact File by Peter Sharpe (Midland Publishing Ltd 1998).

105   Handley Page Halifax: From Hell to Victory and Beyond by K. A. Merrick (Chevron Publishing 2009) and U-Boat Fact File by Peter Sharpe (Midland Publishing Ltd 1998).

106   In response to Borchardt's appeal for help, the inbound, fuel-low U-621 commanded by 24-year old Kapitänleutnant Max Kruschka briefly searched for survivors and was herself attacked by Liberator 'Q-Queenie' on 224 Squadron piloted by Robert V. Sweeny, an American, who toggled twelve depth charges in two runs. These severely damaged U-621 but she reached Brest on 3 June and was subsequently converted to a 'flak boat'. U-621 was sunk with depth charges by RCN destroyers, Ottawa, Kootenay and Chaudiere with the loss of all 56 hands on 18 August 1944. Hitler's U-boat War: The Hunted, 1942-1945 by Clay Blair (Random House 1998) and U-Boat Fact File by Peter Sharpe (Midland Publishing Ltd 1998).

107   Hitler's U-boat War: The Hunted, 1942-1945 by Clay Blair (Random House 1998).

108   U-415 was finally lost on 14 July 1944 when it detonated an RAF mine west of the torpedo net barrier off Brest Harbour and sank. U-Boat Fact File by Peter Sharpe (Midland Publishing Ltd 1998).

109   All five crew members on the Whitley were taken prisoner. Fielder was killed on 31 July 1944 while in command of U-333 which was sunk in a Royal Navy action. U-boat Fact File by Peter Sharpe (Midland Publishing Ltd 1998).

110   Hitler's U-boat War: The Hunted, 1942-1945 by Clay Blair (Random House 1998) / U-boat Fact File by Peter Sharpe (Midland Publishing Ltd 1998) / Conflict Over The Bay by Norman Franks (Wm Kimber 1986, Grub Street 1999). Flight Lieutenant H. W. Skinner and all 12 crew were killed on 18 August when Sunderland W3985/T was shot down in the Bay by Ju 88s. At 1845 hours HQ

received an SOS from him but nothing else.

111 *Conflict Over the Bay* by Norman Franks (William Kimber 1986 and Grub Street 1999).

112 The Halifax was HR792 'A Able' which flew its first operational flight on 15th July 1943 and its last on 9th December 1944, flying 67 operational sorties. After a crash on 13 January 1945 HR792 was SOC and stripped and dismantled and taken to a scrap yard, where it lay until being spotted by a Mr MacKenzie, a crofter from Grimshader. He thought the fuselage would be ideal for keeping his hens in. Mr MacKenzie removed the long range fuel tank, which served the people of Grimshader as a water tank until mains supply became available in the late 1970s. This Halifax later became Halifax *'Friday 13th'* at the Yorkshire Air Museum.

113 U-613 was commanded by Kapitänleutnant Helmut Köppe and was sunk with all 48 hands on 23 July by a US destroyer. Rupprecht Fischler Graf von Treuberg was killed on 24 August 1944 when U-445 was sunk by a Royal Navy frigate in the Bay of Biscay with the loss of all 52 hands. *U-Boat Fact File; Detailed Service Histories of the Submarines Operated by the Kriegsmarine 1935-1945* by Peter Sharpe (Midland Publishing Ltd 1998).

114 *U-Boat Fact File; Detailed Service Histories of the Submarines Operated by the Kriegsmarine 1935-1945* by Peter Sharpe (Midland Publishing Ltd 1998).

115 *Short Sunderland: The Flying Porcupines in the Second World War* by Andrew Hendrie (Airlife 1994, Pen & Sword 2012).

116 *U-Boat Fact File* by Peter Sharpe (Midland Publishing Ltd 1998).

117 *Hitler's U-Boat War; The Hunters, 1939-1942* by Clay Blair (Random House, New York 1996) and *U-Boat Fact File* by Peter Sharpe (Midland Publishing Ltd 1998).

118 *Hitler's U-Boat War; The Hunters, 1939-1942* by Clay Blair (Random House, New York 1996).

119 *Hitler's U-boat War: The Hunted, 1942-1945* by Clay Blair (Random House 1998)/ *U-boat Fact File* by Peter Sharpe (Midland Publishing Ltd 1998)/ *Short Sunderland: The 'Flying Porcupines in the Second World War* by Andrew Hendrie (Pen & Sword 2012).

120 U-546 was abandoned during a naval action on 24 April 1945. *Hitler's U-boat War: The Hunted, 1942-1945* by Clay Blair (Random House 1998)/ *U-boat Fact File* by Peter Sharpe (Midland Publishing Ltd 1998).

121 *U-Boat Fact File* by Peter Sharpe (Midland Publishing Ltd 1998).

122 *Coastal Command Review III/4*, April 1944.

123 *Coastal Command Review III/4, April 1944/They Shall Not Pass Unseen* by Ivan Southall (Angus and Robertson ,1956).

124 *Coastal Command Review III/5, May 1944* and *U-Boat Fact File* by Peter Sharpe (Midland Publishing Ltd 1998) and *Hitler's U-Boat War; The Hunters, 1939-1942* by Clay Blair (Random House, New York 1996).

125 On 18 July 1944 U-672 was depth charged to the surface by the RN frigate HMS *Balfour* 27 miles south of Portland Bill and scuttled due to damage. 52 crew were rescued by an ASR launch and the Commander by an ASR Walrus aircraft. *U-Boat Fact File* by Peter Sharpe (Midland Publishing Ltd 1998).

125 *Coastal Command Review III/5, May 1944. U-Boat Fact File* by Peter Sharpe (Midland Publishing Ltd 1998) and *Hitler's U-Boat War; The Hunters, 1939-1942* by Clay Blair (Random House, New York 1996). Niestlé lists U-240 as lost to unknown causes.

127 In May 1945 U-995 surrendered to the Allies at Trondheim. *U-Boat Fact File* by Peter Sharpe (Midland Publishing Ltd 1998) and *U-Boat Fact File* by Peter Sharpe (Midland Publishing Ltd 1998) and *Hitler's U-Boat War; The Hunters, 1939-1942* by Clay Blair (Random House, New York 1996).

128 *U-Boat Fact File* by Peter Sharpe (Midland Publishing Ltd 1998) and *Hitler's U-Boat War; The Hunters, 1939-1942* by Clay Blair (Random House, New York 1996). On 30 September 1944 U-921 was bombed by Swordfish 'F' of 813 Squadron FAA on the HMS *Campania* escorting Convoy RA 60, 280 miles WNW of the North Cape and SW of Bear Island and was lost with all 51 hands. *U-Boat Fact File* by Peter Sharpe (Midland Publishing Ltd 1998).

129 *U-Boat Fact File* by Peter Sharpe (Midland Publishing Ltd 1998) and *Hitler's U-Boat War; The Hunters, 1939-1942* by Clay Blair (Random House, New York 1996).

130 On 31 May 1942 Sergeant Baveystock was Flying Officer Leslie Thomas Manser's second pilot on the Thousand Bomber raid on Cologne when their Manchester was hit by light 20mm flak and set on fire. And then the port Vulture engine suddenly burst into flames. Oberleutnant Walter Barte of 4./NJG1 had intercepted the Manchester at low level and he delivered the coup-

de-grace with a burst in the engine before flying off to submit his claim for his fifth victory. Manser feathered the propeller and ordered Baveystock to try to put out the fire with the extinguisher. Baveystock did but it was no use. Although he and his crew could have safely bailed out Manser was still determined to try to get them home. Manser steered for Manston on the Kent coast. 'Go aft and jettison everything you can' he ordered Baveystock. He stuffed everything moveable that he could find down the flare chute but it was clear that there was no hope of reaching England. Manser ordered the crew to put on their parachutes and prepare to abandon the aircraft. One by one they bailed out. Baveystock shot a glance at the flying instruments and realized that with the speed down to 110 knots they were almost on the point of a stall. He tried to hand Manser a parachute but his Skipper waved it away. 'For God's sake get out - we're going down' he shouted. He could only hold the aircraft steady for a few seconds more. Baveystock crawled down to the front hatch, doubled himself up and dropped though the hole. The aircraft was now at 200 feet; no time for his parachute to open fully. Baveystock incredibly, survived the 200 foot jump when he hit a dyke. The four or five feet of water broke his fall. Baveystock evaded capture and on the night of 12/13 June he and two others were taken across the Pyrenees and into neutral Spain. Finally, on 6 July all six men sailed home from Gibraltar. They were each awarded the DFM. The award of a posthumous Victoria Cross was made to Leslie Manser on 20 October 1942 after testimonies from all five of the crew. See *RAF Bomber Command; Reflections of War; Cover of Darkness 1939-May 1942* by Martin W. Bowman (Pen & Sword 2011). The award of the DFC to Baveystock followed on 25 January 1944. The citation said: 'This officer was the pilot and captain of an aircraft which sighted an enemy blockade runner on December 27, 1943. After signalling the position, Flying Officer Baveystock determined to attack the vessel. In the face of considerable anti-aircraft fire he raked the ship with machine-gun bullets and then attacked it with bombs which he released on his third run over the objective. His aircraft had been hit but he flew safely back to base. Visibility was extremely poor and the flare path could not be seen; nevertheless, in absolute darkness, Flying Officer Baveystock brought his aircraft down on to the water close to the shore with masterly skill; no further damage was sustained. This officer displayed outstanding keenness, efficiency and determination.' Baveystock received a bar to his DFC on 25 August 1944.

131 *Coastal Command Review III/6* June 1944.
132 *Hitler's U-Boat War; The Hunters, 1939-1942* by Clay Blair (Random House, New York 1996).
133 *Task For Coastal Command.*
134   Ketels survived and later took command of another U-boat.
135 *Hitler's U-Boat War; The Hunters, 1939-1942* by Clay Blair (Random House, New York 1996) and *U-Boat Fact File* by Peter Sharpe (Midland Publishing Ltd 1998).
136 *Coastal Command Review III/7* July 1944.
137 *Coastal Command Review III/7* July 1944/Task For Coastal Command.
138 On 19 July Lieutenant B. Thurmann-Nielson on 330 Squadron RNWAF attacked and damaged U-387 which had left Narvik seven days' earlier. On 9 December 1944 the U-boat was sunk 25 miles north of Kola while operating in the Arctic by depth charges dropped by RN corvette *Barnborough Castle*. U-387 was lost with all 51 hands. *U-Boat Fact File* by Peter Sharpe (Midland Publishing 1998).
139 *Hitler's U-Boat War; The Hunters, 1939-1942* by Clay Blair (Random House, New York 1996).
140 *Coastal Command Review III/8* August 1944. Ivan Southall is the author of *They Shall Not Pass Unseen* (Angus And Robertson 1956).
141 *Hitler's U-Boat War; The Hunters, 1939-1942* by Clay Blair (Random House, New York 1996).
142 *U-Boat Fact File* by Peter Sharpe (Midland Publishing Ltd 1998).
143 *Short Sunderland: The 'Flying Porcupines in the Second World War* by Andrew Hendrie (Pen & Sword 2012).
144 *On the Step.*
145 U-246 was previously believed sunk on 29 March 1945 by the 3rd Escort Group west of the Lizard. *U-Boat Fact File* by Peter Sharpe (Midland Publishing Ltd 1998).
146 *RAAF Over Europe,* edited by Frank Johnson (Eyre & Spottiswoode, 1946).

Index

208